MW01519115

MAKER OF
MODERN
ARABIA

BY

AMEEN RIHANI

BOSTON · AND · NEW YORK
HOUGHTON MIFFLIN COMPANY
1928

PRINTED IN GREAT BRITAIN BY ROBERT MACLEHOSE AND CO. LTD.
THE UNIVERSITY PRESS, GLASGOW.

ABD'UL-AZIZ IBN SA'OUD
KING OF NAJD AND AL-HIJAZ

CONTENTS

		PAGE
A NOTE ON TRANSLITERATION	- - - - -	xi
THE KINGDOM OF NAJD AND DEPENDENCIES (A FEW STATISTICS)	- - - - - -	xiv
A GENEALOGICAL TABLE OF AAL SA'OUD	- - -	xvi

CHAPTER

I. WE SAID : HURAIMALA, BUT ALLAH SAID : DH'RUMAH	- - - - - -	1
II. IN BAGHDAD	- - - - - - -	6
III. IN BAHRAIN	- - - - - -	14
IV. IN A JALBOUT TO OJAIR	- - - -	23
V. THE MEETING IN THE NUFOUD	- - -	31
VI. WITH THE SULTAN ON THE MARCH	- -	42
VII. THE SULTAN ABD'UL-AZIZ	- - - -	50
VIII. BETWEEN IRAQ AND AL-HIJAZ	- - - -	59
IX. THE CONFERENCE OF OJAIR	- - - -	69
X. AL-HASA	- - - - - - - -	90
XI. ACROSS THE DESERT	- - - - -	101
XII. AR-RIYADH	- - - - - - -	123
XIII. IN THE PALACE	- - - - - -	140
XIV. THE TRAGEDY OF SHAMMAR	- - - -	165
XV. THE SA'OUDS AND THE RASHIDS AT PLAY	-	175
XVI. THE BEDU OF NAJD	- - - - -	188
XVII. THE ULEMA OF NAJD	- - - - -	200

CONTENTS

CHAPTER		PAGE
XVIII.	THE IKHWAN	207
XIX.	THE RULE OF IBN SA'OUD	215
XX.	REVENUE AND RAIN AND SOMETHING EQUALLY IMPORTANT BETWEEN	222
XXI.	POETRY AND POLICY	227
XXII.	IBN ABD'UL-WAHHAB AND WAHHABISM	237
XXIII.	WADI HANIFAH	251
XXIV.	THE WASHM	264
XXV.	THE QASIM	277
XXVI.	'ANAIZAH AND BURAIDAH	285
XXVII.	IN THE DAHNA	310
XXVIII.	AL-HAFAR	334

LIST OF ILLUSTRATIONS

PAGE

H.M. King Abd'ul-Aziz Ibn Sa'oud - - - *Frontispiece*

Map showing the new boundaries of Najd - - - xv

The Author on the Mare presented to him by Ibn
Sa'oud - - - - - - - - - 2

Shaqdoufs, in which pilgrims are carried to Mecca - 8

King Abd'ul-Aziz, Ameen Rihani, Sir Percy Cox - 12

The American Hospital, Bahrain - - - - - 14

The Mission of the American Dutch Reform Church,
Bahrain - - - - - - - - - 14

A Village in Bahrain - - - - - - - 16

A Palm Grove in Bahrain - - - - - - 16

Getting Water from the ' Sweet Spring ' under the salt
water of the Gulf, Bahrain - - - - - 20

An Ancient Ruin in Bahrain - - - - - 20

Al-Qatif - - - - - - - - - 26

A Water Spring in Al-Qatif - - - - - 26

The Arab side of the Camp at Ojair - - - - 36

The Bodyguard of King Abd'ul-Aziz - - - - 42

The Wahhabi Host at Prayer - - - - - 48

King Abd'ul-Aziz and the Author - - - - 50

Sheikh Muhammad Nasif - - - - - - 52

Mounted Forces of Najd - - - - - - 56

The Ojair Conference, November–December, 1922 - 76

King Abd'ul-Aziz, Major Frank Holmes, Sir Percy
Cox - - - - - - - - - 80

Map prepared by Major Holmes - - - - 84

PAGE

The Close of the Ojair Conference   -   -   -   -   88

The Donkeys of Al-Hasa   -   -   -   -   -   -   90

The Camp, Al-Hasa   -   -   -   -   -   -   90

The Pottery Market in Hufouf   -   -   -   -   -   92

A Lime Kiln in Al-Qatif   -   -   -   -   -   -   92

The Author's Route   -   -   -   -   -   -   -   93

The City Wall, Hufouf -   -   -   -   -   -   -   96

Market Day in Hufouf -   -   -   -   -   -   -   96

Entrance to the House of the Ameer Abdullah Ibn Jlewy
      in Hufouf   -   -   -   -   -   -   -   -   98

The Palm and the Dates   -   -   -   -   -   -   98

Main Street of Hufouf on a busy day   -   -   -   -   100

One of Ibn Sa'oud's Governors and his Bodyguard   -   100

Around the Fire sipping Coffee   -   -   -   -   -   102

The Summan Desert   -   -   -   -   -   -   -   102

Baddah, the Braggart   -   -   -   -   -   -   -   102

The Guardians of the Cave, Al-Hasa   -   -   -   -   104

The Two Breasts, Al-Hasa   -   -   -   -   -   -   104

The Nufoud at Sunset -   -   -   -   -   -   -   110

No pasture and no water.   Only the hard soil and the
      burning sky   -   -   -   -   -   -   -   -   110

One of the gates of Ar-Riyadh   -   -   -   -   -   124

The Coffee-Hearth in one of the Houses of Ar-Riyadh   124

A Jalib in the Shamsiyah Gardens, Ar-Riyadh   -   -   126

Interior of the Grand Mosque of Ar-Riyadh, with
      Minaret in background   -   -   -   -   -   -   130

The Palace and part of the Souq, Ar-Riyadh   -   -   152

Another view of the Palace -   -   -   -   -   -   152

PAGE

Interior of one of the Courts of the Royal Palace -   -   156

In the Palace at Ar-Riyadh -   -   -   -   -   -   156

At the Review on the day of Faisal's return from Abha   176

The Ameer Faisal, Viceroy of Al-Hijaz   -   -   -   178

H.M. King Abd'ul-Aziz leaving his car   -   -   -   182

The Ameer Sa'oud, the King's eldest son, Governor of
       Ar-Riyadh   -   -   -   -   -   -   -   -   188

The Author in Najd Dress   -   -   -   -   -   -   192

A Motawwa' (Wahhabi Missionary)   -   -   -   -   192

A Motawwa'   -   -   -   -   -   -   -   -   203

An Arab of the Ikhwan with a falcon -   -   -   -   208

Reefs along the Persian Gulf   -   -   -   -   -   208

The 'Arfaj in the Desert   -   -   -   -   -   -   210

A few of the Ikhwan   -   -   -   -   -   -   -   210

Muhammad, one of the Children of Ibn Sa'oud, with
       his tutor, Yousuf Yasin, Editor of the Mecca
       Weekly Paper, ' Umm'ul-Qora '   -   -   -   -   216

A Corner of the Sultan's Stud   -   -   -   -   -   218

A Caparisoned Zelul   -   -   -   -   -   -   -   232

One of the Ulema   -   -   -   -   .   -   -   248

Hazlul, our Chief -   -   -   -   -   -   -   -   265

Hamoud, the Beduin Boy   -   -   -   -   -   -   266

Fares, the Scribe of Hazlul -   -   -   -   -   -   307

Hamad, the Prodigal Black -   -   -   -   -   -   307

Khalaf, our Guide   -   -   -   -   -   -   -   312

Ju'aithen, our Good Scout   -   -   -   -   -   -   320

Misfer-Caliban, our Cook   -   -   -   -   -   -   322

A NOTE ON TRANSLITERATION

WITHOUT a scientific system of transliterating proper nouns and place-names in Arabia, the inconsistencies and the variations, which are so irritating to the scholar and so confusing to the general reader, will continue to multiply. For every traveller, following his fancy or, what is worse, his ear, will add to the confusion. He will hear the Syrian say M'hammed, the Hijazi, M'hammad, the Asiri, Mehemmed; but the muazzen and he who leads in prayer everywhere will say Muhammad. Why not, therefore, follow those who know and observe the rule?

But not every Arabic noun and place-name is as simple as Muhammad. Here is Ibn Hathlain, Sheikh of the 'Ujman, who lives in the Sarrar—a nut to crack. And I could not crack it without a nut-cracker furnished, strange to say, by the Arabists of Oxford. How am I, in other words, to write the name of the mighty Sheikh so that an English reader can pronounce it and an English scholar can trace, through the English characters, the original gutturalisms? Ibn Hathlain, Sheikh of the 'Ujman, who lives in the Sarrar—in these four nouns are five Arabic characters of which the English alphabet is innocent; and the learned Arabists of Oxford, supplying the deficiency, give me an 'h' with a dot under it for the first, a 'th' for the second, a 'kh' for the third, an inverted comma for the fourth, and a dotted 's' for the fifth. They have also gone to the end of the matter and developed a complete system of transliteration, which has been adopted by the Royal Geographical Society.

This system I follow as far as it is possible in a book which is not intended exclusively for the scholar. I do not underdot the 's' in Al-Qasim, for instance, or the 'h' in Al-Hafar, or the 't' in Mutair. Nor do I use the diacritical marks. Instead of Āl (family, house), I write 'Aal'; and instead of Sûq and Nufûd, I write Souq and

Nufoud. The latter form is more pleasing to the eye and is not misleading. On the other hand, I use the ' q ' for ڨ although the American University of Beirût uses the dotted ' k ' instead. I wish that the two Universities, to reduce the difficulties of the writer at least, would agree upon one system of transliteration.

But no system can entirely abolish inconsistencies. It is the business of the writer to convey to the reader the right meaning of a foreign word, its right pronunciation, and the simplest form of spelling it. How am I to make the reader understand, for instance, if I am not using diacritical marks, that harim is pronounced hareem and not ' hayrem ? ' Another instance is Amir. I find in the Dictionary both Amir and Ameer. But the former is stabbed ; and not unless the diacritical marks become popular will the scientific spelling be preferred.

Ulema, on the other hand, can be corrected in its middle vowel and supplied with the inverted comma— 'Ulama. But I have retained the spelling of the Dictionary. It is very difficult for an English writer, unless he be an able Arabist, to get to the correct vowel through the various shades of a syllable in pronunciation. There are even educated Arabs who say Hajrah, for instance, instead of Hijrah, and zikat instead of zakat. Henry Doughty writes mushrakin for mushrekin ; which is saying ' Those who are associated,' when you want to say, ' Those who associate.' And I do not know where he found his justification for so many characters in so simple a word as gazu (raid, foray). Doughty's ' ghrazzu ' is both barbarous and misleading. Even his glossary is in need of correction. Someone, I suppose, will say the same thing about mine.

But I have tried to be consistent only in those words and proper nouns which are not too familiar to be corrected, retaining the old form of Abdullah, Ali, Mecca, beduin, etc. ; but in the rest I am as scientific as the Royal Geographical Society.

A word more about the termination ' h ' and the article ' al ' in certain words and place-names. San'a, for instance, ends with an ' a ' and is written accordingly ; but Al-Medinah ends with a short ' t,' which is pronounced like an ' h.' Hence the ' h ' in the terminating syllable. The article ' Al ' is equally necessary to distinguish it from other cities. For Medinah (Madinah, rather ; but the ' e ' has been there ever since the days of Sale and I am not going to disturb it), Medinah is the Arabic for city, and Al-Medinah, where the Prophet Muhammad is buried, is The City. No one in Arabia, no one in the Islamic world, ever dares, in writing or in speaking, to strip it of the distinguishing article.

The same is true of other countries and cities. You never hear an Arab say, I am going to Hijaz or I am coming from Yaman ; nor do they ever say, We are from Al-Najd, for instance, or Al-Asir. The article in the last two names is as foreign as the want of it in the former two. The reason for this, were we to seek it, would take us out of the subject of orthography. Sufficient for the present to say that I have followed the Arabs in writing ' Al-Hijaz ' and ' Al-Yaman.' But here, too, I am inconsistent ; for I have not conformed in ' Kuwait ' and ' Iraq,' which in Arabic assume the distinguishing mark. But Kuwait and Iraq are now on the Mail Route of the world and are known as such in the Mail Directories of Nations. Would I, therefore, be so fatuous as to seek to correct, in a book of travels, the Mail Directories of five Continents ? It was Mr. Churchill who first said ' Iraq,' and the postage stamps, the most bombastic in the world, are made. Moreover, King Faisal has discarded both the *ighal* and the fez. Let us not quarrel, therefore, about the discarding of ' an article ' of speech.

AMEEN RIHANI.

FREIKÉ, MT. LEBANON, SYRIA.

THE KINGDOM OF NAJD AND ITS DEPENDENCIES

ITS BOUNDARIES.[1]—To the East, the Persian Gulf from Jafourah and Qatar up to Ras'ul-Mish'ab, and north of Ras'ul-Mish'ab to Ras'ul-Qilliyah is the neutral zone between Najd and Kuwait; to the West, the Kingdom of Al-Hijaz; to the South, a line extending from Qonfuzah on the Red Sea, running south of Abha in Asir and south of Wadi'd-Dawasir including Najran, thence easterly around the Ahqaf (the Vacant Quarter) and continuing to the boundaries of Qatar on the Gulf; to the North, the neutral zone between Najd and Iraq (an area the shape of a rhomboid included in the degrees 29 and 30 lat. and 45 and 46 long.), a line thence northerly and north-westerly up to the meeting point of the parallels 39 of long. and 32 of lat., leaving Jabal 'Aneiz to the north, thence south by west to Wadi Rajil and east by south to the meeting point of the parallels 38 of long. and 30 of lat., thus including all of Wadi Sirhan in the Kingdom of Najd, which line continues due south for 25 minutes along the 38th meridian. But the line thence across the Hijaz railway to Aqaba is still under consideration.

ITS POPULATION.—About three million souls.

ITS AREA.—About nine hundred million square miles.

ITS HIGHEST MOUNTAINS.—Jabal Twaiq, J. Aja, J. Sulma.

ITS BIGGEST SAND DESERT, after the Vacant Quarter, is the Dahna.

ITS BIGGEST WADIS.—Wadi'r-Rummah, Wadi Sirhan, Wadi'd-Dawasir.

ITS BIGGEST OASES.—Al-Hasa, Al-Qatif, Al-'Ared and Taima.

[1] The northern, north-eastern and north-western boundaries are based upon the two Treaties concluded between the Governments of Najd and Iraq and Great Britain, and Najd and Great Britain and Trans-Jordania; the first was signed at 'Uqair on the 2nd of December, 1922, the other at Hadda, Al-Hijaz, on the 2nd of November, 1925.

Najd: 内志 (沙特和�(?)).
a central plateau region
of the Arabian Peninsula; formerly an
independant sultanate untill 1932 when
it united with Hejaz to form the
kingdom of Saudi Arabia的志.

Abd'ul-Aziz Ibn Abd'ur-Rahman Aal [1] Faisal Aal
Sa'oud was made Ameer of Najd and Imam of the
Wahhabis in 1902, a year after he conquered and
occupied Ar-Riyadh ; and in the summer of 1921,
when the British Government had decided to make
Sherif Faisal King of Iraq, the Sheikhs and Chiefs of
Najd in Assembly elected the Imam Abd'ul-Aziz
Sultan of Najd and its Dependencies. About five
years later, January 10, 1926, after the conquest of
Al-Hijaz, he was made King of Al-Hijaz by the
suffrage of its people ; and in the same month of the
following year, January 19, 1927, he was proclaimed
at Ar-Riyadh King of Najd and its Dependencies, his
aged father Abd'ur-Rahman giving his sanction,
as he did on the two former occasions.

[1] All-Faisal = Of the house of Faisal.

CHAPTER I

WE SAID : HURAIMALA, BUT ALLAH SAID : DH'RUMA [1]

disapointment

WHEN I was in Lahaj I wrote a letter to His Highness the Sultan of Najd stating the purpose of my travels in Arabia and asking for permission to visit him at his capital. I had little or no hope at that time of ever getting there ; for between me and ' the mighty Ameer and Imam without peer ' were the Indian Ocean, the Nufoud, the Dahna—and the English. But the seas of water and of sand are nothing to the sea of affability and evasion, which was indeed the worse ; and the story of my adventure through it is not without a point of interest—of profit, too, perhaps —particularly to madcap travellers and government officials.

In the letter, which I wrote before I set out for San'a and gave to a well-known merchant in Aden to send to the Agents of Ibn Sa'oud in Bahrain, I asked his Highness to favour me with an immediate reply, so that, in passing through Bahrain on my way to Iraq, I might know what to do. It was my intention, if permission had been granted, to travel first in Najd and then in Iraq, thus saving trouble and time and money.

But when I returned three months after from San'a, I had to put up in Aden, in the oven-like Crater, among the spectres of smallpox and malaria, for six long weeks,

[1] A proverb of the people of Najd expressive of disappointment and resignation. Huraimala and Dhouma (pronounced Dh'ruma) are two cities in Al-'Ared, Central Najd.

R.I.S.   A

waiting for permission from my friends the English to
go to—Najd? No: only to Iraq. For Ibn Sa'oud's
country to them, in those days, was a sort of *sanctum
sanctorum* that could not be approached by anyone outside
of the few who had access to another *sanctum sanctorum* on
the banks of the Thames in London. The Political Agent
or Officer or Resident, on the Red Sea or on the Gulf,
when approached on the subject, is one of three—a
diplomat, a business man, or a mere official. He is either
soft-spoken and evasive, or outspoken and apologetic, or
hopelessly negative and disdainful. I have met the three
in Aden. I said : Najd ; they said : Iraq. I spoke of
Ibn Sa'oud ; they smiled and said nothing. I was
persistent ; they were not assuring. In one letter the
Acting Resident wrote that His Excellency the High
Commissioner for Iraq had granted me permission to
visit Baghdad, and he inquired if I ' propose to go there
at once.' He would have me leave Aden immediately,
being solicitous, I thought, about my health ; but he was
not quite happy in his dictation. ' I consider that the
subject matter of your conversation with me will not be
forwarded by your remaining here any longer,' he wrote.
And in another letter, written in a conciliating mood, he
assured me that there was no objection to my visiting
Bahrain, and asked me, in a *P.S.* to give his salaam to the
Political Agent there.

I left Aden with a mixed feeling of gratification and
regret. It was gratifying to know that the Residency was
not altogether devoid of a human quality even in the
tenor of its political existence. Its private door was open
in the end to the foreign traveller ; its table was set for
him, and the few officers with their chief who welcomed
him were quite human in their curiosity. But why begin
at the other end, the wrong end, when a little gumption
would show that the right end is even less troublesome ?

Alas, in Bombay, too, they began at the wrong end.
For after five days of a pleasant sea voyage, in which the

THE AUTHOR ON THE MARE PRESENTED TO HIM
BY IBN SA'OUD

south-west monsoon had abated its fury—had consented,
I mused, that I be left alone to suck at the red-and-white
stick of gratification—I was met on shipboard by a
special representative of the metropolitan police. My
visit to Headquarters, however, was not followed by anything more unpleasant ; and I found the Commissioner
and his Deputies as amiable as the constable who carries
in his inside pocket a warrant for your arrest. They would
arrest my fond anticipations. I could go no farther than
Iraq for the present. They even evinced a surprise that
I, who am neither English nor a distant kinsman, should
be granted the privilege—it was a privilege in those days
—to visit Baghdad. Indeed, even other American travellers had to wait two or three months in Bombay and were
in the end refused permission to go to Iraq. But I was
not pleased with my privilege.

We said : Huraimala, but Allah said : Dh'ruma. A
commissioner of police is not always, however, on Allah's
side ; but whether I deserved his support or not in Bombay is another matter. 'We have orders to send you to
Iraq,' he said. 'And I think in what they wrote to us
they say that they have not yet received a reply from Ibn
Sa'oud. I shall look up the letter and send you a copy of
it, if you like.' I thanked him for what I thought was the
extreme of official courtesy and went back to my hotel,
where I found some Arab Muslims, merchants in Bombay,
waiting for me. One of them was Hajji Ali Ridha
Zainal, son of my venerable friend the octogenarian
member of the Prayer Club of Jeddah, and his visit
afforded me double pleasure, because he told me (I seldom
failed in those days, whatever the subject of conversation,
to make an inquiry about Ibn Sa'oud) that Abdullah'l-
Qosaibi of the house of Abd'ul-Aziz al-Qosaibi and Co.,
Agents of the Sultan of Najd in Bahrain, had arrived that
morning in Bombay. On the following day, therefore,
I hastened to him, taking Hajji Zainal with me.

Abdullah'l-Qosaibi is an Arab gentleman with a

cosmopolitan manner. He had been of the retinue of the Sultan's son, the Ameer Faisal, when two years before he was the guest of King George in London, and he spoke with a knowing accent. He told me that my letter was received, that it was forwarded in due course to the Imam,[1] and that they had received a reply of welcome, as well as orders to manage for my journey and comfort when I arrived in Bahrain. ' We have been expecting you for a long time,' he continued ; ' you have been delayed on the way, I suppose, or you have changed the programme about which you wrote to the Imam.'

' Neither the delay nor the change is in mine own hand,' I replied.

' Of a truth, everything is in the hand of Allah.'

' And what about our friends the English ? '

Abdullah smiled knowingly. ' We shall welcome you in Bahrain and manage for your journey to the Imam.'

On my return to the hotel I received a note from one of the Deputy Commissioners of Police, enclosing a copy of the following letter, which fairly represents the method of the Circumlocution Office in India :

No. 308—A
    Political Department,
        Secretariat,
            FORT, BOMBAY, 22nd August, 1922.

From
    A. F. KINDERSLEY, Esquire,
        Acting Secretary to the Government of Bombay,
            Political Department.

To
    THE COMMISSIONER OF POLICE,
        Bombay.

Subject : Mr. Ameen Rihani's proposed visit to Bahrain and Najd.

SIR,

    With reference to your letter No. F—2071, dated the 21st August, 1922, I am directed by the Governor in Council

[1] Ibn Sa'oud is the Sultan of Najd and the religious head—Imam—of the Wahhabis ; but his subjects seldom address him as Sultan.

to request that Mr. Ameen Rihani may be informed that permission to his visiting Najd had not yet been received, but is expected at Bahrain ; that there is no objection to his proceeding to Baghdad and that, in any case, it will be necessary for him to proceed thither first.

I have the honour to be,

Sir,

Your most obedient servant,

Sd. J. A. ARRATOON,

for Acting Secretary to the Government of Bombay,
Political Department.

True copy forwarded with compliments to Mr. Ameen Rihani for information.

Sd. W. STUART,

for Acting Commissioner of Police,
Bombay.

The discrepancy between the information of the Political Department of the Government of Bombay and the Bahrain Agency of the Sultan of Najd will be more obvious in the following chapter, *inshallah.*

CHAPTER II

IN BAGHDAD

I WAS not permitted to go to Bahrain.

We said : Huraimala, but Allah said : Dh'ruma. I had learned, however, to accept with equanimity the divine dispensation, going ahead as ordered or led, while reserving for myself the right to turn back and, Allah forgive me, to hit back when the hitting might be of some earthly good. I went to Iraq, but my heart was in Najd.

Two essential truths which I soon learned governed my actions, and, to a certain extent, my opinions in the ancient city of the Abbaside Khalifs. First, the key to Najd from any port on the Persian Gulf was in the hand of the High Commissioner for Iraq ; second, the door was seldom opened to anyone but the English. Nay, only to a few favoured Englishmen who combined at times the interests of the Royal Geographical Society with those of the Foreign Office. Even some of the American physicians in Bahrain were often refused permission to go to Najd on professional business. These are the truths with which I was confronted in political circles. Even my native friends were not more encouraging than the Englishman in office. The Englishman in office ! He smiled at my boldness, my ignorance rather, in Hudaidah ; he blandished and evaded in Aden ; he equivocated in Bombay, and—what will he do in Baghdad ?

After having been received by His Majesty King Faisal in his temporary quarters on the east bank of the Tigris,

I went to the Residency on the west bank to see Miss Gertrude Bell,[1] the Oriental Secretary to the High Commissioner. The Iraqis call her Khatoun, that is, a lady of the Court who keeps an open eye and ear for the benefit of the State. I found Miss Bell had two other loyal troopers—her tongue and her mind—and the manner of being quite at home in Baghdad. Her figure is quite English—tall and somewhat lank ; her face is aristocratic —rather long and sharp ; and her silver hair is not inharmonious with the persistent pink in her delicate complexion.

The first meeting was in her office, and she kept the reins of conversation in her own hand. She speaks Arabic almost without an accent, often mixing it with her English, and emphasizing it with a dogmatic though graceful gesture. Her energy and agility amazed me. She smoked, while she spoke, one cigarette after another ; she rose from the divan and walked up and down the room in—shall I say accelerated ?—animation ; she opened the casement window to let in some fresh air and flounced on the divan again, puffing away and talking, talking, and calling me Ameen Effendi in a most in-gratiating manner. I was pleased. I was relieved. The Khatoun, I said to myself, is still a woman, Allah be praised. I admired what she exhibited of her mind at the first meeting ; and when she unveiled a corner of her heart I was surprised. She almost lifted the whole political curtain to show how sincere she was to King Faisal as well as to the people of Iraq, and to prove that England has always been and still remains the best friend of the Arabs. 'You have no doubt found that out for yourself, Ameen Effendi.'

I was glad that she did not stop for a reply. She went on to speak of—not to ask me about—my travels in Al-Yaman and Asir. She had followed me evidently, as far as official reports made it possible, and I was not

[1] She died in Baghdad in the summer of 1926.

surprised. An English Political Agent or Resident in Arabia sends out as a rule copies of his regular reports to his colleagues in Egypt, in the Soudan, and in Iraq, as well as to the Government of India.

Miss Bell reverted to King Faisal, who in those days was angry with her and the High Commissioner, and would not accept the Anglo-Iraq Treaty. ' I have worked very hard for King Faisal, served him faithfully with all my power. . . . The tribes were against him, the chiefs would not vote for him. I argued with them. I persuaded them. I convinced them. I got them to vote for Faisal. Yes, indeed, Ameen Effendi, I exerted every effort on his behalf. People said : this man is a Hijazi, a foreigner. But I guarantee him, I replied. *Ana'l-kafil* (I am the sponsor). Believe me, Ameen Effendi, I love Iraq almost as much as I love my own country. I am an Iraqi, and I want to see the people of Iraq achieve their freedom and independence while helping us to promote at the same time the country's progress.'

I was enlightened and amused at the *majlis* of the Khatoun. But my admiration for her as a woman could hardly vie with my doubt in her ability to manage the affairs of the new Kingdom, let alone its turbulent tribes. I hasten to assure the reader, however, that she did not, as Oriental Secretary, divulge all the secrets of the Orient at the first meeting. Nor at the many meetings that followed. She refutes, in this sense, what man in all ages has believed, what man has invented, about the lack of secrecy in woman. But this is not the place for an adequate discussion of Miss Bell's qualities and gifts. I bring her into this chapter because, in the days of Sir Percy Cox, she was the keeper of the keys as well as the secrets of State. Principally among the former—what interested me exclusively at that time—was the key to Najd. Would she open the door ?

I was most discreet with the Khatoun when I broached

SHAQDOUFS, IN WHICH PILGRIMS ARE CARRIED TO MECCA

the subject, taking care not to betray aught of the feeling
I had against her colleagues, nor even to allude to the
inconsistency between the attitude of the Bahrain Agents
of Ibn Sa'oud and that of the Political Department of the
Government of Bombay. For I could see that in that
little office, whose casement window opened on the Tigris,
was the springhead of many little currents of authority,
which flowed in every direction and reached as far as
Poona in the Mahratta hills. Her tone and her manner
changed when I asked the first question ; and she did
not answer with the same directness and openness as
marked her talk about the affairs of Iraq. She hesitated,
she ruminated. How was I going to behave in Baghdad ?
Had I come to start another revolution against the
English ? Would I side with one national party against
another ? Or did I come from America as the secret
agent of one of the Oil Companies there ?

These are some of the rumours that floated in Baghdad
and into the office of the Khatoun. But she did not
condescend to ask me one direct question. She would
convey to me, however, by allusion and by inference—
reinforcing with a gesture what, in her own view, seemed
conclusive—that her knowledge about Arabia and England's political policy in Arabia, was all encompassing.
I was no doubt convinced about it, even if I did not say
so. Or she must have read in my silence a disposition at
least to believe. She took things for granted, and I was
to blame. For even in my smile at our first meeting I
was not real, except in the sense that a rope-walker with
a rod in his hand is more true to reality than a man
carrying a walking stick.

To do myself justice, however, I must ask the reader to
bear in mind that I was a traveller who had an almost
insurmountable obstacle in his path. And I would not
capitulate. I would not, on the other hand, equivocate.
True, lest my desire and purpose be thwarted by a woman
in power, I countenanced, without counterfeiting, her

humour. But I did not mince matters in the speeches
I made at the various meetings and receptions in Baghdad
and other cities. Iraq, however, was not my goal. And
when I walked out of the Khatoun's office, there was a
duel in my mind about the realization.

On the following day I went to the High Commissioner,
Sir Percy Cox, who, unlike Miss Bell, would not give me
the pleasure of doing all the talking himself. He asked
me several questions about my experience in Al-Yaman
and Asir, which I answered with circumspection. He
then told me of the recent incident at the Palace when
he went to congratulate the King on his first anniversary.
The demonstration was an insult to the British Government. Nevertheless, he would not have acted as he did—
he would not have exiled the leaders of the Nationalist
Party and closed its newspapers and its club—if he did
not think that the situation was fast becoming unmanage-
able. And suddenly, by no logical connection that I can
remember, Ibn Sa'oud came into the conversation.
There was a little dispute between Najd and Iraq ; there
was also a Treaty under negotiation ; and the High
Commissioner, with these objects in view, was soon going
to visit his friend the Sultan Abdul-Aziz.

I had some trouble in keeping my joy under cover, and
I said, with diplomatic calm : ' You are going then as
a peacemaker between two of the Kings of Arabia.'
' Between more than two,' he replied. ' My desire is to
pave the way for peace and good understanding between
them all.' Not being English I could not further sustain
the attitude assumed. I babbled in an unseemly familiar
accent. ' That is my purpose also,' I said. ' Take me
with you, therefore, to Ibn Sa'oud and I'll serve you in
what I can, in so far as you will permit, without any
charge to you or the British Government.' He laughed
and said something which I did not hear, while the servant,
who had just come in, was announcing, ' Luncheon is
ready, Sir.'

I walked out of the office of the High Commissioner as I did out of his Oriental Secretary's, feeling that my goal was still very far of attainment. Indeed, I was fast realizing that the last of the four barriers previously mentioned *was* the worst. It was not the fault of Ibn Sa'oud, as I have shown, for he immediately sent a letter of welcome in reply to mine, and ordered his Agents to attend to all my needs for the journey when I arrived in Bahrain. But why, under the circumstances, should the English say, Nay ?

Nevertheless, I did not despair. On the contrary, I found in the High Commissioner's words, *I am going to visit Ibn Sa'oud*, a rack to hang my hope upon. I even indulged in the visionary. I saw myself going with him to Al-Hasa : I pictured myself travelling with an Englishman in power. And what matters it if they say, my deluded friends and enemies : Behold him travelling with the High Commissioner—proof enough that he's in the pay of the British Government. I did not care. I had my own point of view, loftier or lower, as you like, which vibrated with a supreme purpose. I would beat the British Government at their own game, and I would see Ibn Sa'oud.

Political meetings and literary receptions, the first, the second, . . . the tenth, were held in Baghdad and reported to the Mandatory Authorities and to Miss Bell. But I was not long in dispelling the clouds of doubt. I did it in the first speech, and the Khatoun was pleased. Blessed be thou, O woman, who art always the first to believe, and who always art ahead of man in thy trust and faith. Miss Bell asked me several times to her home, and she gave a reception in my honour at the Salaam Library, of which she is President. Many distinguished Iraqis and English people were present ; and the President's address was more gratifying to me than the others, not because its words of welcome and praise were few and choice, but because it expressed the sincere feeling of a woman who, like her colleagues, had started on the wrong track, but was quicker to change.

She was still undecided, however, about my visit to Ibn Sa'oud ; and whenever I spoke of Najd she deftly brought me back to Iraq. Have you not visited the ruins of Babylon ?—Did you go to Ctesiphon ?—No, there is no objection to a sojourn in the Najaf and Karbala—The ruins of Samarra are most interesting, etc. And so, for two long months I went up and down and to and fro in the ancient land of Mesopotamia, feeling more like Job than Satan, sick and feverish and sore-minded, even discouraged. Why, the symptoms of nostalgia withal were setting in. I was getting nearer to Syria, and often in the morning I would get up with its name on my lips. It had been no doubt in my dreams. But I kept the secret from the High Commissioner and the Khatoun, and continued to make a show of the doggedness which was rapidly evaporating. I said everywhere, in the Serai, at the Club, at the Residency, at the Palace that I was going to sit tight in Baghdad till I get my permit to go to Najd. War is strategy ; and more exigent of strategy is the war of wills. I am almost certain that if the High Commissioner in those days had an inkling of what was developing, or rather crumbling, in me—if he had known that I was sick of Baghdad and was on the point of deciding to go to Syria—he would have kept me on the same diet another week, applying the salve of promise as usual, and the policy of suavity and evasion would have succeeded.

But Miss Bell, thanks to her thoughtfulness and kindly disposition, came to my rescue in the nick of time. She called me up on the telephone one day and said : You are going with the High Commissioner. This was too sudden, but I stood it well. On the following day, however, Mr. Lloyd George resigned the Premiership, and the fall of his cabinet necessitated that the High Commissioner remain at his post another week or ten days. But I had no post to detain me. So I packed up

H.M. King Abd'ul-Aziz

Ameen Rihani   Sir Percy Cox

and went forthwith to Basrah, where I had a few engagements, and where I was to wait for Sir Percy Cox. From Basrah we were to travel together to Bahrain and thence to Ojair.

I have referred to a phase in my moral and social conduct, which is the fruit of experience in my Arab travels—the fruit of practical wisdom rather—without which I would have lost faith and courage at an early stage of the journey and returned home with a broken spear and spirit. But I have followed the Arabic proverb, *Darihem ma zilta fi dārihem* (Humour them whilst thou art at their home) in a superficial way mostly, or whenever it was vitally necessary for my safety, for the success of my plan, and for the knowledge and information I sought. Otherwise, I was as candid and direct as an unspoiled Arab.

Practical wisdom, too, which was my guardian and guide, led me afterwards to go alone to Ibn Sa'oud. She must have whispered a word also in the ear of Sir Percy Cox, who accepted her advice and telegraphed to me in Basrah to say that he would be delayed another week, and that I might go ahead of him if I wished. It is well that he did so, as you will see, and it is well that I went.

CHAPTER III

IN BAHRAIN

IN Basrah, some of my native friends tried to dissuade me from going to Najd. They admonished, they discouraged. You are not strong enough to withstand the hardships and privations ; you may not be fortunate enough to escape the dangers. Consider the Nufoud, think of the Dahna—you have to cross them riding a camel. Days and nights rocking on a camel in the land of the Bedu and the Ikhwan.[1] They exaggerated the hardships, they magnified the dangers. And one evening, when I was dining at the house of the Mutasarrif of Basrah, Ahmad Pasha as-Sane', who is himself a Najdi and still wears the *aba* and the *ighal*, we were discussing Al-Yaman, and I said that when I entered San'a, I felt that I had suddenly gone back to the tenth century. Whereupon, Ahmad Pasha : ' And you will go back to the fifth century in Najd. You should not attempt this journey—there are many difficulties and dangers—visit Ibn Sa'oud in Al-Hasa and come back.' Here be a warning from a very Najdi. Would I not listen, would I not be persuaded ? I confess that I was assailed with misgivings.

But on the following day an Arab gentleman, who was destined to be my *rafiq* to Ar-Riyadh and my companion there, came to see me at the hotel. He is a son of the sea as well as the desert and has the smoothness and roughness of both—a man who pleases and offends without a thought

---

[1] The Ikhwan—the Brothers—a Wahhabi fraternity, militant and fanatical.

THE AMERICAN HOSPITAL, BAHRAIN

THE MISSION OF THE AMERICAN DUTCH REFORM CHURCH,
BAHRAIN (ON THE RIGHT, DR. AND MRS. DAME)

or a misgiving. The reader will meet, from time to time, Saiyed Hashem, son of Saiyed Ahmad of Kuwait, who was then in the service of the Sultan of Najd, one of the scribes of His Highness's diwan.[1] He had come to Basrah on official business, and chancing to hear of my being in the city he hastened to see me. He came, Allah reward his kindness, at the psychological moment. Or was he sent by Allah to bolster up my courage?

He spoke of the Sultan Abd'ul-Aziz. 'His Highness knows you from the newspapers, which he receives every week, and he is anxious to see you. . . . He is waiting for you in Al-Hasa. . . . Yes, he likes to meet every true and loyal Arab.' These words were music in my ear, and I would have kissed Saiyed Hashem between the eyes, Arab fashion, had I not had acquired, in my Arab travels, a certain gravity of demeanour suited to the native humour. But without hurt to the said gravity, and without detracting from my own ' perfections ' in the presence of the worthy guest, my heart danced with joy and went to the steamer in that happy state. Saiyed Hashem, too, as chance would have it, was returning to Bahrain on the same boat.

One cannot understand the contempt an Arab has for sleeping in a bed, cooped in a cabin, until one sees the well-to-do among them make their little home on deck. The servants spread the rugs and cushions, setting the baggage—boxes and cans, bundles and bales—around the carpets to define their boundary in this little world of a day or a week ; and a few feet away from the improvised *majlis* the iron kitchen is installed. In ten minutes after they had come on board the fire is made—they carry their charcoal with them—and the coffee is soon served.

---

[1] Diwan (with the ' w ' in Arabic, a ' v ' in Persian or Turkish) is in Arabia a room where the scribes and secretaries of an ameer or a sultan perform their duty. The Sultan's diwan is other than the Sultan's *majlis*. The first is a council of state over which he presides ; the second is the place—it may be in the Palace or outside—where he sits, *yajlus*, to receive his subjects.

It is a comfortable little home where the Arab in his robes, seated on his carpet and leaning against his cushion, is quite himself. To put him in a cabin below were a libel upon his estate—upon his heritage of the open sky.

We had a few of these distinguished Arabs with us. But when we anchored before the city of Kuwait, I was introduced to a more interesting passenger, one whom I had met previously in the course of a literary adventure, not unknown to travellers as well as Arab scholars, frequently mentioned by the writers of tales, and made much of by De Sacy and Hammer-Purgstall in their controversy about the Arabian Nights. Here, indeed, is the falcon. Many falcons, who had come from the hills of Persia, were on their way, through Kuwait, to Bahrain. They came on board in their neatly made hoods of leather which covered their eyes, perched on padded poles to which they were bound with leather cords. And they were of various shades of white and brown or white and black, and of a variable temper. Some of them, slightly nervous, would not suffer a touch, a caressing finger ; others yielded in what seemed a condescending and tolerant spirit ; while a few, on the same pole, which their master carried horizontally in his hand, enjoyed the caress, turned their heads in thankfulness, and would have kissed, were they not blindfolded, the caressing hand. The Arabs fly mostly the falcon against game, and they pay in Kuwait or in Bahrain as much as 300 rupees for a well trained bird.

Bahrain, the isle of pearls, is second to Kuwait in importance as an emporium, a commercial station, between India and Najd. It is also a step before the gate —the eastern gate to Najd—where a traveller must stop to transfer from steam to sail if his destination is Qatif or Ojair.

A dapper little sail brought us from the steamer, which anchored about four miles outside the harbour, in the quiet morning hour, gliding over the realm of pearls

A Village in Bahrain

A Palm Grove in Bahrain

before a gentle breeze, and in an undulation of wave that seemed to reflect the canvas swell. The sun had just risen, and Manama was white and pink in the haze, as if it had been built of pearls—so many pearl hills it seemed, rising from their realm above the cerulean blue of the Gulf. The sails, passing each other, flapped like pigeon wings whispering salaam to the Princess of the Pearl Seas of the world.

Nor was the approach disappointing, because Manama did not lose aught of the enchantment which distance lends to the view. From the quay we walked to a large two-story building, which the Qosaibis reserve for their guests and the guests of the Sultan of Najd, and which I and Saiyed Hashem occupied the first day. But on the day following I found myself alone in what seemed like an empty museum. Those spacious and high-ceiled rooms, those large and airy halls, those colonnaded porticos which looked from three directions on the Gulf —I did not know what to do with them. And having come from Baghdad, where we sought the cool of the roofs at night and the cool of the *serdabs*, the cellars, in the day, the contrast was overpowering.

Bahrain is not of Najd ; but the hospitality of Ibn Sa'oud crosses to Bahrain to welcome in the name of the Lord of the Arabs the coming guest. And his generosity sends Qosaibi to you to attend to your needs. He came with a tailor the day I arrived, and on the second day I was an Arab of Najd from tip to toe. But when I went to visit the Shiuokh of Aal Khalifah in Muharraq, I found I had made a mistake in the hospitality I chose ; for being the ruling family I should have given them the priority. I attended every meeting that was held in Muharraq, however, accepted every invitation to dinner, and left the young literati and patriots (you cannot separate the two in Arabia) quite satisfied.

When I entered Bahrain I lost my freedom as a traveller ; I delegated it rather to Saiyed Hashem, who aspired from the beginning to the management of my affairs. It was good of the man to place himself at my service before he had been formally charged to do so ; and I must here set down that from the first day we entered Bahrain to my last day in Ar-Riyadh, our relation, with its slightly intellectual and spiritual contact, was on the whole pleasant and gratifying. In a companionship of several months, however, intervals of depression are inevitable, when even the desert loses its spell and the *rafiqs*, their temper.

When Saiyed Hashem went to Al-Hasa to report on the Basrah mission with which he was entrusted, he carried a letter from me to His Highness the Sultan, in which I informed him of my arrival in Bahrain. And I began, after being left alone, to reconsider all the things, contrary and strange, I had heard about him. As I drew nearer to the man, the mind asserted its priority and anxiety gave way to speculation. My longing to see him, which was like a coruscating pine flame before I arrived in Bahrain, became, after the greatest barrier was broken and the goal was in sight, like the flame of dry pine needles silent and calm.

I recalled what was said in Al-Hijaz and in Iraq : Ibn Sa'oud is a beduin Arab, ignorant and despotic—Ibn Sa'oud is a ruffian, without heart and without religion— he is an impostor who uses religion to further his own selfish aims. And the Ikhwan his men? They are monsters of fanaticism, who slay their fellows and praise Allah. They steal and plunder and call people infidels, and commit all sorts of atrocities in Allah's name. . . . Ibn Sa'oud's cause is a sectarianism which can never succeed outside of Najd. . . . With the political ambition of Ibn Sa'oud there can be no peace and prosperity in Arabia. These charges, which are often repeated in Al-Hijaz and Iraq, have been echoed in Syria and in Egypt.

I recalled also what I had heard in Aden and at the Residency in Baghdad : Ibn Sa'oud is a big man, the

genius of his race and country—an astute diplomat, a
brave soldier, a leader of men, a just ruler—the greatest
and the strongest of his contemporaries. . . . A son of the
desert which throws out from time to time a big man,
real and genuine, a natural genius, who appears suddenly
and dominates with his mind before he dominates with
his sword. . . . Thus the English and some of the Arabs
outside of Iraq and Al-Hijaz.

The first view, which emanates from Mecca and the
sherifs, has behind it a hostility, religious and political,
of long standing ; the second view may be actuated by a
policy of traditional friendship and interest which England
has been cultivating with the rulers of Najd for the last
hundred years.

But here is a story which was told me by one of the few
who escaped at the battle of Tarabah (May 25, 1919).
' After the battle Ibn Sa'oud walked among the dead and
wept. He shed tears, *billah*, and he said : " This is the
burden with which Allah has burdened me. Upon me
is the responsibility of bringing the *mushrekin* [1] back to
the straight path. . . . Would that I were a common
soldier (Shades of Henry the Fifth !) fighting for the cause
of Allah." He wept as he spoke, and his tears had great
effect upon the enemy as well as upon the Ikhwan. . . .
After that battle he received a message from the Government of Great Britain through its political agent in Jeddah
asking him not to proceed any further in Al-Hijaz. He
complied, and ordered his hordes back to Najd. " Ibn
ur-Rashid is making a move against Ar-Riyadh," said he,
" and we must hasten back." He would not let them
know that he the great Ibn Sa'oud readily obeys the
orders of the Ingliz.'

Another story. The beard of a Wahhabi, according to
religious tradition, has to be of full length, that is long
enough to grasp ; but the moustaches are trimmed short.

[1] Muslems who associate saints with Allah in their prayers and inter-
cessions.

One day, at the *majlis* of the Sultan, a beduin remarked that the moustaches of the Imam were not properly trimmed, and he called his attention to them. Whereupon, the Imam sent for the scissors, and said : ' Thank you for advising me.'

A man from Najd, living in Bahrain, told me this story, as I tell it, without comment ; for although an admirer of Ibn Sa'oud, he would not venture an opinion. ' You are going to see him,' he said, ' and a seeker of truth will shut his ears and open his eyes. . . . But I ask you, I beg of you to advise Abd'ul-Aziz, and to urge upon him the necessity of opening schools in his country.' These words, coming from a man who was free from political and sectarian bias, were a revelation. They reminded me of the words of the Mutasarrif of Basrah : ' You will go back to the fifth century in Najd.'

There was another admirer of Ibn Sa'oud in Bahrain who had another plan of reform, and that was Major Dickson, the liaison officer at that time between the High Commissioner for Iraq and the Sultan Abd'ul-Aziz.[1] An Englishman born in Syria, Major Dickson has a love for the Arabs akin to Miss Bell's ; and he thinks Ibn Sa'oud is the greatest Arab of his time—' I have a little of the hero-worshipper in me. But the Sultan Abd'ul-Aziz is the one ruler in all Arabia who has been able to control the Bedu. He knows how to rule them. He has the sword, and he has also a big heart. . . . What he needs is a better administration, and more revenue. I wish he would build a port in Qatif. The commerce of Bahrain and Kuwait with Najd would then be transferred to it.

---

[1] The Sultan had asked that his relations be with the British Government direct, and not through the Government of India. The reason is obvious. The Sultan hates red tape and circumlocution. There are none in his government, and he would cut down as much of them as possible in his business with other governments. Why, for instance, go through the Agency in Bahrain, thence through Simla, thence through the India Office in London, and thence to the Foreign Office to say that he is not dead yet, as rumoured, or that he needs money. The Indian Government was the Dahna desert between him and London, and he cut it out.

GETTING WATER FROM THE 'SWEET SPRING' UNDER
THE SALT WATER OF THE GULF, BAHRAIN

AN ANCIENT RUIN IN BAHRAIN

Of course, we would have a consul there. And the Sultan
Abd'ul-Aziz will admit no consuls in his country. Call
his attention to this matter—show him the benefits of it.'

Here, too, from an English admirer, is a light on the
subject showing another weak spot in the armour of our
hero. But is it a weak spot ? The people of Najd do not
want any foreigners in their land ; and one foot, they
say, brings a thousand behind it. A reasonable excuse.
But what is the reason for the want of schools ? Only
the Bedu dislike education. Only the Bedu are satisfied
with ignorance. Is the Sultan then a beduin—a beduin
of genius with a mind and a heart, and a political ambition guided by wisdom and moderation ? It seemed
to me that I was getting nearer to the truth, and I was
anxious to put it to the test. A week after Saiyed Hashem
left I received the following letter :

In the name of Allah the Compassionate,
                    the Merciful.

From ABD'UL-AZIZ IBN ABD'UR-RAHMAN AAL FAISAL AAL
    SA'OUD to the zealous compatriot and reformer AMEEN
    EFFENDI RIHANI, may his merits endure.

        Salaam and longing. At the most auspicious moment
I received your letter in which you inform me of your
arrival in Bahrain and your intention to come to our end.
Welcome, a cordial welcome. I am extremely pleased,
billah, for I have long desired to meet you, and Time now
brings the realization, praise be to Allah. I am very sorry,
however, because you did not telegraph from Basrah when
you left. And as we have been informed that the steamer
might be delayed, there was a slackness in ordering our
Agent to meet you. For this I ask forgiveness of you.
We are now waiting for you, and we have ordered our
Agent Qosaibi to provide a vessel to bring you to Ojair,
where you will be met by Saiyed Hashem. Accept the
expression of esteem and good wish.

                                THE SEAL.

Written on the 27*th of Rabi' ul-Awwal,* 1341.
        (*November* 17, 1922.)

This, the first letter I received from the Sultan Abd'ul-Aziz, reveals one of the principal traits in his character which his succeeding letters did not belie. The man is absolutely without affectation. His amiability, like his abruptness, is without effort. But amiability and a ruggedness of temper may go naturally even in a beduin ; may be with certain people cunningly, even subtly affected ; or may not be possible at all together. In the first instance we have an uncommon personality ; in the second, a man of parts or a clever politician ; while in the third, whether of rough metal or fine, the person is one with the others of his day, who enjoy or just suffer the common lot.

Now, what is Ibn Sa'oud ? Is he a man of natural amiability and grace, whose power is the outcome of events, the issue of circumstance ? Is he a shrewd politician who overcomes his opponents with generosity and governs his people with expediency ? Or is he of the very few in Arabia, in the world, whose temper, however refined, is seldom wholly free from the primitive note ; who remain simple in power, child-like in greatness— those few who seek their goal in a straight path, gathering wisdom from experience not from books ; free in their likes and dislikes ; honest with themselves and the world ; having the courage to be just, and fearing no one but God ? We are on our way, dear reader, and the truth, hidden behind the golden dunes, beyond that horizon of turquoise blue, will soon be revealed to us.

CHAPTER IV

IN A JALBOUT TO OJAIR [1]

I WAS as glad to leave Bahrain as I was to get to it ; for every hour, after the two great barriers—the sea and the English—had been crossed, brought me nearer to my goal. There remained but a corner of the Gulf which is not accessible to steam and a road that is easy only for the camel. In that corner, south-west of Bahrain, forty miles from Manama, is Ojair,[2] the gate to the land of Ibn Sa'oud. The coast of Al-Hasa can be seen from the south-west end of the island of Bahrain, but the distance is subject to the sail, and the sail to the wind ;—from six hours to forty-eight—sometimes even three days across— as the winds please.

I spent two nights and a day in the jalbout, which was carrying a cargo of rice, and thanked Al-Qosaibi for his thoughtfulness in providing me with a steamer chair. Otherwise, I was a full-fledged Muslim Arab in my mode of travel. A rug and a bag, and my *aba* for cover—this was my bed and baggage. And the servant Rashed, sitting near me, would stretch his neck every now and then to see what I was setting down in the book. A happy

---

[1] The jalbout is a coasting vessel with a long beak and a broad stern, resembling when it is large the *muheila* of Iraq or the *sanbook*—dhow—of the Red Sea ; and when it is small it is much like the *balam* of Shatt ul-Arab. Its name jalbout is, I think, a corruption of 'jolly boat' and it is only called thus in Bahrain.

[2] Al-'Uqair, as it is written in Arabic. But in Najd, as in Basrah, the qaf 'q' in many words is pronounced jim 'j.' Al-'Uqair=Al-'Ujair. I have retained, however, the familiar form, Ojair.

23

democratic—or would you say primitive ?—state. Now
Rashed will make the tea, and sitting on the rug will
serve it fastidiously. But what is he doing ? No, I am
not yet a pure Arab, an unadulterated Muslim, traveller ;
—not until Rashed throws that can of milk into the water.
Condensed milk ! and from the land of the infidels !
The hard biscuits of Bahrain were sufficient, O Rashed.

One of the crew was standing on a bag of rice, which
was his minaret at that hour, and calling the sunset
prayer. They prayed and then sat down to tell stories.
A shepherd in Al-Hasa once lost a sheep. He saw a man
riding on a camel and carrying something that looked
like his lost property. He tracked the camel to the village,
—The story is interrupted by the sudden turn of the wind
from S.E. to S.W. The *nakhouzah* (skipper) at the rudder
gives the order, and the sail swings clean round the mast
to the rhythmic ululation of *Praise thou the Prophet !* ' I
say,' the black-bearded, bright-eyed Najdi continued,
' I say that he tracked the camel to the village and complained to the Sheikh. " What tells you," said the
Sheikh, " that the man who stole your sheep is here ? "
" The footprints of his camel," says the shepherd. And
all the camels, *wallah !* were brought forth, and the
shepherd examining their footprints pointed out the
guilty one. The owner confessed, but he had already
put the sheep to the knife. The Sheikh, therefore,
makes him buy another and orders him in punishment,
wallah ! to give his camel also to the shepherd.' Every
one exclaimed in expansive pitilessness : ' Wallah ! this
be justice.' ' Had he come before Ibn Jlewy,' [1] the voice
was that of a bundled-up shape between two bags of
rice, ' he would have cut off his right hand too.'

Soon after we left Manama the wind subsided and we
weighed anchor in the evening. The babble of the crew
and the soft fresh breeze lulled me to sleep ; but towards

[1] Abdullah ibn Jlewy, cousin of the Sultan Abd'ul-Aziz, is the Ameer
of Al-Hasa.

midnight I was awakened by strains of song, which were siren-like in the distance. The *nakhouzah* had gone out in a row-boat to visit another vessel anchored for the same reason and purpose as ours ; and his men who were rowing him back were singing, *Salli 'ala 'n-Nabi* (Praise thou the Prophet). This was the body and the burden of their song, but the syllables and vowels of the Arabic lent it a soft enchanting air. Of a truth, they could not do anything without a vocal accompaniment, and invariably they brought into it Allah or the Prophet. A little higher or a little lower with the sail—*it-taisir 'al-Allah* (made easy by Allah). To leeward or to wind-ward.—*Allahu! ya Allah!* the head-hand, who would be doing most of the tugging, would cry in a voice denoting great pain, and the crew would reply : *twakkalna 'leih* (we depend upon him).

And here are the traditional chests of the ancient galley set in a horseshoe round the poop, and on one of them is the compass trembling under a broken glass cover. We are sailing 10 of S.W., but we are still in sight of Bahrain. 'The coast of Al-Hasa appears,' said Rashed, ' when Bahrain disappears from view.' The wind was contrary at night, however, and all day following it withheld its favour from our sail. What a depressing sight to a sailor is a sagging sail. But Rashed is not a sailor, and he could only see a hollow stomach in the canvas. ' It is like a camel,' he said, ' after she had been delivered of her foal.' Rashed is too clever to be in the service of anyone in Bahrain. *Awwah!* could he not also patter in English, and did he not know the great cities ? He makes ' fusseclass ' tea ; he can pick a winner on the race track in Bombay ; he speaks knowingly of a ' fluke ; ' he can stand as many hard drinks as Tommy Atkins, and he has in everything, especially in his choice of wives, a ' fusseclass ' taste. He even delivered himself authoritatively on the subject of intercourse. ' Never in the morning,' he warned the crew that sat around him on the rice cargo, ' and never with one above thirty. It is bad for the health. Between the age of fifteen and twenty, that is the choice of a wise man.' Among the crew was a *motawwa'* (Najd Arabic for mulla, religious elder) who was the muazzen of Al-Faras, our jolly boat. He looked at Rashed dubiously when he was holding forth, and in a charming accent accompanied by a wistful smile he said : ' That is best which Allah alone, praised be he, makes attractive.' He had also a sense of humour. When I said, in its Arabic equivalent and an insinuating gesture, that we must have a hoodoo with us, he pointed his finger at me and laughed.

But Rashed towards evening made a discovery which dispelled all the evil spirits that hovered around Al-Faras. He found one among the crew who had a voice and knew all the songs of old Baghdad.

> ' A villainous world whose cup is ever full,
> And he who drinks is ever sorrowful ;
> The days are chains, the taverns are the jails,
> And they are ever full, aye, *billah*, ever full.'

The meaning of Sulaiman's song did not matter. The song itself, with its melancholy strain, bewitched like the sirens' even the wind ;—the wind, which had disappeared for twelve hours, suddenly came upon the scene and danced on the canvas an accompaniment of ironic mirth. But the *nakhouzah's* joy as well as mine was quite real ; for the performance of Sulaiman and the wind continued till after midnight when we had entered the harbour of Ojair ; and early in the morning, before Saiyed Hashem and the Ameer of the Qasr came to meet me, the flag of Ibn Sa'oud, which is green with a white border, and on which is written, There is no God but Allah, was hoisted over the mast.

A good harbour for light craft with a shed for a custom house ; a landing with a big patch of water in it ; a broad open space for the merchandise and camels ; a few tumble-down houses in a long castellated enclosure

A Water Spring in Al-Qatif

Al-Qatif

for a *qasr* (castle) ; a pool of brackish water and a little garden for the Ameer—this is Ojair the principal seaport of Najd. North of it are two others, Qatif and Jubail, in one of which the Sultan would build a suitable harbour to eliminate Bahrain as a stepping-stone between him and the world. This would be possible if a steamship company chose to make Qatif, for instance, a port of call ; but the steamers that almost monopolise the Gulf are English, and one half of the British India Company, the Peninsula and Oriental, is unfathomably mixed up with the British Government. Ergo : Ibn Sa'oud, the mighty Abd'ul-Aziz, has to satisfy the said British Government, prove to it, before he can have a seaport, that his friendship is sound and everlasting.

For the present, therefore, he has to content himself with Ojair and his jollyboats and jollier camels—both of Arab origin, made in Arabia—which ply between the desert and the sea. The jalbouts come from Bahrain laden with rice and sugar from Bombay, oil from Abbadan, cotton goods from Lancashire or Massachusetts ; the camels come from beyond the Nufoud and the Dahna carrying dates from Al-Hasa, sheepskins from Sdeir and the Washm, clarified butter from Al-Kharj ; and they meet, a few score yards apart, on this forlorn coast, exchange their burdens to the profit of the man who leases the Custom House from the Sultan, and return, content with their destined portion of life and lucre, the one to the sea, the other to the desert. I too have waited, like a jalbout or a camel, on the same spot for a Sultan to come out of the desert and a High Commissioner to come out of the sea to accomplish a part of *their* destiny in this troubled political life of the world. That there might be a pact I hoped and prayed ;—and a pipe of peace, which I too might smoke with my English friends.

Meanwhile, the Ameer and Saiyed Hashem would entertain me as generously as the resources of Ojair allow. I was delighted, however, to see a bed in the room, and

my hosts had the perspicacity to read in my eyes the story
of the past two nights and the good taste to leave me alone.
But from my window in the *qasr* I could see the camel
world below ; a multitude of turbulent and truculent
beasts loading and unloading, crouching and rising,
coming and going ; grey old *naqahs* (pronounced naghah
=she-camel) driven by women in red smocks and black
masks for veils ; black giants led by children to the crouching place ; caravans arriving in the early dawn strung
to little white donkeys carrying bundled forms—the
cameleers wrapt in their *abas*—still half asleep ;—and
those on their knees are not idle ; some are enjoying their
breakfast of thorns ; others with their right forefoot in the
tether are hopping forward for a bite or trying to escape
duty ; some are just chewing the cud and sniffing the
air ; others are restless under their burden ; still others
are joyfully shaking their humps, having been relieved
also of their wooden saddles ; and they all grunt and growl,
groan and moan, rumble and grumble, whatever their
occupation be. How then could I sleep ? I could not
get anyone to tell me why a camel's voice has such a
variety of notes. Why, for instance, does the *naqah*, who
is but loafing on her four knees and chewing the cud,
utter such cow-like accents at intervals and then, like a
wolf, lift up her neck to heaven and howl ? And the
guggle in the throat, that death-ruckle—or is it a chuckle ?
The burdened beast and the one carrying a little girl
behind its bare hump are one in this ; but are they expressing a common complaint, a common satisfaction,
or what ? I doubt whether the Arabs ever think of the
camel as having a stomach, and of a thistle diet as a
possible counter-irritant or stimulant. I forgot when in
Jeddah to ask King Husein's opinion on the subject ;
for he knows more about camels and their affections
than a beduin who has tramped behind them for fifty
years.

The boy Majed, who walked behind my *thelul* when I

rode out with Saiyed Hashem to visit the site of ' a very
ancient city ' not far from the *qasr*, which must have been
a village of mud huts built fifty years ago—I know too
well the Arab's sense of time and space (in fact there was
not a stone to be seen and what my companion described
as the ancient city wall is a semi-circular ridge not more
than five hundred feet long) ; but I started to say that
the boy who walked behind my *thelul*, or according to
the standard Oxford spelling *zelul* [1] (my literary friends
in America, who have accused me of eccentricity in the
transliteration of Arabic words, of which I know the
pronunciation and, therefore, how they should be written,
will not blame me, I hope, for following deferentially the
learned Arabists of Oxford)—but what about the boy
that was walking behind my *zelul* ?   And what was it he
said ?   After we had been to the site of ' the ancient city '
even the *zelul* was disappointed and she refused to walk
straight.   She began to ramble and browse.   Whereupon
—now comes Majed and the statement he made, which
confirmed what King Husein once told me : the camel
that browses while walking, is good tempered and patient ;
but the surly one will refuse while on the march even the
luxury of an accacia twig.

We go back to the *qasr*, where the Ameer, who was
waiting for us, tells us more about camels.   The *zeluls* are
of two kinds, the pure Omaniyah, which comes from the
province of Oman and is invariably of a reddish colour,
and the *hurrah* (one of gentle birth) which is a cross between
an Omaniyah and a camel from the country north of
Najd.   The Omaniyah is the faster, and the *hurrah* the
more enduring of the two.   As carriers the black camels
are the strongest and the best.   The Ameer, a tall gaunt
figure with aristocratic calm of speech and grace of manner,
sat on his haunches kneeling on the carpet and kept his
hands joined before him as he spoke.   He did not ask me
questions or volunteer any information ;   and he would

[1] A zelul is invariably a she-camel broken exclusively for riding

sit silent in that manner until 'the honoured' guest 'deigned' to speak.

'At what season of the year,' I asked, 'do the strong winds blow in this part of the Gulf or between Bahrain and Ojair ? '

'During the last thirty days of Suhail [1] (Canopus),' he replied, 'we have a strong wind called *al-uhaimer* (the little red one) ; but when the Pleiades [2] begins to wane, the more violent winds blow and the water increases in the Shott (the river Shtt'ul-Arab).'

'You discover by experience,' I remarked, 'what men of science discover by study and observation.'

The Ameer : ' Men of science often get their knowledge from the reports of men of experience.'

For the quality of his mind as well as the gentleness of his manner the man deserved to be a real ameer living in a real *qasr*. But I must tell the reader, before closing this chapter, that the people of Najd are democratic and do not believe in titles. They are all equal before Allah and in the brotherhood of their Unitarian faith—Wahhabism. If their Imam the Sultan Abd'ul-Aziz, however, chooses to call his Governors, Ameers, which may imply a covert contempt for the title as well as for the undeserving bearers of it, the people of Najd do not object. And if a Najdi wishes to call a tumble-down quadrangle in the desert a *qasr*, his fellow Najdis and the Imam are quite satisfied. The real *qasr*, castle, with these people is the mosque ; and the true ameer is he who fears no one but Allah, who worships Allah alone and does not associate with him either saint or prophet.

---

[1] Canopus, according to the calculation of the Arabs, rises on the first of zu'l-Hijjah (about the middle of June) and continues for a hundred days.

[2] The Pleiades first appears on the horizon in Rabi'uth-Thani (October) and continues till the end of the winter season, when the snow begins to melt in the mountains and the Euphrates is at high tide. Hence, ' the increase of water in the Shott.'

CHAPTER V

THE MEETING IN THE NUFOUD

THE day I left Bahrain Major Dickson told me that the High Commissioner, Sir Percy Cox, will soon leave Baghdad and is expected to arrive in a few days ; and when I got to Ojair I learned from Saiyed Hashem that the Sultan would soon ride out of Al-Hasa to meet the High Commissioner. I looked up in my map, therefore, the distance between Al-Hasa and Ojair—40 miles—and comparing between a ride of twenty hours in two days (for I would certainly have to return with the Sultan) and a rest of two days to prepare me for the long desert journey, I decided on the latter and wrote to His Highness that in crossing I had slept two nights in the jalbout. But if he desire me to come to him or to wait for him where I am, I am in either case ready :—to hear is to obey.

My letter was carried by a *najjab* (a courier on a fast *zelul*) who started in the early dawn and came back the following morning with a reply even more gracious than the one I had previously received. The Sultan left the matter to my own convenience, however, and informed me that they would leave Al-Hasa on Thursday and ride leisurely to be at Ojair Saturday morning. I had been thinking of riding out to meet him ; and in his letter to Saiyed Hashem there was a suggestion which decided me at once. ' It seems to me,' said the Saiyed, trying to be subtle, ' that His Highness the Sultan would imply in his leisurely march that he would like to see you before he

sees the High Commissioner,' ' To the desert, therefore,'
said I, girthing my loins.

And on the morning of Thursday, when the Sultan
marched out of Al-Hasa, we left Ojair, Saiyed Hashem
and I, accompanied by five servants, one of whom—the
comedian of the caravan—had a donkey carrying our
provisions and some firewood. My *zelul*, by reason of the
spangled breast-cloth, the tassled saddle-bag and the
black sheepskin that covered the rug in the saddle, was
the mount of honour. It was also the best in point of
merit, for she tolerated no one ahead of her, except the
donkey whose time-honoured privilege it is to lead the
caravan. But that she was the best did not help me in
my first experience. I was being rocked and shaken and
pinched and scratched at every step. There was something around me I felt, and under me, and before me,
and behind me, which should not be there ; and those
pommels,[1] wooden pegs a foot long standing upright,
knocked me in the breast and in the back every time I
swayed to and fro in the saddle. Nor did the saddle-
frame seem to be adjusted right : it's tipping to the
side, it's sliding from the hump. And it's pinching somewhere, the indecent thing ! Why, even the girth is loose.
' Saiyed Hashem,' I cried, ' O Saiyed Hashem ! ' ' *Ibsher*, [2]
ibsher,' he replied.

We crouched the camels, and one of the servants,

[1] The saddle-trees, which are called *gazalahs* in Arabia, are a part of the
wooden saddle-frame ; and they are knobby and long, not only to protect
the rider from falling, but also for slinging the ropes around them in loading.
Moreover, the *gazalahs* of the Najd saddles are perpendicular and not very
far apart so that the rider is held in the seat, as it were, by a pair of tongs.
The saddle-frame of the north, those made in Damascus, for instance,
are more convenient, for the *gazalahs* are placed at obtuse angles, thus
giving the rider more room and saving him from the knock in swaying.
But in Oman, the land of the thoroughbred *zelul*, they dispense with
gazalahs altogether. Their wooden frames are made in the shape of an
English saddle.

[2] *Ibsher*, literally rejoice, be of good cheer, that glad tidings or a benefit
of some sort is coming to you. It is mostly used in Iraq and Najd in the
sense of ' as you please ' or ' at your disposition.'

obeying the Saiyed's order with *samm, samm*,[1] came to adjust the saddle and tighten the girth.   After which, depending upon Allah, we resumed our march across the golden dunes and soon reached Umm uz-Zarr,[2] which takes its name from the few trees near by and which is the first watering-place on the way.   We stopped and I was the first to descend.   For the ' *samm* ' of the servant did not adjust anything and the *gazalah* had no compunction.

Soon after we ambled out of Ojair we struck into the Nufoud,[3] where the camels must walk at a very slow pace, making deep footprints in the shape of hearts with daggers in them ; for with their hoofs, as they drag them out of the sand, they draw a long straight line, which is the dagger in the heart.   And the dunes, in their formation and their shades of light and colour,—their undulating lines, their curving sides, their slopes, smooth as rose leaves and as soft, their summits so firmly and deeply etched against a shimmering sky, their shades of gold and purple melting away on one side only to form on another, —they are bewildering, they are bewitching.   Like their colours and shades, the dunes themselves shift and change—to all appearance, melt away.   But they only move, carried by the winds, from place to place.

The horseshoe forms, some of whose slopes are ridged, are particularly fascinating ; they curve from the base and continue to the summit in a regular composition, even symmetrical, but broader as the slope rises and recedes.   We came to a spot near one of these horseshoes, where the bare rock was visible—a white rock looking

---

[1] *Samm* is an abbreviation of *Bismillah* (in the name of Allah) and is used in the same sense of compliance—' ready, sir,' ' at your order '—by the people of Najd only.

[2] *Umm uz-Zarr*, mother of the *zarr*, a tree with a large, thick, brittle and heart-shaped leaf, which is poisonous to animals, and a flower like that of the sweet-pea. Its wood is used by the natives in making gunpowder.

[3] This Nufoud, a sand desert between the coast and Al-Hasa, runs from Qatif in the north to Jafourah in the south. Its breadth from where we crossed it, *i.e.* between Ojair and Jishshah, is about twenty-five miles.

like a salt-pan from a distance—which is a lime-stone
formation. There is also a variety of granite under the
Nufoud, for Al-Hasa, geologists say, is a volcanic region
covered with sand. And also, says the engineers, full of
good water which is found in many places between the
sand and the rock strata.

At Umm uz-Zarr the water forms in a few sand-holes
about two feet deep ; and when there is a run on these,
the cameleer or the traveller just arriving digs another
hole for himself,—digs with his hands till the water begins
to ooze—and fills his *qirbah* (water-skin). It does not
take long to find water or to provide oneself with it. In
ten minutes we filled our *qirbahs* and proceeded, the
camels trudging for three more hours, till we had reached
'Alat in the afternoon.

The billowy dunes rose before us and melted away as
we meandered through them, passing a few places that
seemed to exist only in name. Jasrah, for instance, is a
spot distinguished by the bare rocks, which are like little
barren islands in that sea of sand. And the bleached
camel-bones which I had frequently seen along our path
brought us in the end to the very thing they had suggested
—to the tragedy of loneliness and death ! For there was
a camel, which had crouched but recently and for the
last time !—a ghastly sight. It had twisted its neck in
agony and stuck its head, dying, in the sand. The
comedian that walked behind the donkey,—a simian-
browed, foul-mouthed dwarf of the gutters of Basrah,
who had been mimicking the dancers of that city,—did
not cease his antics as we passed it. On the contrary,
his grotesqueness became odious as he twisted his neck
like the ' *mowta* ' who could ' twist her neck like this
camel.' The ' *mowta* ' (motor car) is what they call the
dancer in Basrah. ' For she is light, O Effendi, and quick,
and she spins like a *mowta*.'

When we descended at 'Alat, which is the name for
the elevated region of the Nufoud—about 300 feet above

sea-level and half-way between Ojair and Hufouf—I for one praised Allah aloud. And Saiyed Hashem, hearing me, thought that six hours' ride for the first day was quite sufficient. I even heard him say to the servant that carried his letter to the Sultan informing him of the place of our encampment : the *zelul* has killed him (meaning me). So we are to rest at 'Alat for the night and go forth in the morning to meet His Highness, who is encamped ten miles away from us at Jishshah.

It did not take our men long to get us under the protecting shade of canvas ; and soon after they had dug two holes in the sand, one for the water-skin, the other for the fire, we were seated on a rug eating our noonday meal. Tea and coffee followed the cold roast, which the Ameer of the *qasr* had prepared for us ; and were it not for the flies, which also came with us from Ojair, I might have dozed away my exhaustion. But when the desert heat abates, especially between sundown and dusk, ten minutes of the vastness and freshness of silence dispel the fatigue of a day's travel. At that hour, as the first star pierces the darkness and the arrows of light follow each other, the desert begins to weave its spell and gradually the inward exultation is exteriorized in a sensuous joy. The charms crowd themselves upon sense and vision. The atmosphere, the vastness and the silence are scented messengers of the infinite ; and the world within reach of hand and heart is all beautiful—beautiful to see, beautiful to touch, beautiful to breathe.

After supper Saiyed Hashem and I started to run like children in our barefeet. The servants followed us and one of them suggested that we have a race. Saiyed Hashem said that he would be the judge and I would give the prize. The servants ran back to the tent—a distance of about two hundred yards—and Majed and Rajhan, who fell, tripped by the ropes, one on top of the other, both claimed the prize. Followed the bragging, which is inevitable with the Arabs. And Majed then stood on his hands to prove to Rajhan that his feet were higher than his own head (Rajhan had called him a low-born beduin) ; that he was honest ; did not lie ; did not steal ; and that howsoever he stands or walks, he can beat him in everything—in running, in wrestling, in shooting, in riding, and in. . . . Here we had to intervene. But Majed, unconscious of his vulgarity, persisted. ' And I can beat him dancing too.' Saying which, he started to dance, while the cook and the coffee boy seated around the fire clapped and applauded. Then they all sat down to the usual evening occupation of sipping coffee and telling tales.

They were still around the fire, when I went into the tent and threw myself on the cot in the softly enveloping joy of realization. For have not the days brought about the fulfilment of one of my dreams ? Here is the desert, here are the camels, here are my slaves ; and am I not a neighbour to one of the great ameers of Arabia, the Sultan of Najd ? I felt that I could now fold my hands and let the Golden Dream close my eyes for ever. But I was still half awake when I heard a voice challenging some one passing by ; and then Saiyed Hashem, after exchanging a few words with the men who had descended near our fire, came hurrying into the tent and said : ' Get up, *ya Ustaz*,[1] get up. The Sultan is coming.'

' True ? ' That is all I could say. And I got up instantly to dress, that is to cover my night garment with an *aba* and my head with a kerchief and *ighal*—the convenience of Arab clothes ! And slipping my feet into a pair of sandals I could walk out and say : Allah greet the comer—welcome, the guest.

The servants hurried in different directions to gather

---

[1] *Ustaz*=professor. But its modern acceptation was borrowed by the Cairo newspapers from the French—*maitre*=master—and was first applied to lawyers only. Now, every Muhammad, Mahmoud and Ahmad, who knows anything, is called *ustaz* in Syria and Iraq, as well as in Egypt ; and I have the newspapers to thank for a questionable title which has stuck to me throughout Arabia.

The Arab side of the Camp at Ojair, to the right, Saiyed Hashem

wood for the fire, and I helped Saiyed Hashem to put our ' house ' in order. We spread the rug inside, placed the camel-saddle in the centre as a leaning pillow, and a sheepskin to the right of it for the royal guest—all that is required for the reception of a king in Arabia.

It was a dazzling night, vested with a transparency of atmosphere which revealed the naked, hard-blue sky and through which the dark outlines of the crescent moon were visible ;—a night in which the distances for sight and hearing are bridged by the ineffable purity and calm of the desert ;—a night that gives wings as well as musical charm to the human voice. And what an unearthly charm had the cry I heard at that moment, coming from behind the dunes, in waves of assurance and awe across the meadows of night ! ' *Ya s'aaiyed, ya s'aaaiyeeeed !* ' [1] The criers, who precede the royal cavalcade, announce the coming of the Sultan, or his passing by, so that those within hearing distance may know ; and if anyone has a claim or a grievance, or likes to join in the march, may follow the voice and be a happy one—a little happy one, a *su'aiyed*.

Ya s'aaaiyeeed ! And soon the heights on which we were encamped reverberated with the cavalcade of the Sultan. More than two hundred camels guggled and growled as they were crouching, while the *ikh, ikh* of the riders and the sound of their bamboos on the necks of their mounts, were like the patter of rain in a grove of palms. Soon after, the tents were pitched, the fires were lighted, and the tintinabulations of the mortars in the coffee pestles were heard.

We hastened forth to meet the great guest, but he was quicker in coming towards us, followed by two of his

---

[1] Most of the Arab ameers have criers and words of proclamation by which they are known when they move from place to place or when they go to battle. Ibn 'ur-Rashid's was *ya farhan* (O thou joyful one) and King Husein's, *ya marzouq* (O thou blessed one). There is a humility in the diminutive of Ibn Sa'oud's *su'aiyed*, which implies that great happiness can come from Allah alone, and that a little happiness only can come from the Ameer.

suite. I said ' guest,' for at that moment, by royal choice, the situation was reversed. We first met on the sands, under the stars, and in the light of the many bonfires that blazed all around. A tall majestic figure in white and brown, overshadowing, overwhelming—that was my first impression. Indeed, I was standing near a giant—he is over six feet but admirably proportioned—who took my hand and held it in his own as we walked into our little tent.

The pomp of power, the ostentation of sultans, the magnificence of the Orient—they are not to be seen in Najd. The Sultan wore the usual brown *aba* over a white robe, and his head was covered with the usual red-checkered cotton kerchief, which everybody wears in his country. The only thing that distinguished him from his subjects is the gold-thread *ighal* which is also worn by some of the members of the royal family. And the first thing that dominates in him is his magnetic smile.

He sat on the sheepskin leaning his right arm against the saddle, and the fire outside of our open tent lighted up his rugged countenance, which is offset by a mobile mouth, full but not heavy, and soft brown eyes. He first introduced the two men that accompanied him—his physician, Dr. Abdullah Damlouji, and his relative, and then representative in Iraq, Abd'ul-Latif Pasha al-Mandil.

Without losing time in the ordinary formalities of conversation that follow the salaam, I apologised to His Highness for my delay in coming and said that when I acquaint him with the facts about the matter he would realize that the fault is not mine.

The Sultan : ' We know all that and we consider it very strange. But we did not hesitate or delay in our reply. And how can we refuse to see you and you are a true Arab ? They told us that you are an American missionary coming to preach Christianity in Arabia ; and they told us that you represented certain Companies who desired concessions in Arabia ; and they told us that

you are come from Al-Hijaz and that you are a supporter
of the cause of the Sherif (King Husein), and other things
were reported to us. But we said : if there is evil in the
man, we know how to avoid it. And if there is good, we
know as well how to benefit by it. Aye, *billah !* We are
better informed, *ya Ustaz,* about your mission. Allah
keep thee and bless thee.'

I asked permission to state the purposes that led me
to travel in Arabia and said : ' The first has been fulfilled
in seeing you ; the second will be fulfilled, *inshallah,* when
I write of what I have seen ; and the third can only be
accomplished by your assistance. I am certain, *ya mowlai*
(O my Lord), that Arab unity can only be realized by
a meeting of all the ruling Ameers for acquaintance first
and a common understanding. They are to-day isolated
from each other, if not at war with each other, and no
one has a true knowledge of his contemporary.'

Then suddenly I found myself arguing, pleading for
a cause. It was not my want of tact, but the want of
reserve, I must say, on the part of my royal guest. He
is open-minded, direct, and delightfully naive.

' Who are the Arabs ? ' he asked, with a spark in his
eye, when I mentioned his contemporaries. ' *We* are the
Arabs ! ' he replied, striking the carpet with his bamboo
stick. ' We know well each other,' he continued ; ' I
know them all. The trouble with the Arab is that he will
not do anything in which his own interest is not paramount.
Add to this that the Arab has a bad trait—many bad
traits—and he has fine qualities also—no worse and no
better than other people. You see the truth. . . . I have
to be aware of my own people—the nearest to me.
Treachery we have discovered among the closest of our
allies. . . . Let us not muddle our heads with fine fancies.
I, Ibn Sa'oud, what do I want ? Two things are essential
to our State and our people, two fundamental things :
religion and the rights inherited from our fathers. To
these I add two things, which are deemed essential in

these days : right relationship with the foreigner and right understanding among ourselves.'

A black slave entered carrying in his left hand the coffee pot and in his right the cups. He poured first to the Sultan and then to me.

' Do you know, *ya Ustaz*, that we were the first to invite the Ameers to a conference to discuss our common interests ? You will have the proof of this, *inshallah*. But we shall not trouble you further to-night. You are tired and you need sleep.'

It was about midnight when he said salaam outside our little tent and would not let me walk with him to his own. The bonfires were extinguished, the camp was asleep and silence had filled again the dimly lighted night. I re-entered my tent, which a minute ago was the *majlis* of a Sultan, and not feeling the need of sleep, I lit the candle and wrote in my diary a few pages, from which I copy the following :

I have now met all the Kings of Arabia and I find no one among them bigger than this man. He is big in word and gesture and smile, as well as in purpose and self-confidence. His personality is complex. . . . The shake of his hand and the way he strikes the ground with his stick proclaim the contrary traits of the man. . . . He gives you the report about yourself and then pats you on the back telling you that he knows better. He gives you at the first meeting a bit of his mind and his heart, without fear, without reserve. . . . He knows himself as well as he knows his people. *Hinna 'l-Arab* (we are the Arabs) ! The man in him is certainly bigger than the Sultan, for he dominates his people with his personality, not with his title. . . . Strange, indeed. I came to Ibn Sa'oud with an unburdened heart, bearing him neither hatred nor love, accepting neither the English view of him nor that of the sherifs of Al-Hijaz. I came to him in fact with a hard heart and a critical mind, and I can say that he captured my heart at the first meeting. Admiration, however, and love may not go together all the way. We shall see. I promised to be free and open-minded with him. He gave me the privilege, and promised to be the same with me. . . .

I think I can trust my first impressions, however, and I am not reluctant. Moreover, I have now a gallery of Kings for comparison. . . . And I am glad I came last to Ibn Sa'oud.

It was one after midnight when I went to bed, and about four in the morning when Saiyed Hashem shook me out of my sleep, saying, 'The Sultan is up.' The camp was awake, the fires were lighted, the pestles were grounding the coffee in the mortars, and I heard a voice rising slowly above the hubbub and clatter, rising slowly, quietly to meet the dawn. It was the muazzen, calling the morning prayer. 'Prayer were better than sleep,' he chanted, 'prayer were better than sleep. . . . *La ilaha ill' Allah!*' And in half an hour the Arabs had said their prayers, taken their coffee, laded their camels, and—they silently stole away.

CHAPTER VI

WITH THE SULTAN ON THE MARCH

THE Arabs, especially in Najd, travel mostly at night ; and when they do so in the day, they start invariably an hour or two before dawn. The Sultan Abd'ul-Aziz rises even earlier than his men, is quick in preparing for the march, and is often the first one ready for the morning prayer, which is performed at that hour to avoid stopping for that purpose at dawn. It is one of his military rules, and he is the first to observe it although he has to content himself with two hours of sleep. He is vigorous enough and sinewy enough to do so. Besides, he requires but a quarter of an hour to prepare for the march.

Here I was beaten. For although what is sufficient sleep for him might be sufficient for me, I could not, on my second day in the desert, compete with him in the rest. The royal cavalcade, therefore, started ahead of our little caravan. But as by a miracle, Saiyed Hashem applying the bamboo to his *zelul*, and I, without a thought to what may happen, doing likewise, we caught up in an hour with it as it moved slowly among the dunes that were suffused with the roseate hues of dawn. And the Sultan's golden *ighal* was seen at the head of the cavalcade high above the heads of those who rode in front with him. It was a sign, a beckoning sign. And I had the courage to ride away from my *rafiq*, ' bambooing ' my *zelul* recklessly, and marvelling, as I penetrated through the ranks, at my skill, which seemed to have come to me suddenly as by inspiration. But I must not deny a share

The Bodyguard of King Abd'ul-Aziz

of the credit to my *zelul*, which, being an Omaniyah, did not relax her pace till it had reached her goal and then went gliding neck to neck with that of the Sultan. 'We did not think,' he said, quite surprised, ' that you rise early.'

Thus it was that the first time I said, Good morning to Ibn Sa'oud was from the height of a camel saddle in the Nufoud. And we rode side by side towards the rising sun in a file that ranged from five to fifteen, followed by many more like it, as the cavalcade broke and re-formed without order, some of the servants and black slaves sometimes riding with the soldiers or with the Sultan's entourage. The baggage train—tents and furniture and provisions—went ahead as usual, except for a few sluggish beasts, carrying waterskins and kitchen utensils—pots large enough to take a bath in and metal platters to hold a whole sheep—that were straggling in the rear. No, it was not an army on the march. We were not going on a raid or to battle. The rifles, encased in European leather or wrapt in cloth, were slung behind from the rear *gazalahs ;* and the swords in their scabbards—some of which were carried in native-made cases of leather ornamented with strips of many colours—swung on the side with the long red and yellow tassled hangings of the saddle-bags. We were on the way to a Peace Conference, and every one was wrapt in the *aba* of security and, at that hour of the morning, of pious silence.

The Sultan alone spoke. And like every Arab ruler, he prefers politics to other topics, especially the politics of Europe in the Near East. But he chose that morning to speak of America and its political policy with the Allies.

He asked me to tell him what caused the fall of President Wilson. And when I said, after speaking of the elections and the political parties, that the spirit of partisanship has a great dominating influence upon the nation and the Government, he exclaimed : ' Strange ! And does it not lead them to war ? '

'They solve their political problems by the vote.'

'*Zein* (good). And how many parties have they?'

'Two principal parties and many minor ones.'

'*Zein*. And how does the victorious party satisfy the claims of the others?'

'The minority bows always, *ya Mowlai*, to the majority.'

'But Wilson ruled, and the majority, as you say, is with the ruler. How then did Wilson fall?'

'The majority was not with him in the last election. Many of his supporters deserted him and voted against him.'

The Sultan raised his bamboo stick and stroked lightly the neck of his *zelul*, saying: 'I do not think they did well. Wilson is a great man. And his is the credit for awakening the small oppressed nations of the world. Wilson showed them the way to freedom and independence. He has infused, especially into the people of the East, a new spirit. He has also made America known to us. We did not know America before Wilson. And now that he has spoken truth to the world in her name, she is indebted to him as the world is indebted to her. . . . I have great respect for America, *ya Ustaz*, even if her policy with the Allies now is not the policy of Wilson. . . . America is the mother of weak nations, and we Arabs are of them. . . . A man of good sense needs but a suggestion—point the way to him, and that is sufficient. . . . I invite you to my board, for instance,' saying which he turned to the man on the other side of him, 'but would you expect me to feed you also—to put the morsel in your mouth? It is sufficient, what America has done —what she said to the small oppressed nations—what Wilson said in her name. And the man of good sense is he who strives for himself and profits by the striving.'

As for Europe, the Sultan Abd'ul-Aziz expressed his opinion eloquently and forcefully in a brief word. He said: 'I liken Europe to-day to a great iron door, but there is nothing behind it.' That is why he does not blame America for her isolation. ' It would be strange if she continued as the partner of Europe.' He changed his seat in the saddle, crossing his right foot in front of the *gazalah* to relieve the left, and turning to one of his henchmen, he continued : ' I say, the partnership of America and Europe to-day is like my partnership—the partnership of Ibn Sa'oud—with the Bedu of the North. You see the truth.' He who was addressed nodded in approval.

We had reached the top of a hill, half-way between 'Alat and Umm uz-Zarr, where the Sultan crouched his *zelul* and the cavalcade came to a halt—the first halt for breakfast. We sat in groups on the cleanest and finest of golden sand ; and round mats of palm leaves were spread before us on which the servants placed the food, which consisted of the inevitable central dish of rice and lamb, a roast chicken thrown whole, and delicious Hasa dates. Soon after the servants were seen removing the mats and the leavings to their own various groups. They brought us water and soap to wash our hands. And the Imam—he prefers to be called by his religious title—addressed us in his high-pitched but full voice from his side of the hill, saying : ' Shall we come to you or will you come to us ? '

He did not wait for a reply. But as we hastened to him, he walked slowly towards us, followed by his relatives and his captives,—among them was his brother Muhammad, the Amir Faisal ibn 'ur-Rashid, and the last King of Haiel Abdullah ibn Mit'eb,—whom he introduced. He then sat down cross-legged on the sand, saying, ' this is our best carpet,' and invited me to do likewise. The best carpet, of a truth, in the reception hall of Allah. And while the Imam was holding forth on what he considered to be the only sound basis of every State—religion and justice—the relatives and the captives got up, without any ceremony or word of salaam, and walked away.

' These are Arabs,' said he, pointing to them, ' and

these,' pointing to the blacks who were still eating their breakfast, ' they are also Arabs. I am responsible before Allah for them all. . . . We the people of Najd follow the Prophet, who recognized no differences in rank among Muslems. And we would preserve, above all things, our religion and our honour. . . .'

We continued the conversation as we rocked along, the necks of our *zeluls* gracefully keeping time with each other ; and those who rode around and behind us seemed to be pleased particularly with the talk of the Imam. For he has an alert mind and a great flow of speech ;—is eloquent of tongue and quick-witted. He asked me how England was faring with France, and what were the last demands of Mustapha Kemal. The Arabic translations of Reuter which he receives through his Agents in Bahrain, together with the newspapers of Cairo and Damascus, help him to keep abreast of the times. And as we were speculating on the possibilities of the Conference which was to be held at that time in Lausanne, he reverted to Europe and America. ' Europe,' said he, ' thought of her interests before she made the sacrifice in the War. America made the sacrifice first, and she had no interests to think about. . . . Yes, England is of Europe . . . and I am the friend of the Ingliz, their ally. But I will walk with them only as far as my religion and my honour will permit. . . .'

We camped about ten o'clock at Umm uz-Zarr, the Sultan's tent occupying a central position among many others, of camel hair and of canvas, that were pitched around it. The fires were then lighted and people began to visit each other. I had my coffee with the Imam, who sent for me to continue the discussion about the Ingliz, or as he pronounces it, the Inglaiz.

The man's energy and staying power are amazing. He sleeps but few hours at night and seldom in the daytime. He was in fine fettle that afternoon and particularly animated. But I was exhausted and felt the need of sleep ;

and had I yielded to a sense of shame or false consideration, I do not think I could have continued in the march
the following day. I asked him if he did not sleep in the
afternoon, and suddenly, in the most tender accent,—as
if he had been guilty of an offence for which he would
atone,—he said, rising : ' Forgive us, *ya Ustaz*, we have
tired you.'

But when I returned to my tent I found it full of flies.
Flies in the sand desert,—in that vestibule of the Infinite,
which Allah hath cleaned of everything but the freshness
of the air and the silence—they are the worst of all
abominations ! And where do they come from ? They
ride with you on the *zelul*, on her back, and on your back,
and on your head ; and they get ahead of you to the tent
and crush in you what remains of hope in life.

But Allah, praised be he ! revives your hope at sunset
and you go out to respond to the call of the mauzzen, if
you be a right Muslim, or to the higher voice, which is
whispered through the vast silence at that hour, if you
be a votary of the Universe. And lo, in the dim light that
filters through the invisible stained glass of the Temple
are tremulous shades of lilac and sea-green and violet.
The sand hills undulate with colour ; the sand under our
feet is beginning to cool ; and the horizon itself, lulled
in the mild refreshing breeze, seems to expand with a
sense of satisfaction and praise.

The Wahhabis, standing in two long lines behind the
Imam,[1] were at prayer. The Sultan stood in the centre
of the first row, guarded by a soldier who stands behind
him with sword drawn and does not join in the ceremony.[2]
It was the first time I had heard the Wahhabis pray in
congregation. Like the Christians, they chant, Amen !

---

[1] Imam=leader. He who leads in prayer is also called *imam* like the
Head of the Wahhabis himself. But the title is applied to him only in
connection with prayer.

[2] The great grandfather of the Sultan Abd'ul-Aziz, the Imam Turki
ibn Sa'oud, was assassinated while praying in public, and from that time
was instituted the custom of guarding the Imam on such occasions.

when the *imam* finishes a prayer or an invocation. *Praise be to Allah, the God of all creation !—guide us in the right path —the path of those who do not go astray.* And the voice of the congregation chanting, Amen ! is like the sound of Lebanon bells as they echo down the wadi and across the hills.

Guide us in the right path ! It is only when you travel in the trackless waste, among the ever-shifting dunes, that you realize the full potency of these words. The right path, indeed. All the desires of man, whether in Arabia or in America, are centred in this one wish, to be guided in his ' trek '—to be saved from the desert or the Thing that decoys and devours.

On the morning of the following day a *najjab* arrived bringing news from Bahrain. Sir Percy Cox is coming on a gunboat and will soon arrive. But he is bringing with him, among others, the British Political Agent in Kuwait and Sheikh Fahd ul-Hazzal, Chief of a section of the tribe of 'Aneza in the North. This is what angered the Sultan. For Sheikh Fahd, whose *dirah*, watering and pasture region, is in Wadi Hauran, on the road between Damascus and Baghdad, seems to be a wily Turkefied Arab who draws his revenue from several questionable sources, besides the Government of Iraq, and who had been fomenting raids on the boundaries of Najd. He was even nursing a scheme, which the British Authorities at one time countenanced, of creating an independent State under his ameership—a buffer State—between Najd and Iraq. The Sultan read the letter from Bahrain and showed it, without saying a word, to his brother.

We resumed our march at a slow pace through the very difficult Nufoud in a majesty of awe and silence. The Sultan, who does not always ride at the head of the cavalcade, could be distinguished even without his silk *ighal* ; for he towers wherever he be above the rest. Even his red Omaniyah, I discovered afterwards, was taller and had a higher hump than all her contemporaries.

THE WAHHABI HOST AT PRAYER

In silence we rode ahead ; and for a while, as the camels trudged through the sand, only the squeak of the saddles was heard. Soon a man near the Sultan started to intone verses from the Koran, and the few hundred Arabs behind him, swaying with devotion, chanted in chorus, Amen. The camels themselves seemed to keep time with the rhythmic human movement of body and voice. Their graceful neck performance, when ten or fifteen abreast sinuously sway in unison, is most fascinating.

When the reading from the Koran ceased, the Sultan after a moment of ominous silence spoke. He was addressing the man near him, and his voice rose gradually to a pitch.—' Wherefore comes Ibn ul-Hazzal ? And wherefore comes the Consul of Kuwait ? Do they want to force a boundary settlement upon us ? No one can force anything upon us. *La wallah* (No, by God) ! What was the right of our forbears, is our right. And if we cannot get it by friendly means, we will get it by the sword . . . why should I, Ibn Sa'oud, be made to yield what is rightly mine ? . . . They may spin (this is a favourite word with him, by which he means, to intrigue and plot ; and he accompanies it always with a circular movement of his index finger—a pretty gesture) and spin for their purpose. But I am a man of my word—I speak the plain truth. What have we to fear ? We ask for nothing but our rights. . . . Let them spin, and let the Inglaiz spin with them--spin for them too. I am not a spinner. I am a straightforward, plain-spoken man. . . . The Inglaiz are my friends. Yes, I am also their friend. If they insist—if they say, Do this for our sake—I will set my seal to it. But the folly of the wise is a folly manifold.' And then he quoted the Arab poet :

> ' Let none be with us proud and overbearing,
> For we can be more foolish and more daring.'

CHAPTER VII

THE SULTAN [1] ABD'UL-AZIZ

THE Sultan Abd'ul-Aziz is tall of stature, muscular, sinewy, and of noble proportions ; has the Arab's complexion, but not the physiognomy—a swarthy face, without the high cheek-bones ; has not the Semitic nose, —his is straight but slightly upturned—and is quite modern in his beard and moustache, which he trims, Wahhabi-fashion. His age, from the viewpoint of the calendar, is, at the time I write, forty-nine ; and from the viewpoint of achievement and history—the modern history of Najd—a hundred years may be added to it. He wears robes of white linen in the summer, of cloth in the winter, under a brown *aba* of camel-hair ; goes in sandals ; perfumes himself profusely ; and carries an unstained staff,[2] which he uses as an aid to expression,— with which he underlines a word, as it were, or emphasizes an idea. He has other aids to expression in his well-modelled hands, which are particularly elegant and eloquent in gesture ; and in his dark brown eyes, which throw a soft light on the feeling in his speech when he is in good humour, and which inflame his words when he is roused to anger. His mouth in the former state, like a red rose leaf, becomes in the latter like iron. The lips, shrunk and taut, white and trembling, the colour in a trice disappearing from them, suggest a blade of vibrating steel.

[1] See page xvii.

[2] The Sultan always carries his staff, even in his public *majlis*. The light bamboo stick is used as a whip in riding.

H.M. KING [1] ABD'UL-AZIZ AND THE AUTHOR

[1] See page xvii

Indeed, Ibn Sa'oud in anger changes completely and suddenly. All the charm of his features gives way to a mordant, savage expression. Even the light in his smile becomes a white flame. He is then terrible. He turned to me when he was pouring his wrath upon Ibn Hazzal and the 'spinners'—intriguers, plotters—and asked : ' What do you say, *ya Ustaz ?* ' It was a bit awkward ; for there were three or four camels between us and I had to shout out whatever I had to say. But I could not at that moment think of anything more appropriate than one of the commonplaces of Islam : Verily, Allah is with the patient people. He repeated the words, but not in a tone of resignation ; and pressing his bare heel against the breast of his *zelul,* as he stroked her neck lightly with the bamboo switch, he went at a *dirham* [1] pace and we followed suit.

I confess that I experienced a revulsion of feeling when I first saw Ibn Sa'oud in a fit of temper ; and when he would interrupt me with, ' Hearken ! I will inform thee,' I could hardly believe that I was in the presence of the same man who visited me in my tent in the Nufoud. But his anger subsides, as it blazes, quickly. No sooner does he strike the ground with his staff than he reaches for your heart and frequently overwhelms it in compensation. Even when he realizes that he has been hasty in his words, he confesses it in a kind and often in an amusing manner, which is completely disarming. One of his men was brought before him to answer for an offence he had committed. The Sultan listened to his story and said : ' It is my fault, because I did not warn thee. Therefore, I shall not punish thee this time.'

A living conscience that guides his sense of justice ; a clemency that vies with his generosity ; an alert mind trained in the business of a simple life and, therefore,

---

[1] The *dirham* in Najd and Al-Hijaz is the running pace of a camel, and it is of three degrees : the dirham which is an amble, the dirham trot, and the dirham gallop—*ghārah.*

intensely alert ; a light-heartedness which often dispels
the clouds of depression in his *majlis*—these are some of
the good traits in the character of Ibn Sa'oud. He has
also a sense of humour which is seldom unrefined, and
a pretty wit, which can well turn the weapon of sarcasm.
One of the notables of Najd, a pompous-mannered bore,
used to come into the public *majlis* with a splurge. So
the Sultan, once speaking of him, said : ' He is a quarter
of the world,' and then in a modulated accent, ' the vacant
quarter ' (meaning the great sand desert in the south of
Arabia).

When the camp was pitched in Ojair, the tents of the
High Commissioner and the Iraq Delegation were set
apart from those of the Sultan and his men. It was a
double camp, in fact ; and the European side was
furnished with all the comforts and some of the luxuries
of civilization, which had come, thanks to Al-Qosaibi,
from Bahrain and were there ahead of us. So when we
arrived the Sultan asked me to go with him on a tour of
inspection. Evidently there is no more democracy in
this camp than there is on an ocean liner. He who will
occupy the cabin-de-luxe, however, is not the Sultan, but
his first guest, Sir Percy Cox. And those who will travel,
camp rather on Deck B, are not the Sultan's retinue and
ameers, but the Englishmen who are coming with the
High Commissioner and the Iraq Delegation. They have
even a bath-room under canvas.

We walked through the luxuriously furnished camp,
which he described as the civilization of Ojair. And
when we entered into the reception tent, which was furnished with beautiful carpets and upholstered chairs,
he sat down saying, ' Let us have a little civilization.'
He invited me to a chair, and, clapping for the servant,
he ordered tea.

I took the opportunity at that moment to put in a word,
not for the British or the Iraq Government, nor for the
tribes of Hazzal, but for peace and peace foremost—

SHEIKH MUHAMMAD NASIF
' The Bibliophile of Jeddah ' with his children

for the general good of the Arabs and Arabia—A strong man is never afraid of making concessions in the interest of peace—he who can and would do so is entitled to be counted among the great—I have the honour of addressing one of them now, etc., etc. The Sultan Abd'ul-Aziz is not unamenable to flattery. He knows his strength, of a truth, but he does not disdain a word of recognition or praise. Fulsome praise, however, he scorns.

The tea was served, not in small glasses, Persian style, which is also the fashion in Arabia, but in large cups with milk. Whereupon, the Sultan : ' This is civilized tea. And the Inglaiz drink it, not as we drink our coffee, like this, but without noise, like this.' To the delight of Al-Qosaibi and myself, he gave an illustration of both manners. And then reverting to our serious discussion he assured me that he desired peace, desired it more than any other ruler in Arabia. ' We have to restrain ourselves—all the time. I have to keep my people in check—all the time. You see the truth. Let them stop encroaching upon us, and let them come to us with honest hearts.' He launched into his favourite grievance again, and I was afraid of his getting into another paroxysm of rage. But he didn't. On the contrary, as we were going back to our side of the camp he joked again about the civilization of Ojair. And a little truth lurked in his irony when, arriving at his own tent, he said : ' You see, we are not very far from civilization—a few steps only.'

Here too were beautiful carpets, but no chairs. On one side, however, there was an elevated cushion, a sort of low diwan, covered with a rug, and divided into two seats by the camel saddle. This is the ordinary *majlis* of an Arab, be he an ameer or a cameleer ; and he carries its furniture with him, under him, when he travels. The bedding and the carpet soften his saddle-seat on the march, and serve him as a *majlis* when he camps. I could not help thinking, when I first sat on the bed and diwan of the Sultan Abd'ul-Aziz, with a feeling of something

suppressed,—it was neither amusement nor a reminiscent
gloom, but a little perhaps of both,—of the one-room
diggings of a Bohemian artist in New York, who with a
damask cover or a worn-out carpet makes a diwan in the
daytime of his or her bed.   I must not pursue the comparison, however, lest my bamboozling Bohemians
think that a Sultan of Arabia is stealing their ideas.   But
he too carries neither gold nor silver, nor a watch, nor a
fountain pen : he has no pockets in his clothes.   And yet,
he must know the time, at least, for the purpose of prayer.
One day I saw him pull out from under his pillow a little
velvet-covered case, which he carries in his saddle-bag
when riding, and he opened it to consult the watch therein.
Another article he cannot dispense with, and that is a
field glass.   He must see, and see far, always and ever.
From his seat, with the binoculars to his eyes, he watches
the camp and everything that moves in it, and beyond it,
—watches every shadow, every cloud of dust that looms
up on the horizon. He must know, and be the first to know,
since he must be the first to act or to give orders for action.

' Our life is a problem, *ya Ustaz*.   Upon us the
responsibility of big things and small.   If we do not
continually observe, therefore, we would not be properly
acquainted with our own affairs. . . .   The ameer and
the slave, our eye must watch both to be able to do justice
to both.'

He was then watching a caravan which had just arrived
from Al-Hasa with water and vegetables.   One of the
camels, evidently, was being misused.   He sent for the
head-man to come before him.   ' What is the matter with
that camel,' he asked.   ' Vicious, O thou Long-of-days,'
the man replied,—' Do not take him back with you to
Al-Hasa then.   Turn him here with the *jaish* [1] to pasture.'

And he took up the thread of conversation, saying :
' Our justice begins with the *'bel* (ibel=camels).   He

[1] *jaish* =army. It is applied in Najd collectively to all the camels, *zeluls*
and beasts of burden, of a caravan.

who is not just to his camel, *ya Ustaz*, cannot be just to people.'

Thus often would his attention be turned from the conversation to what would seem an insignificant thing ; a servant or one of the Secretaries would then enter to interrupt again the discussion ; and the Sultan, after disposing of both matters, would go back—that is what used to amaze me—to where he stopped, without asking, What was I saying ? as is the wont of most people under such circumstances. No, I do not remember him asking once this question, although our conversations were always subject to interruptions. He has, in fact, an excellent memory as well as an alert mind. Upon him, indeed, the responsibility of big things and small ; and his is the corrective and effective hand in both.

We had been three days in Ojair when the High Commissioner Sir Percy Cox arrived ; during which time the Arabs were giving the finishing touches to the Civilization they themselves had built—the Civilization of Ojair. The tents were furnished with all the needs of gentlemen —commissioners and scribes and delegates and special envoys—who had come to cement the differences of nations, without losing, on the sand-wastes of Al-Hasa, their creature comforts. Even the dining tent was furnished with luxuries from Bombay and London and Paris and Havana. Of a truth, there were choice fruits from one of the best markets in India—the Crawford Market ; water from beyond the seven, to be exact, the five seas (those who did not like Source Cachet could have Perrier); sealed bottles with the name of Johnny Walker upon them, and, by the Prophet ! big black cigars to smoke in the neighbourhood of the Ikhwan of Najd. The Sultan Abd'ul-Aziz did not, of course, order all these things. He only had to write to Al-Qosaibi that our friends the Inglaiz must not, while his guests, even on the dreary coast of Ojair, miss anything they are accustomed to have in their official or private capacities at home.

They too brought other things with them, principally their dinner clothes. Marvel at these ' Inglaiz ' who do not forget their little formalities in the desert. When I was asked by the High Commissioner to dine with them one evening, I found them all, even the Delegate of the Iraq Government, in smoking jackets, and I was the only one, besides the Sultan, who sat at the head of the table, in Arab clothes. Which pleased him, methinks. But he did not criticize the English, who were not, of course, dressing for themselves only ; nor did he say anything about the Arab-Iraq gentleman, who was expected to put on, at least, an *aba* and *ighal*.

We ate with ' the instruments,' that is, with knife and fork and spoon, that evening ; we drank Source Cachet water ; the dinner was served in the most proper manner ; we had fruits and sweets which never got across to our side of the camp ; and we came out of the tent feeling no better than we went into it. ' We had too much of Civilization this evening,' said the Sultan, as we walked to the reception pavilion, where we said Good night to our civilized friends. His Highness would give them a chance to have their smoke.

And that evening we strolled together, the Sultan Abd'ul-Aziz and I, hand in hand, barefoot on the sand, on the cool, refreshing sand, under the brilliant stars that seemed to come so near to us with their light of assurance and peace. There was, of a certainty, something more than clothes and language that drew me to this man.

I referred at the opening of this chapter to the value in time of the achievements of the Sultan Abd'ul-Aziz. The position he occupies in Central Arabia to-day was occupied by the Ameer Muhammad Ibn 'ur-Rashid thirty-five years ago. Indeed, only thirty-five years ago, his father Abd'ur-Rahman, who still lives, having lost Ar-Riyadh, the capital and the last stronghold of his Kingdom, was an exile with his family in Kuwait. Ten years later (1318 H.—1900 A.D.) his son Abd'ul-Aziz,

MOUNTED FORCES OF NAJD

then twenty-four years of age, joined the forces of Sheikh
Mubarak of Kuwait against their common enemy Ibn
'ur-Rashid. They were defeated at the battle of Sarif.
But that did not discourage Abd'ul-Aziz, who was bent
on the *gazu*—on conquest ;—he dreamed of regaining his
father's kingdom. So he asked Sheikh Mubarak for a
little loan. And Sheikh Mubarak, who would see Ibn
'ur-Rashid crushed at any price, complied. Whereupon,
in the same year of 1900, Abd'ul-Aziz at the head of a
band of twenty Arabs—among them his senior brother
Muhammad—riding on mangy camels sallied out of
Kuwait ; and a few months later, at the beginning of
1901, he captured Ar-Riyadh.

That is the beginning of Abd'ul-Aziz ibn Sa'oud's
career of conquest ; and from the year 1901 to the fall
of Haiel in 1921, his star, though subject to many vicissi-
tudes of darkness, was ever rising. He put the Turks out
of Al-Hasa in the east and out of Abha in the west of
the Peninsula ; he conquered Al-Qasim and the Shammar
Mountains in the north and Wadi 'd-Dawasir and Najran
in the south ; he fought the unruly tribes of Central
Arabia and brought them all back to law and religion :
but he has experienced in that small compass—small,
despite these achievements—of a desert existence, all the
trials and sufferings and privations that may fall to the
lot of man.

One evening in Ojair—we were still waiting for Sir
Percy Cox to arrive—he related of his war exploits in
most picturesque and eloquent speech, speaking of his
defeats with the same gusto as he spoke of his triumphs.
' We have no secrets,' he said, as he blew in his hand,
which he held up to his mouth in the shape of a trumpet.
' I made peace with Ibn 'ur-Rashid—a little peace—
which neither of us was going to observe.' For having
been threatened in the south by his own people, and in
the west by the Turks, he had to do something to smother
the hostile fire in the north. And how he subsequently

conquered Ibn 'ur-Rashid and annexed Al-Qasim, when
he, Ibn Sa'oud was an outcast with nothing but his gun
and a score of men—how Allah had given him victory
when there was nothing but death before him—he told
in a manner which the best of actors might admire. ' The
worst moment in the life of a man,' he continued, ' is
when there is neither fear nor assurance in his heart.'
And he leaned his cheek upon the palm of his hand,
half opening his mouth and half closing his eyes, to illustrate his meaning.

This is Abd'ul-Aziz ibn Sa'oud.   Whatever then one
says of him, he is first and foremost a man—a man with
a big heart and a big soul—a real, rugged, unaffected
Arab.   He has all the virtues of the Arab, magnified to
kingly power ; and he has the Arab's failings, which he
never attempts to conceal.   Without pretentions himself,
he can see through things—sees the thing itself, not its
shadow or its embellishments.   There are no puddles in
his mind, except that dark zone, which in his race is the
result of centuries of uneducation ; and there are no
dark spots in his soul, except those vacuities for which
Al-Islam alone is responsible.   In Europe he would have
been a great King as well as a great leader of men—one
who would leave an enduring heritage of greatness.   As it
is, he is the leader and guide and protector of about
three million souls, most of whom are of the Bedu of all
the tribes.   And these followers, brothers of Ibn Sa'oud,
are scattered over an area of eight hundred thousand
square miles, in villages hundreds of miles from the sea,
in oases hundreds of miles from each other, and in the
open desert, wherever there be a seapage of water or a
patch of pasture land.   A vast kingdom, exiguous in
production as well as in population, with no means of
communication except the *najjab*, and no other guaranty
of security and peace than the religion of Ibn Abd'ul-
Wahhab and the word of Ibn Sa'oud.

CHAPTER VIII

BETWEEN IRAQ AND AL-HIJAZ

WHEN I first met the High Commissioner Sir Percy Cox in Baghdad, he said to me that the purpose of his visit to Ibn Sa'oud was to consummate the Treaty between Najd and Iraq ;—the Treaty which had been negotiated at the Muhammarah Conference a few months before that time, and which the Sultan Abd'ul-Aziz refused to sign, because his representatives at that Conference made an unwarranted concession about the two tribes of 'Amarat and Dhafir that are claimed by the Governments of both Iraq and Najd. It was King Faisal's idea that the question should be referred to a committee of experts, whose decision would be binding on both Governments ; and Sir Percy Cox had come to Ojair to persuade his friend Ibn Sa'oud to sign the Treaty and to accept the decision of the boundary experts concerning 'Amarat and Dhafir.

But it did not occur to the Sultan Abd'ul-Aziz, who had come to Al-Hasa for an entirely different purpose, that the High Commissioner and the Iraq Government were still manoeuvring for the Muhammarah Treaty ; and when he learned the morning we were crossing the Nufoud of the coming of the Iraq Delegation he became wrathful and threatening. He told me that it was he who had asked the High Commissioner to come to Al-Hasa to discuss certain matters of importance, and that he had come to meet him, therefore, in Ojair. As for the two tribes, 'Amarat and Dhafir, he would not have troubled himself to come out of Ar-Riyadh about them. His rights to them are incontestable according to the brief which he had prepared for his Representatives at the Muhammarah Conference, the gist of which is as follows :

First,—When the Kingdom of Aal Sa'oud was dismembered, parts of it fell to the lot of the Turks, while other parts were ruled by Ibn 'ur-Rashid. Later, the present Sultan re-conquered it, established his authority over Najd entire, wrested Al-Qasim from Ibn 'ur-Rashid and put the Turks out of Al-Hasa and Qatif. And he still seeks to regain what remains of the Kingdom of his ancestors and to establish his authority over all their tribes in the north and in the south—everywhere in the Peninsula.

Secondly,—The Dhafir tribe, which now inhabits the Shamiyah district of Iraq, was formerly subject to the authority of Ibn Sa'oud. The Dhafirs migrated northward seeking pasture, and they often return to Najd territory for that purpose. Ibn Sa'oud has the right to levy taxes upon them. As for the 'Amarat and the Ruwala, they are two branches of the great tribe of 'Aneza and they formerly were of Najd, living in the province of Al-Qasim. Their Sheikhs Benu Hazzal and Benu Sha'lan are cousins of Aal Sa'oud and of their subjects.

Thirdly,—When the English entered Iraq, they respected the boundaries which were formerly acknowledged by the Ottoman Government as the eastern boundary, for instance, between Persia and Iraq, and the southern boundary, between Iraq and Kuwait. They have also accepted the *status quo* existing at that time between the Turks and the ruling Arab Ameers, their neighbours, foremost among them Ibn 'ur-Rashid. And as the present Sultan of Najd has conquered the Kingdom of Ibn 'ur-Rashid and exercised his authority over all its dominions and its subjects, urban and bedu, he has a right to those of them like 'Amarat and Dhafir who have moved to Iraq.

I have often heard the Sultan Abd'ul-Aziz say : ' These Arabs are of the subject tribes of our forbears. Nay, they are our cousins.' This last, ' our cousins,' is a standing argument of his against any assumption of independent authority by any of the Sheikhs of the tribes. They are our cousins. Ergo, we must protect them. Ergo, they must accept our advice and submit to our authority. Something like English protection forsooth. As for Ibn Hazzal and Ibn Sha'lan, they are his cousins because they are the Sheikhs respectively of the 'Amarat and the Ruwala ; and these two tribes are, as I said, branches of 'Aneza ; and 'Aneza, as it is written in the books of genealogy and lineage, which, next to the Commentaries on the Koran, are the most esteemed in Arabia, is a brother of Wa'el of the house of Rabi'ah, of which Ibn Sa'oud is a direct descendant. 'Aneza and all its branches, therefore, are cousins, who are entitled to his protection. And they shall get it, whether they ask for it or not, if Nouri the minion of the French and Fahd the minion of the English do not look out. Meanwhile, the sword of Ibn Sa'oud is busy elsewhere, and they need not worry. It should be remembered, however, that north of Jabal 'Aneiz, east and west, between Syria and Iraq, are scattered his cousins the 'Amarats and the Ruwalas, and that stipends and mandates are not eternal.

It was the Sultan Abd'ul-Aziz, as I have said, who had asked the High Commissioner Sir Percy Cox to meet him at Ojair ; but what were the matters of importance which he wanted to discuss with him ? ' People think,' said the Sultan to me, ' that we are receiving large sums of money from the Inglaiz. But of a truth, they have only paid small sums considering our services in their behalf. What we have done for the Inglaiz during the war and after no other Arab could do. And we will keep faith with them, even through loss and injury, so long as they keep faith with us. . . . Be assured, *ya Ustaz*, the Inglaiz are my debtors. But I make no claims. And yet, see what they have done to me—to Ibn Sa'oud their friend and ally. They spin, and spin—spin nets for me.

They have surrounded me with enemies—set up states which they are supporting against me.   The grey-haired one (King Husein) in Mecca, his son Abdullah in Trans-Jordania, his other son Faisal in Al-Iraq. . . .   Ever since Faisal came to Al-Iraq the troubles in Shamiyah (where the Dhafir and some of the 'Amarat now make their home) have not ceased. . . .   And what is Ibn Sa'oud, the friend of the Inglaiz, in the eye of the Sherif and his sons ?   He is a ruffian, an infidel, a bandit.   It is true, *ya Ustaz*, they have said all that—they have said more than that. Albeit, they ask me to make war against the French in Syria.   I will show you.'

He called one of his Secretaries and asked him to bring certain numbers of the *Qiblah*,[1] in one of which is a poem written by a poet of the Hijaz, appealing to him in the name of the Arabs—calling upon him to free Syria from the French—and in the others are virulent attacks upon Ibn Sa'oud the infidel, the cut-throat bandit.   I tried to say something palliative.   ' The newspapers are the same, *ya mowlai*, whether in the Holy City of Mecca or in New York.'   But my words had the contrary effect ; for the soft light had departed from his eyes and the crimson had left his lips.   His anger was rising.   ' Hearken, I will inform thee.   This is written by the Sherif himself, and not by a needy scribe.   And I will show you the contrary of it, written in his own hand.   Bring the last letter that came to us from Mecca.'

Exit Secretary.

' *Hat'igh'hewah.*' [2]

When the Sultan is in anger or when there is a lull in the conversation he calls for coffee.   *Igh'hewah !*   And

[1] The *Qiblah* was a weekly newspaper published and edited in Mecca by King Husein.

[2] *Qahwah*—coffee—with the q softened as usual to gh, *i.e.* ghahwah. But in Najd, following the habit of silencing the first syllable in certain words, it is pronounced gh'hawah, or igh'hewah, with a broad and pompous accent, thus imparting to it somewhat of the majesty which swells the breast of every Arab when he is making or serving or drinking the bitter black brew.

the slave at the door repeats like a stentor, *igh'hewah !*
which is echoed by another slave stationed midway
between the Sultan's tent and that of the coffee maker,
who repeats the order dramatically and with a great
oath attached—*aye, billah, igh'hewah !*

'We will not concede a jot of our rights. And we
ask for nothing which is not ours,—which our forbears
have not always enjoyed. Let the Inglaiz know that.'
Saying which, he struck the carpet with his long staff.

The coffee-bearer enters and, standing like a soldier
before the Sultan, salaams and waits till he had finished
speaking.

'And let the Sherif and his sons know it,' he continued,
emphasizing his words with another stroke of his staff.
He then stretched out his hand in which the servant
placed the cup, after he had poured in it a thimbleful
of coffee. The Secretary then came in carrying a letter
which he gave to His Highness, who, after drinking
thrice in succession, gave it to me to read. I was amazed
—after having read the articles in the *Qiblah*—at the
courteous and friendly tone, nay, at the flattering tone,
of the letter. The style of the Hashemite Diwan, however,
did not change. The Sultan then gave me a postscript—
a confidential note—written by another hand and telling
the true story. Confidential and of good augury, *inshallah.*
King Husein calls the Sultan to the path of understanding
and friendship, and offers him terms of peace based upon
the following conditions : that Tarabah and Khurmah
be given back to Al-Hijaz and that Ibn 'ur-Rashid be
reinstated as Ameer of Haiel.

'Words,' said the Sultan, 'all words. But what
must we believe, the letter or the newspaper ? '

Our discussions were seldom closed before midnight,
and, like the serial, were always ' to be continued.' On
the following day we met in the tent allotted to the High
Commissioner, and all the Rashids were there seated
according to their rank. The youthful Ameer, a *mowallad*

(of Arab and black blood), was near the Sultan, his uncle
Faisal sat next to him, and so on. That they were treated
with due consideration for their rank was also shown by
the coffee-bearer. I have always been the second after
the Sultan to receive the cup ; but the little Ameer of
Haiel, when he was also present, received his before me.
The murderous uncle Faisal was fourth in rank. Thus
does Ibn Sa'oud retain the trust and loyalty of his captive
Ameers. After they had their coffee they got up, without
saying a word as usual, and walked out. ' They are a
melancholy people—a neurasthenic people.' said the
Sultan, ' they do strange things. Something defective
here '—pointing to his head. ' One of them killed himself
—shot himself in the brain, and Faisal, the man that was
sitting there, murdered his own brother, the father of
that boy—yes, the little black Ameer. But we must take
care of them, treat them with consideration.'

' The ruling Ameers of Arabia are not all like that,'
I said, thus opening again the subject of Pan-Arabism.
And I argued for treaties of friendship and peace between
the different rulers as a corner stone, a foundation, to
the proposed unity. Whereupon, the Sultan : ' I am
ambitious—very ambitious. Not for my own sake, but
for the sake of my people—for the sake of all the Arabs.
Nevertheless, I am ready to make concessions, if the
foundation of a unity or a confederation is clearly defined.
. . . What is the good of treaties of peace, if they are to
be considered as scraps of paper ? Who is it that said—
the German wazir, (vizir) is it not so ?—that a treaty is
but a scrap of paper ? That wazir spoke truth, revealed
the truth about all Europe—the truth which the other
European Governments would conceal. Now, should we
Arab rulers imitate Europe in this ? I said to you—and
I say it again—America is right in refusing to enter into
treaties with Europe. . . . We ought to get together, you
say, and define our boundaries at least. *Wallahi !* *ya*
Ustaz, I am the first to respond to such a call. But who

is to call us together ? Will America join England and
France in this business ? If she does, there is hope.
But the Inglaiz ? Well, they are coming to-morrow.
The High Commissioner is coming. I have asked him to
meet me here to consider two questions : the first I have
already mentioned—the grey-haired one and his sons ;
the second is the Kemalist attitude towards Iraq, and
consequently towards the Arabs of Najd. These two
questions must first be settled—I must first be assured—
before I can properly consider anything else. Now,
what am I to do ? I ask you who are travelling in Arabia
to study the conditions of the country, what am I to do
under these circumstances ? You say that you are not
interested in politics. We know.' He touched his beard
and smiled. ' But you have seen the Sherif and the Imam
Yahia and the Idrisi and Faisal—there is politics enough
even in a simple visit to any one of them. What would
any one of them do, if he were in my place ? What am I
to do threatened as I am on all sides ? I ask your opinion.
The Inglaiz, who have surrounded me with enemies,
are coming to-morrow. What am I to say to them ?
What is to be done with them ? I have spoken freely
with you, and I ask you to speak thuswise with me.'

I had already in previous discussions expressed my
opinion about what I thought was the nearest approach
to Pan-Arabism, the only means in fact to it. It is impossible, of course, to do anything without interfering
with British interests or British influence everywhere,
particularly in the Persian Gulf. Great Britain has a
monopoly there, and she wants every other nation to keep
off. Not only that : she tries to restrict, as I have shown,
and often succeeds in restricting, the freedom of travel
in Arabia. Her own officials, with or without the cog-
nizance of the Colonial or the Foreign Office, even go
farther in their zeal. One of them wrote to the Sultan
Abd'ul-Aziz that I was a Sherifian in the service of King
Husein, and that it were wiser if he did not consent to

see me. The Sultan also received letters from Arab
notables, natives of Iraq who are in close touch with the
Residency in Baghdad and are ever ready to serve it,
that I was English in my sentiment and purpose—I was
even accused of being in the pay of the British Government
—and that my Pan-Arab principles were but a screen.
' But I heed not the one nor the other,' said the Sultan.
And now he wanted my opinion—something concrete
and practical to act upon.

' Tell the English,' I said, ' that the time has come when
they should either help the Arab rulers to get together or
let them do so themselves directly, independently.' ' The
Inglaiz,' said the Sultan, ' will do neither this nor that.
And if they did try to bring us together, their mediation
is always suspected and seldom does any good. Sometimes it does much ill. Take an example. Two sheikhs
had a boundary dispute which a Consul of Great Britain
would adjust. The dispute, before the Consul interfered,
could have been easily adjusted by a native expert ; but
when it was submitted to the Consul the claim of each
sheikh was raised manifold. This is natural ; for both
thought—and rightly so—that the Consul would show
favour to one or the other. That is, of a truth, the way
of the Inglaiz. Each party, therefore, reasoned thus :
If the Inglaiz are against me, they will leave me something;
if they are with me, I will get my claim in full. That is the
way of the Arabs, *ya Ustaz*, and that is the way of the
Inglaiz. Allah alone, praised be he, can teach the one
and punish the other.'

' Experience also is a good teacher,' I said, ' and the
Arabs ought to have learned enough by this time to make
them prefer a direct settlement of their disputes.'

' But the Inglaiz will interfere whether they are asked
or not. When you invite them, they come ; and they
come also without an invitation. There is a difference,
however, in the outcome. They were invited into Kuwait,
and, therefore, Kuwait gets nothing from them. They

went into Oman (what is now known as Trucial Oman) without an invitation and made treaties with its Sheikhs, giving them a little money every now and then to keep the peace on the Gulf.'

'Could you not make them keep the peace on the Gulf?'

'That is not difficult.'

'And would they object if you went into their territory like the English, invited or uninvited?'

'We do not have to go to them, *ya Ustaz*; they come to us.'

'Why not, therefore, get them to transfer their allegiance to you, or enter into treaty relations, at least, with you? For with more power on the Gulf, you can get the English to compel the Iraq Government and the Government of Trans-Jordania to respect your rights in the north and the north-west.'

The idea pleased him, and I, expanding upon it, laid before him a plan for the unification of Eastern Arabia, under his aegis and control, from Mascat to the southern boundary of Iraq, including Oman and Bahrain and Kuwait, as well as a treaty with Great Britain in which her treaties with the little Sheikhs would be merged, thus transferring to Ibn Sa'oud the responsibilities and the obligations they implied. On the other hand, he would pledge himself to maintain peace, suppress piracy and slavery, and safeguard the interests of Great Britain on the Arab side of the Gulf. Great Britain, it seemed to me, would not ask for anything more. She would thus, in fact, be creating the Arab block with which to countermine the combined influence of the Turks and the Bolsheviks.

In the midst of this discussion came the Sultan's mail from Bahrain and with it Reuter's Dispatches telling of the approaching Conference at Lausanne.

'If France and England do not agree,' said the Sultan, 'the Turks will get what they want. But what will happen to us Arabs? If the Turks get back Mosul, nothing can stop them from coming down to Baghdad. That is what worries me.'

' It ought to worry the English, too," I remarked.

' The Inglaiz will move to Basrah and let the Turks do what they like in the interior of the country.'

' To keep the Turks out of Baghdad, therefore, and out of Mosul, there should be a treaty of defence between Najd and Iraq.'

The Sultan was on the point of saying something, but instead he called for coffee. There was a momentary silence. His Highness was in a brown study. And then, as if waking from a trance, he uttered a sharp *Hearken ; I will inform thee*. ' When the Inglaiz want something, they get it. When we want something, we have to fight for it. I will put my seal,'—he punched the palm of his left hand with the knuckles of the right,—' if Great Britain says, You must. But I will strike when I can.'

The coffee-bearer poured for the Sultan, who took two sips, shook the empty cup—meaning sufficient—as he returned it, and resumed.

' I will strike when I can. Not in betrayal, Allah be my witness, but in self-defence. What I cede of my rights under force, I will get back when I have sufficient force, *inshallah*. No words can be more plain and clear.'

In sooth. And no man can be more candid and direct.

CHAPTER IX

THE CONFERENCE OF OJAIR

THE tents are wet with dew, the heavy mist has made a paste of the sand, the fog has robbed the dunes of their colour, and the damp, sticky atmosphere adds to the depression and gloom. Ojair, with all its civilization—chairs and tables and silverware and Perrier water and Indian cooks—is not, I agree with the Sultan, worth a pinch of sand. And yet, it is his chief seaport, which he leases to a merchant in Bahrain. It is well, therefore, that he visit it once in a score of seasons to see at least his friend and fellow soldier the old Ameer of the Qasr, who was the first to welcome the Imam and greet him with four kisses, two on the forehead and two on the nose.

There is no kissing of hands in Najd. For to kiss the hand of a fellowman were an impiety, because you have to stoop to do so ; and the Najdi bows the head only to Allah. But they kiss the Imam on the tip of his nose—a kiss of love ; and to be able to do this, the Imam being the tallest man in the land, they all have to raise their heads, which suits their Wahhabi lofty-eyed Unitarian humour.

But kissing or no kissing, Ojair hath no charms for the Sultan Abd'ul-Aziz. He was tired, moreover, of scouring with his binoculars the watery horizon.

We were all, in fact, getting tired of waiting for an English official to arrive. But the Arabs had another complaint against Ojair. The Arabs, who seldom linger much at any place, who are always travelling, nomadizing, said that Ojair was like a foreign land. It made them home-sick. Indeed, the camp was a market of melancholy, a hive of sighs and groans. The black slaves themselves were as audible and as gloomy as the rest.

Even my own tent, which harboured the one man among all these Arabs who was really far away from home and country and who had more right to complain of nostalgia than anyone else, was deeper than the others in gloom, not because of himself, however, but because of his companion Saiyed Hashem. I asked my friend of the sorrowful countenance to tell me what was the matter.

'Is there anything besides the air and the dreariness and the English?'

'Nothing of that, *ya Ustaz.*'

'Is it anything that can be overcome? Can I be of help against it?'

'If you were a barber, my dear *Ustaz*, and you had scissors, and you desired to please me, you might do so.'

I opened my bag forthwith, and said: 'Three conditions, two of which are fulfilled. Here are the scissors and here I am. Do you want your hair cut?'

'No, my dear *Ustaz*. This beard is getting too long for my wits, and is making my life miserable—blackening my days.'

But I did not succeed in whitewashing them. For after I had trimmed his beard to conform to the Wahhaby doctrine—made it round and short—the sorrowful Saiyed said: 'How weak is man, *ya Ustaz*, and how flimsy his excuses, when he is overcome with emotion. I tried to conceal my sorrow in my beard, but I did not succeed. You beautified me, Allah beautify your days, but you could not make me forget. Praise the poet who said:

" Conceal not that to which thy heart is thrall ;"

He had touched a string in my own heart, which, in spite of distance and time, would fain reply :

" But speak thy love, for we are lovers all."

' I had a most beautiful wife, *ya Ustaz*, with a beautiful mind, a beautiful taste, and a beautiful passion. She was the sole occupant of my heart and home. But I was permitted to enjoy her only two years, and then—she was snatched from my hands by the bawd Death. I left Kuwait, therefore, and came to Najd seeking oblivion. But in Ojair the memory recurs. Ojair brings me nearer to Kuwait and sorrow. . . . O thou Huwaidy, bring *ghahwah*.'

And when we were at the Sultan's *majlis* that evening, the *majjab* arrived from Ar-Riyadh bringing the mail in a package, which was opened by the Secretary. There were letters for some of the men and the servants with him. Those for himself he opened, glanced at them nonchalantly, and threw them to the Secretary who was seated cross-legged on the carpet awaiting orders. One letter, which he knew from the superscription, wrought a change in his mood. After reading it he turned to me, and in a tone of sadness which half concealed his anger : ' It is from home, from our people. And they complain of distance and absence.'

For four months he had been away from them, and every mail that comes out of the desert carries words of longing and love and reproach. Moreover, the climate of Al-Hasa does not agree with him, and the air of Ojair is deadly.

' We would forthwith return were it not for the High Commissioner, who is our friend. I like Sir Percy Cox and respect him. But he is slow, very slow in coming. And this lethal air of Ojair, and this lonesomeness, which, without you, *ya Ustaz*, would have been insufferable. We the people of Al-'Ared [1] cannot endure the damp air of the coast. We have had enough of Ojair, we are sick of it. And we shall return, if Sir Percy Cox does not arrive to-morrow. Aye, billah ! we shall return. *Hat-i-gh'hewah*,' (bring coffee).

[1] Al-'Ared, the Najd Province of which Ar-Riyadh is the capital.

The servant at the door, vehemently : ' *Igh'hewah !* '
The slave outside, in a lugubrious echo : ' *Igh'hewah !* '
The man around the coffee fire, confirming the order
with an oath : ' *Aye billah ! igh'hewah.*'
And while we were returning to our tent that evening,
we passed by the public circle which any one might join ;
and there were freemen and slaves around the fire, sipping
coffee and listening to one of them chanting poetry. They
made room for us, and soon I found myself joining the
chorus, which repeated with a sigh the rhyme or word
that marked a pause in the chant.

> I wish I were his camel,
>   To carry his food and his clothes ;
>   *Chorus :* His clothes.
>
> I wish I were his steed,
>   To bear him away from his foes ;
>   *Chorus :* His foes.
>
> I wish I were his pen,
>   To write and repeat what he knows ;
>   *Chorus :* He knows.
>
> I wish I were his sandals,
>   To go with him wherever he goes.
>   *Chorus :* He goes.

' Fine, *billah !* fine.'
' But they were said in praise of Ibn 'ur-Rashid.'
' And what though they be ? They speak the heart
of a friend I have beyond the Nufoud.'

> O thou who exiled Love,
>   Why hast thou forgotten me ?
>   *Chorus :* Forgotten me.
>
> Love has tied me into knots,
>   And none can untie me—none but he.
>   *Chorus :* None but he.

' Fine, *billah !* fine.'
' Pour *ghahwah*, O thou Abd'ur-Rahman.'

Said Abd'ur-Rahman, as he was pouring the coffee :
' We Arabs cannot endure severance and long absence.'

Said another in a footnote, making the matter very
plain : ' Abd'ur-Rahman means that we cannot endure
being away from the harim. We desire women all the
time. And he whose desire is strongest of all desires is
the Imam. Allah sift the Ingliz ! ' [1]

About the second hour of the gibbous moon the following
evening, when we were discussing the underground water
courses of the desert, we heard the tooting of a horn in
the harbour, and the Sultan, who was ever ready with
his binoculars, saw a speck of light moving towards the
quay.

' It is the yacht of the High Commissioner,' said the
Sultan ; and he was quick with his orders.

Horses were sent down to the beach ; and he, accompanied by his slaves, who had quickly donned their red
robes and sworded themselves, rode down to meet his
friend Sir Percy Cox. A number of self-appointed body-
guards followed, and others walked down leisurely to
have a look at, rather than to meet, the illustrious guests.
Soon after, they were all seen coming up the hill, the
Sultan and his friends the ' Inglaiz ' surrounded by a
motley multitude, most conspicuous of which were the
red-robed slaves, who lost none of their splendour in the
moonlight. On the whole it was an impressive scene, but
not imposing. The disorderly Arab crowd never is.

They alighted before the reception tent which was
made brilliant by the Lux [2]—arc-light—and once inside
the dignity of the subject was restored. Sir Percy, who
was invited to enter first, modestly chose his own seat,
taking the chair on the left of the Sultan's, while the one

---

[1] The Arabs of Najd seldom or never curse like the people of Syria, for
instance, or of Egypt, When they want to vent their anger against one,
they say, Allah sift him ! that is, Allah sift the evil out of him.

[2] The arc-light, which is much in use throughout Arabia, is mistaken for
electric light. The Arabs call it *atrik*, corruption of electric, and give it a
plural full of musical syllables—atarik.

on the right, which in ordinary circumstances would have been mine or the Ameer of Haiel's, was immediately occupied by an old Arab, hook-nosed and blear-eyed, who, although he sat throughout silent and head bowed, held my attention, fascinated me. And whatever I said that evening must have been stupid ; for every time I spoke he lifted his head from his breast, peeped out of his *koufiyah*-folds surreptitiously and ducked again as quick as he had turned. The contrast of the straight-eyed, open-hearted Sultan with this dark-visaged crouching-like-a-leopard Arab was most striking. He sat huddled in his chair, wrapped in his *aba ;* his eyes wandering across the carpet, as if looking for something he had lost ; his head buried in his stooping shoulders and tilted downward, as if listening to voices coming from the ground. And all the time he fingered nervously his amber beads.

Not until the Sultan spoke did I realize that he who sat between me and himself was none else than Ibn ul-Hazzal—Sheikh Fahd Chief of the 'Amarat tribe of 'Aneza ;—the very Hazzal whom the British and the Iraq Governments find it necessary to subsidize. And yet, they are both England's friends, the lion and the lynx. What strange bed-fellows are thine, O Britannia ! But there, seated to the left of the Sultan, is thine own lean-visaged, blue-eyed son, whose lipless calm conquers every eloquence, overcomes all argument, and whose business now is to make peace between the lynx and the lion.

Sir Percy first spoke apologizing for the delay. The Sultan accepted the apology and went straight, as is his wont, to the heart of the subject. ' I am not afraid of the man,' he said, ' who has religion and honour in his heart. But he who has none——' He shook his hand as if to keep back something very offensive. Sheikh Fahd, who had sipped his coffee, held in his hand the cup which the coffee-bearer received, and pouring another drop into it placed it in the same motionless hand of the same impassive figure.

'These nomad Arabs, O worthy Commissioner, are never satisfied unless they have some *gazu* ' (raids)—the Sultan addressing Sir Percy still had his back turned to Sheikh Fahd—' and they cannot like a strong Government. They have no respect for authority. They are the friends of a weak Government, which lets them do as they please, and which, above that, pays them a monthly allowance. . . . But these Arabs fear only the sword. Draw the sword in their face and they will obey ; sheathe the sword and they will ask for more pay.'

This is not the conventional manner of receiving a guest or opening a Peace Conference. The straight-forwardness of the Sultan, which his staff helped to drive home, would have been indeed fatal had he not himself had a clear vision of his objective. In the current phrase, there was method in his madness. He wanted Ibn Hazzal to realize that he, Ibn Sa'oud, is as direct and frank with the English as he is with the Arabs. After stepping therefore on everybody's toes—the Iraq Government's, Great Britain's, the tribe of 'Aneza's—he hastened to administer an assuaging balm. How well he can do this, I have already remarked. It is indeed rare that the debonaire of a Parisian and the abruptness of an American should be so coupled in an Arab.

'Sheathe the sword, and they will ask for more pay.'

Whereupon, he turned to Sheikh Fahd, smiling his bewitching smile, and said : ' Is it not so, O Fahd ? We Arabs know each other.' Every one laughed except old Fahd, who sipped his coffee, shook his head, and buried it again in his breast. His glance shot against the carpet and obliquely upon the High Commissioner, as if he would say : why did you bring me here ?

This was the first meeting of the Conference of Ojair. But on the following day the Sultan and Sir Percy Cox had a private conference, which was followed by open and secret sessions, attended by the Delegation of the Iraq Government and also at certain times by Fahd ul-Hazzal. The relations between Najd and Kuwait were discussed at special meetings between the Sultan and the British Political Agent there, Sir Percy Cox assisting at times. There were also informal meetings in my own tent, attended by interpreters and boundary experts and Secretaries who came in for a chat or a secret smoke. The Conference lasted five days. And five months later, I met in Baghdad the Sultan's agent, who had come to the Residency to urge the payment of the sum of money agreed upon in cancellation of the yearly stipend of sixty thousand Pounds Sterling, which the British Government was paying to Ibn Sa'oud. But this was not the only question that was settled at the Conference. I quote from my diary to show also the *modus operandi*.

November 28, 1922.—The Sultan and Sir Percy Cox had a *tête-à-tête* this morning, and Sir Percy came out of the tent with a long document in his pocket. Half an hour later, when I went to see him, he gave me the said document to read and translate for him. It was an argument in support of the Sultan's claim to the 'Amarat and Dhafir tribes,[1] written originally in the form of questions and answers, for his Delegates at the Muhammarah Conference. If they ask you so and so, make the following reply. If the British Delegate insists on a certain point, ask him if he is speaking for the Government of Iraq or for the British Government. If he says, For the Government of Iraq, say : We can make no concessions. If he says : For the British Government, say : His Highness the Sultan will accept on compulsion. ' But they know that even then, there will be trouble. The control of the nomad tribes is not always possible, and—as they know—is not always desired.' I read and translated this slowly, but the High Commissioner did not seem inclined to dwell upon it. The Sultan Abd'ul-Aziz is a man of awkward surprises. . . .

November 29.—A false move was made to-day by the High Commissioner. Following a long conference with the Sultan, he sent for Abd'ul-Latif Pasha al-Mandil, who is acting as adviser to His Highness, and after a brief discussion, he gave him a rough draught of certain proposi-

[1] A summary of this document is given in the preceding chapter.

THE OJAIR CONFERENCE, NOVEMBER–DECEMBER, 1922

Seated : Sultan Abd'ul-Aziz Ibn Sa'oud and Sir Percy Cox, High Commissioner of Iraq
Standing, left to right : Fahd'ul-Hazzal, Chief of the Aneza Tribes ; Sabih Bey, representing the
Government of Iraq ; King Faisal's delegate to Ibn Sa'oud, Abdullah ibn Misfer ; Sir Percy
Cox's Private Secretary ; Major Moore, Political Agent at Kuwait ; Colonel Dickson, Liaison
Officer at Bahrain

tions to take to the Sultan. They were, of course, in English. His Highness, therefore, sent for me. It is regrettable that neither he nor the High Commissioner has a good interpreter. Doctor Abdullah's English is as bad as the British Secretary's Arabic. . . . I translated the two drafts to the Sultan.

I.—A letter which he is asked to write to King Faisal in reply to a letter which he, the Sultan, is supposed to have received from the King. ' Relying upon the assurance made to me by the British Government in my Treaty with them, I accept the pact of the Muhammarah Conference.' This is the gist of the reply.

II.—A letter to Sir Percy Cox informing him of the letter which he, the Sultan, wrote to King Faisal, and that of the assurances relied upon one should be in reference to Clause II of the Treaty, where the words ' any foreign Power ' should include the new-formed Kingdoms of Al-Hijaz, Trans-Jordania and Iraq. That is, England shall protect the Sultan of Najd in case of any attack made by any or all of them against him.

The Sultan's ire was aroused. Who told the High Commissioner that he is afraid of the Sherif and his sons ? He wants no protection against any Arab, and he resented being told—in a lead pencil draft—what to write to King Faisal or to the High Commissioner. . . . Two or three Arabs came in, while I was translating, and he motioned to them with his hand. They passed out of the opposite door of the tent.—' We are afraid only of Allah.' The muazzen was calling the noon prayer, and His Highness got up saying : ' We will pray.'

December 1.—The Sultan and the Iraq Delegation have come to an agreement about the desert boundary. A neutral zone in the shape of a rhomboid has been defined and accepted.[1] Evidently, after the Conferences he has had with the High Commissioner, the Sultan has become less intransigeant. He has perhaps been offered a more substantial substitute for ' Amarat and Dhafir, than that strip of territory which was made common pasture and watering ground for the neighbouring tribes in both Najd and Iraq ;—common ground for quarrel and strife. For who shall water his camels first, and who shall have the best pasture, but the strongest ? It is not peace, but only a

[1] See Map, p. xv.

makeshift. The Sultan would call it a little peace, such as
he often had with Ibn 'ur-Rashid. . . . I wonder what is
happening at Lausanne ? Are they making peace there,
or, like us, just a little peace ?

December 2.—Sir Percy Cox is doing his best, no doubt,
to settle the boundary disputes between Ibn Sa'oud and his
neighbours. But the Kingdom of the Wahhabis, whose
limits the Sultan Abd'ul-Aziz has stretched in every direction
to the breaking point, is most difficult to define. His Highness speaks of almost every tribe as ' our cousins '—they
were subjects of his forbears. From the oasis or Jibrin,
south-east of Ar-Riyadh up to the 'Amarat west of Baghdad,
and from Ojair and Qatif westward to Abha in Asir and
Tabouk on the Hijaz Railway, every tribe is subject to his
authority and owes him tribute. Who's going to dispute
it ? He speaks of peace and says that he fears only Allah.
I'm afraid that he also fears losing his annuity. It is no
doubt the strongest argument, this annuity, which the
High Commissioner can use in support of any or all of his
peace propositions. The Sultan gave away his 'Amarat
and Dhafir tribes, made a present of them to Iraq. And
for what ? I remember, when he was on his high camel in
the Nufoud—I was riding beside him—how he swore by
Allah to defend his inherited rights and quoted martial
poetry to boot. He was mentally rattling the sword. . . .
It is disappointing in a way. For I believe that this man
has many of the elements of greatness ;—he is strong,
fearless, unequivocating. And although his mind is subject
to storms, he thinks clearly and is honest in his likes and
dislikes. . . . He knows what he wants, and—what is best
—he knows how much he can get of it at a given time.

December 2.—*Evening.*—One of the most hopeful signs of
this Ojair Conference for Arabia—the only hopeful sign,
indeed—is the autograph letter of King Faisal to the Sultan
Abd'ul-Aziz—his ' beloved Brother.' The letter is carried
by a special envoy, Abdullah ibn Misfer, and is couched in
the most friendly terms. The reply, which Ibn Misfer is
carrying back, is even more so. . . . This is a most hopeful
sign. For if King Faisal repudiates the policy of his father,
and makes a pact with Ibn Sa'oud, the foundation of Arab
peace and unity is laid. . . . I do hope they can get together,
and better without ' the good offices ' of the British Government. . . . The Sultan is sincere in his desire to meet King

Faisal, but I know that he is not feeling well. Besides, he has been too long away from his capital. Another ' besides : ' he prefers that the meeting should take place between him and a brother Arab, without the intermediary of British Officials. But I'm giving away the secrets of the Conference. It is fortunate that there are no newspaper men in this wilderness to ruin a good cause.

December 3.—The last paper, in connection with the settlement, I translated to the Sultan, is a cable dispatch which Sir Percy Cox is sending to Mr. Churchill (then Secretary of State) suggesting that the boundary line between Najd and Trans-Jordania in the Jawf should be so drawn as to include Qoraiyat 'ul-Milh (villages and salt mines) in the territory of Ibn Sa'oud. These villages are claimed by the Sultan as a part of the Jawf ; and Sir Percy Cox, in addition to the dispatch, which is definite about Meridians and Degrees, also made a definite promise to see that the Sultan's demands are fulfilled. This is a part of the compensation made to him for conceding to Iraq his right of sovereignty over the 'Amarat and Dhafir. We take from Ibn Sa'oud to satisfy Iraq, and we take from Trans-Jordania to placate Ibn Sa'oud.

Aside from the boundary and tribal disputes that were temporarily settled, and the neutral zones that were established between Iraq and Najd and between Najd and Kuwait at this Conference, there was also certain financial and economic forces, inevitable in any national or international conference of these times, pressing for consideration. To be specific, there is oil, it is thought, in the Province of Al-Hasa, and the oil-man, like the archæologist of our day, is willing, on a sporting chance, to dig anywhere. But before digging there must be a concession —and thereby hangs a tale.

The man that sought this concession had his tent pitched between the two camps ; not far from our side, however ; and he frequented the tents of both the Sultan and the High Commissioner. He also came casually to see me and Saiyed Hashem. Now, having mentioned myself in this connection and having furthermore alluded to the state of propinquity that existed between our tent and his, I shall tell the story, which is not without interest, from the beginning.

Saiyed Hashem was acquainted with this gentleman before I was. They were in Basrah together. And when I left that city on the S.S. *Barjora* he happened to be on board ; he was the only other saloon passenger. So at a little table set for two—the steward's own inspiration —we had our tea together that afternoon ;—and there was no ice to break ; we had to speak. He told me that he was travelling in those parts for his health. I told him that I had come from America to travel in Arabia for my sins. He was surprised at the English tongue in an Arab dress—particularly a tongue into which had crept some of the slang of New York—a tongue which revived in him pleasant, very pleasant memories.

He, too, had been in America, had travelled all over America, and liked immensely the American people. Too effusive, I thought, for an Englishman. No, he is not an Englishman. That was the first thing I discovered. He hails from the antipodes—spent many, many years in the East—worked with Herbert Hoover in China. Herbert Hoover—a second surprise. And he tells me more about him. ' Hoover was not long in bossing a job he undertook. A man of decision, of quick mind, impetuous but not nervous, full of ambition and grit. He seldom hesitated in making up his mind. He would go down a mine, for instance, look it over and say whether it was worth working or not. I once inspected a mine and thought it was good. I asked Hoover to go down and look it over. He did ; and when he came up he told me that it was no good. "I wouldn't spit on it," he said. Hoover is like that. He wasted no time or energy on what *he* thought was of no value.'

Later I saw my fellow-passenger speaking with Saiyed Hashem, and I was surprised that he knew him. But there were more surprises for me in our second conversation, which I opened with a commonplace remark about

H.M. KING ABD'UL-AZIZ   MAJOR FRANK HOLMES   SIR PERCY COX

the heat in Iraq. ' It is worse in Asir because of the dampness,' he said.

' And you have travelled in Asir ? '

' I visited the Saiyed Idrisi in Jaizan.'

' And you lived in that fort—the guest-house ? '

' Two weeks.'

' Then you know Dr. Fadl 'ud-Din in Hudaidah.'

' Very well. I lived with him in that big house there.'

Something of annoyance was working itself into my surprise. That this man, who does not even speak Arabic, should have been to those places before me !

' And do you intend to visit Ibn Sa'oud ? ' I asked with a suggestion of malice.

' I have already seen him in the Hasa,' he replied ; which was exasperating. But I had schooled myself in outward calm during my travels. He then launched into a eulogy of Ibn Sa'oud, and was mighty glad that I too was going to see him. We exchanged cards after that. And to the reader I now introduce Major Frank Holmes, of the British Navy during the War, an associate of Mr. Hoover before the War, and a traveller after the War, travelling for his health in Arabia !

At Bahrain he went his way and I went mine. But the day I arrived at Ojair, Saiyed Hashem, by the usual Oriental circumlocution, mentioned the name of my fellow-traveller in connection with a certain document which His Highness the Sultan wanted me to examine. Ha ! so the Major is travelling for his health ! The Saiyed brought the document with him, and I was to criticize if necessary the translation and give my opinion moreover of its subject matter.

Now, there being but one decent room in the Qasr, that which I occupied—the Saiyed lived downstairs with the Ameer ;—and there being but one lamp, which was in my room ; and I having come out of the jalbout exhausted and feeling the need of rest and sleep, we agreed to read the document together in the evening.

But in the afternoon, just in time for tea, who should pop in but Major Holmes ? He had just arrived in a *jalbout* from Bahrain, bringing with him his Somali servant and an interpreter. He wore over his European clothes a thin *aba* which concealed nothing ; and over his cork helmet, a red kerchief and *ighal* which made his head seem colossal. But in this attempt to combine good Arab form with comfort and hygiene he certainly looked funny. He was no longer a mystery to me. The document and this second visit to the Sultan indicated concessions and economic schemes.

' Our paths will cross again,' he said, after expressing his regret for not coming to see me in Bahrain ; ' I know they will. I have a fondness for that great country of yours.'

But Saiyed Hashem was in a pickle. The double problem he now had to solve was where to lodge the gentleman, and where, if he were to share my room, were we to read and discuss his document. The Saiyed hurried down to the Ameer ; and putting their heads together, they arrived at the proper solution. A moment later the Major was called out, his interpreter following. Another moment, and enter Hashem and Holmes, smiling and exuberant. The advice was that he the Major should proceed to Al-Hasa ; and if he rode all night he would get there on the following day and have an interview with the Sultan before he started for Ojair.

Major Holmes was much pleased.—' Good-bye, we'll meet again—I'm sure we will.' He bestrode a mare with a sore shank and a caving haunch, which the Ameer of the Qasr had provided for him, and slowly moved off towards the Nufoud, followed by three white donkeys carrying his interpreter, his Somali, and the baggage.

Later in the evening I regretted his going; for I certainly should have enjoyed the Major more than his document, on the twenty pages of which were his twenty signatures in full. Of what interest to me, in sooth, is a concession to drill for oil and minerals and salt in the Province of Al-Hasa ?

For the sake of the Sultan, however, I read the document and the execrable Arabic translation, clause by clause ; and, summoning from the past my long neglected business sense, I was able, I think, without hurting the prospects of Major Holmes and his Company, to make a few suggestions.

With the suggested changes, I strongly recommended the contract. I had to send my report in writing, and be quick about it, so that it should get to the Sultan ahead of Major Holmes. This was the job that kept me up that night four hours by a smelling, blinking kerosene lamp, while my fellow traveller, bent on the accomplishment of his mission, was trailing his white caravan under the stars, in a country as strange to him, on the surface, as its people and their language. But he knows what's in the bosom of the land, this man ; can see the invisible streams of water that flow from the Persian mountains under the Gulf, through the veins of the Hasa soil ; can track the bubbling oil and the sparkling minerals to their depths and beyond ; —has the modern Argus eye of science and finance. And for his knowledge, his energy, and his pluck, which after all are the compensations of our modern civilization, all honour to him and success.

We did meet again, as he predicted. For he loomed up on the horizon unexpectedly as usual, and incorporated himself into the Ojair Conference. I therefore resume the story, quoting from my diary.

November 30.—Major Holmes has come back from Al-Hasa and has pitched his tent near our side of the camp. He eats with his own people, however, although he does not share their confidence. The Anglo-Persian Oil Company also wants the concession for which he has applied ; and the A.P.O. has the British Government behind it—is virtually the British Government, who hold 70% of its shares. . . . For this reason, principally, the High Commissioner says to the Major : ' Go slow about the Concession. The time is not yet ripe for it. The British Government

cannot afford your Company any protection.' But yesterday, Abd'ul-Latif Pasha showed me a letter which he had
just received from his friend, Sir Arnold Wilson (President
of the Anglo-Persian Oil Co. at Abbadan), in which he says,
that he is coming soon to see the Sultan and 'maybe we can
strike a deal about oil.' Evidently, it is not untimely for
the A.P.O. to negotiate for a Concession.

December 1.—Major Holmes came to see me this morning
and went so far as to speak of me as 'a friend at Court.'
I told him that I had already given the Sultan my advice
in the matter, and that I had no axe to grind. But I
believed that the less a Company applying for a Concession
had to do with politics the better for the Sultan.

December 1.—*Evening.*—They would monopolize Ibn
Sa'oud. Not even an Englishman, outside the Bureaucracy,
shall have a share in him—shall even get a chance to see
him. Their Sentries at Bahrain and Bushire shall see that
no one cross to Ojair without explaining to their perfect
satisfaction his business. The Americans there are not
permitted to cross from the Island Hasa-ward, without
permission from the Resident at Bushire. If Dr. Dame
gets a call from Qatif, the patient may die before he gets
his permission from the British. Why all this barbed-wire
around Ibn Sa'oud ? Surely, it does not help to promote
British interest, nor does it ennoble the British name. If
these minor officials are following orders from Whitehall,
then Whitehall ought to be better guided in its Colonial
policy ; and if they are acting independently, overzealous
in the interest of the Government or their own, then Whitehall should know and should take immediate action in the
matter.

December 2.—*Evening.*—Major Holmes and his Contract
are now in the hand of the High Commissioner. 'I see the
justice of certain objections he made to our additions and
conditions,' said the Sultan last evening to me. 'But I have
entrusted the matter to my friend Sir Percy Cox, and I
shall accept what he and the Major agree upon.'

December 2.—*Evening.*—Saiyed Hashem comes to me,
before the close of day, with a bit of bad news about the
Hasa Concession. Sir Percy Cox has asked the Sultan to
write a letter to Major Holmes saying that he cannot give
his decision till he had made certain inquiries of the British
Government and consulted with them about the matter.

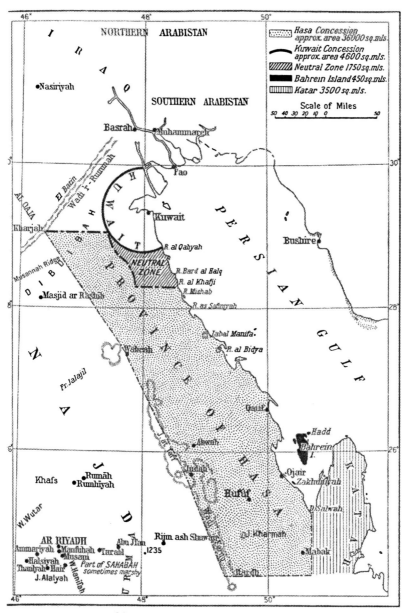

MAP PREPARED BY MAJOR HOLMES

He sent a copy of the letter to be written, with a lead pencil note to Dr. Abdullah, saying : Will the Sultan please write letter in the above terms to Major Holmes and send me a copy of it. . . . Saiyed Hashem told me that three times the Sultan refused, and three times the High Commissioner insisted. . . . The letter was finally written.

Ar-Riyadh—The Palace.—Whenever the Concession was mentioned.—' Your Highness is sovereign in your land, and you have a right to give a Concession to whatever Company you please, so long as it is English. Your Pact with the British Government does not bind you to accept the Company they prefer. Here are two English Companies, one of them practically owned by the British Government, while the other has nothing to do apparently with politics, is free from all Government influence, and you have a right to have your own choice in the matter. . . . The least of politics with Capital the better for Arabia. Concessions given on a purely business basis and with a purely business motive, without any political tags to them or any lead pencil suggestions from British Officials concerning them—these are best for the Arabs and for the English.'

Baghdad, April 10, 1923.—Here is Major Holmes again. He has been waiting all this time for a decision from somebody—from the Sultan, from the Residency, from the Colonial Office—about the Concession. Nothing has come —nothing favourable—and he has cold feet. He is packing up and returning home. ' My own Government is against me,' he said. But I know that the Sultan is well disposed— I left him so—towards him and his Company ; and I told the Major to change his mind and go back to Al-Hasa. The Sultan will soon be there. ' I will give you a letter to him, and I'm certain you'll get the Concession. . . . Never mind what Sir Percy Cox says. . . . By all means, accept the invitation of Lady Cox to tea, and tell her you are going back home. . . . Say Good-bye, too, to Sir Percy. For if he suspects that you are going back to Al-Hasa, he might get ahead of you to the Sultan with one or two of those lead-pencil notes of his. . . . I leave in a few days for Damascus and thence to Freikè. Good-bye and good luck.'

Freikè, Mt. Lebanon, August, 1923.—I have received a letter from the Sultan Abd'ul-Aziz in which he says that he has granted the Concession of Al-Hasa to the Syndicate of Major Holmes.

This, my dear reader, is the story of that Concession, which, to tell faithfully and comprehensively, I had to carry you, forestalling time, to Ar-Riyadh and Baghdad. We now come back to Ojair to witness the closing scene of the Conference. On the morning of December 3, 1922, the air of Ojair was light and fresh, the sun of Ojair was abundantly warm and caressing, and everybody in Ojair was in good humour. Even blear-eyed Sheikh Fahd, who had forgotten the cudgelling administered to him by the Sultan and was glad to have asked His Highness for some Oman *zeluls* (which must now be adorning the pasture of his Wadi Hauran), condescended to speak to me—satisfaction breeds sympathy—and, apologizing for not returning my visit, he invited me to his *dirah* and promised to entertain me there ; and the Delegate of the Iraq Government, he who would not forgo his dinner coat in Ojair and was the most miserable man at the Conference, complaining all the time of the air and the water and the sun and the sand and the dreariness and the loathsomeness of Ojair, asked me if I was really going to Najd and shook his head in pity ;—even if the sand of the desert were to turn into gold he would not walk ten steps towards the Nufoud ;—Baghdad for him, and the comforts of Civilization, all the time ; while Major Frank Holmes, in spite of the letter he had received from the Sultan, which, however, was offset by a visit of His Highness, who came in person to his tent to say, Farewell, and to comfort him, was still nursing his hopes and smiling ingratiatingly at Sir Percy Cox ; and His Excellency Sir Percy, realizing that I was really going with the Sultan, asked me if I did not intend to go also to the Vacant Quarter. ' Evidently,' said I, ' you want to get well rid of me.' He laughed and hastened to correct the ungracious remark by saying to the Sultan : ' We leave him now in your care.' Whereupon, His Highness, even more graciously, as he laid his hand on my shoulder : ' The *Ustaz* is a Nadji now ; he is of us.' Everybody, in sooth, beamed contentment ; and those who had cameras availed themselves of the occasion. Soon after, they all rode down to the landing, where a jalbout was waiting. Also a motor launch to see that the sail boat is not delayed on its way to the *Cyclamen*, which was anchored ten miles out.

Ojair is not likely to go down in the history of International Conferences ; but the peace of the world was as much dependent upon it as upon that of Lausanne. For if Ibn Sa'oud invaded Iraq—he had almost done so the year before—and if he chose to sack the two Holy Cities of the Shi'a, Karbala and An-Najaf—Wahhabism justifies it—then ancient Mesopotamia will be ablaze, and, being dowered with Oil, not only the East, but the West will also be drawn into the conflagration. Let us, therefore, remember that in the year of grace 1922, when at Lausanne, the diplomats of Europe were trying to solve the Near East problem, something has been done to secure peace and goodwill in a section of the Near East, which is second in importance only to Constantinople. But did it end well?

Behold, the sun and the sand in the civilized part of the camp have again the undisputed freedom of the desert. The tents are down, and so is Civilization—the breakdown of Civilization, indeed ! and none of its sons has remained to do it reverence. A few shrewd and enterprising members of our camp, however, are busy in and around the Quartermaster Department. Saiyed Hashem himself has also done a little salvaging. Here he comes with an armful of bottles of Perrier water, followed by two slaves carrying some live chickens and a crate of eggs.

How convenient it is to enjoy Civilization for a day, and then to be able to say to it, Begone ! Lo, and as fast as the Arab can fold his tent, it goes. Chairs and tables and beds, knives and forks and plates, and a bathroom under canvas !—short has been your tenure in Ojair. And no one, alas ! seems to regret your ignominious end. For

THE CLOSE OF THE OJAIR CONFERENCE
The Sultan (left) escorting Sir Percy Cox to the beach on his departure.

there they are, thrown pell-mell, scattered on the sand, with all the carelessness and recklessness of which an Arab is capable. Arab vandal ! Outside of his own kit, which consists of a saddle and a saddle-bag, an extra *aba* perhaps and some dates and water, he cares for nothing. knows not how to care for anything—breaks and rips and tears and ruins with a single throw. Tighten that strap—zip ! it breaks. Fold that bed—and lo, the bed-cloth and covers and pillows are on the sand scattered in every direction.

The Sultan has given his orders to move, and our part of the camp is also falling. Falling too my energy, for I am carrying a heavy cold with me. One of our servants who coughed incessantly would not go back to his home in Al-Hasa, where, if he remained in bed a few days, he might recover. He would remain with us : he was persistent in his devotion :—and he would come in at night—it was too cold outside—to do his coughing in our little tent—after he had closed and tightened all the flaps ! That is what I got for trying to doctor the lout. He took my salt and my quinine, and he stuck around, day and night, till I took his cold in return.

CHAPTER X

AL-HASA

In Najd as in Al-Yaman, it is not wise—it is even considered unseemly and irreligious—to speak of infection or contagion ; for you hurt the poor sick one when you tell him that he is likely to give his disease to his brother man, and you offend moreover against the dogma of predestination. I caught the cold of our servant Rajhan, but Saiyed Hashem, who slept near him in the tent on the same rug, did not. He would not argue the matter with me, however, for he is a bit of a philosopher himself, and he is acquainted with Darwin. ' I have read Darween,' he would say, whenever he found it necessary to prove his superiority. He is acquainted with him, through the medium of Buckhner, who is the only door, in Arabia, to Darwinism. Not for this reason, however, would I ascribe certain simian traits to my *rafiq*.

There were three coughing travellers in our caravan— Huwaidi the cook had also caught Rajhan's cold—when the necks of our *zeluls* were stretching and swaying towards the Nufoud ; and Saiyed Hashem, in a sympathetic mood, joined the chorus. I was sorry when I first heard him, for I thought that he too had been infected. I was amused the second time I heard him, for I saw him grin ; but the third time, when he persisted in commenting with a grotesque exhibition of his teeth upon the imitation, my anger was aroused. Nevertheless, I was not inclined to speak ; it was sufficient that I was coughing. And I continued to cough silently—in solitary misery sometimes,

THE DONKEYS OF AL-HASA

THE CAMP, AL-HASA

but often in company with Huwaidi and Rajhan—till the joke began to pall. My mind had already dwelt upon mimics and monkeys and other ancestral landmarks of biology ; had even tried to cover with the fig-leaf of charity the shame of my *rafiq :* but I could not help venting myself at last. ' You are a monkey of the monkeys of Darween,' I exclaimed ; and he laughed merrily, laughed uproariously, laughed triumphantly. It never occurred to him that he could thus prove the Darwinian theory. ' You have made a discovery, *ya Ustaz*. But you could not have done it without me.'

The Arabs have a sense of humour, which in some of them, as in Saiyed Hashem, is alternately coarse and refined. He had to have his cigarettes, for instance, which he would smoke secretly in the tent, after lacing tightly all the flaps. And he would generously share them with those who dared ' to let their freedom out of the cage,' as he would say. ' But I do not let it fly out of the tent. I close all the doors.' He dug a hole in the sand, under the carpet, where he kept the precious boon hidden ; and some of those who used to come to uncage their freedom had to pay for the privilege. ' The Secretary is a good man, *ya Ustaz*, lovable. But I always make him take off his turban and I give him three slaps on his shaven skull and three slaps on the nape, before I give him a cigarette.'

About sunset, after we had left Ojair, stopping at Umm 'uz-Zarr for water, we pitched our camp where we had done so before—at 'Alat. The Sultan and his Wahhabi host, who had arrived ahead of us, were standing in long rows, saying their prayers. Their silhouette, half in shadow and half glowing in the light of the sundown, as we came up the hill, was sublime. But curious enough, after the *imam* had finished his prayer, the chanting of ' Amen,' carrying me back to New York, recalled in my mind a ferry-boat blowing its horn in a fog.

Outside of San'a, no Arabs have I seen who pray as

much as these Wahhabis. But, in fact, they are strictly
following the Koranic precept—five prayers a day.[1] A
Muslim may combine one or two of the prescribed five,
however, if he is travelling ; that is, he may pray at sunset
the evening prayer also, or he may combine the noon
and the afternoon devotions with that of the sunset.
The most difficult part of the performance for a foreigner
is the kneeling attitude. The Christian kneels upright ;
the Muslim rests, sits down on his haunches, which
involves a twisting of the ankles, if you do not want to
break your toes. I could not, much as I tried, maintain
this attitude more than thirty seconds. And yet to a
Muslim, even at home or in a *majlis*, this is a restful as
well as a respectful way of sitting. I have seen even
children do it with admirable ease and grace. And of
all the rulers of Arabia, King Husein is, in body, the most
pliant and agile. It was a rare delight to see him in that
devotional attitude, seated—kneeling—before me as he
would in a mosque, and to listen to him speak of camels
and chameleons. But he often changed his position when
he started to talk politics, twisting his body to suit—
inadvertently perchance—the twist of his mind.

Camping at 'Alat unleashed the braggadocio of Majed,
and stirred up in him the spirit of rivalry ; for, although
he realized that poor sick Rajhan was in no condition for
a running match, he still had him on his mind ; and,
remembering what I had said to him, before leaving

---

[1] These are : the morning prayer, which must be said at dawn a little
before sunrise, the noon prayer, the afternoon prayer, the sunset prayer,
which must be said a little before the sun goes down, and the evening prayer.
The reason why the first and the fourth prayer should be said a little before
the sun rises and sets, is connected with a superstition about the Satanic
horns of the sun at the moment of rising and setting. Abu Hanifah, one
of the five leading Commentators, was explaining this to his students one
day, when a venerable old man entered and sat down among them. The
lecturer, who was seated with his foot stretched out, drew it in respectfully
and covered it with the edge of his robe. ' At any moment of the dawn,
before the sunrise,' said the Master. ' And what if the sun should rise
before the dawn ? ' asked the venerable-looking old man. The lecturer
replied, ' Abu Hanifah will then stretch his foot freely and care not.'

THE POTTERY MARKET IN HUFOUF

A LIME KILN IN AL-QATIF

Ojair, about his teeth, he would be his superior in everything. ' The teeth of Rajhan,' I said, ' are white like the
daisy petal ; yours are dirty.' And I gave him the hand
mirror, which he held up to his face dejectedly :—' A
poor " *b'dewi* " ' (beduin). And when he saw the reflection of his teeth he grinned, and then grinned at his grin,

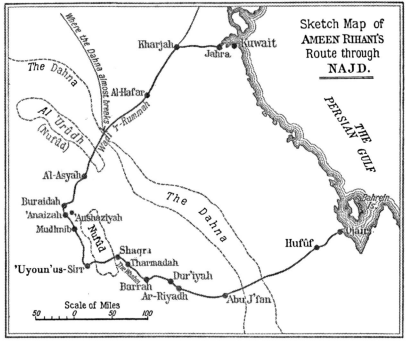

Sketch Map of
AMEEN RIHANI'S
Route through
NAJD.

THE AUTHOR'S ROUTE

and, dropping his jaw in mock mortification, said :
' The teeth of a " *b'dewi*." But you shall see.' So, at
'Alat, even as he was unloading the camels, he began in
a monologue : ' I can beat him running, and I can beat
him wrestling, and can beat him tumbling, and I can beat
him riding. And why should his teeth be better than mine?'

I saw him a few minutes later take in his hand some
clean sand, which he thrust into his mouth ; and after

making a paste of it there, he proceeded to rub his teeth assiduously, religiously, so that, in a few minutes, he had achieved a little success. 'They are not yet as white as the teeth of Rajhan,' I said. 'There is plenty of sand,' he replied, as he repeated the operation; and not long after, when we were seated in front of the tent, he stood triumphantly before us.—'I can beat him running, and I can beat him wrestling, and I can beat him——' he grinned to reveal his white teeth. And this was followed by one of his buffooneries. 'I'm a poor man—a b'dewi —a destitute.' Whereupon, he turned a somersault, laid flat on his bosom, and began to kick the air with his feet. He slept where he performed, with only an *aba* for a cover, and was the last in the morning to get up.

When we pass 'Alat, the Nufoud breaks up and the dunes recede westward and southward as we traverse a strip of hard soil—sand and gravel—to the saline field, about five miles long, preceding Jishshah. Here is what looks like salt on the surface and potassium, perhaps, underneath. And there, as we sight Jishshah, is the first palm grove of Al-Hasa, which is about thirty miles from Ojair. The town itself—about two thousand souls—is in the foreground, and behind it and the palms is Jabal Sanjan, while south-east of it are four mounds looking like pyramids in the desert.

We crouched our camels under the palms, near an abundance of running water, and not far from Jafr, another walled town but bigger than Jishshah, where a Souq or Market Day is held every week. One of our men went there and soon returned with two plates full of fresh dates, very delicious—and very dirty. I had a few put into a cup and sent to the stream; but one of the soldiers in our escort pointed to those in the plate, saying: 'We prefer them like that.' Dirt may be a cultivated taste, but I'm making no effort at cultivation. I read in my Diary the following: 'I cannot set down here what I suffer from that one source in all Arab travel—dirt. I'm afraid of discouraging myself, and I'm but at the beginning of my long Najd journey.'

Although there is an abundance of water in this oasis, the method of cultivation is even inferior to what I have seen in Al-Yaman ;—does not imply much energy on the part of the inhabitants. I saw them scratch the soil with the puny pre-Babylonian thing like a plough ; and yet, it did not seem to need more than that. The palm, which is the essential source of living, flourishes without much care, is blessed, it seems, with an abundance of the divine, self-uplifting energy of the Universe.

' The palm,' I said to Saiyed Hashem, ' is the mother of the Arab.' Whereupon he quoted the Prophet : ' *Honour your cousin the palm*,' which has the flavour of St. Francis d'Assisi. The Prophet must have said many wise things about the camel too. But the most startling word was uttered by a man from Najd, who is now a Pasha in Basrah and a man of wealth and ideas. *He* would kill the camel to civilize the Arabs. One might as well say also : Cut down the palm to make them work. But the palm and the camel are the mother and the father of Arabia. The one may die a natural death by the introduction into the country of electricity and steam ; the other can be made doubly productive by a modern method of cultivation.

Not only the few oases of Al-Hasa can be made doubly productive, but the whole province—that long strip of land from Kuwait to Qatar and from the Gulf to about fifty miles inland—can be made a garden of date-palms by digging bores of from two to three hundred feet, and running eight-inch pipes through the country for irrigation. Indeed, there is artesian water, not only in Al-Hasa, but in many other parts of the Arab Peninsula. An American engineer submitted to King Husein an astounding irrigation scheme. He proposed to tap the undercurrents of the Nile and send across the Sinai Peninsula and down through the very heart of Arabia to the Persian

Gulf, a river—a river of water ! [1] And he could have the
work completed, he said, in five years. King Husein
thought that he was mad. But the Sultan Abd'ul-Aziz
cherishes the hope that Al-Hasa will see, even in his own
days, a modern irrigation system, which shall bring its
oases together, thus transforming its desert waste into
gardens of date-palms, or still better into rice-fields.

But what little there is of cultivation now is very
luxuriant, considering the abundance of water and the
richness of the soil. The fruit gardens, on either side of
the road, between Jishshah and Al-Fudoul, a distance of
about seven miles, are suggestive of those of Damascus.
But from Al-Fudoul on the soil changes, the white
barrenness almost overwhelming the little patches of
green ; and the only conspicuous landmarks on the way
are two abandoned forts built formerly by the Turks.

Two hours after we left Jishshah, about sundown, we
arrived at Hufouf the Capital of Al-Hasa. Outside the
city wall are several threshing-floors where people were still
threshing and winnowing rice. We entered the first gate
to the outer town and then through another gate to the
old Hufouf, where we were lodged. The Sultan had
arrived ahead of us, of course, and he sent a messenger to
say that I was no doubt as tired as himself and that we
had better, both of us, retire early. Tired ? I was more
than tired. I was on the point of collapse, not from a heavy
cold or from exhaustion but from a sore, which had
started the day before, and was filling me with dis-
couragement. How am I ever to get to Ar-Riyadh ?

On the morning of the following day, as soon as the
Sultan sat—*jalas*—that is, when he was ready to receive,
he sent for me. I walked down the dingy narrow street,

---

[1] In ancient times, says the geologist, before the process of desiccation
had created the deserts of Northern Arabia, a great river descending from
the Harra of Khaibar along the bed of Wadi'r-Rummah and the Batin,
must have flowed into the Persian Gulf. But I read in the *History of Aal
Sa'oud* by Ibn Bushr of Najd that in the year 1780 this river flowed and
inundated the city of 'Anaizah.

MARKET DAY IN HUFOUF

THE CITY WALL, HUFOUF

following the sword bearer to a house as common outwardly as the rest ; passed through the court in which
was a multitude of people sitting in line around the walls ;
ascended a stone stairway, on every step of which were
several pairs of sandals, and lo, I stood in the door of a
long baronial hall, where His Highness was sitting. But
what struck me first with awe was the august assembly
of Arabs—about two hundred devout Wahhabis filling
the stone benches and half-kneeling before them along
the four sides of the hall,—still carrying the bamboo stick
of travel, and listening silently, intently to the reading
from the Hadith. It was an imposing scene. And the
Sultan, at the end of the hall, seemed to me distant,
indeed, and forbidding. But the man with whom I rode
through the desert and had many a long conversation in
his tent was now sitting in state and listening, like the
most devout of his subjects, to the sayings of the Prophet.

I walked up to him while the reader was still reading,
feeling, I must admit, a little disconcerted ; but he stood
up to receive me and offered me the vacant chair to his
left. He himself sat on a raised diwan, resting his bare
feet upon a footstool. We exchanged, in a low voice,
brief words of salaam and joined in the general silence
and attention. Something of restraint marked the wonted
graciousness of his manner. But I do not think there
were three in the whole assembly who gave a thought to
the stranger. Some of them, who were not with us in
Ojair, looked at me surreptitiously, but they were,
nonetheless, apparently absorbed, like the rest, in the
sayings of the Prophet.

When the Sultan had enough of these sayings he ordered
coffee ; and in the interval, those who had entered during
the last reading, came up to salaam, some of them kissing
him on the nose. After we had coffee, the reader began
again, this time reading in another book—*The History of
Arabia* by Tabari. The story of Az-Zabba' Zenubia,
(Queen of Palmyra) is, indeed, most marvellous, is more

like a modern novel, full of thrilling adventures, as Tabari tells it.   It is also interspersed with pithy sayings, commonplaces, pithily expressed, which afterwards be- came proverbs.   The reader theatrically emphasizes this point.   *Who reins his ire accomplishes his desire.*   Following which, in a tone much like the ghost's in Hamlet : ' And it became a proverb.'   Whereupon, the august assembly would nod, and the Sultan, turning to me, would say something about the wonderful wisdom of the Arabs. No other people in Arabia, except it be the Zioud of Al-Yaman, so honestly and wholeheartedly live in the past.   I can imagine the same assembly a thousand years ago of the same silent, proud and self-satisfied people.

The hall of audience, simple and dignified, is not without a touch of design, a decorative effect, which is of special appeal to the Arab.   There is so little in his land beyond the austerely simple—I speak of his studied efforts in architecture and dress—that a touch of decoration is always highly prized ;   the gold thread, for instance, exquisitely wrought around the neck and down the front of the *aba ;* or the carved lace-work in stone, which was the vogue in the Baghdad of the Khalifs, and is now imitated in plaster.   The hall of audience is about 100 by 25 feet, with windows on both sides and pointed arches three in a row spanning it, dividing it breadthwise into three sections.   One walks under the arches to salaam the Sultan or, when he is not visiting Hufouf, the ruler of Al-Hasa, Abdullah ibn Jlewy.   The decoration, which is plaster, consists of a zone of dedal-work above the windows, with a variation of the motive around them from top to bottom ;   while about three feet above the zone are square openings in lattice, into some of which is incorporated a sort of coat-of-arms or arabesques in bas-relief.   This motive is repeated in circles on the sides of the arches dividing the hall, and the effect is very pleasing.

After the reading, which takes place every morning and every evening from the same three Books : namely,

ENTRANCE TO THE HOUSE OF THE AMEER
ABDULLAH IBN JLEWY IN HUFOUF

THE PALM AND THE DATES
' Honour thy cousin, the Palm.'—The Prophet Muhammad

The Hadith, Tabari's *History of Arabia,* and *The Life of the Prophet* (when one book is finished it is re-read again), I walked with the Sultan to another building—the new Serai—which the ruler of the Province, his cousin Sheikh Abdullah, is having built. It has four baronial halls, the largest of which, on the ground floor, is 150 feet long, and is designed for general assembly ;—for salaam and coffee and a loafing, when there is no reading, of fifteen minutes. Upstairs are the other halls, for special audience and for business.

Of ancient architecture there is little or nothing in Hufouf ;—no trace of the Carmathians, nor any ruin to tell of the Khalifs of either Damascus or Baghdad. I have only seen the old Mosque, a square building of 60 by 60 feet, built of stone covered with plaster, and spanned by a single dome. It is called the Mosque of Ibrahim, because it was built, as some believe, in the beginning of the last century, when Ibrahim Pasha defeated the Wahhabis and occupied even Al-Hasa. I think it is two hundred and fifty years older, dating back to the first occupation of this part of Arabia by the Turks,[1] and was perhaps built in the days of Sultan Murad, the Conqueror of Baghdad. More interesting to me, however, was the view from the roof of the archway or inner gate. There, outside the wall of Hufouf proper, was the broadest street I have seen in Arabia, and the busiest,—a broad and very attractive street with arched arcades—the Rue Rivoli of Al-Hasa. More of the place I have not seen ; more about it I know not. For much as I desired to visit the environs of Hufouf, Mubarraz, for instance, and the hot springs, I could not—it was a physical impossibility. Indeed, dear reader, the few days I spent in this old town of the

---

[1] The Ottoman Turks, who first entered Al-Hasa in 1520 A.D., considering it as a part of Al-Yaman, lost it when they lost Al-Yaman in 1557 ; and not till 313 years later, in 1870, did they reconquer it, calling it the Province of Najd. But their rule, which never extended beyond Hufouf westward, came to an end in the winter of 1913, when the Sultan Abd'ul-Aziz put them out of the Province and established his own authority over it.

Carmathians—the ancient Bolsheviks of Arabia—were dedicated to Aesculapius and to Muhammad Effendi.

Aesculapius you doubtless know. My business with him was the outcome of a contact which a foolish resoluteness —obduracy—would not own at the start and would not subsequently try to overcome. No, it was not the *gazalah* of the camel saddle, but the saddle itself, the very breast-bone of it, which impudently penetrated, through carpet and sheepskin and cushion, to the entity enthroned upon them. Another day, another hour, in fact, after we came within wind of Hufouf, and I would have been violently dethroned. Morally, of a truth, I was ; and to reinstate myself I had to check every ambulatory impulse and surrender myself for a few days to the God of healing. Here it was that Muhammad Effendi was the Chief Steward of the god.

Muhammad Effendi of Mosul, erstwhile of the Turkish regime, is now one of the best Finance Secretaries of the Sultanate of Najd. But that is not what recommended him to me. Muhammad Effendi is also the best cook in the Sultanate, Moreover, Muhammad Effendi has taught all his wives and his nine daughters the fine art of cooking. It was by virtue of the covered trays, which were sent on the heads of slaves, three times, four times a day, from his house to ours,—the fastidiously prepared dishes, the delicious tit-bits, the flesh-pots delicately seasoned, the meat and crushed wheat-balls which recalled my own Lebanon kitchen, the mysteriously embalmed confections, the stuffed and spiced dates, the sweetmeats and the sherbets indescribable,—it was by virtue of these master-pieces, produced by the collaboration of Muhammad Effendi's wives and daughters that my days with Aesculapius were shorn of their sting, were even made joyful. Allah keep thee and thy wives, thou best Treasurer and Cook of the Sultanate of Najd, and Allah send thy nine daughters nine good husbands.

MAIN STREET OF HUFOUF ON A BUSY DAY

ONE OF IBN SA'OUD'S GOVERNORS AND HIS BODYGUARD

CHAPTER XI

ACROSS THE DESERT

Two names, marking milestones on the journey from Al-Hasa to Ar-Riyadh, stood out most prominently in my mind and were like two beacons in my heart, when we marched out of Hufouf through the Najd gate. These were Rujmat'ush-Shwai'er (Cairn of the Little Poet) and Abu Jefan. The first marks the entrance to the Dahna, the great sand desert ; the second is the first watering place after we leave the Humaidah wells, which are a few miles outside of Hufouf. At these wells we filled our four large waterskins, which were carried by two camels, and the *qirbahs* (small waterskin), one of which every one carries with him. Drink deep from the good, clean fresh water of Humaidah,—the incomparable water of Al-Hasa, —for not until you get to Ar-Riyadh will your eyes behold *aqua pura* again, and not until you cross the Dahna to Abu Jefan,[1] a hundred and fifty miles away, will you see another well.

The Sultan Abd'ul-Aziz, accompanied by the men who came with him to Al-Hasa, went the day before ahead of us ; for he could not, having been four months away from his home and Capital, travel at a walking pace ; and he would not, considering my own disadvantages, force me to the *dirham* with him. ' We are going ahead to prepare for your coming,' he graciously said. And he left me with a goodly crew. Saiyed Hashem, who, having read ' Darween,' was in doubt about his soul and,

[1] Pronounced Abu J'fan.

therefore, didn't much care what became of the souls of others. Huwaidi the cook, who, having spent the heyday of his life in ' cosmopolitan ' Basrah, looked with disdain upon the ragamuffins of Najd ; Majed the ' *b'dewi*,' who could stand on his head even upon the hump of a trotting camel and quote the Koran, thus standing, as perfectly

BADDAH,
THE BRAGGART

as a learned Wahhabi sheikh ; Baddah the guide, son of the fierce tribe of 'Ujman and braggart of the first water, who would acknowledge the superiority of no one, not even the philosopher Saiyed Hashem ; Rajhan, Huwaidi's assistant, who coughed and quaked every time he was asked to do something, and who preferred to take the camels to pasture when we camped, because he would thus avoid Majed and loaf to his heart's content :—these were my *rafiqs* and brothers of the road.

The first day out, what lingered of my cold had departed ; but the carbolated vaseline was still necessary. Nevertheless, we rode at a slow walking pace six hours in the daytime and three hours at night, coming to a plain called Na'lah, where we slept. It was a pleasant spot, in a hollow of sand, sheltered from the wind. But on the following day the name as well as the aspect of the plain changed ; and my bed the second night in Rubaidah was on a ground of unmitigated stoniness. We were traversing the Summan, that hard and barren and shadeless plain between Wadi Farouq and the Dahna, which is to the natives of many localities and names. But to the traveller they signify nothing. Wadi Farouq, however, is conspicuous ; for it runs north by south between the rolling soil to the east and the table-land to the west of it.

Of the scabrous Summan, which is about fifty miles across, I remember nothing but the stones under my mattress at night and the terrible ordeal of one of our camels. On the second day, after we had our supper, we

AROUND THE FIRE SIPPING COFFEE

THE SUMMAN DESERT

waited for the moon before starting our night march, and then proceeded to pack and load. Everything went well, till the turn of the last camel, which was to carry the two other skins of water. He was a black beast with a tendency to viciousness, who had given the men some trouble the morning they started to load him in Hufouf; and in the Summan that evening he seemed to prefer the stones under his knees to the load on his back. He was in no mood for business. The two skins were lifted to the wooden frame, slung on its *gazalahs* and tied, while he growled and groaned; and when he was asked to rise he refused. The bamboo switch was applied with decision and firmness but he would not budge. Two bamboos were broken upon his hide; he growled incessantly, hideously; and moving only his neck he made several attempts to defend himself. But his teeth bit at the air and the night.

The 'third degree' was applied. His head was held by Majed, his mouth was opened by Huwaidi, while Baddah took handfuls of earth and stuffed them down his throat. The perverse, vicious one refused nevertheless to lift a knee. The fourth and last resource—yea, there is a 'fourth degree' of torture among camel-kind (man and beast are in this of the same species)—this last resource was within reach. Our fire was still burning; and Baddah taking a stick that was blazing on one end, dug it under the camel's tail. He uttered an unearthly cry, groaned, roared of his anguish to high heaven; and flinging on his side, he overturned his load. The water, from the skin which was under him, flowed on the ground. I felt the cold sweat on my brow. I was veritably sick. The delay, the torture of the camel, and now, the crowning of calamity—half a skin of water gone. Which may mean that we shall have to travel night and day to cover the dry distance to Abu Jefan.

What added to the plight was that the other camels, which were left to themselves, roved far afield; and I myself had to do, in a poor way, some herding. I know, at least, the herdsman's cry. *Waw reimaw, w-a-aw reim-a-a-w!* Slowly, they came to a point and were brought back by Majed. Meantime, the Inquisition continued ; and the suffering one, having thrown off his burden, rose to his feet. They walked him a little and beat him again down to his knees. Whereupon, they poured some water out of the full skin into the half-empty one to equalize the load, and lifted them again to the saddle-frame amidst the renewed groans of protest and appeal. And Baddah, tired of torturing him, was inclined to mercy.—' Up good beast—up camel—thou cursed of both parents, rise ! Thou foul one, thou foolish one, thou vicious one ! rise—rise up ! " But Huwaidi, whose ruthlessness was not yet spent, came forth with another stick of fire. I had run to recall Saiyed Hashem who had gone ahead of us, and when we returned the poor beast was moaning and turning on his hams, while Majed and Baddah were clinging to the waterskins.

' Stop ! ' cried Saiyed Hashem, who would try another method of persuasion, ' Leave him alone—stand away from him. Now, wait.' And by the Prophet ! the camel was not slow in responding. He seemed to find a soothing something in the new voice ; and, getting up of his own accord, he quietly, silently and slowly walked away. I thanked Saiyed Hashem. But Baddah said that that is what he was going to do—let the beast alone—when Huwaidi came again with the fire. ' A stick of it under the tail of you and the tail of him ! '—this from Majed. But Huwaidi, who had such deep contempt for Majed— for everybody, in truth—lifted his raucous voice in song. It was worse, *billah*, than the groan of the camel, and there was no trotting away from it at night. We had to stick together and follow the guide. It was an arduous, painful march, and we did not stop for an hour's sleep till two after midnight.

The sun on the third day was not, perhaps, more intense than it was the two days preceding ; but, owing to

THE GUARDIANS OF THE CAVE, AL-HASA

THE TWO BREASTS, AL-HASA

fatigue and lack of sleep, it was to me more insufferable. I was becoming impatient—impatient for the Dahna, as if the Dahna were the end of our journey. Baddah seemed concerned only about the Shioukh. Every time we met some Bedu going to Al-Hasa he stopped them, asked them for their news, and then : 'Where did you meet the Shioukh?'[1] But I started from the morning to inquire about the Cairn of the Little Poet. Strange, how anxiety and impatience keep the goal away, multiplying, as it were, the distance between it and yourself. We had to pass through Malsouniyah and Baidhah and Jasrah—names of localities in the Summan, which are not to be found even on a big map of Arabia—before we got to the Cairn of the Little Poet. O Shwai'er, the shadows are snuggling up to us, are hiding under us, are running towards the east away from us, and thy Cairn seems farther than Ar-Riyadh. But why question the dumb horizon, why lay thy faith in shadows, why even look at thy watch ? Look into thine own heart, and gather up what patience thou findest therein to have the courage at least to ask again. 'Ahead of you,' said the herdsboy we met in the afternoon, 'very near.' Which meant a ride of six hours more ; and when we passed the Cairn, it was veiled, alas ! with the veil of night.

Humaidan, the Little Poet, who lived about a hundred and fifty years ago and made satirical rhymes in the dialect of the people of Najd, lampooning everybody ;—even himself when he no longer could do justice to his wife ; even his wife—the mother of his children—who forgot his bounties in the prime of his power ;—he seems to have eloped with a young one in his latter days, carrying her behind him on his *zelul* across the Dahna. But before they had been out of its last fringe of sand, they were overtaken by the girl's brothers and cousins, and a battle

[1] Shioukh—plural of Sheikh—is another title of the ruler of Najd. It was originally applied to him by the slaves of the Palace when he and his male relations would be together.—Here come the Shioukh—there go the Shioukh. Now the plural is applied to the Sultan alone.

ensued. The Cairn marks the spot where the poet was killed.

We rode on for another hour before we descended. And I flung myself, from sheer exhaustion, upon the sand, where I slept like a top and did not wake up till the wind of dawn had bitten me through the boots. I have experienced in December the weather of two seasons and two zones. About midday, the flies, which travel with us to the end of the earth, begin to buzz, singing a hymn to the tropic sun ; and I raise my *aba* over my head, holding it out at both ends to protect my eyes as well as to attract a little breeze. What would be the wrath of the sun in July if this be his temper in December? But at night the December winds are unmistakable. They are dry, however, and invigorating. No ill reaches you, un-sheltered as you are, with the soft sand for a bed and the sky for a cover. And how welcome is the morning fire ! though often, in our hurry to start on the march, we left it blazing behind us.

After we had crossed the Dahna, I was disappointed —disappointed because it ended in a day—disappointed because I had but two nights' sleep in it. And where are the dangers? Not while a good guide is with you do they cast out their luring nets ; and Baddah, after all, has proved his metal. He has also a voice with a gamut of tones from the squeak of a rat to the roar of a lion. His imitations were perfect and delightful. ' By the father of thee,' he cried, imitating the broad ' stage ' voice of the Bedu, ' we're at the head of the D'hana.' And when we came to its western end : ' *Walhamdulillah !* (Praise be to Allah) we strode th'D'hana—we're out of th'D'hana.' Even as the Arabs of old, whose poet says,

' We go forth through the Dahna, light and clean,
    And come back heavy laden from Darin.' [1]

But to me, of all the vast stretches of desert I have

[1] Darin, on the Persian Gulf, near Qatif, was in the past an emporium like Kuwait to-day, and famous for its pearls.

crossed, the Dahna, which is the most feared, is the most hospitable and is also beautiful. Except at its edges, it is a white desert and has no dunes. Nor is it a barren waste. It has good pasture even in the summer ; and man and beast, providing the *qirbah* is full, may cross it breadthwise, of course—leisurely, too,—without any danger. I have seen in it, here and there, even before the fall of rain, patches of green—a tall herb, like the ele-campane, and the trailing colocynth. But of withered shrubbery and parched thorns, which the camels prize and at which they snatch as they go, there is an abundance. For the benefit of man, too, there is plenty of wood. When I say, 'wood,' I speak the language of the Bedu, who call a shrub a tree and a stick a log. But these are sufficient for the purpose of the wayfarer. In parts of the Summan we could not find a root ; in others, only shrivelled grass ; and in each place we had to use camel dung for fuel.

The Dahna is hospitable even to the most delicate of created things. I saw on the greyish, parched-up shrubbery, skipping from twig to twig, and tripping lightly upon the sand, the pet bird of the Arab poets, the *warqa'*, which resembles only in form, the fire-tailed humming bird. But the grey wing, of the warqa' and its long tail are fringed and lined with black. Other birds also, among them the grey partridge, come to the Dahna for the winter season and tarry till the middle of Spring.

Herdsmen drive their flocks to this great sand desert for pasture, and across it to the Hasa market :—flocks of goats as well as camels ; for the goat, too, can go without water for many days. I have also seen cattle crossing the Dahna ; which is only possible, however, with an accom-panying water-carrying camel corps. But of all things, winged and hoofed, animate and inanimate, wings visible and invisible—aye, even the four winds of the compass (Does any of the winds that blow over Arabia ever come from America ?)—of all things, I say, that have shared the highway of the Dahna with me, nothing had travelled such a distance to it as the human being that is responsible for this narration, and quantities of cotton cloth—bales marked Aden, Bombay, Bahrain—which, through many trans-shipments, had crossed the seven floods, coming all the way from Massachusetts, and were being carried by the ships of the desert to Ar-Riyadh.

The width of the Dahna,[1] where we crossed it, is about twenty-five miles, which we covered in eight hours ; and when we crouched our camels towards sunset at its western end, we held to a fringe of its soft red spread for the evening. Besides, the dunes along the edges were of too rare a beauty to leave behind at sundown. Those dunes, before which we lighted our fire—the fire of adoration ; those delicate and exquisite forms with outlines as sharp as steel and as soft as unspun silk—are they sentinels at the gate, behind which is a vastness of fear and death, or are they ushers in the vestibule ? Do they express words of warning or of welcome ? Whatever they be, they stand there full of loveliness and beauty, concealing in their heart the mystery of the desert, and weaving the spell that lures and destroys whosoever comes unarmed—without a *qirbah* and a guide.

That we might spend a whole day at Abu Jefan we got up at midnight and resumed our march in the light of a waning moon, through a level plain dotted closely with clumps of earth and grass. My *zelul* Zabia, whose rhythm in walking and mine in swaying had reached together a degree of harmony sufficient to establish peace between us, threaded her way through the tuberosities of the plain without over-tripping, or disturbing my sleep. What a wonderful thing to have accomplished, I thought as I opened my eyes at the break of dawn and looked around for my *rafiqs*. They too were nodding as they swayed. Our *zeluls*, with the halter on the neck, as the Arabs say, kept close together and seemed to know the

---

[1] More about the Dahna when we cross it again on our way to Kuwait.

road. To be sure, after a march of six and a half hours, they brought us in the early morning to what looked like the end of the plain. All around, for some geological reason I know not, it had caved ; and we stood over a ravine, about fifty feet deep, along the sides of which are ledges of rock.

In this ravine are the wells of Abu Jefan, which were already crowded with travellers and herdsmen seeking the water. We walked our camels down, and under one of the ledges of the fault—that is, I think, the geological term—my tent was pitched for the first time after leaving Ojair. And for the first time, after leaving Al-Hasa, I had two hours of sleep on a cot and afterwards a decent wash.

The water at Abu Jefan is good—when it is clean. But this can hardly be expected in the winter season, when, after a day's run on the wells, of which there are five, they become almost empty, and the Bedu go down in their barefeet and dirt to scrape what remains in the dark puddle of the living liquid surface. At night, they only half fill up again ; for the underground streams which feed them are very thin at this time of the year. But in the summer the wells overflow, and are then the meeting places of the tribes. Here they gather, bringing their flocks, their merchandise, and their politics with them.

At the close of day, two of our *qirbas* were found empty, and Majed was asked to fill them. ' Samm ! ' Saying which, he skipped down the jutting rocks, friskily like a goat to the bottom, which is about thirty feet deep ; and in a few minutes, shouldering the two skins, he clambered up again a model of mud-bespattered sacrifice. But the colour of the water in the *qirbas* was a dark yellow. ' This is for Rajhan,' said Majed, to dissipate my fear, ' and this is for Huwaidi. Praise be to Allah, your *qirbah* was filled at noon. Observe.' Saying which, he poured out a drink for himself. The water was tolerably clean.

The second day out, however, it will become mud-pure like the rest ; for the leather skins are seldom washed. And when they are, they are seldom rinsed, so that the water often becomes rancid. Oh, the purity of the white sand of the Dahna and the red sand of the Nufoud. It has been with these Arabs ever since they began to speak in poetry, and it has taught them nothing. On the contrary, the desert has killed in them the sense of taste, while the other senses, in their tribal development, have become anomalous. Thus, the Arabs hit back. They have conquered the desert by the will to do away with the comforts of life ; and they have become inordinately bold and fierce and proud, because they can cross ' th'D'hana ' with just a *qirbah* of water and a poke of dates.

So Saiyed Hashem, philosophizing around the fire at Abu Jefan.—' If the great Darween saw our Bedu, he would have found the missing link.' Baddah wanted to know who was ' Dawreen.' ' Darween is father of the monkeys,' replied Saiyed Hashem.   ' *Billah!* and hast thou ever seen a monkey ? I saw them in Al-Yaman. And *billah!* they do like us.' ' We do like them,' retorted the Saiyed. ' They are our ancestors.'—' Speak not thuswise. I am an 'Ujmani, son of the brave 'Ujman. Thou art a Saiyed, a descendant of the Prophet, Peace upon him. But the monkeys may be the ancestors of the people of Al-Yaman. Allah knows better than Dawreen.' ' D-a-arwe-e-n,' corrected Saiyed Hashem.   ' Hearken, Allah keep thee. This Dareen may have seen many monkeys, but if he ever visits the 'Ujman tribe, he would know that there are some people in the land of the Arabs who are not the brothers nor the cousins of the monkeys. I Baddah am an 'Ujmani, and I can drive myself against fifty of the monkeys of Al-Yaman—the monkeys of Qahtan—and slay every one of them *billah!* before I breathe twice.' He had done a like great deed in Basrah one day, after he had gulped down a whole bottle of whisky. One man

THE NUFOUD AT SUNSET

NO PASTURE AND NO WATER. ONLY THE HARD SOIL
AND THE BURNING SKY

of a party of twenty insulted the 'Ujman.—' And I drove
myself against them, *billah!* and made them all run—
except the one who insulted the 'Ujman. I brought his
head with me to Al-Hasa.' He then told us that after an
absence of a month from his wife he gave her fifteen
favours, and an extra for the sake of the Prophet. ' And
on the following day,' he continued, ' I had to carry a
letter from the Imam to Ibn Jlewy,—a very important
letter. " Like the lightning," said the Imam, and *wallah,
billah!* I rode out of Ar-Riyadh at dawn and prayed the
noon prayer the following day in Hufouf, stopping three
times, once in the Dahna and twice in the Summan, to
rest the *zelul.*' [1]

The distance between Hufouf and Ar-Riyadh is a little
over two hundred miles, which the *najjabs* can cover in
three days, riding at a brisk pace fifteen hours a day at
the least. It may also be done in two and a half days,
riding eighteen hours a day. And they do it cheerfully,
although they brag about it enough to beat a Tartarin,
and resolutely ; stopping for an hour's rest or sleep only
where there is pasture for the camel. We have ridden,
at an easy pace, eight hours a day and from three to six
hours at night, which even to Saiyed Hashem was a good
test of courage and endurance. But I do not know of a
people outside of Arabia, who are so hardened to long
marches at a *dirham* (trotting or galloping) pace as the
people of Najd. Miles at a stretch ! The *zelul,* its halter
upon its neck, *dirhaming,* while the rider, his hands in the
air, his arms akimbo—this is the sportsman's manner—
is dancing in the saddle, darting up and down like the
shaft of an engine—it is a wonderful, a memorable sight.
Especially when they go in groups, ' light and clean,' as

[1] The Arabs of Najd reckon the distances by their daily prayers. When
one of them asks another : what is the distance between such and such a
place, the reply would be somewhat as follows : ' *Wallah,* O my brother,
if you start after the noon prayer, you will say your evening prayer there.'
Or : ' The distance is just a little ride between the two prayers,' *i.e.* the
afternoon and the sunset, or the noon and the afternoon, prayers.

their ancient poet said, each carrying his own *qirbah* and a few dates in his saddle-bag to cross the Summan desert and the Dahna in two days. But I felt like a Veiled Thing riding in a *shaqdouf*, and carrying four big skins of water for the same journey. It does not matter if the water was spilt on the way. The motive and the fear were there. But strange how they too were shaken out of my heart as we rode forth, coming at last to Abu Jefan, the providing and protecting deity of the traveller.

I have even befriended my *zelul* Zabia, who not only would let me sleep on her back but would also eat out of my hand. I gave her dates—a chunk as large as a grapefruit is the least you can offer a camel—and she chewed at them—ordinary camels just swallow them— and stretched her graceful neck for more. Zabia has a long reach and a cultivated taste. But, although she found no more in my hand, she patted it with her upper lip and closed upon it her nether—every fear of the camel I had tucked away in my bosom, from my infancy till that day was swept away, and I was as proud as a ' b'dewi ' crossing ' th'D'hana ; '—Zabia, I say, began to lick my hand with her big tongue and to suck at my fingers. What a wonderful moment ! To have conquered a camel with a chunk of dates,—to have, moreover, made of her a friend. I went to bed full of the joy of this triumph, and I got up in the morning still full of it. I would reward Zabia, therefore,—I would give her a rest.

Saiyed Hashem, erstwhile a fisher of pearls, still retained something of the sporting spirit ; and when I suggested a walk, he was delighted. ' To Ar-Riyadh,' he said, ' let us walk to Ar-Riyadh.' Now, a good map is indispensable ; but when it is a question of roads or of heights, I know of no map of Arabia that is perfectly reliable. The one I carried, an excellent work in many details, showed but one road westward from Abu Jefan. *There are two*. We struck out, leaving the men packing and loading, and followed the road before us. We walked

an hour, happy as larks, till we came to the point where
the table-land ends, falls precipitantly into the plain.
There is the *aqaba* (steep incline), which we were told is
three hours' walk from Abu Jefan. Ah, we have caught
the Arabs exaggerating distances in the reverse manner.
It's only an hour : we know : we have watches. But
the Arabs say, It is three. They should have said, It is
ghraiyeb [1] (very near). We were still happier in the
discovery. The *Bedu* we met on the way told us that that
was the *aqaba*. There is no mistake about it. And we
were on our way to Ar-Riyadh ? Aye, *billah !* The map
says so, too.

On, therefore, we went, descending the *aqaba* and
proceeding through the plain. But Ar-Riyadh, according
to the map, is N.W. of Abu Jefan ; and I noticed from our
shadows that we were going in a south-westerly direction.
I began to doubt, but I kept silent. Soon we heard a
voice—in the wilderness forsooth—repeated twice, three
times, but saying nothing—just shouting. It sounded like
that of Majed. Saiyed Hashem replied, woh ho ! woah !
at the top of his voice. There, to be sure, was Majed
galloping on my Zabia ! and with him the braggart
Baddah. They motioned us to stop. What has happened ?
The vicious camel again ? beaten by Huwaidi to death ?
What is it ? Baddah, with anger in his face and voice :
' You have mistaken the road. *Billah !* Come back.'
The camels crouched for us ; and, with him and Majed
as *radifs* (back-riders) behind us, we trotted back to Abu
Jefan. The right road has to be resumed at that juncture.
The road we had taken would have brought us to Yamama,
about seventy-five miles south of Ar-Riyadh.

When we reached Abu Jefan I felt like a truant
brought back to duty ; but, nevertheless, I still wanted to
walk. Saiyed Hashem was in the same mood. So we
got down. Huwaidi had gone ahead cursing everybody ;

---

[1] 'Nothing is far for the Bedu. Everything is *ghraiyeb*.'—Majed, the
B'dewi.

Baddah and Majed rode our *zeluls* ; and we resumed our tramp. We had lost two hours of the day, but that did not matter. The Dahna and the Summan were behind us, and Ar-Riyadh was only two marches away.

Soon after we had debouched, ascending from Abu Jefan, we came to a vast plain that recalled at the first blush the Summan. But the Summan, in comparison, is meadow-land. Before us was a desolation, wild, and forbidding and hopeless. Not a blade of grass, not a broken twig, not a dried-up root : it was even black and stony ;—the nearest I had yet seen to what is called the Harra, or volcanic soil. The stones under our feet were small and sharp, of colours ranging from bronze to ebony ; it was lava drift. And in places there was a resonance in the ground, which seemed hollow beneath.

We trudged along to reach the *aqaba*, the right *aqaba*, which is, of a truth, more than three hours' walk from Abu Jefan. I was walking in my riding boots—a burden. We sent Baddah galloping to overtake Huwaidi to make him stop ; for all the water was with him, and we were getting thirsty. Baddah in a few minutes disappeared ; and for one, two, three hours, we saw no more of him. ' They are base, these Bedu, and treacherous,' said Saiyed Hashem. ' They will let us walk the whole day without water.' We decided, therefore, to send Majed after Baddah. And in a few minutes, Zabia going at the last degree of the *dirham*, he, too, disappeared behind the sloping horizon.

When you are travelling, tramping, athirst and without any assurance, through a vastness of lava drift, you welcome any fall or rise in the land before you. An open horizon is like a sentence of death : a hillock or a ridge on the horizon holds out a hope. For is it not likely to reveal something different ? No : one circle of our little Harra, like Dante's Inferno, was as bad as the other (even worse to us, considering the drop in the thermometer of our endurance). And here was an infinity of the series.

Saiyed Hashem lost his temper, and introduced me to a new vocabulary. The servants were the objects of it—bawds, sons of bawds !

He wanted water, and I was dying of thirst. Fortunately I had placed in my pocket, the night before, a few lemon-drops. I gave my *rafiq* one, and moistened my parched tongue with another. A curious effect of thirst and fear : we had marvelled at some alabaster stones and bits of quartz we found on the way ; and when I gave Saiyed Hashem a lemon-drop he looked at it curiously. ' That is a pretty stone,' this in earnest ; ' where did you find it ? ' ' Put it in your mouth,' I said ; ' it tastes good.' And our little laugh was a break in the monotony of terror.

Majed did not come back ; the *aqaba* seemed farther away than ever ; the sun was nearing the zenith ; the atmosphere vibrated and gleamed with the noonday heat ; and there was not a sheltering shade, not even a stone big enough to sit down upon in that vastness of desolation, that eminent domain of Death. About two and a half hours after we left Abu Jefan, however, the soil in places changed into a soft mould—here is where the ground sounded hollow ; and an hour later, when I was on the point of collapsing from thirst and fatigue and despair we came to the end of the table-land—the break in the plain—the rift in the earth ;—the tumbling, crumbling wall, which is called the *aqaba !*

It is, indeed, a wonderful geological phenomenon. The whole section from south to—I know not how far north—is such a crumbling wall ;—the Harra comes abruptly upon the plain ; falls from a height of about three hundred feet, and with a crash. And what a welcome sight is the green-vested field below. More welcome to us at that moment, however, was the sight of our camels—the whole caravan—at the foot of the *aqaba* waiting for us. ' Bawds,' cried Saiyed Hashem. And while he was venting his ire upon them I took the water they had offered me—from what skin they drew it

and where they got the bowl they poured it in, I knew not
and cared not ; but I closed my eyes and gulped down
the yellow contents of that filthy vessel, and praised Allah
sincerely, as sincerely as a right Muslem.

We then rode to a grove of *salam* trees (a species of
acacia) in Wadi Terabi, as that plain is called, and made
our halt for the day. An hour later, Huwaidi having put
to the knife the sheep we had brought with us from Abu
Jefan (no one could prepare a meal quicker than that
Basrah churl), we sat down to a mess of rice and lamb.
Here I shocked everybody by eating raw meat. I even
awed them. Indeed, as soon as I began to cut up the
lamb into little pieces and eat them thus with my bread,
I had established without any forethought a certain
savage superiority over them ; and they became thence-
forth more respectful. I do not know how the custom
of eating raw meat in Syria originated ; but I am certain
it did not come from the Arabs, for nowhere in Arabia
is it known.

Between Hufouf and Ar-Riyadh, the soil, although
variable, has one thing in common—barrenness. And
the landscape is most dismal, except in the Dahna, and
particularly the edges of it. The Summan, from the
point of view of the camel, is tolerable ; the Dahna is
enjoyable ; the plain between Abu Jefan and Wadi
Terabi is execrable ; but from the point of view of man
they are all one :—over them all have swept the burning
blasts of desolation.

Although Wadi Terabi, with its thin patches of *salam*,
seems more promising, and is more inviting for a walk,
I decided that I would not separate myself from the party
again. Besides, I was annoyed with Saiyed Hashem, who
said that in our walk yesterday he was neither tired nor
thirsty ; that he was anxious about the water for my sake ;
and for my sake, too, he lost his temper. He had caught,
from Baddah, it seemed to me, the germ of brag ; or, if
I have wrongly doubted his veracity, he must have some-

thing of the *jinn* in him. So I said to him—this around
the fire under the *salam*, when the assertive mood bloomed
with great *billahs !*—' A man who can walk from here to
Ar-Riyadh (about fifty miles) without getting tired, or
thirsty, and without ever losing his temper on the way,
cannot be human, *billah !* And I prefer to walk with one
like myself, who gets tired, and thirsty, and is not imper-
vious even to despair.' Whereupon, everybody, even the
lazy Rajhan, spoke in defence of Saiyed Hashem. He
was my *rafiq*—a human like myself—he spoke the truth—
a walk of fifty miles is nothing—the Arab can do it in a
day, without tiring, without thirsting—the Arab, Allah
keep thee, is in this like the camel. ' And it is not
possible to get angry while walking,' this from Majed.
' It is only while sitting—sitting with the devil—doing
nothing—that I get angry. And then, I get up and walk,
or I ask some one to wrestle with me—rise, thou Rajhan,
thou oaf ! (Rajhan with his elbow pushed him away).
Very well. I will walk on my hands and beat thee walking
on thy feet—like this—come !' Thus Majed, with one
of his merry performances, closed the argument about
walking to Ar-Riyadh.

On the following day, seeing me urge Zabia with my
heel, he drove his camel, which was carrying the tent and
the luggage, close to me and said : ' Zabia is the best
zelul in the land of Najd ; touch her lightly with the
bamboo—thus. But not with thy boot. Zabia is the
princess of th'*bel* (ibel=camels).' We had traversed the
salam patches in the plain and were launched again into
what seemed an endless vast, the circles of terror, softened
by a ridge or an undulation, following each other ; and
I was anxious to get through even at a *dirham* pace. Soon,
however, we came to a stretch of sand overgrown with
the green *harmal* (elecampane) and the '*arfaj* of the last
season. This bush, green or dry, is the favourite of the
camels. So we walked our mounts, even let them stray
as they list to graze.

Between these sand patches are dark, black spots in the plain—the most interesting hitherto, and the most fatiguing for man and beast. The ground, which is also of sand, is covered with a sprinkling of stones, of shades ranging from dun to ebony, and of an infinite variety of forms. Some look like ossified chips of wood ; others like parts of miniature statues ; while others seemed to retain a memory of animal bones—broken stone clubs, as it were, hollow like pieces of iron pipe. What are they ? Fossil remains, or lava drift, or the hundred million pieces of a shattered meteorite ? Whatever they are, not a blade of green grows among them.

Nor in the next circle, which is whiter than white sand ; —a lake of dry loam ;—a floor covered with plaster, as it were, and checkered in cracking, made into a mosaic by the sun of last summer. It is in sooth an arabesque floor on which we rode ; and it still bore here and there the footprints of a camel and a man who had passed when the soil was still impressionable from the last spring rain. A rare thing, the footprints of yesteryear, even of yesterday in a country of changeless grit and ever shifting dunes. But these two impressions, after the rain had gone for the season, were caught and preserved by the sun. More curious than this loam soil, however, was a strip of sand not far from it, abounding in pebbles and looking like a beach or a river bank. But when did the river last flow through this arid land, or when did the waves of the sea roll over it—these are questions which I myself cannot answer.[1] All I can say is that in a day's march we came upon four different features of soil : i.e. gravel, loam, sand, and lava. All of which are characteristic of lower Najd. But the Arabs divide the country between Al-Hasa and Ar-Riyadh into Summan and desert, that is hard soil and sand.

[1] Says the geologist : ' Between Abu Jefan and Ar-Riyadh are found fossils which represent the remnants of a marine fauna, which thrived over a considerable area of what is now Arabia during the Jurassic period.'

Between Abu Jefan and Ar-Riyadh there is one well at Al-'Uqlah, where we descended a little before sundown, and the camels were turned to pasture. Evidently, my *rafiqs* were also very hungry, for they all helped Huwaidi to cook the supper. But I did not have to wait. For the past three days my stomach had turned against the concoctions of the Basrah cook ; and the quarter of lamb, which dandled from his saddle and was before my eyes the entire day, still looked inviting. I got to it with my jack-knife, therefore, and out of the neighbourhood of the bone, where no fly could penetrate, I carve out my supper. After the raw meat, the dates—Honour thy cousin the palm ! This, for the last three days of the journey, was my diet. But on the first two days I partook heartily of the bounties of Muhammad Effendi of Hufouf, especially of his meat and wheat-balls, which might have been sufficient for the whole journey had Baddah a less ravenous appetite.

One morning I saw him put a whole roast chicken in his saddle-bag for the noonday meal (we ate as we rode) ; and when later I asked him for a piece of it—a drumstick, a wing, a bone—he stroked one palm against the other and smiled—all gone ! Of dates, however, we had an abundance, and I always carried some in my saddle-bag. When travelling in Arabia, if you breakfast on dates and take a good drink of water before you start, you will not thirst or hunger during the day. This is the rule of the Bedu, and I found it quite sound.

But Baddah is not of the Bedu, and he, therefore, breakfasts on *khabis* (mess), which is even more nutritious than dates. Here comes Huwaidi with some of it on a *clean plate !* What has happened ? My raw-meat defiance must have had its effect. And his *khabis*, which looks like maple sugar, but soft, is good. It is even better cold and hard ; for it keeps. A mess, indeed, is *khabis*, which consists in its ordinary form, of four ingredients—flour, water, sugar, and butter—and in its form *de luxe*, of six.

To make the first, the flour is placed in the kettle over a good fire and stirred—dried—till it begins to smell ; the water, with the sugar, is then poured over it and stirred well till again the smell—another variety—is evident ; whereupon, the rarefied butter is added and stirred assiduously till the mess gives forth its pungent aroma and becomes consistent.   To make the second, a kettle is not necessary.   For after the mess is kneaded into a paste, and rounded and flattened into a cake, it is cooked in a sand pit, which is covered with fire.   Thus, after it is done, are added to it two more ingredients—ashes and sand. Besides, it has a pleasant burnt flavour.

A plate of *khabis*, and we were getting near our goal— the Arab, without reading in books, knows the value of the psychological moment.   For although we had travelled five hours the night before, following in the darkness the sleeping guide Baddah ; and although Majed, the most illuminate of vagabonds, could not bring us back to ' the white flames,' [1] the road, till we had strayed a few miles from it ; and although we had slept but two hours on a ground as hard as the Summan and were up in the early dawn to resume our march ; yet, with a mess of Huwaidi's *khabis*—and the goal drawing near—I was completely reconciled.

And there, after we had traversed Wadi Slaiy, which runs north-east, by south-west, and which glows with a richness of green—a waste of green rather, for the camels touch not the *harmal ;* and after meandering for a couple of hours amidst hummocks of hard clay and basalt ;— there, as we come to the last ridge on the horizon, a few miles beyond, is the silhouette of the oasis of Al-'Ared— there is Ar-Riyadh !   Of all the scenes in my Arab travels that gave pleasure to the eye or to the soul none was more pleasing and more welcome than this—the Capital of

---

[1] ' How is the road,' a night-traveller asks of a beduin. ' Flames before you,' he replies ; or, ' white and broad as the neck of a camel.' The poetic exaggeration in both instances, from the little to the big and from the big to the little, is characteristic of the Arabs.

Najd among the palms. For I had really suffered much and endured much to reach it.

Saiyed Hashem asked Baddah to go ahead of us and announce our arrival. ' Samm ! ' said the 'Ujmani, and after taking his ' official ' green jerkin out of his saddle-bag and dusting it he put it on, then tightened his *ighal* on his head, and gave his *zelul* the rein. We followed slowly till we came within the shadow of the city wall, where I descended, praising Allah, and kissed a tuft of green. What a magnificent green did the lucerne exhibit on that afternoon ! It seemed to glow with a supernatural beauty. And there is the palm, my cousin, indeed, my most beloved cousin, come out to meet me.

Baddah soon returned to say that we were to crouch our camels at the Palace gate ; which meant that I was to live in the Palace. So my brothers of the road quickly changed their travelling clothes ; and Majed and Hu-waidi in their immaculate white garments looked like Mullahs. Even Saiyed Hashem donned a clean *zuboun* [1] of cashmere, and I wore mine over my riding breeches and boots. Thus, in the shadow of the city wall, on the fringe of a field of lucerne, we made ourselves presentable ; and getting on our high camels again, we entered the City solemnly and decorously, in garments spick and span, as if we were coming to fetch the bride.

[1] The split robe, which is worn under the *aba* or the *jubbah*, is called *imbaz* in Syria and *zuboun* in Najd and Iraq.

A TIME SCHEDULE OF THE JOURNEY
FROM OJAIR TO AR-RIYADH [1]

FROM OJAIR TO HUFOUF

First Day : Left Ojair at noon. Arrived at 'Alat in the Nufoud at sunset.

Second Day : Left 'Alat 8 a.m. Arrived at Jishshah 12.30 p.m.

„   „   Left Jishshah 3 p.m. Arrived at Hufouf 6.30 p.m.

FROM HOUFOUF TO AR-RIYADH

	Day March Hours.	Night March Hours.	Total.
First Day : Slept in Na'lah - - -	6.15	3.	9.15
Second Day : Slept in Rubaidah - -	8.		8.
Third Day: Slept in the Dahna - - -	8.45	5.	13.45
Fourth Day : Slept in the Dahna - -	7.	6.15	13.15
Fifth Day: At Abu Jefan			
Sixth Day : At Terabi	3.30		3.30
Seventh Day : At Al-'Uqlah - - -	7.	4.15	11.15
Eighth Day : At Ar-Riyadh - - -	7.		7.
	47.30	18.30	66. Hrs.

210 Miles in 66 hours in 8 days.

Average : 3¼ Miles an hour ; 8½ hours a day.

The Najjab's Average Schedule.

210 Miles in 45 Hours in 3 Days.

Average : 4⅔ Miles an Hour, 15 Hours a Day.

[1] This road was crossed in 1912 by Leachman and in 1917 by Philby.

CHAPTER XII

AR-RIYADH

The only conspicuous sign of architecture that meets the eye, as we approach the city from the east, is the high tower of the Palace ; and the only voice we hear, as we enter the city gate, is that of the moaning *saqia*, which in Najd is called *gharb*. Even as we go through the principal street to the Palace square the men look up incuriously, as they pass, and the children gape in silence. There were crowds, squatting along the walls or just visiting in the street ; but there was no bustle and no visible sign of business. Even the square, which in the morning is a busy scene, was at that hour almost empty, except that part of it immediate to the Palace gate.

There, was a spectacle—the first of its kind I had seen in Arabia.

Along the Palace wall were clay benches in double tiers filled with people, who had come out, I first thought, to see us ; and the idea of an open theatre, a full audience, and a show which had arrived from the desert, afforded me, the principal character, a moment of amusement. But I had forgotten that the Arabs are incurious. And not until I had inquired did I know the intent and purpose of these people sitting solemnly outside the Palace and in the court and corridors within. They were waiting, not meekly or beggarly, but like personages who had an appointment with their sovereign lord. Indeed, some of them had the mien of princes ; others, whose rags were most conspicuous, were dignified enough with the inevit-

able bamboo stick, the curved end of which they held up
to their lips, vacantly or pensively it matters not. But
nothing seemed to require emphasis or even speech at
that hour; so those few hundred, mostly of the Bedu, sat
there solemnly, I say, and silently, rubbing the bamboo
against their lips and waiting for their second daily meal
at the Palace.

Thus, about five hundred people come to the Palace
twice a day, in the morning and in the afternoon, for two
square meals. Some of them carry, concealed under
their *abas*, kettles or wooden platters for the purpose of
taking some rice and lamb to their kith and kin in the
black booths outside the city. These people have nothing
to do in times of peace; they form a part of the Sultan's
standing army, as it were, whom he has to feed and clothe
and keep content. And there are many among them,
who, moreover, receive an allowance in money. Indeed,
there are many pensioners in Ar-Riyadh, which is in a
sense like Mecca, whose people live on the munificence of a
religious tradition austerely observed.

There are many beggars, too. At the back door of the
Palace, every day at sundown, they gather and swarm,
the bundled shapes, the female multitude, the black
spectres of poverty and disease; each carrying a bowl or
a platter of earthenware or copper or wood; some with
their babes sucking at their leathern breasts; others with
two or three children innocent of a rag;—they crowd at
the Palace gate for the daily donation of rice and meat—
for the leavings, in fact, of the men, whom I have described.

The Arab man, of a certainty, does not beg; never
comes down from the high camel of his pride to stretch
out a begging hand; never surrenders the bamboo of
his dignity even to the imperious spectre of hunger: but
that same pride and that same dignity do not prevent him
from sending out his wife or his child to sing at the doors
of charity and affluence. Thus many have I seen and
heard in the streets of Ar-Riyadh; although I have been

THE COFFEE-HEARTH IN ONE OF THE HOUSES OF AR-RIYADH

ONE OF THE GATES OF AR-RIYADH

told that there are no beggars in the Capital, and that
those who are seen begging are of the miserable Bedu who
camp outside the city wall. But how is one to know when
the beggar-woman enjoys the advantage of concealment ?
In sooth, the luxury of the veil ! Whether of the Bedu or
of the city Arabs, the voices that issue, uttering invocations
of poetic beauty, from behind that veil, as its captives sit
before the big bolted door with a bowl in hand, were to
me, even in the most doleful strains, full of quaint charm.

> ' On the bounty of Allah, ye who live,
> Of the bounty of Allah, give, give.'

> ' May the bough of the Jannat tree
> Bend low to thee.'

. . . . .

> ' Sweet fruits from the branches fall
> At your feet, O hear my call.'

> ' Hunger singeth at thy door,
> Allah give thee more and more.'

For half an hour the voice sometimes sings, before
anyone comes to the door with a little rice or a piece of
bread.

Other plaintive voices, which are heard in the city,
come from behind the city wall, from the moaning *gharbs*
in the palm-groves and gardens. But they give whilst they
moan, as they take from the bounties that flow under the
oasis of Al-'Ared and give to the thirsty soil. The *gharb*,
which is to be seen in every palm-grove around Ar-Riyadh,
is worked on the same principle as the *cherd* of Iraq and
the *saqia* of Al-Yaman. It consists of a wooden structure
with wheels and spindles built over the mouth of the
jalib ; [1] and the two ropes, one on the spindle, the other
on the wheel above, which are attached to the waterskin
at its two ends, are drawn by a donkey or a camel down
an inclined plane ; so that when the end of the plane is
reached the skin is lifted full of water ; and because the

[1] Correctly speaking, *qalib*, which is the Arabic for well. But the 'qaf'
or 'q' is in some words pronounced in Najd 'jeem' or 'j' as Oqair,
pronounced Ojair.

rope attached to the bottom of the skin and run on the
spindle is a little shorter than the one attached to the neck
and run on the wheel, the skin is lifted bottom up and the
water is poured into a trough or direct into a cistern for
the purpose of irrigation. The length of the inclined plane
is in proportion to the depth of the *jalib*, which is sometimes eighty feet deep, reaching to the living rock, and
built solidly of dressed stones ; while the *gharb* has as
many wheels and spindles as the capacity of the *jalib*
requires. The biggest I have seen is in the Shamsiyah
palms outside the city. It has two slopes, one on each
side, and twelve sets of wheels and spindles working
twelve skins, which are drawn by twelve donkeys, six on
each slope. The work is fascinating to behold. While
six donkeys are running up the slope to let the six skins
down the *jalib*, their twin-six are walking down the other
slope and thus lifting to the level of the spindles six skins
full of water, which look like gargoyles as they pour their
silvery contents into the troughs.

The oasis of Al-'Ared at the foot of Jabal Twaiq
(pronounced Twaij) is oblong and about twelve miles
from north to south. It has no running streams of water ;
but there are a few good springs, and, judging from the
many *jalibs*, an abundance of water under ground.
Ar-Riyadh is situated on its north-eastern side and is
built on one of the ribs of J. Twaiq, whose bare rocks are
seen in some of its streets. But there are no houses one
would say in those streets ;—no houses visible. And the
mud walls, which are from twenty to sixty feet high, can
vouchsafe no sign of human habitation, through the small
windows or apertures at the top, beyond the gaze of man.

The houses are within, built, as a rule, around an
unpaved court, a kind of patio, but without a fountain
or a tree or a flower plant. Nothing seemed to echo so
faithfully the aridness and the dreariness of the Summan
desert. I have not seen an aromatic plant or a single
flower within the mud walls of Ar-Riyadh. Nor have I

A Jalib in the Shamsiyah Gardens, Ar-Riyadh

seen a blade of grass in the cemetery outside the town. The austerity of Wahhabism, in life as in death, is in this sense most appalling. I can understand, however, the religious reason for a barren cemetery. The superstitious Arabs worshipped even the trees near the tomb of a *wali* (saint) ; and Ibn Abd'ul-Wahhab, in his orthodox unitarian passion decreed that there shall be no trees whatsoever in a graveyard ;—nor any flowers—so his followers—not even a blade of grass. But why this lugubrious graveyard note in their homes ? I cannot assign any religious reason for it.

The aesthetic feeling is not, however, entirely be-numbed ; for it finds expression in the dedal decorations in plaster on the walls, and on the doors in an abandon of colour. It was always with a manifold pleasure, an ecstasy produced by the law of reaction, that I stood before one of those doors arabesqued in blue and green and yellow primaries, as if it were a famous canvas. Nor is it devoid of real artistic merit. The designs are infinite in variety, following the caprice of the artist ; but there is always a harmonious scheme uniformly, geometrically conceived and deftly carried out. Also a motive, be it just a line of red and yellow dots ; or when more elaborate, a half a circle in yellow containing three or four almond shapes in red and blue. A door thus painted, with its central panel of rhomboids and circles in brilliant blue and red, which is the dominating note, is on the whole most attractive. From our point of view, however, it would seem overwrought ; but the barbarous suffers not by it. On the contrary, considering the severity of the surroundings, the spacious and almost empty rooms, the white walls though decorated, the high ceilings, which are covered in the houses of the well-to-do with cotton cloth, a wealth of elaborately conceived and highly embellished designs in brilliant primaries, is a necessary foil, the only balance, in fact, which is adequate and appealing. It is an oasis of colour to the soul.

There is nothing, however, of the barbarously beautiful in the decorations on the wall, which are exquisitely conceived, but somewhat roughly at times executed. Here, on the whole, is an artistic expression of the other side of the Arab's nature—his subtle and delicate humour. The wall, after being plastered, is covered with another layer into which the designs are cut. The reception hall in the Palace is an excellent example of this art ; its walls, which are decorated in zones and panels from the floor to the ceiling, the white plaster over a fawn-coloured ground, look as if they were covered with Valenciennes lace.

But the principal feature in the home of a Najdi, whether in Ar-Riyadh or in 'Anaizah, is the fireplace in the reception room, or what they call the *qahwah* ; for here the host receives his guests and makes coffee for them. This fireplace—is it not proper to call it the coffee-hearth ? —is generally an oblong pit at the end of the room, about ten inches below the level of the floor, with two raised seats on either side of it for the host and his assistant, and shelves behind it for the coffee utensils. When the fire begins to blaze and the coffee, roasting, mingles its pungent smell with that of the smoke, the place assumes a venerableness of hospitality and the guests experience a pleasant sense of comfort.

Another attractive feature, besides the fire-place and the decorations on the walls, is the gallery with which some of the reception rooms are adorned. The First Secretary of the Sultan invited me to tea *and* coffee at his home, which is outside the city wall set in the midst of a palm-garden, and is within a poem in plaster. But the best stanza in the poem is the Qahwah or reception room, with its lace-work and panels in white fresco on a fawn-coloured, granulated surface ; its painted rafters dotted like totem poles ; and a gallery with colonnades all around. This gallery, which is about twenty feet from the ground and is itself about fifteen feet high, supporting the roof as well as the ceiling, is furnished with windows on three sides, thus making the *qahwah* below very cool in summer.

The streets of Ar-Riyadh are like all those I have seen in Arab towns ; but they are not so bad as Hufouf's, nor so good as San'a's, nor so dirty as those of Karbala. They are unique in the sense that in places they have a pavement of live-rock—the visible bones of old Twaij.

But the Souq is insignificant. Nowhere, as far as I could see, was any article of food offered for sale. Nor any clothes. I went out with Saiyed Hashem one day to buy a black *ighal*, but we did not find any *ighals* at all. Which did not surprise him. ' Why should people pay money for food and clothes,' he said, ' when they can get them for nothing at the Palace ? ' Half the Souq, therefore, is public property, a Soviet institution within the Palace, under the management of Shalhoub, Chief Steward of the Sultanate of Najd. The other half is a junkshop scattered to pieces, or divided into twenty or thirty booths set in two rows, between the main square, where firewood is sold, and the minor one in front of the Grand Mosque, where one can buy green lucerne—a luxury—for one's camel. And between the firewood and the lucerne is the junkshop, where the luxuries are more conspicuous than the necessities. Carpets, for instance, and swords, and scented soap made in England. I even found a second-hand thermos bottle, which I purchased for half of its price, and which, unlike those I had bought in Bahrain—Made in Japan—did not break on the second day of the journey.

Those who did most business, it seemed to me, were not the shopkeepers but the hawkers, the circulating auctioneers. Everywhere in Arabia, auctioneering is in vogue. If you have anything to sell you give it to a hawker, who hastens to the Souq with it, and is mighty quick about his business. See him run, carrying an *aba*, and crying, Twenty reals ! [1] And there is another, with a silver-

[1] A real is a Marie Theresa dollar, which is worth about 45 cents.

hilted hack sword : Five *liras* (gold pounds), five *liras !* You have to run after him if you wish to acquire the precious steel.   But the camel auctioneer cannot run. He stands by his crouching beast and cries : Twenty reals ! As cheap as his fodder, *billah !*   Even such a thing as a mattress—apparently new—I saw one day trailed in the dust by a lusty hawker : Only five reals ! Pray upon the Prophet, only five reals !   One man stepped upon the mattress to make the hawker stop, and offered four reals. The hawker jerked it away, pulled it over his shoulder, and resumed his trot and his cry : Only five reals ! Pray upon the Prophet, only five reals !   They never mention the article, and they never stop to bargain. See with your eyes ; hear with your ears ; and if you desire possession, come forth and quickly with the reals, or you are a dis-appointed man, even though you do pray upon the Prophet.

In the absence of musical instruments, however primi-tive, in Ar-Riyadh, and in the absence of song, however crude—both being tabooed—the voice of the circulating auctioneer and that of the muazzen were to me a welcome change from the growl and groan of camels in the public square.   What was even more pleasing was that the two voices never conflicted ; for although the hawker has the freedom of the Souq from sunrise till sunset, there are intervals of silence which he with the multitude must observe.   These intervals are inaugurated by the muazzen, who has the floor—of the minaret—five times a day. Marvel of devotion !   For as soon as the muazzen lifts his voice calling the Faithful to prayer, the hawker ceases at once, the Souq is closed, and silence profound reigns over the city.

The minaret of the Grand Mosque is misleading in its modesty.   For, judging from it, I had thought the Mosque itself to be like many of the *masjids*,[1] the interior of which

---

[1] The Grand Mosque, *jame'* is for general assemblies, especially on Friday. The *masjid* is a local mosque.

INTERIOR OF THE GRAND MOSQUE OF AR-RIYADH WITH MINARET IN BACKGROUND

is seen through the streets. Indeed, the *masjids* of the Wahhabis are severely simple, inside and out. The architecture is based on simple lines and right angles : a mud wall without ; a mud floor, with perhaps a mat or two, within ; a few steps for a tribune ; an alcove for a *mihrab ;* and the minaret is neither tapering nor high, but resembles a piece of cubist stage scenery. All that redounds to the glory of man is banned—it is not consistent with true religion. Anything like music or singing or decorative art that tends to exhilarate the spirit and lift it to what may be pride, is likewise taboo. Christian asceticism of the Middle Ages, this it is, but without the sackcloth and ashes. The Prophet has said that there will be after him seventy different sects in Al-Islam, and that only one of them will escape hell-fire and win Al-Jannat. The Wahhabis believe that they are the favoured sect. But they try not to reflect their pride in their mosques or in anything else.

The Grand Mosque is simple in design and in a way crude ; but as an original work of architecture, sublime in its very austerity, I have not seen its like anywhere. It occupies a space of about 125 by 100 feet, which is divided lengthwise into three sections : one in the centre, an open isle at one end of which is the entrance, at the other the minaret ; and to each side of the isle is a section of the Mosque composed of columns and pointed arches. The left section is ten columns deep, the right is three ; and each line consists of twenty-five. The effect is very imposing, even bewildering.

The first impression recalled in my mind the Mosque of Cordova, although the Wahhabi temple is but a crude replica of the Omaiyads' of Andalusia. Its columns are of stone, some of them of rubble and plaster, and are not more than nine feet in height ; its arches are angular and pointed ; its ceilings to either side of the open isle are of palm rafters, and its floor is spread with pebbles. The simoom winds can raise no dust in this open temple to Allah. Here is Wahhabism rising in its most ascetic and austere aspect to the sublime. By far the best expression, in sooth, of the sublime in Ar-Riyadh. Under the Mosque is a replica of the surface structure for the winter.

Yes, I have discovered, even before I visited the Mosque, that there is a winter in Central Arabia ; and I did not come prepared for it. Thinking that January in Ar-Riyadh would not be as truculent as he is in New York, for instance, I brought no heavy clothes with me, and I am not accustomed to the dogmatic warmth of a split robe, no matter of what material. As for the *aba*, it only helps to store up in its ample folds a layer of air, which serves no purpose of isolation. The atmosphere is penetrating, and inside and out, its teeth are very sharp. At night the *aba* serves as an extra covering up to a certain hour ; but towards morning, when the thermometer descends to twenty above zero F., I got cold feet in more than one sense of the word.

But those half-naked natives, does their piety keep them warm ? Long before one can ' distinguish the black thread from the white,' about four o'clock in the morning, the voice of the muazzen is heard, and every right Muslim —every Wahhabi—has to get up and—to the Mosque. There is a roll-call in every *masjid*, it must be remembered, and a fresh palm switch ! [1] It is not so hard for them the early rising, as there is little or no ceremony of wash and dress. The *aba* is thrown over the shoulders, the head is covered with a kerchief and—slip on the sandals and go. As for the morning ablutions, they are done in a left-handed superficial manner.

No, Ar-Riyadh is neither Aden nor Bahrain ; and I should have known that when one is 1800 feet above the level of the sea and is between the 25th and the 26th degrees of latitude, and furthermore, when one is not accustomed like the Arabs to go barefoot from infancy,

[1] More on this head in a succeeding chapter.

one requires at least a pair of woollen hose. The chief
Steward of the Sultanate, Shalhoub, I have seen wearing
a long fur coat under the dogmatic *aba*. Wise man,
Shalhoub. I have with me but a raincoat, however,
which I may yet need. But the cold—my fingers, as I
try to write, tingle ; and as the sun never peeps into the
large and airy and freezing apartment I occupy, I must
run out to find it.

If one could shake off at will the habits as well as the
customs of civilization ! I could then sleep in my clothes,
and I would not place myself under any obligation to a
cold and windy wash-room. It contained what the Sultan
Abd'ul-Aziz called a samovar : *i.e.* a large tin vessel for
water with a pipe running through it for a fire to keep it
warm. But the servants had an idea that the fire was not
needed till the sun had come into the wash-room to warm
up its atmosphere for them. So Ar-Riyadh is not better
in this than Paris or London.

The only parts of the body that Arab clothes help to
keep warm are the head and neck. The *gutrah*,[1] especially
if it is of Indian cashmere, is an excellent scarf as well as
head-kerchief ; but my ends would continue to tingle,
and the camel-hair *busht* [2] which the Sultan gave me
was of no use. I had to seek the bounty of the sun to be
able to tell of the bounties of Abd'ul-Aziz.

On certain days there was a general distribution of
clothes. Three thousand *bushts*, made in Iraq, in Syria,
and in Persia, were given away to those who needed them
and those who did not : the Sa'oud families, the Rashids
and their households, the employers, the servants, the
slaves, and those who came twice every day for their
meals—soldiers, beggars, illustrious citizens of Ar-Riyadh
—every one received his *busht* and *zuboun* of a quality
becoming his rank, and, pink of generosity ! a flannel
shirt to boot.

---

[1] The head-kerchief worn under the *ıghal* is called *koufiyah* in Syria,
somadah in Al-Hijaz, and *gutrah* in Najd and Bahrain.

[2] The *aba* is called *busht* in Najd and Bahrain and Iraq.

The women, too, get their share of the bounty of the State. Speaking one evening to the Sultan of these gifts, he replied : 'And the harim, Allah keep thee, are a problem. Their needs and demands we must always heed.'

This wholesale distribution of clothes takes place twice a year, in winter and in summer. And many of the beneficiaries, I was told, often sell what they do not need. That is why there are so many hawkers and circulating auctioneers in Ar-Riyadh. A *busht* of camel hair, worth 150 rupees, is sold for a hundred. Good rugs, also the gift of the Sultan, find their way to the Souq, and are disposed of at a price which otherwise would be compromising.

But the good cheer and geniality of the Sultan Abd'ul-Aziz have taught the natives of the Capital nothing ;— have not affected in the least their saturnine and sanctimonious spirit. Those who used to visit me at my quarters in the Palace or ask me to tea and coffee at their homes, were not from Ar-Riyadh ; and those whom I often met at the *majlis* of the Sultan and who are natives of the Capital would not even look at me in the street. One of the Ulema to whom I was introduced by His Highness I chanced to meet one day outside the Palace. '*Salaam 'alaikum*,' I said. ' H'm ! ' he replied, without raising his head. And every time I met him afterwards I deliberately sought to irritate him by giving him the salaam ; but he ceased to say even, H'm.

Not only towards a Christian, but towards all non-Wahhabi Muslims, are they thus ; and the motive is not entirely religious nor entirely temperamental. There is much in it of both, and little or nothing else. Even Saiyed Hashem found them to be inhospitable and unsociable ; and those who come from the north, from Al-Qasim and Haiel, to live in Ar-Riyadh, suffer from loneliness at the beginning and then from the surly and fanatical humour of the people.

Thou shalt not smoke. Thou shalt not sing. Thou shalt not wear silk robes. And if one is found in his shop, or dawdling in the street during the time of prayer, he is insulted by the zealous mosquegoer, or at least looked upon askance. Impious churl—child of calamity and perdition ! That is why Saiyed Hashem, who was not a zealous mosquegoer, never ventured abroad at that hour. But he did wear his *zuboun* of barred silk, now and then, to assert his independence and his superiority. ' Every one of them,' he would say, ' is a proof of the theory of Darween.' And he would go to the house of one of his friends, a haven of freedom and *keif*, where he uncovered his head and his heart, sipped tea and coffee, and smoked cigarettes to intoxication. He could not get intoxicated on anything else in Ar-Riyadh ; for unlike Jeddah or San'a or Hufouf there is no liquor of any kind in the city. Nor anywhere else in Southern Najd at least. Even those who travel to the coast towns, as Kuwait, for instance, and Basrah, and are there initiated into booze, seldom bring a bottle with them. It is moreover true, that of the thirty thousand inhabitants of Ar-Riyadh, nay, of all the people of Najd south of Al-Qasim, hardly anyone ever tastes a drop of liquor.

But even in the most sacrosanct quarter of the Capital, where the Ulema live, one is likely to find some tobacco, hidden in the bottom of a chest, for a surreptitious moment of *keif*. Outwardly, of course, the law is strictly observed and enforced. Asceticism and piety are ever watchful and alert. If one is seen walking in that quarter through the street with a swing of the shoulders or a sweep of the garment, he is forthwith reprimanded for his arrogance. If one laughs freely in one's house, some one will soon knock at the door.—Why are you laughing in this ribald manner ? No one in that quarter ever dares to miss, except for a reason of sickness, one of the five daily prayers in the *masjid*. And as for tobacco, the culprit, when he is discovered smoking, is summarily dealt with.

No pity has the piety of the Ulema ; no mercy in their ascetic justice. ' But,' said one of the *zkirts* of the Palace, ' they are secretly a lecherous people. The walls of their houses cry out against them.'

Now I must tell you what is a *zkirt*. The Arabs all over Arabia are divided into two grand primal divisions— urban and Bedu, the nomads and the city folk. And the *zkirt*, who may be black or white or yellow, a slave or a freeman, is an Arab and Muslem ; but, strictly speaking, he is neither of the city nor the desert, neither of the Bedu nor of their less truculent urban cousins. The *zkirt* is of the Palace and for the Palace. He is of a class by himself —a distinct species. He lives and loafs and grazes in the Palace—when he is employed. He hovers around the Palace, when he is not. In the former state, he walks behind the Sultan and carries his sword in his hand ; in the second manifestation, he squats at the Palace gate with his sword across his knees. He may have a wife beyond the Dahna and another beyond the Twaij hills ; or he may have a dozen on a Prophet's promise beyond the Universe. But this latter, the eunuchized *zkirt*, from the viewpoint of the Palace, is as good as his wiving brother. Both have a complex personality ; for they can go without going, having a thunderous voice ; they can see with their ears as well as their eyes, having an imagination ; they can carry the yoke with the same philosophic calm as they carry the sword ; and kissing the horn of Satan with the same devotion as they kiss an angel's wing, they have always an eye for Allah, as honest as the Prophet's, and another for the main chance.

The *zkirt* travels with the Sultan or by himself with the Sultan's messages ; by reason of which he sees the world and tastes of it in Bahrain or in Kuwait or in Damascus. Some *zkirts* have even the good fortune of going to farther springs—of dipping their buckets in Baghdad or in Bombay. Thus they acquire a gift of gab. Also a gumption which enframes a silhouette of wisdom. Having

these accomplishments, the desire to show them, if only
for the pleasure of reflecting the wonders of the human
mind, becomes natural. But they cannot do so while
travelling with the Sultan, or loafing at the Palace, or
galloping across the desert. They therefore ever long to
travel with the Sultan's guests ;—foreign guests—Christian
guests preferable. For then they can put to good use
not only their knowledge, their skill, their gumption, but
also that cosmopolitan spirit, which stands on the best
two legs in the world—freedom and toleration.

Having told you what the *zkirt* is, you will better
appreciate his dictum upon the Ulema. And in addition
to that dictum I give you the following. To the Sultan's
Diwan came every afternoon a certain one whose business
evidently was to sit down and say nothing. And he sat
with his hands folded across his breast, his head bowed,
his white beard shading his fingers. He wore no cord—
ighal—upon his head-kerchief, one end of which he wound
around his neck like the Bedu. His sandals and his long
staff he left at the door outside. One day, when he was
thus adorning the Diwan, I was discussing with the
Sultan the modern history of Najd, and I asked about a
certain battle. His Highness, who did not remember the
date of that battle, turned to the man and asked : ' Do
you remember the date of that battle, O Sheikh Fares ? '
The Sheikh lifted his hand and waved it, shaking simultaneously his head. Later, the discussion turned to a
question of religion—something about dealing with the
infidels—and the Sultan again bespoke the assistance of
Sheikh Fares, and again he waved his hand and shook
his head. His Highness supplied the footnote : ' You
do not know.' The head shook again. Sheikh Fares is
one of the Ulema, one of the doctors of learning (theology
and jurisprudence) of Ar-Riyadh. When I walked out
of the Diwan with the Sultan, he smiled satirically and
said : 'The Ulema do not condescend to speak to us.' The
Ulema, forsooth ! The Mildew, rather, of Arab Learning.

Here is another picture from the heart of Arabia. A boy of twelve, with a black slave behind him carrying a sword, followed by a retinue of a dozen people walking solemnly at a respectful distance :—the son of a noted Sheikh going out to take the air. Or it may be one of the Rashids, for that matter, coming to the Palace for his dinner. The spectacle does not vary. A man walking alone followed by an entourage of slaves and attendants —Arab grandeur ! The Mildew of Arab Grandeur, stalking through the centuries with Allah and the Prophet in its heart and nothing but the *gazu*-complex in its head.

Here is a third picture. Says the Arab poet, describing those who walk with an air : They trail the garment of pride. Which I always thought was a figure of speech. No ; it is a testimony as well as an inspiration. For custom among the Arabs, no matter how old and hoary —the older, the stronger—asserts itself with an adamantine will. In literature, in religion, in poetry, in their everyday speech, Custom has soldiers and apostles. Hers is the very breath of these people. Nothing in their features has changed, nothing in their dress, nothing in their speech. Behold her trailing the garment of pride ! How often has the living illustration been forced upon my unwilling and astonished gaze. Even the poorest among the women-folk, when she steps out of her booth or hut, will prove the truth of the poet's words. How often, indeed, have I seen her in dirty rags carrying a basket of camel dung on her head, and with a corner of her *aba* pulled across her face, ' trailing the garment of pride.' The Mildew of Arab Pride sweeping the streets with a ragged trail a yard long.

Having endeavoured to give a faithful picture of Ar-Riyadh and its people, I must not omit, what in itself is the most telling passage, a word said to me one evening by the Sultan Abd'ul-Aziz himself. He feels that he is a stranger in his own Capital. People come to his *majlis* every day without leaving an impression to cherish.

Between them and himself there is no contact of mind or heart, not even of soul. And the chasm ever yawns. He would not live in Ar-Riyadh a single day were he not the ruler of the country. He is, in truth, far above the ablest and the best :—a palm tree in a field of stubble— a lone pine in a wadi of brambles and thorns.

CHAPTER XIII

IN THE PALACE

' HE who sees with the eye of his head only is a churl,'
said the Sultan Abd'ul-Aziz ; ' but he who sees also with
the eye of his heart is a man.' Now, it has been my
studied purpose, where spontaneousness often found but
vacancies behind closed doors, to see with both eyes
throughout my travels in Arabia ; to see more, in truth,
with ' the eye of the heart,' even though I had to penetrate
through a hundred veils of tradition and custom ; but
when I came up against a stone wall of faith, or when I
stood before the transparencies of a mildewed human
existence, I turned my head more in sorrow than in
despair. Nevertheless, I persisted ; although I have
often wished that I did not have an eye in my head.
How true is this about my struggle with Al-Islam, and
through it, and for it, Allah knows better than my friends
and readers. And since it has been my lot to be in
Ar-Riyadh on Christmas Day, the contrast between the
faith of my fathers and that of my Arab cousins was
irresistible. Thus, then, do I prove myself a Christian,
although in the past I have seldom tried and never cared
to do so. Let us, by all means, shun religious contro-
versies. I owe it at least to the readers of this book that
no such barren medievalism be imposed upon them.
But I do not think it out of place to repeat here what I
said to myself on that day. I can do it like a phonograph,
for I have it set down in my diary. I transcribe the
following :

Ar-Riyadh—*Monday*—Christmas Day, 1922.

I have not the least doubt about it : a religion of love, and mercy, and tolerance, is better than a religion which is imposed by the sword. . . .

.   .   .   .

The Wahhabis or the Ikhwan, for instance, will shed blood for a dogma about the unity and oneness of God. Practical religion has nothing to do with it. You are an enemy of Allah, if you associate anyone else with him in your devotion, and your life and property, therefore, are forfeit—are mine, for I testify that there is no God but Allah.

Whether the spirit of tolerance has come to us in the west from our religion or from science and education is not the question. We have had our religious wars ; we have experienced what the Arabs in Central Arabia are going through to-day ; and we have survived it, and evolved chastened from it—developed into civilized beings who make no pretensions about divine knowledge. To turn the other cheek may be against human nature as it is to-day ; but a tooth for a tooth—' one evil to combat another '—is the law of the jungle, is a blot, to say the least, on the name of a people who have had a Prophet to teach them justice and love and equality ; and who also have a literature that reflects the higher virtues of the soul and the mind. . . .

On this day a lone Christian in the heart of Arabia, with doubts manifold in his heart and a catholicity of belief withal, turns his face to the north, towards the hill of Galilee, and bows down in a spirit of devotion that has shed its theology, and in a spirit of love that excludes no one in this little world of ours.

The above was written when I was in the lap of Dame Malaria, who enveloped me, saturated me, with the heat of her love. And the Sultan Abd'ul-Aziz, our Christian brother, came to see us, carrying the latest medical invention, a thermo-index—it registers both the heat of the atmosphere and the human body—in one hand, and a bottle of lime juice ! in the other. His face was sunshine in the room, and his words were draughts of clear spring water. ' This will tell thee—hold it in thy hand—how

many degrees thou hast above the health heat,' he said ;
' and this,' holding up the bottle, ' will soften and cool
the inward of thee. . . . Didst thou *eat kinkina* (quinine)
to-day ? Allah keep thee, and ward the evil from thee !
eat of the kinkina three times a day.' Allah keep thee,
my dear Abd'ul-Aziz, my noble friend, my good doctor
and nurse, I am eating nothing else.

What I *had* been eating ? It seems incredible that at
the Sultan's board the year round rice and lamb are
served twice a day. In my case, a chicken was served
with the rice—two chickens, in fact, every day boiled
like the rice and served on a platter. They use little salt
in their food or their bread. Of a truth, I found salt more
precious in Ar-Riyadh than, say, sugar, which was plentiful at Shalhoub's stores ; but they use it mostly in the tea.
Pastry or sweets or dessert of any kind is seldom made.
As austere as their religion is their board—pardon, their
tray.

Breakfast is the meal I most enjoyed ; for I had eggs,
which I boiled myself (I could not get any one of the
servants to understand so intricate a matter as the boiling-
point of the water and the minute that followed of time) ;
milk and tea I also had together with a plate of excellent
sweet butter and another of honey. At noon, I took a
bowl of *laban* (lactoferm) which the Arabs call *rowb*, and
a cake of bread, thus dispensing with half of the daily
bounty of chicken and rice. Huwaidi, who insisted on
sticking it out at the Palace with us, once gave me a happy
surprise. He came in with a handful of small, plum-like
tomatoes. I could scarcely believe my eyes, and I confess
I could not wait to have them cooked. A salad was out
of the question, for there was neither oil nor vinegar.
So with a little damp, coarse blackish salt I ate the six
tomatoes, and felt as if I had dined at the Café de Paris.

Nothing mattered, however, so long as I kept well.
But Dame Malaria kept coming and going, and I was
fast becoming a wire burning to white heat of cerebration

—nothing else. Strange how she sharpens the human faculties Dame Malaria ; for not until she began to visit me did I become completely conscious of my surroundings. The large room I lived in did not see a ray of sunshine the day long ; but the fever helped me to discover that it was also damp, and that on the wall-side of the *masnads* was something like mildew. Moreover, the dust was everywhere ;—on the diwans, on and under the carpets, on the table, on my cot and clothes ;—it found its way into the room through a dozen places besides the four windows. And there would come Huwaidi with his thumb stuck in a bowl of milk. How often has he reminded me of the story of the man who ordered a cocoanut. As for Saiyed Hashem, who was responsible for my comfort, he was no longer useful. The melancholia was upon him ; for he could not smoke a cigarette at the Palace, and he had not yet found a wife.

Indeed, the only visitors, besides the Sultan Abd'ul-Aziz, that brought any cheer were the birds. They would flit in and out, perch on the red punka, pick at the table, trip on the carpet, twittering freely and volubly about their own troubles, I suppose, or their joys. My own no longer existed : the troubles were becoming a matter of form, the joys a matter of fancy. Bed linen I had long since forgotten ; the only piece I found in my bag was a pillow-case, which I had to turn inside out to conceal from my feverish eye the mark of a month's use. My washing was done once by Huwaidi (who would dare to suggest that a woman, though a toothless black hag, should come into the Palace for this purpose ?) and once by his yoke-fellow D'heim. After that I wore out a piece of clothes and threw it to the dogs.

Yea, I was fast being reduced to the necessity of upholding in practice the native tradition. It is a luxury in that part of the world to have a complete suit of clothes ; —an *aba*, for instance, a *zuboun*, a *gutrah* and *ighal*, and an under garment. The latter you may wash yourself, say once a week if you are religiously clean ; once a month if you are indifferent ; once every season if it lasts ; and never at all if Allah and the Prophet are all that you care about in the world. I am speaking of the people, what in the west we call the masses. Among those above them, as well as the many who live in the Palace—and *on* it—one beholds flowing and scented garments, and as clean, occasionally, as those worn by the Sultan himself. The white linen *zubouns*, with broad but not tapering sleeves, which His Highness wore at Ojair, and which he wears in Ar-Riyadh when the days are warm, I particularly admired. But clothes no longer worried me, especially when Dame Malaria began to frequent my apartment.

Nor would Malaria, for that matter, if she came alone ; but she and neuritis are unbearable. I did not need the Sultan's thermo-index to tell me that she was coming : Neuritis announced her and remained with her. Indeed, to speak plainly, and for the benefit, perhaps, of nerve specialists, the neuritic pains always told me that the fever was mounting, and they were seldom wrong. Alone, neuritis had become a customary nuisance with intervals of agony—spells of acute pain, which lasted from fifteen to thirty minutes ; with malaria, the intervals disappeared, or they stretched, accurately speaking, into one long continuous paroxysm. Add to this a heavy cold, indigestion, and the ascetic atmosphere of Ar-Riyadh, and you will get an idea of what it is to be in Central Arabia.

You get sick like a saint with only God as your visiting physician and bitter memories of distant friends as your nurse. There is nothing that anyone can do, except it be a sympathetic word or an assuring smile. But the Arab, as a rule, will withhold, or will not care. A stoic by nature and breeding he lives, and he gets sick, and he dies in the same stoic spirit. A camel falls exhausted in the desert and is left there to die. The poor beast

sticks its head in the sand, agonizes, and dies. A man falls
sick and is treated in the same manner. Dark, very dark,
indeed, were those days ! And there was no other alterna-
tive, since I refused to die, but a month of travel ahead
of me, or the Dahna and the Summan behind me for a
retreat.

But having told you of the hard-hearted Arab, I must
revert again to the great exception, the Sultan-Com-
forter Abd'ul-Aziz. He it was who visited me every day,
bringing always something with him—quinine, fruit-salt,
biscuits, even books. Of all the tokens of his thoughtfulness and kindness, however, nothing was more welcome
and more serviceable than an oil-stove, which was brought
to me from the sanctum of the harim itself. It shone with
a hundred loving eyes in my room ; and it spoke with a
hundred tongues, when my own was tied with the fever,
of the incomparable Abd'ul-Aziz.

Among the books he brought for my entertainment,
' when the fever goes out,' is a MS. *History of Aal Sa'oud*,
or how Wahhabism was founded, how it developed, and
how, under the great Sa'oud his ancestor, it conquered
almost the whole Peninsula. It is written in rhymed
prose, and every page reeks with blood. I give an example:

> In the year . . . the Imam marched with his men against
> the city of Huraimala, because its people, who had embraced
> the unitarian creed, had too soon renounced it. He met on
> the way a company of roving Bedu of the *kafir* (infidel) tribe
> of . . ., attacked them, killed ten of them, and carried off
> their sheep and camels. He then proceeded to Huraimala,
> and reaching its palm gardens at night he descended there
> and divided his men into two forces, the attacking and the
> *kamin*, that is, those who lay in ambush (the business of
> the *kamin* is to cut off the line of retreat when the enemy is
> drawn out and attacked). The historian proceeds :
> ' And ere the night had folded its sail and the dawn had
> shed its veil, when the eye of sleep and ecstasy in the city
> of apostasy was languishing still, under the *kohl*' of hidden
> ill, the Imam charged with his men, and the cry went up as
> from the lion's den : but the inhabitants in their fright

R.I.S.   K

preferred the cover of night to an open fight. Thus Allah willed that the streets of the city with their blood be filled : it was, in sooth, a day of butchery and woe for Allah's foe, and a day of glory without boast for the unitarian host. And the booty was great : hundreds of sheep and camels and much that is precious and light in weight. Withal— thus Allah decrees—they cut down the tallest of their palm trees.'

In every *gazu* or battle there is some such punitive measure as cutting down the palm trees to teach the enemy courage, I suppose, so that he will come out the next time and fight in the open. They were great days. The first Imam, Abd'ul-Aziz ibn Sa'oud, conducted in person five or six, sometimes ten, *gazus* every year, and in places so distant apart as Al-Hasa and Bisha beyond the Dawasir wadi—a distance which the fastest *zelul* cannot cover in less than twenty days. But his namesake and descendant Abd'ul-Aziz ibn Abd'ur-Rahman has done the same, has even surpassed him in these modern times. With but a handful of men, in certain instances, he had to fight his way or hold his own against the superior forces and the German-Turkish cannons of Ibn 'ur-Rashid.

One day he came in bringing with him a section of the map of Arabia, in English, to show me the distance between Haiel and Ar-Riyadh ; and it occurred to me, as I was examining the map, that I could render him a little service by translating it into Arabic, that is by writing under the English the names of the towns, the hills, the wadis, etc., so he himself can refer to it direct. He was pleased with the idea ; but he was reluctant, considering my condition, in accepting. He would not give his guest, his sick guest, such trouble. ' But when I recover,' I said, ' I might not be inclined—I may not have the time.' ' Very well,' he said, laughing ; ' we will send the map. It might help you to chase the fever away.'

There were three other sections as big as the one I had seen ; and when I put them all beside each other I saw what a task I had before me. Here was the biggest map—

Scale=1 : 1,000,000—of Arabia extant, the one mentioned in the Treaty between Great Britain and the Sultan of Najd. But regarding the transliteration of Arabic nouns, it was full of inconsistencies and mistakes. More annoying than the learned Arabist's caprice, however, was the delay of the servants in getting me the necessary material for the work. In the first place, I had to have a reed pen and red ink ; for black or blue ink would not readily show under the black print, especially in crowded districts like Al-Yaman and Asir. Well, it took a day to get the ink and a day to get the pen.

The translation done I had to have glue or mucilage or paste to make the map whole. Three servants were therefore sent out in different directions ; the Palace stores were ransacked ; so, too, the shops in the Souq ; and three days later a brown powder was brought, which was beaten in hot water into a paste. All's well. Fortunately, I had a pair of scissors ; so I did not have to wait another day before I could cut the margins of the sections and paste them together. But I had to have two sticks to roll upon them the two ends of the map, so it could be hung as the Sultan desired on the wall of the Diwan ; and I could think of nothing better, more to hand at least, than palm ribs. But Huwaidi, who volunteered his service in this matter, disappeared for two days, and on the third day he showed up empty-handed. In my exasperation I became feverish. 'But wherefore hurry and tire thyself,' he said, in assuaging accents. 'Allah protect thee and give thee health. I have hurried for thy sake. But we had to send out to the palm gardens, cut the branches, whittle them to make them even, as thou hast said ; and then, since the nail must go into them, we must keep them a few days in the sun to dry.' I shall take a week's vacation, therefore,— thanks to thee, O Huwaidi—while the palm rods are being seasoned. And then—I had almost forgotten the cord. But what matters another day's delay ? After all

I think the job was well worth the gold watch, which His Highness gave me the day after the map was hung on the wall of the Diwan.

In poetic haste, I allowed my fancy to dwell on a vacation of a week. But I had forgotten Saiyed Hashem, who still came to see me in the daytime ; for in the evening, that he might smoke a cigarette, he went to the house of one of his friends, where he also slept. Now, one day, when I was waiting for Huwaidi's palm rods and incidentally shivering with the chills, he came in lugging an Arabic typewriter. ' Teach me, *ya Ustaz*,' thus abruptly, ' how to write on this machine.' He would not wait till the fever which followed the chill had subsided. But placing the typewriter on the table he began to pound the keys as if they were his enemies. So I decided, choosing the lesser evil, to give him a lesson ; but when I saw the machine I realized that neither my handling nor the hammering of the Saiyed could make it work. It was clogged and smudged and encrusted with three years of dust and rust. ' This needs cleaning first,' I said. ' Very well, clean it for us,' he replied. I could not put him out of the room ; for he was, after all, one of the Sultan's Secretaries. I could not be unkind to him, even in words ; for he has been very kind to me in Basrah, in Ojair, and across the desert ;—and in vain did I offer my fever as an excuse that day. He could not understand why an extra degree of heat in the body should hinder one in so trivial a matter as cleaning a typewriter. Moreover, he had to write a very important letter to the High Commissioner in Baghdad ;—and I would not, surely, delay the business of the Sultan.

An hour to remove the dust and part of the rust of three years ; an hour to teach Saiyed Hashem how to write the superscription of a letter ; and continuously after that, till the time of the Sultan's evening visit, the slow *trak, trak*, fell like missiles of red hot steel on my ears and nerves. He would not even remove the machine outside.

Still worse, his questions : Why does not this letter work
—why does not the roller roll ? And I had to get out of
my bed to show him why.

Once I enjoyed what had happened. I laughed at the
indescribable scramble and confusion and tangle of the
types. The ribbon had stopped moving ; and he had
dug a hole in it ; and one type got stuck therein ; and
two or three were tangled above it ; and others were up
in arms protesting at the whole disgraceful business.
But why did the ribbon refuse to move when it had not
reached its end ? There was about half of it on each
spool. I made peace between the types first, separating
them and putting them quietly in their places ; after which,
rolling the ribbon backwards, I discovered the cause of the
tragedy. And I laughed. Saiyed Hashem stared at me
and then at the poor machine in stupefaction. The ribbon
had in previous days undergone some unwonted hammering at that particular point, so that finally it gave way
—it broke ; and the ingenious typist, with a thought not
to economy so much as to expedience, sent to his harim
for a needle and thread, and sewed it together ;—sewed
it so tightly and thickly as never to break again and never
incidentally to pass through the ribbon guide ! Fortunately, they had other ribbons at the Palace ; and on
the following morning there was a knot of spectators in
my room watching the operation of replacing the old by
the new.

At another time—I had earned ˋa reputation at the
Palace for doing odd jobs—Saiyed Hashem and Huwaidi
came to me pleading together for assistance. They spoke
despairingly of water and soap and flannels.—What ?
I have not begun to take in washing yet.—No, *ya Ustaz*,
we would not have you descend to such menial labour.
Allah preserve you in your dignity, we come to ask the
assistance of your mind only. And again they reverted
to the flannels—the woollen flannels of—the Sultan—
Abd'ul-Aziz ! Ha, the Sultan is involved, and the neck

of my *rafiq* as well as that of my cook is in the noose. I
promised my assistance. Whereupon, Saiyed Hashem
calmly related of his plight.

When in Basrah he bought for the Sultan half a dozen
woollen flannels, which being of a coarse material had a
peculiar unpleasant smell ; and to His Highness, who
always, as I have said, perfumed himself extravagantly,
the smell by contrast was more offensive. He would not
therefore wear the flannels until something had been
done to deodorize them. And Saiyed Hashem, who was
charged with the business, gave them to Huwaidi to
wash. Huwaidi, in conscience, did so with soap and
water vigorously ; but after he had finished with his
material—after it had dried—he saw with amazement
and trepidation that it had shrunk woefully. What is
to be done ? Stretch the flannels ? He did so with all
the strength of his shaggy arms, but they would not
remain stretched. Now, Huwaidi was in cosmopolitan
Basrah, and he had seen or heard of the flat-iron there.
Fortunately, too, there was an iron at the Palace. Forthwith, therefore, he gets it and applies it. But it would
not work in Ar-Riyadh as he has seen it work in Basrah.
Travel had apparently robbed it of its virtue. Now,
the questions I had to solve and the miracles I had to
perform were many indeed. Why will not the flat-iron
work ? Why will not the flannels remain stretched ?
What can be done to reinvest the one with its virtue, the
other with its size ? Can we by bringing the iron to bear
upon the flannel make it shake off its kinks and stand out,
in its deodorized state, as it did when it was tainted, a
full-sized garment fit for a Sultan ? Huwaidi appealed
to me pathetically. Saiyed Hashem was in the suds.

The flat-iron and the flannels were brought before the
Inquisition. 'Where is the fire ? ' I asked. Huwaidi did
not think that the iron needed a fire. 'Where is the
water ? ' He did not think it needed water. 'Where is
the cloth ? ' He did not think it needed a cloth. Saiyed

Hashem enveloped me with wondering, admiring eyes. I had no doubt risen in his estimation even higher than 'Darween.' But what a miracle of evolution ! The live coals were put into the iron ; the cloth was spread on the table ; the water in a bowl was at hand, and I was in an instant transformed from a Syrio-American Arab into a Chinaman. Each flannel was stretched on the table and I spouted water at it like a whale. After which I applied my finger to my tongue and then to the sole of the flat-iron in the most expert manner ; it was fit for action ; and with a neuritic arm, forsooth, I drove it against the drenched thing and brought it back to its factory virtue. My *rafiq* and my cook wanted to embrace me ; but I could not prevent them from kissing my hand in gratitude.

Two days later the Sultan was wearing one of those flannels ; but their obtrusion down to the wrists, even in a man, spoiled the aesthetic value of the broad open sleeves of the robe. It was cold, however,—as cold as 10 above zero in New York ; but in Ar-Riyadh 50 F. in January—it never fell below that in the daytime— had upon me almost the same effect. The Sultan also complained ; and I am certain he enjoyed the flannels. But unlike the time in Ojair when I trimmed Saiyed Hashem's beard, and His Highness learning of it said that he would gladly submit his own to my artistic care, he did not on this occasion say anything about the flannels. Evidently Saiyed Hashem, to save my own dignity, did not hesitate or blush to say that he had done the job himself. And the Sultan rewarded him with a silver watch. He showed it to me.

' Is it the habit of the Sultan,' I asked, ' to give away watches—only watches—as rewards ? '—' No, *billah !* he gives away everything—clothes, food, money—you have seen with your eyes—even slaves and slave-girls. He has Christian girls also. Ask him for one. *Wallah, ya Ustaz,* he will present one to you.'

I had, in fact, heard of the Georgian women in Ar-
Riyadh, and when I went to visit the Sultan's father,
the Imam Abd'ur-Rahman, who is about eighty and dyes
his beard with *henna*, I was told that he had in his harim
two Gurjiyahs (Georgian girls) and that one of them had
recently given him a son. I do not know how many real
Georgians, who are much prized in Najd for their alabaster beauty, were among the Armenian girls that were
bought in Syria in the year of the red terror, when many
thousands of that race were expelled from their homes
by the Turks and driven east and south into the wilderness.
The traders of Najd, who are always travelling between
Al-Qasim and Damascus, bought seventy or eighty
Armenian girls that year and sold them as slaves in Haiel,
Buraidah and Ar-Riyadh. The Sultan purchased some
of them, gave away a few to his relatives and friends,
and had two with him in Al-Hasa when we were there.
They have been made to embrace Al-Islam these girls,
and were taught the Koran. The Chief Steward of the
Sultanate of Najd, the Quartermaster-General and
Finance Minister, Shalhoub, once told me a story which I
would have deemed incredible had it been told by and
about some one else. But the burly and ever busy
Shalhoub, who would have one of his children, ' a boy
of inflammable wit,' educated at the American University
of Beirût, is a man of veracity and in spite of his position
of modest demeanour. Nor does he indulge in ribaldry
or brag. He had come to see me when I was sick,
bringing with him a package of tea packed in India—
' the best quality,' he said, ' in our stores.' Saiyed Hashem
then came in, and as he was still looking for a wife he
prodded the dear man with questions about women and
slave-girls. Whereupon, to escape the prodding he told
the following story.
    Said Shalhoub : ' The Sultan Abd'ul-Aziz, Allah
lengthen his days, once presented me a Gurjiyah. She
was brought to him from Buraidah, and after he had

THE PALACE AND PART OF THE SOUQ, AR-RIYADH

ANOTHER VIEW OF THE PALACE

'entered upon her,'—one night only—he gave her to me, sent her to the house. And when I went to her room on the evening of that day I stood before the door with my heart in my hand (that is, trembling with fear) ; I entered, *bismillah*. But what I beheld—*wallah, billah !* every word I utter is truth—what I beheld tied my tongue, and I felt moreover as if I had received a blow on my head. I sat down and gazed upon her as upon an image.

'She held down her head after she had seen me. And I—never in my life have I seen or heard of such beauty, such august beauty. Her skin ?—white as alabaster. Her hair ?—like cataracts of melted gold. Her lips ?—red as a pomegranate seed. Her forehead ?— lofty and glowing like the dawn. And those honey-coloured eyes, so soft, so demure, so appealing to the honour of man. And I have nothing, O long-of-days, O *Ustaz*, but my honour that is of any worth. Yes, *billah*, I still have something more, which the years I thought had smuggled away from me. I sat before that image of beauty like a child—I tell you, like a child— and I felt the flame of shame upon me. I was ashamed to touch her, or to approach her, or even to speak to her. I got up and walked out of the room ; and on the following day I sold her to a man from Kuwait for four hundred reals, aye, *wallah*, only four hundred.'

Saiyed Hashem looked at Shalhoub significantly, dubiously, and laughed. And Shalhoub, getting up to go : 'I swore by Allah, *ya Saiyed*. Are you a believer ? Fear Allah then, and doubt not a believing brother.' A few days later the doubting Saiyed came to me and said : ' *Wallah*, the story of Shalhoub is true.'

But the Sultan Abd'ul-Aziz is not always milk and honey to Shalhoub, nor does he always offer him odalisques of ineffable—untouchable—beauty. One day His Highness took me up to the roof of the Palace to show me the tower from which the great *atrik*—incandescent lamp—sends out at night penetrating white rays to the palm-groves encircling Ar-Riyadh ;—a beacon to those who come from. the desert or from the wadi.   But Shalhoub is the keeper of the key to the tower, which was then closed.   He was therefore called, and straightway he appeared.   ' Where is the key ? ' the Sultan asked.   The Quartermaster-General mumbled his reply.   ' Get it,' His Highness darted out.   ' In haste, Allah hasten thine end.'   And Shalhoub running down the stairs tripped and fell on his hands : ' Allah has heard thee, O thou long-of-days,' The Sultan laughed.

He cherishes his Finance Minister and therefore likes to bully him.   But it goes at times even beyond that. Once he committed a grave mistake, and the Sultan's ire was unleashed.   He is terrible at such moments.   His word, which is law, is likely to be anything save death. For this is in the hand of the Judge ; and in his, too, when he sits in judgment.   But he was very angry, in that instance, with his Chief Steward and Finance Minister Shalhoub ; and after cursing him and his forefathers back and forth he exclaimed : ' Go ! Walk to Al-Hasa barefoot.'   And poor Shalhoub, a man in the sixties, set out there and then, leaving his sandals at the door.   He walked until he had reached the Dahna— two days—when a *najjab* with the Sultan's order overtook him there and brought him back.   It was after that, me-thinks, that he presented him with the odalisque—the golden odalisque whom he did not deem himself worthy to touch.

Yet, he is a man of real worth, and to the Sultanate of Najd of great service.   He has to feed from 200 to 300 guests a day ; he has to provide 150 families, the Sa'ouds, the Rashids, and the fallen Eminences of Ar-Riyadh with provisions ;—rice, butter, coffee, sugar, dates, flour, wood, charcoal, tea, and an extra allowance in money for meat ;—he has to keep account of the *zeluls* and camels that come and go ; to dole out also oats for the horses—

more than fifty grooms gather at his door every day about sunset ; and he has to pray five times a day and devote, Allah keep thee, an hour to his harim.

Of a certainty, Shalhoub is the busiest man in Ar-Riyadh, in all Najd, except of course the Sultan Abd'ul-Aziz ; for he, in addition to his own work, has to supervise the work of Shalhoub. Everything, the smallest detail, goes through his hand. The Master of Ceremonies makes a list every day of the visitors who arrive—their names, tribes, towns, also the object of their visits, is set down—and presents it to the Sultan (the copy of one of the lists, which the Master of Ceremony gave me as a souvenir is of more than a hundred names). Now the Sultan goes over the list, marks near each name, what the man is to receive in clothes, in provision, and in money. He knows the place and rank of every one it seems, and his gifts are always appropriate. The list then goes to Shalhoub for execution—Shalhoub the Upright, Shalhoub the Virtuous.

I visited him one day in his office, that is in his stores, on the ground floor of the Palace. He sat on a rug crosslegged with bags of silver before him and two book-keepers to his right, while to his left were two clerks, one of whom had charge of the clothes, the other of the money. Shalhoub counted out the rupees or the Marie Theresa dollars to those who came with orders, and then handed to them the clothes. ' Write in the book,'—this to the book-keeper of the treasury, ' Ahmad ibn Jaber of Tharmadah, 250 rupees. And thou write,'—this to the book-keeper of the stores, ' A Persian *busht*, an Indian *zuboun*, two cotton *gutrahs*.' And so, throughout the day, saving the intervals of prayer.

He took me around, showing me the various Departments : provisions—flour and rice and dates ; the saddlery—everything that is needed for the *zelul* and the pack-camel ; the ammunition—rifles of every make, old and new, and hundreds of boxes of cartridges ; the coffee, tea and sugar store ; the tents ; the rugs ; the clothes—*gutrahs* and *zubouns* and *bushts ;* and—another article which you do not find at Wanamaker or Selfridge —a store of large metal vats, five feet deep by two feet in diameter, all full of clarified butter.

This butter is one of the three articles of food, of which they consume immense quantities in Central Arabia ; the other two are rice and dates. Shalhoub showed me three qualities of rice ; and of the best, which is for the Sultan and all the Sa'ouds and the Rashids, he had a stock of over five hundred bags (200 lbs. each). The rice is cooked with the butter, steeped in it ; and the Arabs are lavish, wasteful, in the use of both. They never serve rice in plates, but always, even to one guest, in large tray-like platters of metal or wood. Eat what you can, and give away what you can't.

But most amazing of all of Shalhoub's departments is the booty-room, where old pieces of brass-ware, odds and ends of rusty cannons and guns, bits of rugs, metal water-cans, army boots, belts, broken swords, and what not, are thrown pell-mell, heaped on top of each other. One large box was still unopened. ' What is in it, O Shalhoub,' I asked. ' *Wallah,* I do not know. I have not yet had time to open it.' The confusion and disorder, however, are not the exclusive features of this great junk-shop only ; but everywhere in the other departments I found something akin to them, something that suggested the junk-shop—and much that was covered with dust. But Shalhoub's idea of the matter does not exactly correspond with ours. ' Everything is kept in order, and clean,' he said. Which reminded me of the beduin who came one day, when we were crossing the desert, to our leavings of rice ; and after he had made away with what was left, he wiped his greasy hands with the edge of his long tapering sleeve, saying : ' The Bedu are clean—cleaner than the *hadhar* (town Arabs).' After all is said, however, it's a colossal job, that of Shalhoub ; and his responsi-

INTERIOR OF ONE OF THE COURTS OF THE
ROYAL PALACE

IN THE PALACE AT AR-RIYADH. THE SULTAN ABD'UL-AZIZ
AND CANNONS TAKEN FROM THE TURKS, IBN UR-RASHID
AND IN THE HIJAZ

bilities are great. But here again his own idea of the
matter does not exactly correspond with ours. ' I do
most of the work,' he said, in a plain, matter-of-fact
manner, ' A simple thing. A thousand comes in : we
write it in the book. A thousand goes out : we write it
in the book. And the result,' he stroked one palm against
the other,—' nothing.'

Besides the stores on the ground floor of the Palace
are the refectories, and a waiting hall where the visitors
are received before they are admitted to the *majlis* upstairs. The Palace itself was not built on a preconceived
plan ; but it grew in a free and spontaneous manner,
which is often short-sighted and quite characteristic of
the Arabs. It took me many days to find my bearings
in it, so tortuous are its halls and corridors, and so ramified.
There are at least ten big buildings connected together,
not by subterranean passages, but by high walled bridges.
The Sultan can thus make his daily tour without being
seen or without going through the streets. There is a
bridge from the Palace to the Grand Mosque ; a bridge
to the Harim ; bridges between the houses of the several
wives and concubines, etc. Some of the citizens of Ar-
Riyadh also indulge in this caprice, or rather enjoy this
convenience. One house is built, and as the family grows
with the growth of the harim another house is necessary,
which often has to be built across the street and connected
by a bridge with the main establishment. Looking
immediately around the Palace, from its tower, you get
the impression that Ar-Riyadh is a city of bridges ; and
looking southward as far as the oasis of Al-'Ared reaches,
about five miles, you behold in the haze the spectral
form of the ancient town of Manfouhah.

After showing me the tower, the Sultan took me through
another wing of the Palace to show me on the parapeted
roof of an adjacent building the cannons and machine
guns. These were about fifty in all, of English and German make, which he had won from the King of Al-Hijaz.

as well as from the Turks and Ibn 'ur-Rashid. They were all kept clean ; and the men who were in charge realizing this looked very proud. But the Ikhwan, who have a deep contempt for cannons—they prefer cold steel—have no objection to them as booty. One of their favourite feats of heroism is to stride the gun while it is being fired and slay the gunner at his job. How else can they conquer the *mushrekin* and win *Al-Jannat ?*

On our return from the artillery exhibition, the Sultan, wishing to show me that he also cared for books, ordered Shalhoub who accompanied us to open a certain room. But the Quartermaster-General opened the wrong room, and we were in the drug store instead of the Library. The stock-room rather, which was full of boxes from England—boxes full of medicines—opened, half-opened, broken, and all in a state of woeful neglect. ' These are the boxes of Dr. Mann,' [1] said His Highness with a tinge of disdain. No, they care not very much for medicine the Arabs of Najd. Besides, there was at that time but one man in Ar-Riyadh, Dr. Abdullah—and he was in Al-Hasa—who understood the use of these drugs. Waste, sheer waste. The books in the adjacent room reminded me of a corner in a second-hand book-shop, where the odds and ends, stray leaves and torn volumes are left pell-mell to the mercy of the moth and the dust.

His Highness would do better I thought if he showed me a corner of the harim quarters. He must have read my mind ; for on the evening of that day, instead of calling on me as usual, he accorded me the privilege of sipping coffee with him in one of his very private apartments—after the odalisque from the north had vacated it. I do not think His Highness realized that he had been cruel. For although a Christian girl had embraced Al-Islam—but why dwell further on the subject ?

[1] Dr. Mann was the representative of the Sultan of Najd in London ; and he and Major Holmes came together to see the Sultan in Al-Hasa three months before I was there.

Sufficient for thy sins, the perfumes of the Gurjiyah and her diwan.

The apartment is on the floor below, and we had to go through a labyrinth to reach it. A lamp hung in the vestibule which led to a pleasant little room, furnished as usual with carpets, cushions, and *masnads*. It has no windows, not even apparently an aperture. But the Sultan, who does not disdain to show the hidden virtues of his living rooms, got up and pulled a cord which opened a square aperture in the wall near the ceiling. ' For the sun and air,' he said. He then pointed to a sword which was hanging on a peg. ' It is the most cherished of all my possessions.' He ordered a slave to bring it down. The hilt is of chased gold, the scabbard of silver ; and since it is the sword of the Great Sa'oud it must be more than a hundred years old. The blade looks even older. The Sultan took it in his hand and told us how he killed with it one of his bitterest foes. It was a revenge—a lawful and honoured custom. ' I struck him first on the leg and disabled him ; quickly after that I struck at the neck ;—the head fell to one side—the blood spurted up like a fountain : the third blow at the heart :—I saw the heart, which was cut in two, palpitate like that.' He illustrated with a shiver of his hand. ' It was a joyous moment—I kissed the sword.'

He then brought out a leather case of perfumes, and insisted on perfuming me from the various bottles : one on my beard, another on my *gutrah*, a third on my breast —and they were all as heavy as undiluted ottar of roses. As for Saiyed Hashem, he helped himself to them all recklessly, without a thought to what was happening to his *rafiq*. The room itself reeked with the dazing essences ; my head began to swim ; I was ready to faint. The Sultan laughingly chided Saiyed Hashem—' a Saiyed never knows his limits,' he said,—and offered me a fan. He then ordered a glass of water for me. ' While Your Highness is giving orders,' I said, indulging the banter of the

moment, 'please order Saiyed Hashem out.' I little
thought that he would do so in earnest; and I felt a
satisfaction, when the Saiyed was at the door, of being
able and willing to intercede for him.

The laughter was refreshing, reviving; and I was able
to ask the Sultan a few questions, and take notes as usual
while he related of a certain battle in his career of conquest, the causes and results of which were not clear to
me. He is an excellent *raconteur*, and I have no doubt that
he tells all the truth—all the truth that an honest monarch
can possibly tell, when he feels that he personally is not
yet finished with history. More than once he looked at
the clock; and as soon as it struck four (9 p.m.) he
stopped. No one after this hour and no affairs of State
can claim his attention or favour. During his evening
visits to me he seemed to know instinctively when to get
up; and invariably as I looked at my watch it was nine
o'clock or five minutes before or after. This is the harim
hour, and he must go to one of his wives. A word he
often said, in connection with the one waiting for him
and his evening visit to me, which cannot be rendered
into English. The nicety of it is in the pun and the
alliteration.

Before going out that evening he showed us through
the Gurjiyah's apartment :—the bedroom with a bed and
mosquito-netting, the dressing-room, the bath-room, and
a private stairs leading to a reception chamber which
gives on the roof. The full moon saw us salaam and
separate, he going through the iron gate across the
bridge and we going back to our quarters between high
roof-walls, and walls even higher of envy and desire.

On the following day we got a better view of what was
beyond the iron gate; for continuing our tour of the
Palace, the Sultan still acting as guide, we crossed three
roofs, two bridges, and several corridors to his own private
apartment, from which we beheld a row of four or
five massive buildings columned and crenelated. 'That

is the harim,' said His Highness ; ' each one has a house
of her own.' In the vestibule—a sort of ante-chamber—
where we had coffee are two doors, one leading to the
private *masjid* where the Sultan prays—he goes to the
Grand Mosque on Friday only—the other leading to the
apartment which no woman ever enters. It is furnished
like the other we have seen, except that it has also a
fire-place and niches with doors decorated in red and
yellow and blue. There is an adjoining room, which is
used as a wardrobe—his robes were hanging on pegs—
and a bath-room divided into two sections, one containing
the samovar, the other a tub and metal-pans. The water
is brought in skins, which is the custom, without exception
in Ar-Riyadh. But in the Palace my attention was
called to the cast-iron pipes which carry the waste water
under ground outside the city.

The Sultan, I have said before, is a man of surprises.
Out of his private apartment he led us across a roof and
a bridge to a house, in the corridors of which as we entered
there were some women. They scampered like sheep
when they saw us. But one of them in a red robe and
a black veil, which she pulled quickly over her face, found
herself right in front of the Sultan, and did not know
like a lost lamb which way to turn. His Highness waved
his staff in the direction of one of the doors. ' Stupid
slave-girls,' he said, ' who cannot see what is even before
them.'

We were passing through the servants' quarter adjoining
another private apartment. The Sultan preceded us into
the vestibule, and hearing a noise within sent ahead of
us one of the accompanying blacks. We followed half
a minute later, and as usual we were greeted with the
unctuousness of Oriental perfumes ; and the usual
furniture—carpets, cushions, and *masnads*. The apartment
consists of the same number of rooms, whose windows are
latticed, and the door of one of which was closed. For
the lady had to hide till the stranger—an infidel, withal—

had seen her living quarters,—had been, in fact, through her prison. The ceiling of these rooms, as well as the two grand reception halls, are covered with red or dotted cloth to match the covers of the cushions. There is also a punka in the living room, and an alcove in one of the adjoining rooms for the bedding. In very truth, I was in the apartment of one of the Sultan's legal wives, and the servants who scampered away from us as we came in attend exclusively upon her. I was told afterwards that she is the ex-wife of Sa'oud ibn 'ur-Rashid, the third from the last ruler of Haiel, and that the Sultan Abd'ul-Aziz married her and adopted her children as a political measure.

Before leaving us that day he showed me the place, a gallery of one of the quadrangles below, from which I might take a picture of the wedding feast. For there was a wedding in the Palace the day or the night before ; but I had heard nothing of it or about it, since weddings like funerals in Ar-Riyadh now take place quietly without any singing, ululuing, or music. The groom is a young Sa'oud—a boy of thirteen, in fact ;—' he wanted to get married,' said the Sultan nonchalantly, ' and we got him married,'—and his wife is his cousin a girl of twelve. The Sa'ouds rarely marry outside of their own house, except it be into the house of *the* Sheikh (*i.e.* the descendants of Ibn Abd'ul-Wahhab).

The marriage ceremony like everything else in Wahhabism is very simple. The parents of the bride and the bridegroom gather at the house of the former, where the formula is pronounced in their presence by a sheikh or a judge. A few days after the visitors and the invited guests come to the house of the bridegroom, where they are entertained with coffee, tea, and Turkish delights, and are perfumed and incensed. They then accompany him to the Mosque to pray and thence to the house of the bride's parents, where a similar reception is held. After which he is conducted into a private apartment, where for the first time he meets his bride, and where after the marriage is consummated he may live with her for two or three days, before he takes her to his own home.

The relatives of the married couple as well as their parents slay sheep and camels for those who may come besides the invited guests. Every one is welcome. And it was the Sultan, in this instance, who had to give the wedding feast. Over three thousand people gorged themselves at four or five sittings with rice and lamb. Shalhoub supplied the exact figures. ' Wallah ! ' he swore, ' they gave me but one day to prepare ; and you saw the result. . . . O yes ; we have vessels that hold a whole camel—We slaughtered eighty sheep and thirty camels. And we emptied twenty bags of the best rice.'

Besides the refectories three open courts in the Palace were filled. People of all classes sat in rows opposite each other, and a sort of table-and-tray combined made of metal was placed over a round mat between each group of ten or fifteen. No sooner was this done than the lines formed into circles. The large trays of rice and lamb were then brought in, and every one tucked his sleeves and waited for the Sultan, who sat among one of the groups, to begin. He had to give a sign. He spoke. He uttered a prayer. And it was the shortest and the most effective prayer I have ever heard. ' Think of Allah,' said he in a loud voice, ' and Allah will think of you.' The hands of the guests were held still for a moment over the bounty of the day, and then they fell to, silently digging into the rice and tearing at the meat.

Saiyed Hashem and I were watching from the gallery above ; and I tried, by setting the camera in one of the loopholes of the crenelated parapet, to take a picture. Light there was still ; and also many watchful eyes among the Ikhwan, who resent being photographed. Hence, alternately through hesitation and haste the attempt failed. But the joy of the adventure was at the end of the feast, when the Sultan came up and surprised us on the stairs. He laughed like a schoolboy who had taken part in a successful conspiracy against the school-master.

Later towards evening I met Shalhoub, the wise and virtuous and strenuous Shalhoub, and he spoke thus : ' Thou hast seen with thy two eyes. Now write down in thy book, for what I tell thee is truth—write, Allah keep thee ! Every king in the world is supported by his people ; but the people of Najd are supported by their king.'

CHAPTER XIV

THE TRAGEDY OF SHAMMAR

THE once ruling house of the indomitable tribe of Shammar, the house of the Rashids, that gave the Mountain south of the Great Nufoud its ameers and Haiel its rulers, had reached the zenith of its power and entered upon a state of moral corruption about the time of the first appearance in Central Arabia of Abd'ul-Aziz ibn Sa'oud. It had even started on its downward course ; and neither the Turks before the War, nor the Germans during the War, nor King Husein after the War, could help to check it.

The defect was more than political ; it was mental and moral, and it had become hereditary. Self-slaughter is scarcely known among the Arabs ; hysteria and hypochondria do not as a rule develop among those who live in the open and on the *gazu ;* but in Haiel, for reasons that are only partly known, they had become quite common, especially among the women of the ruling house. And the hereditary results are tragic. Muhammad ibn Talal, the last ruler of Shammar, is a melancholy Dane without the Dane's philosophy and cowardice. Abdullah ibn Mit'eb, who surrendered to Ibn Sa'oud three months before him, is a sullen idiot in spite of his brilliant eyes ; Faisal his uncle is a smiling villain, a Richard III, without that Richard's unctuous talk. But let me begin with the First Chapter of this Shammar Tragedy.

And the First Chapter begins with the death of Abd'ul-Aziz ibn Mit'eb ibn 'ur-Rashid, whose sway extended

over most of Central Arabia when his name-sake Ibn
Sa'oud was still an unknown quantity in Kuwait, and who
later by ill chance while at war with him was killed in
battle. His own forces and those of Ibn Sa'oud had
fought in the afternoon without any gain to each other
and had returned after sunset to their respective camps.
But Ibn 'ur-Rashid who slept but little that night went
from one section of his camp to the other planning and
preparing for the following day ; and in the darkness
that precedes the early dawn, he drove his charger into
what he thought was another part of his own camp.
Alas, he was in the camp of Ibn Sa'oud ; and the men
he was arousing and urging to battle recognized his
voice, turned upon him, and riddled him with bullets.

Compared with what had preceded it in the history
of the Rashids, this was a natural though stupid death.
For his father Mit'eb was killed by his two nephews
Bandar and Badr, the sons of Abd'ul-Aziz's uncle Telal ;
and Bandar and Badr were consequently put to death
by the other uncle, the great Muhammad, whom Charles
Montagu Doughty met in 1875. ' *Ya Muslemin* (O ye
Muslems),' cried Muhammad in the public square of
Haiel, exonerating himself : ' *Wallah !* I have killed
them only to save this,' and he struck his neck with his
hand. ' They sought to slay me, but I got ahead of them.
And do you think, *ya Muslemin*, that they who slew my
brother Mit'eb would let me escape ? '

But I must tell you, before going further, that there are
two branches of the house of the Rashids, the Abdullahs
or the ruling branch, and the 'Ubaids or its rival for
power. Now, Abd'ul-Aziz left four sons, Mit'eb, Mish'el,
Muhammad, and Sa'oud (the last was with his maternal
uncle Ibn Sibhan) ; and there was a triumvirate of the
'Ubaids, the brothers Faisal and Sultan and Sa'oud,
sons of Hamoud 'Ubaid, who sought to destroy the ruling
House. So after the death of Abd'ul-Aziz they tucked
their sleeves and started in earnest. Nothing seemed

easier and more humane than relieving his youngsters of
a throne which was doubtless going to be a bone of
contention between them. The 'Ubaid brothers, therefore, arranged a hunting excursion and invited their
three cousins, Mit'eb and Mish'el and Muhammad.
The party was properly escorted ; but most of the servants
and slaves were of the 'Ubaid households.

Bismillah, they rode out of the city to the hunt, in
sooth ; but the quarry of the three 'Ubaids was not that
of the three Abdullahs. It was not a contingency ; they
did not have to look for it, chase it, worry it out of its
covert, or fly the hawk at it. It was there before them ;
and when behind a rib in the open field the city was lost
to view, each one of the 'Ubaids leaped from his saddle
to that of one of his cousins and slew him outright as
planned. Not one of the accompanying escort said a
word or lifted a hand, except in the praise of Allah. That
was the first breach in the rule of the Abdullah branch of
the Rashids—the end of the First Act of the Tragedy of
Shammar, which begins with the death of the father and
ends with the assassination of three of his sons.

The Second Act begins with Sultan ibn Hamoud ibn
'Ubaid on the throne as Ameer of Haiel. But his reign
was short owing to the eagerness of his brother Sa'oud to
succeed him. Seven months only was he allowed to toy
with power ; and then—the fatal moment having too
soon arrived and Sa'oud being unprepared—nothing
better was possible than strangling. A drop scene to set
up a new throne and give me a chance to tell of what
happened to the fourth son of Abd'ul-Aziz, he who was
with his maternal uncle Ibn Sibhan.

The Drop Scene is a street in Al-Medinah. And
behold, the aforesaid Ibn Sibhan with his nephew Sa'oud,
the scion of the Abdullah branch, the rightful heir to the
throne. They had heard in their flight of the recent assassination in Haiel, and anticipating a second and a third
of the same 'Ubaid house, they were planning to return.

Meanwhile Sa'oud ibn Hamoud ibn 'Ubaid ibn
'ur-Rashid was on the throne of Shammar ; and the
planning of Ibn Sibhan—he had to muster a few rifles
for a *coup d'état*—took a whole year to mature. To be
exact fourteen months after Sa'oud 'Ubaid assumed the
ameership, Sa'oud Abd'ul-Aziz arrived in Haiel with his
uncle and his men. And forthwith they stormed the
Palace and seized and murdered Sa'oud ibn 'Ubaid.
Haiel applauded and gave the sword of State to its rightful
heir. Before closing the Second Act I must have another
drop scene to tell of the third triumvir, of Faisal the
smiling villain, whom I had the pleasure of meeting in
Ojair and Ar-Riyadh. He it was who went to the Jawf
as governor : he made himself Ameer of the Jawf, while
his brother Sultan was Ameer of Haiel. And he was
eminently satisfied with his lot, considering the first
assassination in the Capital. But when the second took
place and the son of Abd'ul-Aziz on the shoulders of the
revolution came to his father's throne, Faisal fled from
the Jawf and hied him eastward, and hied him southward,
and did not stop till he had reached Ar-Riyadh, where
he bespoke the clemency and favour of Abd'ul-Aziz ibn
Sa'oud.

The Third Act of the Tragedy of Shammar begins with
Sa'oud ibn Abd'ul-Aziz on the throne of Haiel and a
woman—Fatimah Sibhan—behind the throne, and ambitious black slaves under it. Nevertheless—and perchance because the woman counterpoised the slaves—
that throne withstood for several years the storms of time,
which mostly came from the south—from the Ikhwan of
Ibn Sa'oud. In sooth, Sitti Fatimah, that veiled power
behind the throne of Haiel was for fifteen years the
bitterest enemy of the rising power of the Wahhabis in
Central Arabia. She was the backbone of Sa'oud ibn
Abd'ul-Aziz who fought for many years Abd'ul-Aziz ibn
Sa'oud, and did not die like his father in or out of battle.
Alas ! he was fated to die like his three unfortunate

brothers. For in the rival branch of the House of Assassins appeared another claimant to the throne in the person of Abdullah ibn Talal, who was unspeakably treacherous. He had not the courage at least of the hunting Triumvirs.

One day the Ameer Sa'oud as an idle hour weighed upon him rode out of the city, not on a hunt, but just for target practice, accompanied by his *rajajil* (servants and slaves and friends), among whom was Abdullah ibn Talal. And while he and this Ibn Talal were practising, the *rajajil* were busy gathering wood for the fire, making coffee, and attending to the mounts. Only one slave remained in attendance, and he was absorbed as much as the Ameer in the target. Now comes Destiny to direct the two shots and to blind the slave. The Ameer raises his gun ; Ibn Talal who is standing behind him raises his ; and the two go off simultaneously, one bullet making a hole in the bull's-eye, the other penetrating a man's head. The black slave, who was there to protect this man, was watching with wide open eyes the target ; and it was only when he fell dead before him that he realized what had happened. But he was not given a chance to move or cry out. Another bullet from Ibn Talal's gun laid him flat and still near his Master.

By this time another slave had seen the tragedy, and calling to his fellows they hurried to the scene. With them was also young Abdullah ibn Mit'eb ibn Abd'ul-Aziz, nephew of the murdered Ameer. So Ibn Talal, now that he was heading for the throne, had to remove him also. But the slaves protected young Abdullah, and in the battle which ensued one of them was killed and several wounded. Ibn Talal was indeed an excellent shot ; but every time he sought Abdullah he found a slave between him and his own lead. And victory was finally to the slaves, who would not hear Ibn Talal's plea for mercy. Thus, with two murders and a shining example of a slave's loyalty to his master, ends the Third Act of the Tragedy.

The Fourth Act begins with Abdullah ibn Mit'eb on the throne of his grandfather Abd'ul-Aziz. But neither the power of Sitti Fatimah, the great Fatimah Sibhan, nor the bravery and trust of the slaves of the Palace, nor the divided strength of the tribe of Shammar through which Wahhabism has driven the wedge of a unitarian creed, could save this young Ameer from the ever increasing and ever beating storms of Southern Najd. He had to surrender, and it did not take him long to decide. Now he is an honoured guest at Ar-Riyadh. It is he, the dark-eyed dusky Ameer—he has a touch of the tarbrush in him—of whom I have often spoken.

But Haiel after his surrender continued to hold out against the siege of the Ikhwan ; and in this interval of conflict and fortitude appears another Talal, brother to the murderer and murdered Abdullah, who thinks he can save Shammar and reinvest with glory the House of the Rashids. He did so in a measure for three months. Indeed, Muhammad ibn Talal, the last Ameer of Haiel, was so brave and daring that he was admired even by the Ikhwan. But he was fighting against great odds, and he too had to surrender.

Thus ends the Tragedy of Shammar ; not as it began and as it continued throughout its three first Acts in individual murder, however atrocious and treacherous, but in a devastating siege—in famine, and fire, and a torrent of blood.

This last Talal is he who was a prisoner in the Palace, and who was given his freedom on the occasion I was told of my visit to the Capital. Not from the Sultan had I this, but from one of his Secretaries. One day when we were making the tour of the Palace the Sultan, stopping before a door not far from my own quarters, said : ' I will tarry here a little.' He stopped afterwards to see me. ' Ibn Talal,' he began as he came in, ' he is a fool, an idiot. I want to give him his freedom as I did to Faisal and Abdullah, but I am afraid he will kill himself. He

is always making gestures before his own eyes and
talking to himself. And what did he do th' other evening ?
He is I think—there is nothing in his head. He dressed
like a woman and went out of the Palace and into the
street. We have to keep him under guard for his own
sake. . . . No, I do not think it is a trick to escape. For
whither can he escape ? '

Two days later he was set free. But previous to his
coming to the *majlis* to receive his freedom, new garments
were sent to him, and a fitting head-gear. He looked
every inch an ameer, as he walked into the grand audience
hall. A prepossessing youth, tall, bright-eyed, about
twenty-five, and of a firm expression. He sat down next
to the Sultan, his hands folded across his breast, and
listened to a sermon. Aye, the Sultan Abd'ul-Aziz can
also sermonize and even become a bore.

' You of the house of the Rashids, all of you, are as dear
to me as my own children. You live here as I live,
neither better nor worse—your clothes are like mine,
your food is like mine, your horses are even better than
mine. No, *wallah !* there is nothing in the Palace which
you may not have.'

All the Rashids were present, and His Highness rubbed
it in.

' Will anyone of you say if he has ever desired aught,
which is under my hand, and did not get it ? '

No one spoke.

' And you Muhammad, it was your own stupid action
that forced me to treat you as a prisoner. *Wallah, billah !*
all the time you were incarcerated I was in grief for you
—in grief, *wallah !* as if for my own son. You should have
the good sense to not listen to women. Everything you
do will be reported. . . . I know everything. . . . Apply
your wit to your own good—avoid every path that may
lead to intrigue—be loyal as I am friendly—and *wallah,
billah !* any ill that befalls you will stir my heart before
my tongue to your help. You are now one of my own

house. And all the resources of defence, which in time
of danger I use to protect my harim, and my children,
and my people will be put in force to protect you ;—to
protect all of you of the house of the Rashids.'

He spoke with effect and with undoubted sincerity.
One or two, I noticed, were weeping. The *majlis* was full,
and the most solemn moment was when the Sultan stood
up, every one following suit, and gave Muhammad ibn
Talal his hand.

' I give you the pledge of security on the book of Allah
and the life of his Prophet on condition that you be loyal
to us, and that you lend not your tongue, nor your hand,
nor your presence to such as would intrigue or plot
against us.'

' If I swerve from the path you have designated,' said
Ibn Talal, ' cut off my head.' Whereupon, he kissed the
Sultan on the tip of his nose and on his forehead.

A voice then spoke.

' Allah lengthen thy days and strengthen the pillars of
thy reign.'

It was the head of the House of the Rashids, the sur-
viving triumvir Faisal.

But they were not all happy, as I learned afterwards,
in the freedom of their cousin Ibn Talal.

A SUMMARY

Abdullah ibn Ali ibn 'ur-Rashid, founder of the house, the
Ameer of Haiel and Shammar in the days of the first
Sa'oud, about 135 years ago. A good ruler—died a
natural death.

Talal, his son—morose and worldly—seen by Palgrave—
committed suicide.

Mit'eb, brother to Talal—killed by his two nephews Bander
and Badr.

Bander—killed by Muhammad, who also killed Badr and his
four children.

Muhammad, called the Great—ruled from 1870 to 1897—
had some of the qualities of a great man—was seen by
all the European travellers that came down from the
North to the Jawf and Haiel and upper Najd—ruled all
of Central Arabia—died a natural death, and childless.

Abd'ul-Aziz ibn Mit'eb—ruled from 1897 to 1906—had
heroic qualities—was feared and liked—was killed in
battle through his own mistake in the engagement of
Rowdat-M'hanna.

THE 'UBAIDS COME INTO POWER

Sultan ibn Hamoud—one of the Triumvirs who killed the
three sons of Abd'ul-Aziz—ruled seven months—was
killed by his brother Sa'oud.

Sa'oud ibn Hamoud—one of the Triumvirs, ditto—ruled
fourteen months—was killed by Sa'oud ibn Abd'ul-Aziz.

THE ABDULLAHS COME BACK TO POWER

Sa'oud ibn Abd'ul-Aziz—ruled about ten years—was ruled
by a woman and by his slaves—loyal friend to the Turks
—was killed by Abdullah ibn Talal.

Abdullah ibn Mit'eb ibn Abd'ul-Aziz—a *muwallad*—surrendered to Ibn Sa'oud in the siege of Haiel.

Abdullah ibn Talal—ruled three months—fought bravely
during the siege—surrendered on the 29th day of Safar,
1340 H. (November 2, 1921).

Shammar is absorbed by Ibn Sa'oud.

The Sultan Abd'ul-Aziz lectures Ibn Talal and rubs it into
the Rashids.

THE HOUSE OF THE RASHIDS

THE ABDULLAH BRANCH

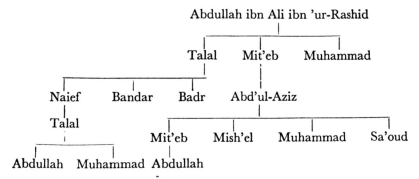

Abdullah ibn Ali ibn 'ur-Rashid

Talal   Mit'eb   Muhammad

Naief   Bandar   Badr   Abd'ul-Aziz

Talal

Mit'eb   Mish'el   Muhammad   Sa'oud

Abdullah   Muhammad   Abdullah

THE 'UBAID BRANCH

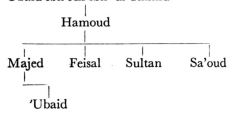

'Ubaid ibn Ali ibn 'ur-Rashid

Hamoud

Majed   Feisal   Sultan   Sa'oud

'Ubaid

CHAPTER XV

THE SA'OUDS AND THE RASHIDS AT PLAY

HORSE-RACING and target-practising are the two principal sports of the Arabs of Najd. But when there is a match or a race in Ar-Riyadh it takes place early in the morning, before sunrise, and the Sultan Abd'ul-Aziz is among the first to arrive. One evening he asked me to accompany him on the following morning—early, he said, but did not state the time. Now an early January morning in a Christian country, even to a labourer, cannot possibly mean before seven—a Christian hour. I kept my watch under my pillow. But I was awakened by a knock at the door at a quarter to six. 'The Imam,' said the servant, 'will be soon at the Palace gate.' Quickly, therefore, to get there ahead of him, I washed and dressed, putting on my *ighal* as I hurried out. But I was crestfallen when I saw him before me walking towards the gate. He had also asked Saiyed Hashem and another of the Diwan. But he did not wait.

'They can follow us,' he said, as he stepped into his carriage, an old one-horse victoria,—the only one in Ar-Riyadh,—which squeaked and lurched most disgracefully. It was most surprising to see that this man, this warrior who had fought many battles and defied and overcome many dangers, was afraid of being thrown out of a puny vehicle. More than once he clutched at my hand and held it like a child. And when something in the harness snapped, as we were crossing a ditch, and the driver descended to see to it, His Highness stepped out,

saying : ' When you fix it take it back.' And then to me :
' We will walk ; it is more safe.'

We crossed a field of stubble to a ridge—the grand
stand—where a few hundred spectators had gathered.
Beyond the ridge was an undulating stretch of gravel
soil—the racecourse. But the grand stand it seemed to
me was exclusively for the people. The Sultan and his
entourage sat on the hard ground, a little to the side of it,
where the slaves had spread two *abas*. Sitting in a kneeling posture on one of them, His Highness invited me
to the other, while the Rashids and the Sa'ouds were
ranging themselves in a line to the right and to the left
of us.

About a hundred yards from us was the starting and
finishing point, where the competitors on their horses
had gathered. There were also the judges. But the
race was in a straight line, a distance of thirty-five minutes,
going and coming, *i.e.* about a mile and a half from the
starting point and return. They measure by the eye of
course, using certain landmarks, and placing judges there
to designate the course.

The horses started at a brisk walking pace and continued
for ten minutes, when they disappeared behind the crest
of the undulation in the ground ; and twenty minutes
later they appeared on the same horizon coming back
at the same pace. No, it is not a walking race, but one
preceded by a walk of a couple of miles. For when they
were within about three-quarters of a mile from the starting
point, they spurred their horses to a gallop—that was the
beginning of the race.

The Sultan with his binoculars to his eyes was the most
interested and the most interesting spectator. He saw,
and he reported, and he waxed enthusiastic. ' The red
is ahead—the white is second.' Riding the red was his
son Sa'oud ; on the white was Abdullah ibn Mit'eb. It
was a race then between the Sa'ouds and the Rashids.
' The red—the red ! ' cried the Sultan Abd'ul-Aziz.

AT THE REVIEW ON THE DAY OF FAISAL'S RETURN FROM ABHA

' *Ghawwaak Allah ! ghawwaak !* (Allah give thee strength).'
He shouted out, and he gesticulated. But the red and the
white were neck to neck. The Sultan rises to his feet ;
and Faisal ibn 'ur-Rashid also rises and dashes forward,
urging the white. ' *Ghawwaak, ya Abdullah, ghawwaak !* '
he cried, waving his bamboo stick. And then, in triumph :
' the white—the white is first.'

So in truth it was, although the red was but half a
neck behind. The Sultan nevertheless continued in a
spirit of delightful abandon to cheer the winners and to
jeer at those who came last. ' Who is behind thee, O
Swailem ? Why so fast, O Sufan ? Haste is of the
Shaitan ! '

The race entailed little or no accounting ; for there
were no entries and no betting :—only prizes,[1] which
were paid in English gold on the spot by the Sultan's
treasurer. To the Rashids went the first prize—and the
glory of the day.

The people dispersed as they gathered, and as they had
witnessed the race, in a quiet manner ;—quiet and impassive ;
—a behaviour on such occasions hardly to be desired. Nor
was this because of the Sultan's presence as a spectator.
At another time, when he himself was of the spectacle,
they were the same. It is the Arab crowd even when it
goes out to meet a hero.

And there was a young hero, the Sultan's son Faisal,
returning from the burning plains of Tihamah and the
frosty mountains of Asir, a distance of seven hundred
miles—thirty days' travel. He was sent to Abha at the
head of an army five thousand strong on a punitive
expedition ; for the garrison there had rebelled, and
behind the rebellion was a plot, which was traced in a
straight line to Mecca—to King Husein. After restoring
the authority of his father in the mountains, therefore,
he marched down towards the sea with Konfudha as his

---

[1] The prizes, in Pounds Sterling, were as follows : First, 15—Second,
10—Third, 5—Fourth, 3—Fifth, 2.

objective. But the soldiers of King Husein had two allies
which the warriors of Najd could not overcome. They
succumbed to the heat and pestilence of Tihamah, and
betook them back to the mountains, where they were
pursued by the enemy and not by his allies, and where
they had their revenge. The soldiers of King Husein
retreated to Tihamah just as the Ikhwan of Ibn Sa'oud
had retreated from it. But in Abha, the capital of Asir,
the victory of the youthful Faisal was complete.

So when he returned to Ar-Riyadh the people went out,
early before sunrise as usual to meet him. Word was
sent the day before that he would arrive at a certain place,
only a few miles from the Capital, where he would pass
the night. His father went there to meet him and ride
with him, as he entered the city, at the orthodox hour of
dawn.

At that hour, indeed, about five thousand people had
gathered outside the city wall to meet and greet the hero
of Abha. And I gave then, as I give now, my whole-
hearted suffrage to the hero elect. For even though he
accomplished nothing, when he got there, the march from
Ar-Riyadh to Tihamah on the sea, through the rugged
mountains of Asir, at the head of five thousand of the
Ikhwan, is for a boy of eighteen a most heroic deed. On
much less than that some grown-up 'political' heroes
of the War have won their laurels.

It was a day of rejoicing. But here again I find a point
of resemblance between these Arabs and those people in
the West who would befriend and dominate them. They
both take their pleasures sadly. Even the octogenarian,
the Imam Abd'ur-Rahman, came out to meet his grand-
son, and was as sombrely grave as anyone in the crowd.
But he did not have to sit on the hard ground as did the
Sultan his son at the horse-race; for there was a
reviewing place, furnished with carpets and leaning
cushions, which he and his *rajajil* and some of the Ulema
occupied.

The Ameer Faisal Ibn Abd'ul-Aziz Ibn Sa'oud,
Viceroy of Al-Hijaz

A detachment of cavalry—the vanguard—passed before them followed at a little distance by Faisal, who came galloping at the head of his staff. He carried a spear in his hand and was dressed in what suggested to me a knight of the Middle Ages. A handsome boy, lean of visage and pale, bearing the stamp not so much of fatigue as of care ; and withal a calm and dignified expression. He stopped before the reviewing place, descended and salaamed his grandfather, who embraced him with an undue fondness, kissing him several times in the face.

Immediately after that he returned to the saddle to continue the *'ardhah* (review), which consisted of charging up and down, a distance of about four hundred yards, shaking the spear or the sword, and uttering the war whoops of the Ikhwan. ' Knight of the Unity, am I —brother of those who obey Allah ! ' The people re- plied, exclaiming : ' *In'em, in'em !* (grace be to thee).' It was the one and only form of demonstration. But they did chat in low voices, and here and there in a subdued laugh was evidence of a disciplined merriment. There was also, apart from the male multitudes, the usual line of black bundles—squatting women—from which little whispers emanated and now and then an ululu (*lu lu lu*) [1] for the returning hero.

Following Faisal came his father the Sultan Abd'ul- Aziz, charging at the head of a detachment and crying : ' Allah is one ! There is no God but Allah ! ' He was stern of aspect, full of the importance of the moment ; not as a father might rejoice on the return of his dearest son from a long journey, fraught with danger and peril, but as a commander-in-chief coming out to meet one of his generals returning from the war. Nay, as a fellow- soldier—one of the Ikhwan. He told me afterwards that

---

[1] ' *lu lu lu*,' from which, no doubt, is the ululu of the Dictionary, is not in Arabia, a wailing as of mourning women, but, on the contrary, a cry of joy.

he had to go out to meet Faisal in that manner ; for if he sat with his father to review the forces he would weep. He chose therefore to march into the city with him as one of his men.

A camel corps headed by a standard-bearer—always the most picturesque section of an army, even in Arabia —came marching behind the cavalry. But Faisal's army, according to the custom in Central Arabia, was disbanded on the way. For there are no accommodations, no military quarters, in the Capital or in the big cities. When a *gazu* is announced they come, the rifle-bearers, like confluent streams from the different towns and tribes to the meeting place, which is generally a watering ground; and when the *gazu* is over the booty is distributed equally among them after setting aside one-fifth of it for the State, and they return forthwith every one to his own town or tribe. But those who join the army in distant parts and those who have no home, as in the case of the three hundred odd soldiers with Faisal, they come to the Capital.

The Sultan Abd'ul-Aziz on his white charger was an intense example of concentrated energy and purpose. He could hardly rein the fiery steed for a snapshot. ' He has killed me,' he said, none the less, smiling, as he held him facing the camera. And I think he is glad that in his little journeys out of Ar-Riyadh he no longer has to ride a horse, or a camel, or endanger his life in that rickety victoria. Aye, it came when I was there, the ' trombil.' Two ' trombils,' in fact, propelled by their own benzine from Hufouf across the Summan, were in the company of a caravan of a hundred camels laden with clothes and foodstuffs from Bombay. But through the sands of the Nufoud and the Dahna they had to appeal to the ship of the desert.

Eight camels tugged at the two cars, while their engines were also doing their bit, to pull them through ;—tugged for an hour at a time and were relieved by eight others. In fact ten cases of benzine, in addition to the energy exerted by sixteen camels, were consumed in the business. But when they reached Ar-Riyadh the enamel of one of the cars had cracked and began to fall off ;—the effect, I suppose, of the sun.

Thus for the first time in the history of Najd, since the false prophet Musailamah threatened to fly in Wadi Hanifah—and was believed by some of his followers to have winged himself to Yamamah by night—the Capital of Al-'Ared turned out its population at the tooting of the horn to witness a real miracle. And beyond the city gate the Bedu crawled out of their black booths and timidly approached the jinn-propelled wonder when it stopped ; some of them dared to stand before it ; and one girl, who came with her mother, was glad to discover that it did no harm—' it eateth not human beings.' She touched it with her own hand and ran back to tell of her discovery.

Indeed, the arrival of the automobiles put every other event in shadow ; and they alone could stir up the stagnant waters in the soul of the people. They ran to see ; ran with a gesture ; ran with a gleam on their faces ; ran with a cry ! Wonder of wonders ! The Poet of the Palace, too, who was not stirred to the rhyme even by the return of the hero of Abha, came to me with a stanza, of which the following is a passable translation :

> My caravan from Bombay comes
>   Across the Dahna and the dunes ;
> And with it wondrous things, for which
>   I've waited many moons.
>   I've waited, and my hope had got the swoons.
> For when the ' trombils ' foundered in the sand,
> The Ikhwan danced a midnight saraband,
> And wished and prayed that they would never land ;
>   But my camels to the rescue went
>   And bravely saved the ' trombils '
>   And towed them to my tent.

The levity of the poet aside, I give the following, which may be of interest to motorists and political road-makers.

Most of the ground from Ojair to Ar-Riyadh, with the exception of the Nufoud—about twenty miles—and the Dahna—about twenty-five miles at its southern extremity —is level and can be made with a little expenditure quite suitable for motors.   Here and there, a ridge or a *sayl* (water bed) obtrudes ; but to the road-maker this is a trifle.   The only place where a road with ramparts has to be built—two or three inclined planes and curves—is at the *aqaba*, about ten miles from Abu Jefan, where the table-land falls into the plain of Terabi.

The Sultan Abd'ul-Aziz himself began to explore the country around Ar-Riyadh, riding every day in a different direction, east, south, and north-east mostly from twenty-five to a hundred miles.[1]   One day he was late in returning and the people were much alarmed.   The black slaves leaped to their horses and galloped out of the city in every direction ; the women came out of their seclusion ; and the Palace square was filled with an anxious multitude of both sexes.   About an hour after sunset, however, the toot of the horn was heard and everybody praised Allah. But the Sultan that evening was reprimanded by the elders for thus ' perturbing the breasts ' of his loving subjects.

A few days after the cars had arrived he invited Faisal ibn 'ur-Rashid and myself to ride with him, while into the other car were packed about a dozen children.   We were going on an outing, I realized ; for the Sultan on such occasions always takes the children—his own and the Rashids—with him.   About a hundred people that day, including the *rajajil*, accompanied us riding horse-back ; and some of them raced with us, when the speedo-meter was registering two, three, four above forty miles ; but when the Indian chauffeur, seeing a stretch before him that was as good as asphalt, increased his speed to fifty-five, the Arab bloods were left behind.

[1] After the conquest of Al-Hijaz, his aged father Al-Imam Abd'ur-Rahman came to Mecca in an automobile ; and the Sultan himself, become a road-maker, has been able to motor to Al-Medinah, and from Al-Medinah to Ar-Riyadh, and thence back to Mecca.

H.M. King Abd'ul Aziz (third figure from left)
LEAVING HIS CAR

We went in an easterly direction about ten miles from the palm-groves, till we had reached an elevation topped with a massive rock, which is carved by the storms of time into a sort of triumphal arch about twenty feet high and twenty deep. Under this arch the Sultan has his outings, of which he is very fond, particularly for the sake of the children. They were clambering joyously up the hill, when we descended from our car ; and Faisal, whom the Sultan had chafed on the way, said to me : ' Abd'ul-Aziz is dizzy.' Overhearing which, the Sultan parried with the remark : ' Faisal speaks the truth only when he says, " I am hungry." ' And as we were going up the hill he drew from his bosom a paper rolled like a scroll. ' See what is here, and praise Allah,' he said, as he unfolded it ; and Faisal, taking the sheet with his two hands, gazed at it rapturously, and lifted it to his lips. It was the picture of a girl's face—a coloured print —advertising perfumery.

After we were seated under the arch, the children were brought before him to salaam ; and there was a baby of two among them, whom the slave had carried before him on the horse. This was at that time the youngest of the Sultan's children. The others, about ten, were not all his. But he kissed them all, and pointed to four of them, saying : ' These are the children of Sa'oud (Ibn 'ur-Rashid) ' [1] ' But they are all ours—there is no distinction.'

The *rajajil*, who were preparing what was brought for the luncheon, now went around with plates of white sweet butter, and dates, and thin round loaves—leaves rather—of bread, which they call *raqiq*.[2] The butter is the best I have ever tasted, and the Najdis eat it with the dates as well as the bread.

' Nothing have we here,' said the Sultan, ' that will satisfy Faisal. He prefers the meat always—and he has

[1] See chapter XIII. p. 162.

[2] In Syria they call this bread *marqouq*, which is the past participle of the same verb : to make thin.

a fondness for heads.'   In both remarks His Highness was
punning, and he was particularly cruel in the latter.
For many years had passed since that fatal day, the day
of the famous hunting party outside of Haiel.   But he
qualified his remark after a pause, after it had its effect,
by saying : ' sheep's heads, which he pulls to pieces with
wondrous skill.'   Faisal smiled and said nothing.   But
His Highness pursued him : ' His handful of rice, *ya
Ustaz*, goes into his mouth like a cannon-ball.   He is a
hero at the spread.'   Faisal dug the *araak* [1] tooth-brush
into his mouth, rubbed it up and down, and said : ' After
all this, you will give me that picture, aye, *billah*.'   ' That
is all you deserve,' said the Sultan, throwing it over to him ;
and he with those around him stopped eating to look at
and admire the beautiful face.   Meanwhile, His Highness,
in an aside to me : ' We joke with Faisal.   But of a truth,
O my friend, he eats—he eats ! '   The repetition was in
an intense whisper.

The servants now came with big bowls of *rowb* (lactoferm), which were passed around from hand to hand.
And after the coffee was served, the Sultan called for the
race and insisted that Muhammad ibn Talal should join
it.   Muhammad reluctantly obeyed.   The entries being
only ten this time there were but three prizes ; and the
race, which started from the starting point without a
preliminary walk, was about a mile forth and back.   We
watched it from the hill-top, and the Sultan with his
binoculars was as usual the most enthusiastic spectator.
Again the Rashids won the day ; for Ibn Talal came
first and Ibn Mit'eb second.

About that time some one whispered a word into the
Sultan's ear, and he announced the noonday prayer.

[1] The *araak* is a tree from which sticks as big as lead-pencils are cut and
dried and used as tooth-brushes.   The Arabs call them tooth-picks.   But
rubbed once or twice against the teeth, after peeling about half an inch of
the stick at a time, the fibres loosen up a little, and you have a hard bristled
brush.   There is something also in the wood which has the virtue of a tooth-
paste.

I walked outside the arch to the shady side and waited there till the Sultan called me. After the prayer came the last and, as usual even in Arabia, the best number on the programme. The Sultan has a magneto-electric machine which he uses as an exercise ; but he had discovered that it can also be used as an entertainment. 'Get the box,' he ordered. And forthwith it was brought, together with a metal vessel, which was filled with water and placed before him. We sat around in a circle ; and he started the performance by taking a pound sterling, showing it to us in the manner of a professional magician, and dropping it into the water, together with one of the wooden handles to which the wires are attached. Following which he asked most professionally : 'Who can take the *lira* (sovereign) out of the water ? ' No one approached. 'Take it out, and it is yours,' he continued, as he turned the crank of the machine.

A formidable black slave took up the challenge. 'Grasp at this,' said the Sultan, giving him one of the handles. 'Hold it tight. Now, with your other hand take the *lira* out of the water.' The slave obeyed ; but as soon as his fingers touched the liquid—the Sultan was still turning the crank—he jumped to his feet. We all laughed ; but the laughter of His Highness rose high and shrill above the mass. 'Who will take the *lira* out of the water ? ' he resumed. And the operation was repeated with increasing merriment. Some of those who tried trembled before the current was turned on ; and one had a trick —evidently it was not his first attempt—of dipping his hand into the water before he held tightly to the other end of the coil. But although it was nimbly accomplished, the Sultan detected it and would not give him the money. Another competitor for the prize was so dogged and determined that he would not let go ;—he could not let go ; and in his confusion he overturned the vessel and dragged the machine with him. No one volunteered to bring it back. Of a certainty, there was something satanic in it.

But the Sultan called to Ibn Talal, who got up and brought the box back to its place. He was then asked to sit near it, which he did. ' Grasp the two handles,' said His Highness. And the hero of Haiel took them both in his right hand and, with his left, quickly snatched the gold piece out of the water. ' Put it back,' said the Sultan, laughing. ' I can do that myself. You must take each handle in each hand, thus.' He did so, and the Sultan turned the crank. Ibn Talal did not let go, but heroically stood the current about twenty seconds. I tried it myself —it was not strong—and stood it well. Then Faisal and others tried it and seemed to enjoy it. After which we all held hands and shared the vibrations in a communal spirit.

But the performance was not finished. The royal magician lifted his hand and commanded attention. I was asked to turn the crank. And while I was doing so he dropped the end of one of the coils in the water, grasped the other with his right hand, and quickly with his left, without fumbling,— having previously cast a furtive glance into the bottom of the vessel,— he lifted the *lira* and held it up, in the same professional manner, before the wondering and admiring gaze of all.

Now, the last on the Programme. The Sultan turned a pin in the machine, which intensified the current, raised it to its highest point, and asked Ibn Talal to take hold of the handles in both hands. He did so, and His Highness turned the crank. I counted by my watch the seconds—five, six, seven—the young Rashid dropped the wires. Then one of the Sa'ouds took them up, but could not hold them more than five seconds. Faisal shivered and surrendered before the third. Others who tried, did not go beyond the record of Ibn Talal, did not even make it. Which seemed to annoy the Sultan. He therefore grasped the two handles, asked Ibn Talal to turn the crank, and asked me to count. After ten seconds,

—he had no doubt practised at home—I looked at his face. It was calm. Twelve, thirteen, fourteen—he still maintained his calm, but he let go the wires.

Here he was pleased to end the performance and the outing of that memorable day.

CHAPTER XVI

THE BEDU OF NAJD

THE Bedu of Central Arabia are as uncontrollable and inconstant as they are superstitious ; and being most susceptible to religious influence every ambitious leader has deemed it wiser to use upon them the sword of Allah instead of his own. Thus in the early days of Al-Islam they followed the false prophet Musailamah ; and in the tenth century they flocked under the standard of the Carmathians and, with their leader Abu Taher, entered Mecca in triumph ; but when the Carmathians were destroyed thousands of the Shi'ah of An-Najaf and Basrah, fleeing the persecution of the Baghdad Khalifs, came down to Al-Hasa, and many of their religious practices, especially the worship of saints and shrines, were introduced among the Bedu, who carried them far into Central Arabia. A sort of polytheism, a heathenism thus became rampant ; and the instruments of this polytheism, the Bedu themselves, who made the mission of Ibn Abd'ul-Wahhab inevitable, and who fought against it during his days under the Ameers of Al-Hasa and the Ameer of Ar-Riyadh Ibn Dawwas, afterward became the most bigoted votaries and the most fanatical protagonists of Wahhabism.

When Muqren, the ancestor of the Sa'ouds, ruled in Al-'Ared his authority did not extend beyond a few towns and a few tribes. Even the city of 'Uyainah, which is about twenty miles from Dir'iyah, the Capital at that time, was governed by Ibn Mu'ammar of Najd for the Benu

The Ameer Sa'oud Ibn Abd'ul-Aziz Ibn Sa'oud,
Governor of Ar-Riyadh

Khalid Ameer of Al-Hasa. But Muhammad ibn Sa'oud ibn Muqren and Muhammad ibn Abd'ul-Wahhab were contemporaries who saw the wisdom of becoming allies. Ibn Abd'ul-Wahhab needed a sword for his unitarian faith, and Ibn Muqren needed a new faith to sharpen upon it his sword of conquest. The two met and agreed. After which began the establishment among the Bedu of the creed of the one and the authority of the other. It was the sword of the great Sa'oud, however, which conquered almost all of Arabia in less than a score of years, and·spread Wahhabism in the cities and in the tribes from Wadi 'd-Dawasir to Haiel and from Al-Hasa to Asir.

But I have said that the Bedu are inconstant, ever shifting withal ;—flyaways who have no pockets in their garments nor in their hearts ;—brigands or brothers of the road for a day. Allah himself, sans houris, cannot hold them. They touch and go, defiling, despoiling, destroying. And with a grand gesture they call upon Allah to witness their impeccability. Him they forget not and betray not —his name is ever on their lips, even in the most villainous exploits—and though they forget and betray the whole world. But religion is not Allah. To their superstitious souls religion is a garment which they may wear right side out, or inside out, or both sides out, if they are unduly constant, and then about the time of the summer solstice cast it away. Even so their allegiance to this ameer or that ; for are they not all Arabs, the ameers, and living in the boundless land of the 'Arab ? [1] What to the Bedu, therefore, is the difference between Ibn Sa'oud and Ibn 'ur-Rashid ? And what though the Prophet Muhammad chide them in the Book. ' We believe,' said the Bedu, in one of the Suras of the Koran. ' Say not, We believe,' said the Prophet ; ' say, We have become Muslems ; for ye are not capable of belief.' Thus, even in the days of the First Arab in History, they took their religion left-handedly. Hence their recurrent apostasy. Their

---

[1] 'Arab is the plural in Arabic of the singular 'Arabi.

oath of allegiance, too, is a lip-flower which may wilt in
a day. Hence their recurrent treachery.

After the death of the Great Sa'oud many of the tribes
who had become Wahhabis renounced their faith and,
consequently, their allegiance ; and from the days of the
first Abd'ul-Aziz—more than a hundred years ago—till
the days of his namesake and descendant the present
ruler, the Bedu have always been an intangible element,
evasive, elusive, mysterious ; a rifle in the service of the
Ameer to-day, a dagger in his back to-morrow ; soldiers
of the *jehad* where there is loot and security ; while in
times of danger they are but poor sick armless mortals
hugging the peace of Allah in their booths of hair. Let
them hear the ring of gold, however, and they will swarm
forthwith like flies around a leg of mutton. And they
will fight for Allah and Ibn Sa'oud—provided the loot
is big and the danger is small. In their recurrent defec-
tions and apostasies during the past hundred years they
had also drifted from the unitarian faith—even from
Al-Islam—and had become again heathenish or frankly
irreligious.—Why should we perform our ablutions ? We
need the water to drink. Why should we fast in Ramadhan ? The whole year to the Bedu is a Ramadhan.
Why should we pray ? Allah, who manages the affairs
of the 'Arab and the 'Ajam,[1] hath no time to hear us.

So Ibn Sa'oud Abd'ul-Aziz found the Bedu of Najd
when he appeared on the stage of modern history. They
were the most elusive, the most exasperating, and in
some instances the most implacable enemies. They
fought against him with Ibn'ur-Rashid ; they were
instigated against him by Ibn'us-Sabah ; they allied
themselves against him with his own kinsman the once
captive Sa'oud, whose mother is of the 'Ujman tribe ;
and some of them, the Qahtans in southern Najd, for
instance, and the 'Ujmans in Al-Hasa, waged war against

[1] The 'Ajam (pl. of 'Ajami) are the Persians ; but to the Arabs all the
non-Arab people of the world are 'Ajam, that is foreigners.

him on their own account and would not submit to his authority till he had humbled them in the dust. But apostasy, treachery and desertion were always anticipated ; and they always recurred. Indeed, the Bedu robbed Ibn Sa'oud of many a night's sleep. They were the most difficult problem which in his career of conquest he had to solve. And he solved it.

He solved it in an original manner along modern lines. And herein is Ibn Sa'oud the Sultan Abd'ul-Aziz a reformer, whose like Arabia has not seen since the days of the Prophet. Even the Prophet Muhammad did not conceive of the reform which was accomplished in these modern times in Central Arabia. Three things had to be done to bring the Bedu within the pale of authority, to keep them there, and to make them behave :—three things, two of which had been tried by his great predecessors and were only temporarily successful. So he would add a third. He would (1) conquer the Bedu ; (2) make good Wahhabis of them ; and (3) chain them to the soil.

The work of conquest and that of proselytising went practically hand in hand, although the one sometimes preceded and sometimes followed the other. Having thus brought the flyaway miscreants back to law and to religion, he conceived of domesticating them to keep them under control. If the beduin sold his camels, and lived under a roof, and had a patch of land to cultivate, he would become more amenable to authority and more respectful of the law. So the work of domestication started with the building of new towns. Every tribe or section of a tribe was allotted an area of land near a water-spring, where the sheikh moved with his people, raised mud-walls and roofs, and began their new life by tilling the soil.

These new towns are called *hijar* (pl. of *hijrah*=emigration), that is, their inhabitants have emigrated from the desert, from nomadism, and settled down to an agricultural life. The devotees have another interpretation :

the *hijar* are havens of faith and salvation ; those who have
settled in them have emigrated from the world to God.
They have been inspired, or persuaded, or forced to do
so by the Wahhabi missionaries (*motawwa's*), every one
of whom is a Peter the Hermit. They
are saturated with the unitarian faith,
fired with the militancy of it. And
Wahhabism, the simplest form of religion, has always appealed to the
Bedu, who scarcely know the fundamental principles of Al-Islam ; for
although they know not how to make
their ablutions properly or how to pray,
they can say, at least, that Allah is
one, alone, unassociated with any prophet or saint, and that is sufficient.

A MOTAWWA'
(WAHHABI MISSIONARY)

These recent recruits to Wahhabism, the emigrants of
Allah, are the material of which the Ikhwan are made.

But a difficulty presented itself. In the western part of
Central Arabia big sections of the two important tribes,
Harb of Al-Hijaz and 'Utaibah, embraced Wahhabism,
sold their live stock and settled on the soil. The selling
of the camels was first encouraged, nay ordered, because
it argued against the nomad life and helped to make
converts for a religion and a roof. But these new converts
were always more eager to fight for their faith than to
cultivate the soil which they had acquired. And when
there was no *gazu* they did nothing but pray. The
hijrah became a hermitage ; and the Sultan Abd'ul-Aziz
realized that a burden of idleness and poverty, worse in
its concentrated form, was threatening his State. So he
got his Ulema busy. And they searched the Hadith and
the Commentaries for sayings and traditions sanctioning
wealth. After which the *motawwa's* were sent forth.
Now that the converts are under roofs you may initiate
them into the second degree of urban or agricultural life.
They, therefore, persuaded them to hold on to their

The Author in Najd Dress

lawful wealth, and urged upon them the necessity of work to conform to the tradition : *A rich believer were better than a poor believer.*—Abu Bakr the first Khalif did not disdain wealth. He had eight thousand horses and camels. And why should Allah deny any of you, the true believers, the unitarians, the bounties he bestowed upon Abu Bakr ? But you must work. And you may trade, even as did the Prophet, peace upon him ! But to trade, you must have stock and you must have provision. Turn ye then to breeding and to cultivation, and you will all become rich believers, *inshallah.* The argument had its effect.

About seventy *hijrahs*, with a population of from two to ten thousand each, have sprung up after the Wahhabi revival in about ten years ; and some of these new towns have become successful rivals, as centres of trade, of their old neighbours. Irtawiyah, for instance, which prides itself on being the first *hijrah*—it is in Al-Qasim east of Buraidah and was built in 1912—is now the biggest and most flourishing settlement ;—an important grain centre in the neighbourhood of the Dahna. Likewise is Dukhnah west of Al-Qasim and Gatgat in Al-'Ared south-west of Ar-Riyadh. But the Arabs of those new towns—the Mutairs of Irtawiyah, the 'Utaibas of Gatgat, and the Harbs of Dukhnah—are most warlike and fanatical.

Indeed, the *gazu* instinct is still very strong even in ' the emigrants of Allah '—the *hijrah* Arabs. It takes more than a settled population to eradicate it ; which the Sultan Abd'ul-Aziz does not, perhaps, deem necessary at present. ' The next emigration for the people of the *hijrahs*,' I said to him once, ' will be from ignorance to education.' ' Everything will come in its time,' he replied. Like Al-Yaman, Najd is without schools ; but unlike Al-Yaman, it is without any industry. If a new generation were given an elementary education, they might prefer the loom to the rifle, and then be able to make their own *abas* at least. Al-Yaman, in this sense, is much more advanced.

Every one of the new towns has a *hima*, or pasture ground ; and the population might now be divided, like that of the city, into three classes ; the majority, however, are the Bedu who have become farmers ; then there are the *motawwas'* (missionaries, priests) and the merchant class. But for military purposes, although the division is also into three classes, it is different. The first class are those who are ever ready, with rifle and *zelul*, to respond to the call—the jehad ; the second class are the reserves, who in time of peace are herdsmen and journeymen ; while the third class of the male population are those who remain in the towns to keep up its trade and agriculture. Even these are likely to be called to arms. This triple division, in other words, corresponds to what is generally known as the regulars, the reserves, and the recruits, or what the Turks call the *nazam*, the *radif*, and the *nafir*. In Najd it is the Sultan's right to call out the first two classes ; but the *nafir*, or mobilizing the civil population, is announced by the Ulema when the country is in danger.

It is a fact, however, that the Bedu, even of the *hijrahs*, sometimes get tired of waiting for a call ; and they sally forth, the *gazu* instinct asserting itself, on their own account. One day a party of six, their *gutrahs* drawn across their faces, covering the mouth and nose, came galloping into Ar-Riyadh, crying out, Praise be to Allah ! and firing their guns in the air. They descended at the gate of the Palace, where they were met by one of the assistants of the Master of Ceremony, who wrote their names and the purpose of their visit on a slip of paper and sent it up to the Sultan. They had come all the way from a *dirah* near Al-Hijaz bringing joyous tidings. Their people had defeated in a great battle the soldiers of King Husein (the great battle was likely a fight between the herdsmen of the *dirah* and the sentries on the border), and they had come to report and—incidentally—get a largess.

When I asked the Sultan about them, he said in a bored manner : ' Bedu—they come every day—a quarrel or a raid, one or two killed on both sides, some camels and sheep taken as booty. And they come here firing their *bundoqs* and troubling our head.' They are, nevertheless, received as conquerors, and, after a week or a month of hospitality in the Capital, they go back to their distant *dirahs* with royal gifts of clothes and money.

It is preferable, I think at times, to give an account of a certain matter, in this strange Wahhabi polity, together with the Sultan's reaction to it, instead of boring the reader always with an analytical study of motive and purpose. Here then is a case of what I might call acute Wahhabitis, on which the Sultan sheds some light. When the *Life of the Prophet* was being read in the grand *majlis* one evening—the reader utilized to the utmost his dramatic powers—a beduin in the audience uttered a cry and leaped to his feet. ' Allah, Allah ! ' and with his hands in the air he rushed at the hall-clock, which hung against the central pillar ; but before he could do it any damage, he fell prostrate on the carpet. I was sitting near Ameer Sa'oud, the Sultan's son, who, presiding at that reading, ordered the reader to stop. And the victim was carried out, groaning and uttering through his teeth unintelligible things. The audience dispersed with little or no concern. I ventured to suggest some cold water. No : it was sacrilege to interfere. The hand of Allah was upon him—a state of bliss devoutly to be wished for.

But the poor man was in an apoplectic fit, and he continued to pant and froth at the mouth. I continued to suggest cold water, and one of the black slaves daring to heed was also daring enough to interfere with the work of Allah. He applied the cold water to the man's face, who instantly came to ; and his feverish lips instinctively found the edge of the vessel. He must have been very thirsty ; for he gulped down the water and seemed after that quite well.

Now the Sultan, coming in at that moment, was told of the incident, and he spoke thus : ' It is the Ikhwan spirit—a wonderful thing is their zeal and devotion. Often it happens during the reading, when the name of Allah or Al-Jannat or Juhannan is pronounced, that they sob, they cry out, they faint, and some of them struck with the divine grace die at the moment.' The Sultan spoke in a matter-of-fact manner and was not moved in the least by his son Sa'oud's recital about the matter.

But in a different accent, it seemed to me, did he later at my apartment tell us more about the Bedu.

' The Arabs of the North,' he said, ' are heavy of foot and stolid ; the people of Najd are quick, light, wiry. They snap and break not. Like our camels. The *zelul* of the North is strong but slow ; that of the south is fast, although he has not so much enduring power. But the people of Najd are like the Bedu in hardship and adversity. We train ourselves in endurance. We put up with much that is hard and onerous. It is our land, our habit of life, our destiny—all one. We have to be always ready and fit. I train my own children to walk barefoot, to rise two hours before the dawn, to eat but little, to ride horses bareback,—sometimes we have not a moment to saddle a horse—leap to his back and go ! This is the Najdi— the Najd spirit—the Najd condition of life. Especially the Najdis of the South—we are like our Bedu in this.

' The people of Al-Qasim are traders and are not, therefore, so hardy and brave as the people of Al-'Ared or the Bedu of the Kharj country. There in the south are the hardest and most truculent of the Bedu ; the Benu Murrah and the Dawasir are savages. In their quarrels they thrust their *jambiyahs* (daggers) into each other, and draw them out exultantly '—the Sultan illustrated the following by drawing his finger across his teeth—' and lick the blood. They are madmen in the fight. Bravery is something common among the lowest of them. In the days of peace they come to us for every-thing—food, clothes, money. But in times of war the poorest and meanest among them makes not a demand. It is a shame with the people of Najd to ask for anything when we are at war or on a *gazu*. They gather up their own, pull down the *bundoq*, saddle the *zelul*,'—here he snapped his fingers. 'Our little serves much during war. We used to go four or five days without food— just a date to suck at for a little nourishment and moisture.'

He described graphically how he and a handful of his men, after going three days without food, sat one evening in a village to a meal prepared for them by the poor sheikh. They ate voraciously. 'But after I had my fill,' said His Highness, 'I smelt something bad—very strong. I looked around—nothing. I bent a little over the dish —it came from the dish—the noisome smell !' He had to get up and run out to throw up the meal.

Once they rode thirty hours at a stretch without dismounting ; for they had to occupy a certain spot, which was also the objective of the enemy, who would prevent them from taking possession of the wells. It was a race for the water. 'A thousand camels on the march—a brisk, even pace—the murmur and buzz of the motion—the squeak of the saddles—a concrete body, moving, moving like a stream of water down a slope, without a single pause.' The Sultan held out his hand and moved it in a vibratory motion to illustrate the march. It was a dramatic recital. Of a certainty, the Sultan Abd'ul-Aziz, as I have already said, has dramatic powers. His gestures are most effective ; never exaggerated or redundant. And his long white staff contributes nobly to the performance. He strikes the ground with it, when he wants to emphasise a point ; he leans his head upon it when he wants you also to ponder ; and he holds it across his knees to crown an eloquent pause.

Often, after those delightful evening hours, my mind would revert in comparison to the other Arab rulers I have known. There is a smugness in the Imam Yahia, an unctuousness in the Idrisi atmosphere, an incontinent complacency in King Husein ; but in this Ibn Sa'oud, the bluff and breezy manner is always charming. And his sincerity I have never had any cause to doubt. Hence the difficulty in understanding at times his attitude towards certain matters pertaining to the Bedu and the Ikhwan. But there is nothing vague or inconsistent in the following, which is his reply to my question of how he manages to keep the Bedu under control.

' We raise them not above us,' he said, ' nor do we place ourselves above them. We give them when we can ; we satisfy them with an excuse when we cannot. And when they go beyond their bounds we make them taste of the sweetness of our discipline.'

A LIST OF THE *HIJRAHS* (NEW SETTLEMENTS) OF THE DIFFERENT TRIBES OF NAJD, WITH THE QUOTA OF FIGHTING MEN OF EACH TOWN

Note.—The quota given is, as a rule, one-third of the male population, or those who respond to the first call—the jehad.

THE MUTAIR TRIBE		THE RUQAH SECTION OF THE 'UTAIBAH TRIBE	
Name of Town.	No. of Men.		
Irtawiyah - - -	2000	Name of Town.	No. of Men.
Imbayedh - - -	1000	Gatgat - - -	2000
Fraisan - - -	1000	Ad-Dahna - - -	2000
Mulaih - - -	700	As-Sawh - - -	300
Al-'Imar - - -	700	Sajer - - - -	800
Al-Ithlah - - -	1000	'Arja - - - -	2000
Al-Irtawi - - -	600	'Usailah - - -	300
Miskah - - -	800	Nifei - - - -	1500
Dhuraiyah - - -	800		
Ash-Shi'b - - -	400	THE BARQAH SECTION OF 'UTAIBAH TRIBE	
Qariah the Upper -	1500		
Qariah the Lower -	1000	'Urwah - - -	1000
Sudair - - -	700	As-Sanam - - -	1000
Nukair - - -	1000	Ar-Rawdah - -	700

THE HARB TRIBE

Name of Town.	No. of Men.
Dukhnah - - -	2500
Ash-Shubaikiyah -	1000
Ad-Dulaimiyah - -	1000
Al-Qorain - - -	700
As-Sadeqah - -	600
Hulaifah - - -	300
Hunaizal - - -	700
Al-Buroud - - -	1000
Qibah (pronounced J'bah) - - -	2000

SHAMMAR

Al-Jafr - - -	2000
Rowdh'ul-'Uyoun -	1000

HUTAIM

Binwan - - -	1500

AD-DAWASIR

Mushaireqah - -	1500
Al-Wusaitah - -	800

AL-'UJMAN

As-Sirrar - - -	2000
Hunaiz - - -	1000
As-Sihaf - - -	800
Al-'Ujair - - -	700
'Urairah - - -	1300

THE QAHTAN TRIBE

Name of Town.	No. of Men.
Al-Hayathem - -	1800
Al-Jufair - - -	300
Al-Hisat - - -	800
Ar-Rayn the Upper -	2000
Ar-Rayn the Lower -	2000

IN THE KHARJ

Adh-Dhubai'ah - -	800
Al-Bida' - - -	800
Al-Munaisef - -	600
Al-Akhdhar - -	500
Taibism - - -	400
Ar-Ruwaidhah - -	400

AL-'AWAZIM

Thaj - - - -	1500
Al-Hasi - - -	1000
Al-Hannat - -	1000
Al-'Atiq - - -	700

BENU MURRAH

Benak - - -	1000
Ubaireq - - -	1500

BENU HAJIR

'Ain Dar - - -	1000

There are also several *hijrahs* of the two tribes of As-Suhoul and Subai'.

CHAPTER XVII

THE ULEMA OF NAJD

THE Ulema are the power that holds the Sultan and his people together—the medium of control. But they seldom meddle in politics ; their chief and sole concern, it seems, is to see that the Five Pillars of Al-Islam—prayers, the *zakat*, the *hajj*, the fast of Ramadhan, and the testimony that there is no God but Allah—are maintained inviolate, strictly in accordance with the Koran and the Sunnat. It may also be said that to the Wahhabis the Sunnat is as essential as the Koran, not only in their daily religious practices but in all the business of life.

How the Prophet Muhammad lived :—what he said and did ;—from the broadest rule to the minutest detail of conduct ;—from the loftiest to the most frivolous ;—how, for instance, he prayed and how he trimmed his beard and his finger nails—that is the Sunnat. The Wahhabi lives and dies by it. Everything he says and does he must be able to justify by the Sunnat or the Koran, —more by the Sunnat, in fact, than the Koran. He bows the head only to Allah—Sunnat. He wears no silk garments—Sunnat. He decorates not the mosques—Sunnat. He kisses not the hand of the Imam or the Sultan —Sunnat. He associates with Allah, in his prayers, no prophet or saint or other mortal. Said the Prophet Muhammad : ' Say not, " By the help of Allah and the Prophet," but say : " By the help of Allah *and then* the Prophet." ' Which finds its application in the daily speech of the Wahhabi. ' Were it not for Allah and then

for thee (the Sultan) we would have lost the battle.'
Writes the Master of Ceremony in his daily list : ' So
and so has arrived and he desires of Allah *and then* of thee
(the Sultan) a *busht*, a *zuboun*, and some coffee and rice.'
How the Wahhabi Ulema receive and verify the Sunnat,
however, I shall tell in another chapter. Suffice it here
to say that they are the guardians of it as well as of the
Book ; and the Sultan is the first to acknowledge this
right and to accept, within its province, their decrees.

Beyond that they seldom go : beyond that the Sultan
has *carte blanche*. He may make a dozen treaties with
infidel Powers ; he may call the people to a *gazu* or a
jehad, as the case may be, whenever he deems necessary ;
he may grant a concession to an infidel corporation to
exploit the oil and mineral wealth of the country : but
he cannot with immunity change a tittle in the Koranic
law or directly abrogate, even modify, a religious custom.

At the beginning of his career the Sultan Abd'ul-Aziz
got the leading Ulema and the chiefs of the tribes together
and addressed them thus : ' You owe nothing to me,'
this, to the chiefs : ' I am like you, one of you. But I am
appointed to direct the affairs of our people in accordance
with the Book of Allah. Our first duty is to Allah and
to those who teach the Book of Allah, the Ulema. I am
but an instrument of command in their hand. Obedience
to God means obedience to them.' A shrewd and subtle
policy of control and command. The Ulema were
pleased, the Chiefs of the tribes, whose *amour-propre* was
thus saved, were pleased ; and the people, urbans and
Bedu, gave willingly, religiously, their undivided allegiance
to the unseen power through the Ulema and the Chiefs.

Yes, the Najd Government is a theocracy at the head
of which is an Imam, who is supposed to be controlled
by the Ulema. As long as the cardinal principles of
Wahhabism are preserved, however, there is no control
and no friction. But the harmony between the white-
turbaned gentry and the sandaled Sultan ; the implicit

obedience of the people, whether it is expressed direct or
through a spiritual medium ; and the peace and prosperity of the State, arising from both and resting upon
both—these sometimes suffer from the zealotry of the
Ulema or the insurgency of the Bedu.

At the beginning of the proselytising movement some
of those who were converted undertook on their own
account, for both worldly and otherworldly reasons, to
convert others.   Which meant that they slew whoever
refused the unitarian faith and carried away his live
wealth.   Had this state of anarchy and rapine been allowed
to spread, the theocratic system would have been nipped
in the bud and the Wahhab-Sa'oud partnership would
have failed.   But the proselytising, murdering, plundering
Bedu offered, in justification of their conduct, one of the
principal articles of their creed.   It is the duty of a Wahhabi to wage a *jehad* against the *mushrekin* (all non-
Wahhabi Muslems).   The Imam could not deny that ;
but he must subject it to Government control.   So he
convenes the Ulema, and puts to them the question [1] of
whether a recent convert has a right forcibly to convert
others.   Not unless he is ordered by the *motawwa'* was
the answer.   Hence the decree, based upon this decision,
which was immediately obeyed.

The *motawwa'* is third in the order of the Wahhabi
hierarchy, the first being the Imam, the second the
Sheikh.   The word literally means, broken into obedience,
—one taught obedience to Allah.   The Sheikh (one of the
Ulema) gives out decisions in religious matters and the
Koranic law ; the *motawwa'* teaches the people the practical side of religion—how to make one's ablutions, how
to pray, what to read from the Book at the different
prayers, etc.   He is also an agent of the Imam, that is the
Sultan, in both civil and religious matters,—in such matters
rather, as are (1) originally, or (2) executively of a civil

---

[1] These questions, upon which the Sultan bases his decrees in religious
matters, are sometimes so worded as to elicit the desired answer.

and religious nature. An example of the first is the *zakat* money, which the *motawwa's* collect from the Bedu and from the inhabitants of the new settlements, *hijrahs*; an example of the second is the forementioned decree, which was sent to them for enforcement.

A MOTAWWA'

But both the Ulema and the *motawwa's* often in their zeal overstep the bounds of reason, and the Imam has to interfere. Flogging, however, not only for smoking cigarettes and failing to go to the mosque but for other heinous offences, often takes place in the Capital. I have witnessed one such. Two sword-bearing blacks, with palm-sticks, ribs, newly cut, led to the public square a bearded man, made him lie on the ground, flat on his bosom, and standing on either side (other sword-bearing blacks kept back the crowd), they started to thwack him across the bareback. The blow, according to the law, must not be so strong as to cut nor so light as not to be felt. So they applied the palm, one on each side, varying the direction of the blow, while another man counted. The crowd watched with grim satisfaction. And when sixty was reached, the thwacking stopped. But some one cruelly added : Allah lead thee in the right path ! Sixty thwacks for smoking a cigarette.

There was a trial of course, and the evidence was conclusive. The Wahhabi judge is very strict, and according to his light very just. He can also be lenient to first offenders, whether in smoking or remissness in prayer. But even in Ar-Riyadh, outside of the exclusive Ulema quarter, Mahallat'ush-Sheikh,[1] one may smoke secretly, of course, and at ease. When he is detected, however, and the case is proven against him by sworn

[1] The Quarter of *the* Sheikh, that is Ibn Abd'ul-Wahhab, the founder of Wahhabism, where live his present-day descendants, most of whom are of the Ulema class.

witnesses, he is consigned without hesitation to the blacks, who enforce the decision in the public square. But detections outside of that particular quarter seldom occur; and when they do, witnesses are not readily to be found. It is in Mahallat'ush-Sheikh, therefore, that the olfactories are ever keen on the scent and the informing instinct is seldom sluggish. One of the men of the Sultan's Diwan, a Saiyed from Al-Medinah, was not comfortable in the house allotted to him and was looking for another. ' I know a house that will suit you,' said His Highness, ' but it is in Mahallat'ush-Sheikh, and they are very strict there. You will have to pray in the *masjid*.'

But I was told that at every *masjid* in Ar-Riyadh there is a list-call every day, morning and evening. And when anyone of the regular attendants is absent a committee is sent to his home. If he is sick, they offer their assistance ; if he has overslept himself, they offer their advice ; if he is remiss, they pronounce a warning ; if he is absent a second time, they give him a lecture and a rating ; and if in spite of all this benign tolerance he persists in his remissness, the palm-switch is applied without hesitation or mercy.

This is the truth about the bigotry of the Wahhabis of Al-'Ared, in fact, of Ar-Riyadh,—nay, in one particular quarter of Ar-Riyadh. And the farther we move away from that quarter, from that City,—the farther from Al-'Ared, north or west, we go,—the farther we are from the bigotry of Najd Unitarianism, the strictness of its discipline, and the cruelty of its decrees.

But the Ulema of Ar-Riyadh, whom the Sultan Abd'ul-Aziz uses to consolidate his State and maintain his control over his subjects, are not frequently given to taste of ' the sweetness ' of a higher discipline. Every now and then he draws the sword of a dominating personality to keep them in their place ;—not only to check their zealotry, but to show the people, even if he has to be despotic, that they, the Ulema, are not the supreme power in the State.

That is what happened when I was in Ar-Riyadh. Three families, about thirty people, were banished from the Capital, from all Najd, by order of the Sultan.

'*Cherchez la femme*,' even in the ascetic city of Ar-Riyadh ! And my *rafiq* Saiyed Hashem was principally involved, was really the cause of the calamity. I have more than once in the preceding chapters alluded to the man's distracted state. He sorely wanted to get married. His work in the office corroborated his half-uttered, half-concealed desire ; and the Sultan encouraged a search. About ten days later, after setting the harim of some of his friends at work, the Saiyed came to me to say that he had discovered the most beautiful girl in Ar-Riyadh and had surrendered, through the female intermediaries, of course, his heart.

But in social affairs the genius of Ar-Riyadh has an English name :—Mrs Grundy. Now, Saiyed Hashem is of Kuwait, which is not a Wahhabi country ; which is, moreover, notorious for its immorality ; he is, therefore, a foreigner with obscure lineage—not of a known tribe or family ;—and besides, he is not a Wahhabi. He is of the *mushrekin !*—an infidel. The family of the girl hesitated, refused. But the Sultan, who was informed of the matter, sent a word to them, which they obeyed. Saiyed Hashem, therefore, proceeded in his business. The consent of one of the girl's brothers was obtained, and the *mahr* (dowry) was paid and accepted.

A week passed, during which my *rafiq*, the happiest man in the world, rented a house and acquired some furniture. But the day before the great event, alas ! he also acquired a toothache, which rounded out his cheek, and the marriage ceremony was postponed.

Meanwhile, the Capital was shaken from its lethargy by the rude hands of gossip and scandal ; and the Ulema had much to do in the matter.—What is Abd'ul-Aziz proposing ? Whereto is he leading us ? He brings the *mushrekin* among us and would marry them into our best families. We are on the way to infidelity and destruction. This must not be. Abd'ul-Aziz should be advised, should be warned, etc. This was the tenor of the protestation which reached the Sultan, and which was previously dinned in the ears of the girl's mother and brother. A change of mind followed. The big brother swore [1] that if his sister married the foreigner and infidel he would divorce his wife ; the second brother took the same oath ; and their brother-in-law did likewise. Three divorces was this marriage of Saiyed Hashem going to cause.

But they had accepted the *mahr*, which makes the refusal contrary to law. Still the Sultan did not insist. He would not cause three divorces in a family, nor would he force a marriage contract. But he would hold the mirror up to the people :—he would chastise ignorance, and bigotry, and fanaticism. And he would teach the Ulema a lesson. He was already conceding much to them.— They will lead us, he argued, to ruin and destruction if we permit them to go to the end of their sanctimonious imbecility. Here is a Muslem like themselves, even better in rank, lineage, and personal acquirements than themselves. . . . But they shall know what it means to listen to the Ulema when the Sultan desires the contrary.

The Sultan, therefore, acted immediately and summarily, as is his wont in serious matters. The two brothers, their brother-in-law, and their families were ordered not only to leave Ar-Riyadh but to leave Najd. ' If anyone of them is found in the city after sunrise to-morrow I will slay him.' He further also declared that he would accept no intercession in their favour. So they gathered their few belongings, and on the night of that day, in the spectral reflections of a new moon, they went away in the direction of Al-Hasa. The Ulema and the whole city bowed to the decree, and no one dared even to intercede.

---

[1] This oath among the Muslems is legally binding, and the divorce, which must follow, is lawful.

CHAPTER XVIII

THE IKHWAN [1]

THEY marched up and down the city square, the infantry with swords drawn, simulating a charge, followed by the cavalry. Their weapons glittered in the morning sun, and their cry : *Sami'in, lami'in !* (hearing and gleaming, *we come !*) filled the air. No drums, no bugles, not a musical instrument of any kind : only the sword and the Book. It was not the Sultan's army, however, but its raw material—the principle of its perpetuation.

The Masjid-School boys marched up and down the city square, the boy scouts, one might say, of Wahhabism ; and they were celebrating the *khatmah* [2] of one of them who had finished reading the Koran. Thus do they in Wahhabi land. A graduation is a demonstration, a rehearsal of battle. The infantry running barefoot, followed by a squad of cavalry, the Koran graduate riding among them —this is an Ikhwan army in little. And their cry : Hearing (*and obeying the call to a jehad*) and gleaming (*we come, our swords gleaming*), is the prelude to the war-cry of the Ikhwan.

It is the only form of commencement in Ar-Riyadh : and the graduate, no matter how much he excels his fellows, cannot be much different in spirit than the man I met one day in the Palace ground. I was taking a picture, when he stood before me and said : ' Take my

---

[1] *Ikhwan* is the plural of *akhu*=brother.

[2] *Khatmah*=seal, or last act or word. Hence the *Khatimah*, or closing Chapter of the Koran, with which the student finishes his course.

'aks (reflection).' 'Bismallah,' I replied, pointing the camera at him. 'This too,' he remarked, touching the dagger at his side. He was afraid I might leave it out. And when I snapped him he walked away saying to his companion : 'He took the dagger in the *'aks*. I would have it in his heart.' This is characteristic of the Ikhwan spirit. He is a true brother !

And the Ikhwan, the roving, ravening Bedu of yesterday, the militant Wahhabis of to-day, are the white terror of Arabia. They wear a shirt of cotton sheeting, often unbleached, with long tapering sleeves ; a *gutrah*, which they throw carelessly over their heads, folding it sometimes around the neck ; and seldom an *ighal*. Their arms ? Just a rifle, which may be of any European make, old or new ; and their ammunition they carry in cartridge belts and bandoliers.

The *motawwa's* go in white shirts also, over which they sometimes wear a *busht ;* and instead of throwing the *gutrah* loosely over their heads, they wind over it a strip of white cotton cloth, two-fold at the most, in the form of a turban. But it often looks as if the man had tightly bound his head to alleviate a headache. This white band, however, is the distinguishing mark of a *motawwa'*. But they all carry sticks or staffs, from the Sultan down to the lowest of the Thespian-voiced Bedu ; and most of them go barefoot. The few sandalled ones, in travelling, carry their sandals in their packs or in their saddle-bags.

But that symbol of Arab dignity and pride, the stick, is never discarded. They even go into the *majlis* of the Sultan with it, and use it, as the Sultan himself, to indicate their mind.

In days of peace, scarcely anyone in Najd carries arms ; only when travelling, the rifle in its case is slung behind on the *gazalah* of the camel saddle. No, not one have I seen, on my way from Ojair to Ar-Riyadh, shouldering a gun. The standing army in this sense is not in

An Arab of the Ikhwan with a Falcon

Reefs along the Persian Gulf

evidence, as it is, for instance, in Al-Yaman. But when a *jehad* or a *gazu* is announced the rifle as well as the *zelul* is ready.

And they dash forth, the Ikhwan, streaming and gleaming, *sami'in, lami'in !* seeking the heads of the *mushrekin ;*—bent on making brothers by the swords,— frantically fanatical Unitarians—Puritan Copperheads ! And the Sultan Abd'ul-Aziz is a Cromwell in the sense that he has made these people and fired them with un-extinguishable enthusiasm for Allah and for Najd. He has imbued them with the spirit of conquest ; he has led them to battle and taught them sacrifice. About them are related, by friend and foe, strange heroic deeds and rare stoic achievements. Also unspeakable atrocities. The demons of religion they are called by some ; the heroes of Al-Islam, by others.

It is their faith, a living, glowing, flaming faith, which makes the blood of a brother fallen in battle sacred in their eyes. Through it they behold Al-Jannat ; and with pious ecstasy they put their fingers in the wound and stain the edges of their garments—The winds of Al-Jannat are blowing ! Ye seekers, in haste for the sowing ! Ye seekers, in haste for the mowing !

They are all fond seekers—seekers of Al-Jannat and the houris. Indeed, however pure, and simple, and lofty is this Wahhabism, this Najd Unitarianism, there is nevertheless in it that element of gross sensuality which permeates Al-Islam. The Ikhwan complex is not much different in this sense than that of the mullas of An-Najaf or the Saiyeds of Al-Yaman. Their spiritual system is infiltrated with *Huri*-ism. Their Allah, beyond a certain spiritual Nadir, becomes a sort of Hotel Manager in Huridom. It has never occurred to any of them, nor even to their great teacher Ibn Abd'ul-Wahhab, that the as-sociation of Al-Jannat and the Huris with Allah, vitiates in practice at least the very idea of unity and oneness. But they will tell you—the Ulema, I mean—that they

worship but Allah ; that reward is not desire ; that
desire is not devotion ; but that devotion and realization
may become one in the *jehad* as soon as one falls dead in
battle, and later separate.   I have talked with some of
the Ikhwan and found such reasoning beyond them.
They fight for Allah of course, but the reward is uppermost in their mind ; and even when they realize that the
fight for Allah is also for Ibn Sa'oud, the reward—the
booty—is nonetheless uppermost in their minds.

Herein Ibn Sa'oud the Sultan Abd'ul-Aziz also has
penetrated into the heart of the matter ; for he has
subjected to the strictest discipline the gathering and the
distribution of the booty of war.   Not one of the Ikhwan
ever dares to conceal anything, no matter how valuable
or trivial.   After the sacking of a town or the taking of a
gazu party, they come with the booty—valuable things,
money, live wealth—and lay it before the Sultan or one
of his generals for common distribution ;   and every
brother, *motawwa'*, beduin or other Arab receives his
share of four-fifths of it, the other one-fifth going to the
Imam or the State.   That is the Koranic law.   No
partiality, no favouritism is shown ; no special advantage
or privilege does anyone, not even the Imam, enjoy.   It
was the way of the Prophet Muhammad ; and it is the way
of the Sultan Abd'ul-Aziz.   This equality of treatment,
as well as the democratic spirit that prevails in the rank
and file, tend to keep the Ikhwan always fit and ready—
ready at any moment to die for Allah and Ibn Sa'oud.
Indeed, theirs is an unextinguishable flame of faith and
loyalty.   But is there anything else ?—a soul with any
feeling in it for one outside the fold ?—a mind with any
reasoning quality no matter how thin ?   Take Nawwar,
a fair specimen of the species.

He had a camel, which at an evil moment he hired to
a servant in the Palace who wanted to accompany us to
the Qasim.   So we had two companions ; for Nawwar
tramped behind his camel and now and then rode behind

THE 'ARFAJ IN THE DESERT

A FEW OF THE IKHWAN

his customer, who was a *zkirt*.[1] Now once a *zkirt* is in
the open desert he will light his pipe and raise his voice
in song ; and singing as well as smoking is banned in Najd,
especially in the new settlements, from one of which
comes Nawwar. But our *zkirt* would sing, and all that
Nawwar could do was to repeat the CXIII Sura of the
Koran—*I fly for refuge unto God from the evil things he hath
created*, etc. But when he saw him light a pipe he leaped
to the ground, exclaiming, ' Deliver us, O God, from
the devil ! Deliver us, O God, from hell-fire ! '
Every one laughed, but he continued to repeat the invocation.

Otherwise, Brother Nawwar was a good *rafiq*, a silent,
energetic, and very obliging man. He helped the servants,
he took the camels to pasture, he gathered wood, he blew
in the fire, and he ate but little. But never, throughout
the whole journey, ten days and nights, did he speak to
me or even once reply to my salaam. One day, when an
attack of fever kept me in bed and Nawwar was standing
near the door of my tent, I said in a self-pitying tone,
although my desire was just to annoy him by speaking,
' O Nawwar, I am ill to-day.' Whereupon, turning his
face towards me, he exclaimed, ' Praise be to Allah ! '
which I thought was the height of insolence ; and as
my stick was at hand, I threw it at him, hitting him in the
head. But he said nothing.

Later in the day, when I got up, I found him standing
near the fire,—' Hearken, O Nawwar, thou art a good and
pious man, and I, thy *rafiq*, am ill to-day ; and we want
to resume the march, which is not possible with illness.
Wilt thou not, therefore, mention me in thy prayer—
pray for my quick recovery ? ' He did not speak. I
continued : ' Wilt thou not pray for me, O Nawwar ? '
He remained silent. I persisted : ' I am thy brother of
the road, and I wish that thou wouldst mention me in thy
prayer.' He turned away apparently much vexed. I

[1] See Chapter XII, p. 136.

took hold of him by the sleeve—my fever was no doubt rising—and I spoke in earnest.

—'Hearken, O thou Nawwar. Thou art one, and we are fifteen. And we all smoke and sing. If thou dost not pray for me, therefore, and ask Allah for my recovery, we will slay thee, *billah!* even as Misfer has slain this sheep.'

I think he was terrified, for his lips moved, and I heard him saying : ' Allah deliver us and thee from hell-fire.' Which was the extreme of politeness on his part, and of tolerance. He did not pray for my recovery. No. But he kindly associated me in his invocation for deliverance from hell-fire. Nawwar is a true brother. And every one of the recently converted Ikhwan is a Nawwar.

But there are those whose Wahhabism is older and ·therefore milder. They salaam the foreigner, smoke occasionally in secret, sing when they are in the desert,[1] and do not blame Ibn Sa'oud for befriending the infidel Ingliz. One of these, a wealthy citizen of Ar-Riyadh, said to me : ' Syria is very progressive. The *Bedu* there are more advanced than our *hadhar* (townfolk) ; but our Islam is better than theirs. We would save every Muslem from the fire (of hell) ; but Allah, praised be he, will save whomsoever he please.' This is the sensible view.

Another class of the Ikhwan, mostly of the Mountain of Shammar, who adopted the unitarian faith during the siege, or a little before or after the fall, of Haiel, share also this view, although the motive may be either fear or interest. They are as tolerant as the Sunnis, and the new Brothers say that they are false.

---

[1] I do not think anyone in Arabia, be he a Wahhabi or a Zeidi or a Shafe'i, can resist the temptation to lift his voice in song once he is in the open desert. We were discussing this subject one evening around the coffee-fire, and one of the men told the following story about the Sultan Abd'ul-Aziz. ' We rode out of Al-Hasa with the Shioukh,' he said,—' we were about twenty—and when we entered the Dahna Abd'ul-Aziz took off his *ighal* and *gutrah* and put them in his saddle-bag. He then looked around and said : " There are no Ikhwan with us. He who has a good voice will now let us hear it." We started to sing, *wallah!* and Abd'ul-Aziz was most pleased.'

Among the men with whom I have lived two months, in my journey from Ar-Riyadh to Al-Qasim and Kuwait, were represented the three classes of the Ikhwan. Indeed, I had with me the mad Brother, the sensible, and the tolerant. Besides, one of the latter was a man of quips and gibes, who every time he lighted his pipe would take a puff and hand it to his neighbour, saying : ' Smoke, ya Ikhwan ! There is no smoke in Al-Jannat.'

But in times of war there is no difference among them. Every one is a *Warrior of Unitarianism, a Brother of those who obey Allah.* And in times of peace every one is a philosopher of the simple life ;—a stoic in endurance and submission, in adversity and pain, in poverty and piety. You meet a Brother on the road tramping barefoot, carrying nothing but a staff, the wind blowing through his tattered garment ; and he may have been walking for three days without tasting of bread or dates. You greet him, ' *Salaam alaikum !* How art thou ? ' And with dramatic accent and assurance, as if he were performing on the stage, he replies : ' In health and well-being, Allah be praised.' This is the solid virtue of the Ikhwan, nay, of all the people of Najd ; for in spite of the poverty and privation that gnaw at the heart of Arabia, they are content and satisfied. Seldom do you hear them utter a word that savours of despair, even a word of complaint.

And the Sultan Abd'ul-Aziz is in everything their Imam: the brave, the pious, the patient, the sensible, the insane —he knows them all, deals fairly with them all, uses them all, knowing the value of each, for Allah and the sovereignty of Ibn Sa'oud. In truth, he puts the different Ikhwan to their right use ;—the sensible are for service, the tolerant for commerce and foreign politics, the mad for battles of war. The case of the last class, however, becomes at times very critical. No, he cannot always keep the brothers of Nawwar under absolute control, because of the vast distances in Najd and the primitive means of communication. In a word, then, the Ikhwan are a power, a terrible power, which needs to be regulated and put under a modern system of administrative control. Otherwise, such raids as have taken place on the borders of Iraq and Trans-Jordania will always recur much to the discredit of the Government of Najd. The raid in the autumn of 1922, for instance, was not ordered or sanctioned by the Sultan ; and he did not accept the excuse of the Ikhwan of Al-Jawf for it. He had the chiefs brought to Ar-Riyadh, where he kept them in prison for three months.

They were set free when I was in the Capital and brought before the Sultan, who spoke to them thus : ' Think not, ya Ikhwan, that we consider you of much value. Think not that you have rendered us great service and that we need you. Your real value, ya Ikhwan, is in obedience to Allah and then to us. When you go beyond that you will be punished. And do not forget that there is not one among you whose father or brother or cousin we have not slain. Aye, *billah !* it was by the sword that we have conquered you. And that same sword is still above your heads. Beware, ya Ikhwan. Encroach not upon the rights of others. If you do, your value and that of the dust are the same. . . . We took you by the sword, and we shall keep you within your bounds by the sword, *inshallah.*'

CHAPTER XIX

THE RULE OF IBN SA'OUD

JUSTICE is the foundation of the State ; and of forms of justice there is that which appeals and that which repels. Both are necessary of course even in the most civilized countries ; and of both I have witnessed in Najd such examples as are rare elsewhere in Arabia. The truth is that nowhere in Arabia, outside of Najd, is the saying, *Justice is the foundation of the State,* so honoured in theory and in practice. The justice of Ibn Sa'oud ! We hear the word on sea and on land, as we travel to Najd and through it. It is the watchword of caravans everywhere the Sultan rules, from Al-Hasa to Tihama and from the Vacant Quarter to the Jawf.

In sooth, the justice of Ibn Sa'oud is but the Shar'—the Koranic law—the justice of the Prophet. The difference between the Shar' in Najd and in other Arab countries, however, is that in the former it is summarily enforced, and without favour or discrimination. The rule of Ibn Sa'oud is no respecter of persons. To the judge, as to the executioner, all the guilty heads and all the guilty hands are one. Indeed, many a right hand in the early days of the Sultan Abd'ul-Aziz's reign was cut off for petty larceny ; and many a head fell to the ground for an offence which, in other countries and under different circumstances, might have been extenuated, even pardoned. Such justice is no doubt appalling to the more civilized who live under the protection of codes which enumerate and classify crimes and misdemeanours, but are not as effective in the application, though more fruitful of pity and mercy, as the primitive jurisprudence of Najd.

I have related in a preceding chapter of a flogging I witnessed in Ar-Riyadh ; but I did not say that for two days after that I felt sick at heart. When you know the Arabs of the desert, however, and realize what margins of impunity surround their condition, you will find the summary process, the ruthless process necessary for their control. But here is a beautiful example of the justice of Ibn Sa'oud. When we were in Ojair we needed quantities of wood ; and the Bedu, knowing of the scarcity and the need as well as the exceptional circumstance—a Conference and English guests—took advantage of the situation.

One of these woodmongers with four camel loads stopped one day before the tent of the Chief Steward and asked two rupees a load. The ordinary price is half a rupee. They bargained, the cameleer and the Steward, without raising their voices, and the price was reduced to a rupee and a half. The Steward refused to buy. The woodmonger drove his camels away. The Steward called him back, offering a rupee a load. No. Five rupees for the four loads.—No, *wallah !* Life to Abd'ul-Aziz, you will give me six.

Were they bought ? No. Were they requisitioned ? No. And we needed wood for the many coffee and kitchen fires. ' Bawd of a *b'dewi !* ' cried the Chief Steward, as the cameleer switched his camels and walked away behind them. ' Were it not for the Shioukh,[1] I would have chastised him.' I can imagine what would happen if a Turkish General were camping at Ojair and his army needed wood. But, ' were it not for the Shioukh,' the Chief Steward might have acted like a Turk.

Justice is the foundation of the State ; and one of the first manifestations of justice is security. Now, hardly is

[1] The Sultan. See footnote, p. 105.

Muhammad, one of the Children of Ibn Sa'oud, with his tutor, Yousuf Yasin, Editor of the Mecca Weekly Paper, 'Umm'ul-Qora'

there in the happy lands of the Mandate, even in the big cities of Europe, such security as we find to-day in Najd. I am not exaggerating when I say this ; and I offer not my own experience as a proof of what I say.   For although I have travelled five months in the heart of Arabia, crossing twice the Dahna, once from Al-Hasa to Ar-Riyadh and once from Al-Qasim to Kuwait ; and although my bags with locks broken were with the baggage train, which was often ahead of us ; and although, among my men were several of the Bedu, nothing, not even a sheet of paper, did I lose.

But I offer not my own experience, which is exceptional, as a proof of the security that exists wherever Ibn Sa'oud has sway.   The Arabs themselves who travel in Najd testify to this.   For caravans may traverse the country of Ibn Sa'oud from one end to the other, from Al-Qatif, for instance, to Abha in Asir—about seven hundred miles— or from Wadi d'-Dawasir in the south to Wadi Sirhan in the north—about eight hundred miles—in perfect security and peace.

I gave a little example of the justice of Ibn Sa'oud, and I now give a few examples of the security that also characterizes his rule.   In the days of the Turks one could not travel in Al-Hasa without a military escort and the paying of *khuwwah* (tribute) ; and the road from Ojair to Hufouf —the principal trade route to lower Najd—was the most dangerous.   An Arab merchant had to pay tribute four or five times before he safely made the journey of forty miles.   The 'Ujman came from the South ; the Benu Murrah from the edges of the Vacant Quarter ;   the Munasir from Qatar and beyond ; the Benu Hajir from the neighbourhood of Al-Qatif and Kuwait ; the Dawasir from beyond the Dahna ;—and they all hovered around this road—the road of the merchants and wealth—and held it partitioned among them in the names of their respective Chiefs.

Even the pearl-fisheries along the coast of Al-Hasa were

not safe. The Benu Hajir and the Munasir are also good sailors and divers ;—therefore, good pirates and pearl thieves. They collected tribute from the skipper of every pearl-fishing craft that came their way or was within their reach.

But take a merchant from Bahrain who would be going to Al-Hasa for trade. Before he set foot on the Ojair coast he had to pay tribute to the 'Ujman ; from Ojair to the first palms—five miles—and fifty reals tribute to the Munasir ; from the palms to Umm'uz-Zarr—five miles and fifty reals tribute to Benu Murrah ; from Umm 'uz-Zarr to 'Alat—another fifty reals to Benu Hajir ; and so on, till the poor man reached his destination with an empty purse and if he was so fortunate alive. Moreover, much of his merchandise was often stolen. And when Turkish soldiers were sent out against these predatory Bedu they were beaten by them, taken prisoners, stripped of their belongings, and sent back naked to Hufouf. After which one of the victorious Bedu would ride into the city on a soldier's horse and have him shod under the very eye of the authorities.

Even our servant, the ' b'dewi ' Majed, he who cleaned his teeth with sand and ' pit,' would have slain me had he met me in those days, in the Nufoud, just to get my boots if I had nothing else. He himself said so to me. ' But the rod of Abd'ul-Aziz,' continued Majed, ' is long and strong. It can reach from the Gulf to Al-Hijaz.'

As we were crossing the Nufoud we saw a crouching camel, which had succumbed under its burden. In fact, it was dying, and its owner had gone to Hufouf to bring another beast to carry the merchandise. He might be gone two, three, five days ; and on his return the ravens might be picking at the carrion ; but the merchandise he will find intact. Indeed, there is more security in the desert of Arabia to-day than there is in the big cities of Europe and America. How was the miracle achieved ?

A Corner of the Sultan's Stud

By returning to the Shar', as I said, and by enforcing it with stern impartial justice.

The Sultan Abd'ul-Aziz is not alone in this. His governors imitate him, vie with him. One of these in particular has made himself famous in Al-Hasa—famous for his Roman justice. Indeed, when Abdullah ibn Jlewy, cousin of the Sultan and Governor of Al-Hasa, occupies the seat of judgment, he permits neither pity nor mercy to sit with him. He sits alone, and he deals out undiluted justice to all who come before him. The name of Abdullah strikes terror in the heart of the Bedu ; with it mothers frighten their babes. His word is law from the ends of Al-Qatif down to Wadi Jibrin in the Vacant Quarter ; and only by amputation and decapitation, with a single eye for justice, was he able to achieve this power. Quicker than his royal cousin the Sultan and more uncompromising he has made the Square of Hufouf a cradle of terror.— Take him to the Square ! And soon after, the sword of the executioner gleams, and a hand or a foot or a head falls in the lap of judgment. *Walhamdulillah !* Justice nods in approbation.

One day a nomad Arab came to complain of a boy that insulted and struck him. 'Would you know him,' asked the Ameer, ' if you saw him ? ' ' The Arab said, 'Yes.' Whereupon he ordered that all the boys of that quarter be brought before him ; and the complainant, when this was done, pointed his finger at the offender. ' He is the son of the Ameer,' some one whispered to the man, who quickly then murmured some words, which he intended as an excuse and a revocation. But the Ameer would not have it. He asked the boy if he had insulted and struck the beduin. ' Yes,' the boy replied. Whereupon he ordered one of his men to bring a green-palm switch and two others to hold the boy flat on his bosom. ' Take the switch,' said the Ameer Abdullah, ' and have your right.' The complainant refused and apologized. The Ameer then took it, and with his own hand gave his son a sound thwacking. ' If we do not begin with ourselves,' he said, ' we cannot be just to others.'

Some men of the tribe of Benu Murrah, who came one day to the Palace in Ar-Riyadh for food and clothes, departed after receiving them in the direction of Al-Hasa, and finding a drove of camels on the way made off with them. The herdsman complained to the Sultan in Ar-Riyadh, who dispatched a *najjab* to the Ameer Abdullah. And the Ameer, when the *najjab* arrived, dispatched four hundred of his men, a hundred in each direction—north, east, south, west—to search for and capture the thieves. In less than twenty-four hours they captured also the stolen camels. And when the Benu Murrah were brought before the Roman-Arab, there was a question, and there was a reply, and there was the word : To the Square !

There, before a gathered multitude, the executioner and his assistant perform their duty in a swift, ingenious, and most expert manner. The condemned is neither blindfolded nor bound ; but he is made to kneel down and watch the assistant executioner dance with a sword before him. The dance fascinates him ; distracts him (which is the real purpose of it) from the executioner who is standing behind ; and a moment after the sword-play comes the sword-work. The executioner pricks the condemned in the neck, under the cerebellum ; the condemned jerks his head forward, thereby stiffening the muscles ; whereupon, quick as a flash the sword falls, and with a single blow the head dances on the ground. A memorable event, which becomes the talk of caravans hundreds of miles away from Al-Hasa.

On the morning of that terrible day, the sword of the executioner flashed eight times in the Square of Hufouf, and eight heads of the Benu Murrah danced on the ground. . . . O thou herdsman, my camel has gone astray, hast thou seen it ?—Here is thy camel, O my Brother, grazing among my own ; come and take it.

Justice is the foundation of the State. And all the

forts which were built by the Turks in Al-Hasa are now abandoned and in ruin ; for caravans may travel eight hundred miles from east to west and eight hundred miles from north to south in Wahhabi land, praising Allah and praying for long life to Ibn Sa'oud.

CHAPTER XX

REVENUE AND RAIN AND SOMETHING
EQUALLY IMPORTANT BETWEEN

THE story is told in Al-Hasa that one of the Bedu who once
found an English sovereign bought with it in Hufouf a
box of matches. He thought it was a copper piece. But
English and Turkish pounds, although scarcely known
among the Bedu and rarely to be seen in the cities, are
kept in chests for a day of drought in Najd. The coins
that circulate are the rupee, the Marie Theresa dollar,
and a copper piece struck in Oman by one of its Sultans
of the last century. The copper piece is sovereign in the
bazaar, because for every M.T. dollar one gets sixty
coppers, each of which may be sufficient for one's daily
dates. But the Bedu value silver the most, probably
because it is more familiar to them. Of a certainty, the
chiefs receive their stipends in silver ; for he who pays,
whether the Sultan or the Sultan's Ally, must think it
wiser to divide the bounty into pieces and thus make it
seem multitudinous. When the Allies were anxious to
stop the contraband going through Kuwait to the enemy
in Damascus and Palestine, England sent Mr. Philby to
the desert with bags of silver for that purpose. Who,
indeed, but the hired Bedu can intercept the Bedu of
contrabandism ?

That was an item of revenue which Ibn Sa'oud used
as it came in those days, but did not depend upon it.
There was also the annual stipend of £60,000, which was
discontinued in 1923. Plausibly, this was a war measure ;

but it was calculated to serve a deeper and more enduring
—an exclusively British—purpose. You agree to keep
out of the coast territories—Kuwait, Qatar, Oman—says
the Treaty between the British Government and the Sultan
of Najd, and we agree to pay you so much every year.
That is the contract and the consideration. But when the
consideration ceased in 1923 the Sultan did not send his
Ikhwan to occupy Kuwait or Qatar or Oman. And the
Government of Great Britain, whatever might be said
of its ways and means, prides itself upon its judiciary and
still considers Blackstone as one of the pillars of Jurisprudence. Now, a contract—we still follow Blackstone
—without a consideration is 'a nude pact,' is void. The
Sultan of Najd has, therefore, a perfect right to occupy
Kuwait and Qatar and Oman, which he can do with
little or no fighting. But he has not done so. He has
occupied Mecca instead.

The revenues may be divided into two classes, the
certain and the contingent. Of the former are the custom-
duties, of the latter is the *zakat* in kind.

As for the *zakat* in kind,[1] live stock mostly, I cannot
better describe it than the Sultan himself. ' When we get
enough rain,' he said, ' the flocks are doubled and the
people of Najd are happy. But in years of drought they
are poor and wretched. You see the truth. We live by
the blessing (*of heaven*), while others live by money.'

Thus, as the blessing is contingent, is even sometimes
withheld, the Sultan, for the sake of his people, has to
continue his career of conquest, or enter into an alliance
with some rich power to increase his revenues. Was it
for this reason that in our political discussions he often
reverted to America—as often as he spoke of Europe as
an iron door with emptiness behind it? Not only Ibn
Sa'oud but all the other Arab rulers believe that Europe

---

[1] The *zakat* in kind is collected, as a rule, on the basis of 10%, that is
one camel or sheep out of ten ; and when one has less than ten, the pro-
portionate sum in money is substituted.

is bankrupt, is impotent, is dead. That she will recuperate, regain her moral and material strength, they cannot believe.

But America?—that is another question. Here, however, is something I have heard which is new to me. Not that I am ignorant of the work of American Missionaries, good or bad as it is ; but I have not heard before that America, both as a nation and a Government, wants to Christianize the whole world. That such an archaic notion should ever get into the head of the Government is absurd ; but that it should inspire a certain class of people to a work which is Christian in its inception, humanitarian in its results, is quite natural.

The Sultan does not always indulge as King Husein in parables. But we were all very anxious to know what had happened at Lausanne, and he was holding forth on the politics of Europe and the East. America, England, France, Germany—that is the order. The affairs of the world cannot be readjusted and peace firmly established unless America takes a hand in the matter earnestly and sincerely. Germany will then recuperate and the balance of power will be again established in Europe. That is the Sultan's idea.

But what is America doing to-day ? Where does she stand as between England and France ? He told us a story to illustrate the question. It is the custom of the Arabs at a meal that no one touches the meat before the host, who pulls it apart and gives pieces of it to his guests. Now, a blind sheikh of the Muntafiq Arabs of Iraq who loved none but his own tribe, and who often had a circle of guests at his spread, always informed himself before distributing his favours.—' Who is sitting at my right ? ' —' A Muntafiq,' some one would reply.—' Out upon thee, thou man of little worth, thou betrayer of thy friends. No morals hath a Muntafiq, nor generosity.' Saying which, he would give him a good piece of meat.—' And who is sitting to my left ? '—' A Bahri (a man from one of the coast tribes).'—'You are of an honest tribe,' he would say, waxing generous in speech, ' noble and straight-forward. You keep your pledges and honour the true and brave. Take this.' And he would offer him a bone. That is America to-day with England on her left hand and France on her right.

The Sultan then told us another story. A traveller in the East came one day upon a people who live in huts and dig their graves in front of their doors. He wrote something in his note-book and inquired of one of the inhabitants : ' You are poor, that is evident. But why do you dig your graves before your doors ? ' The hut-man replied : ' To be always near our God, for he is all we have,' And the Sultan added : ' Such are the people of Najd.'

Therefore, Allah does not forget them entirely. For to save the hut and water the grave he sends them, every now and then, a little rain. And no people in the world are so thankful for little bounties. When the sky is over-cast the Bedu especially are profuse in the praise of Allah ; and when the first drop falls they are the first to utter a cry of joy. It is, indeed, the beduin who watches the soil for the first blade of green, and the sky for the first leaden cloud ; for he it is who in times of drought suffers most.[1] His camels and his sheep begin to fall one by one, dying of both hunger and thirst. He moves to other *dirahs* (districts), but they drop on the way ; he too often shares their lot. One night it rained in Ar-Riyadh, and it was Majed the beduin boy who woke me up early in the morning to give me the glad news. He had neither camels nor sheep ; but he had the instinct of his tribe. ' Rain ! ' he exclaimed joyfully. ' Allah is bounteous, Allah is merciful.' I walked out on the roof and found the ground slightly moist. A few drops had fallen ; but the sky held forth a bigger promise, and the change in

[1] But the loss to the State is manifold. Beside the *zakat* in kind it once lost in a year of drought, the Sultan told me, seven thousand camels.

the atmosphere made that January morning unusually pleasant. The thermometer was 67 F. ; the birds were particularly demonstrative ;—there was a touch of Spring in the air. But on the following day we were all disappointed both with the thermometer and the sky.

The rain that does most good in Central Arabia is the *wasmi*, or that which falls in August and September. It revives the pasture which had been scorched by the summer sun, and offers the herd a sustenance for the autumn. The winter rains, which should follow two months after, give the country its spring. But it is the break in the long torrid season which saves the Arab of Central Arabia and his live stock. Indeed, were it not for the August and September rains, they could not hold out against a torrid season of six or seven consecutive months.

It would thus seem that the rain in Najd often solves a political problem which may otherwise baffle the statesmen of the Foreign Office in London. For if it falls in plenty and at the right time, the green pasture keeps the Arab in his *dirah*. But in a year of drought or little rain he has to move, seeking nourishment for himself and for his flock. And he has to take it wherever he finds it ;— often too he has to fight for it. Hence the raids of one tribe by another. Hence the wars between the tribes. It is often a question of life and death, and politics have little or nothing to do with it. Politics in Central Arabia are often a pretext for a raid or a war.

CHAPTER XXI

POETRY AND POLICY

NAJD is the native country of many of the ancient poets who wrote heroic verse—the *Mu'allaqat*, for instance ; and in Najd to-day the language of poetry and heroism is not extinct. It is more vigorous in the vernacular, however, for the classics are feebly echoed by the academic poet and often misquoted. Nevertheless, they are still highly esteemed, judging from the fact that they are often quoted—it must be so, if they are often misquoted—and written in ink and in lead-pencil on the walls of the *qasrs* and some of the homes I have seen. The quotations in the Palace are significant. On one of the walls of the vestibule to the reception hall, inscribed above the door, is the following couplet :

> ' Strange that a distant people should thee aid,
> When thou hast been by friend and foe betrayed.'

This is a tell-tale quotation, especially to those who are acquainted with the modern history of Najd. In it is epitomized a whole chapter of the intrigues and the treacheries, by his own kinsmen as well as by the Bedu, to which the Sultan Abd'ul-Aziz was often exposed, and against which he drew the sword and welcomed the aid during the War of a distant people. Distant, indeed, was the Ally of Ibn Sa'oud—distant in race, in country, in religion ; and nothing but policy and interest it seems could foster any relation, create any bond, between them.

As interesting, too, is the motive which prompted the

Sultan to have the couplet written at the entrance of his *majlis*. Would he thus continually remind his erstwhile enemies, taunting them with his distant friend and ally, of the dangers he has passed, the hostilities he has overcome, repeating the rhyme much in the spirit of the soldier who looks into a mirror to see his scars ? There is a melancholy in the Sultan Abd'ul-Aziz which, however, is like a hidden scar, poignantly reminiscent.

But more interesting than the couplet and the motive in publishing it, is the fact that policy and interest can overcome, even in Najd, even in Al-Hijaz, the most ingrained prejudices of race and religion. Call them national bonds and sacred ties ; but in the face of a dominant political passion or when the vital interests of a nation are at stake, they are, from the ruler's point of view, like gossamer floating in the breeze of tolerance.

At the entrance of the *majlis* there is also a quatrain which reflects a noble trait, not only in the Sultan Abd'ul-Aziz and the Ikhwan, but in all the people of Najd. It expresses really certain traditional traits of the Arab everywhere—generosity, self-respect, valour, and the love of glory and praise. I said ' traditional,' because in certain parts of Arabia they have so become. But in Najd, among the town-folk and the Bedu, the poet whom the Sultan has honoured by having his rhymes written above the door of the *majlis*, is not quoted in vain.

> ' Either a life of noble aims and deeds,
>   Which men may praise and model for their weal,
> And travellers tell about ; or death that speeds
>   The end of this rust-eaten heart of steel.' [1]

From every part of Najd they come responding to their Sultan's call and repeating the lines, or in their own

[1] Here is the literal translation :

Either a life irreproachable, praiseworthy,
Which those who travel in the mountains and the plains shall tell
    about,—
A life in which desire is fulfilled—or death
To bring repose to a heart become weak from the effect of rust.

words, the sentiment of the poet. The order goes out of Ar-Riyadh, carried by *najjabs* to the farthest ends of the Sultanate, that the rendezvous shall be at a certain well or in a certain vale at a certain day. And on that day many thousands of the Arabs—of the cities, of the new towns, of the desert encampments ;—each riding his own *zelul*, armed with his own rifle, girded with his own ammunition, and carrying his dates and a *qirbah* of water ; —at the appointed time and place they all gather around their Sultan-Imam and offer all they have, for Allah and for Najd.

' In the *jehad*,' said the Sultan, ' they ask nothing of us ; but in days of peace we have to give them everything.' I have related of the giving—the general distribution of clothes and money—in a preceding chapter ; and I have often wondered, not so much at the generosity of the man as at his confidence and trust in the Eternal and Inexhaustible Source of all bounties. Else how could he ever hope to continue in a country that has no wealth to speak of, and in a Government that has no permanent substantial revenues ? There is an autocratic-democratic, in other words, a paternal Government, which is to be sure, free from clerkship and bureaucracy, but is innocent, on the other hand, of any modern administrative method ; there is a land three-quarters of which is sand desert and gravel waste with exiguous possibilities for breeding stock ; there is a population two-thirds of which are Bedu, who in spite of the new settlements have not yet taken to industry ; and there is, at the bottom of everything, a tyrannical climate, whose summer is annihilating, whose winter is faithless, and who sends every now and then a year of drought to stab a poor nation in the back.

Nevertheless, the people of Najd are strong to-day in the strength of Sultan Abd'ul-Aziz ; they are happy in the enjoyment of the two dominant virtues of his reign— security and justice ; and they never despair, even though they see with their own eyes the rock bottom of the spring of his bounties.

These are truths devoid of poetic magnification. And if you wish the truth of the poet about this great and generous Arab I give you the line of Zuhair Ibn Abi Sulma, who must have had a prevision of Ibn Sa'oud when he wrote :

' When he beholds thee coming, he is too rejoiced to speak ;— As if thou comest with the gift which thou thyself dost seek.' [1]

There are even those who come with gifts to Ar-Riyadh and go back the richer for them ;—those who are not of the Sultan's subjects, they come from anciently distant places and tribes to make their salaam. Ibn Swait of the Dhafir from Iraq ; Ibn Mijlad of 'Aneza from Syria ; Ibn Naif of Benu Ali from Al-Medinah ; Ibn Dakhil from the Ameer Nouri Sha'lan ; Ibn Muwaishir from the Jawf ;—they all came when I was there, folding slowly the miles, travelling by night and by day, impelled by a motive of admiration or of fear—a religious or a political motive—to pay their respects to the Long-of-Days, the Sultan Abd'ul-Aziz ibn Sa'oud.

But I had almost forgotten the smallest and most distinguished of the visiting guests, a boy of fifteen, who came with a retinue of sheikhs and slaves and a gift of ten beautiful Oman dromedaries ;—came riding across the many deserts from Dubai on the Gulf to Ar-Riyadh —a distance of twenty-five marches—bringing the salaam of his father, the biggest of the sheikhs of Oman, Sultan ibn Zaied. And this son of Ibn Zaied carried a big bejewelled sword, walked barefoot, and wore, as another mark of distinction, an embroidered head-kerchief of Cashmere weave. The slaves, wearing *bushts* of flowered Indian fabric and tunics of glowing colours, were as usual better dressed than the master.

[1] Literal translation :
When thou comest to him, thou wilt see him much rejoiced,
As if thou givest him what thou art asking for.

But the *zeluls*, naturally the best of their kind, which is
the best of camelkind, were the most beautiful I had seen.
The long graceful neck, the sharp mouth and nose, the
gazelle-like head, the small hump, the long back, and the
most elegant of all her elegant lines, that of the stomach,
from the breast curving upward to the top of the hind-
legs—these are the distinguishing features of an Omaniyah, which is sold in Najd for thirty or forty pounds
sterling. What the ten *zeluls* cost the Sultan is a different
matter. Here is what I find on the gratuity list of Ibrahim
the Master of Ceremonies,[1] written in the Sultan's own
hand, under the name of Hazza' ibn Sultan ibn Zaied :

> Eight thousand rupees, seventy Pounds Sterling, twenty
> rifles, and two mares ;

and to each of his twenty-five men a suit of clothes and
a bag containing from one hundred to five hundred
rupees, according to his rank.

In the history of the Sa'ouds there was no other ruler
I think who was so generous. The Sultan Abd'ul-Aziz
does not, therefore, in his generosity try to live in accordance with an ideal expressed in the following quatrain
written above the entrance to another *majlis* in the Palace.
I said, ' an ideal ; ' but it is only a mixture of wisdom and

[1] Ibrahim ibn Jumai'ah of Haiel, who fought against the Sultan in the
war with Ibn 'ur-Rashid and is now one of the ablest and loyalest of his
men, accompanied Mr. Philby—was the Ameer of his escort—to Wadi
'd-Dawasir. So I asked him one day to tell me the story of the adventure
of ' the infidel Nisrani ' among the fierce and fanatical Arabs of the Wadi,
which Mr. Philby related in his book, *The Heart of Arabia*. His story and
that of Ibrahim are in the main the same. But the difference is between
the learned Englishman and the Arab who is nigh illiterate ;—the difference
in character deserves this footnote. It seems that Mr. Philby is hard to
manage ; and he did not realize that the Sultan had exceptionally honoured
him when he detailed the Master of Ceremonies to be the Ameer of the
escort. Ibrahim and Philby disagreed—disputed routes and schedules—
quarrelled ; and the learned Englishman in relating of this, is unkind.
He attacks the Arab, criticises him in a language which he cannot read. It
is most unfortunate. But what did Ibrahim say ot Philby ? I asked him
more than once to tell me the story of the quarrel, but he refused. All he
would say is that Philby is very irritable. ' His temper is not good. But
he is generous. He gave each of the men from four to ten Pounds.'

folly which the peoples of the Orient have always accepted
as an ideal. Nor am I justified in the generalization ; for
they have discarded in Japan, and they are fast discarding
even in China, the deteriorated and deteriorating half
of the social scheme. It is mostly in the Islamic world,
therefore, that the mixture continues with renewed force
to produce its fatal effects ; sterilizing the mind, the soul,
and the heart of its people ;—so much so that a new idea
does not nourish or refresh the mind ; a new remedy does
not appeal to the soul ; a common affliction does not
revive in the heart a communal feeling and lead the
various nations, the various tribes, at least, through the
lanes of reason and progress up to the citadel of common
defence.

I repeated one day in the *majlis* of the Sultan the
quatrain that is written on the wall outside :

> ' Although we are of a noble line,
>   We do not on our line depend ;
>   We build as our ancestors built
>   And do as they did, *to the end*.' [1]

In the first half of the quatrain, as I said to His
Highness, is solid wisdom, a noble sentiment, a good
principle of conduct ; and I honour the people of
Najd because they live up to this ideal of the poet.
Certainly, the glory and power of the Sa'oud House is
built upon it ;—the Sa'ouds are self-made and democratic ;
and we live in an age which accords to the self-made and
democratic, whether of nations or individuals, the first
place of honour. But the second half of the quatrain :

> ' We build as our ancestors built
>   And do as they did, to the end.'

Here is the gross folly. Here is the swamp from which
issue all the germs of our social, political and religious
diseases. We might even analyse these two lines, and

---

[1] By Al-Mutawakkil Al-Laithy. The translation is literal, only that the
last italicized word is mine.

A Caparisoned Zelul

concede that the idea expressed in the first line is still necessary, can still be of benefit, to the Orientals.   No, we cannot entirely and absolutely renounce the past, and there is no harm in building as our ancestors built—in having, for instance, monarchical governments. . . .   The Sultan : ' We build, *ya Ustaz*, as our ancestors built ; but we do more than they did.'—' Thou hast said well, O thou Long-of-Days.'   Wilt thou, therefore, order that the verse be corrected so as to read :

> ' We build as our ancestors built
> And do *more* than they did, to the end.'

It will then re-light in the people of Arabia the flame of a new life.   The reverence for our ancestors is not complete unless it is coupled with a striving to surpass them— to prove ourselves worthy descendants.   For consider what they achieved in an age deprived of the scientific instrumentalities of progress which distinguish our own ; and consider what they *would achieve* if they were in our place and time.

The Sultan Abd'ul-Aziz is considering all these things, and is conducting his affairs in the light of such consideration.   He has already in reconquering the kingdom of his fathers, in fortifying it with justice and security, and in the revival of Wahhabism, which is the source of both, justified himself in saying, *We build as our ancestors built*. Moreover, in establishing the *hijrahs* and securing the Bedu on the soil ; in utilizing the talents of those around him, irrespective of their religious zeal or indifference ; in giving the Hasa Concession to an English Company ; in bringing automobiles to Ar-Riyadh ; and in employing Syrian doctors, military officers, and engineers — in all these innovations he confirms his own statement that he is doing more than ever did his ancestors.

And he does not much care in so doing about the Ulema ; for they have no right to interfere, when religion is not involved, in the internal and the foreign policy of the Sultanate. For although he has, as they say, strong sectarian feelings, though he must be as the Imam of the Wahhabis a strict Unitarian, he knows when and where to relax—when and where to be tolerant in the interest of his country and his people. One of the Ulema, now and then, thus vents his grief : ' In the days of thine ancestors, O thou Long-of-Days, the world was not troubled with all these problems.' The Sultan smiles and goes ahead towards the fulfilment of his purpose. I have shown how, at times, he treats the Ulema and the Ikhwan to keep them in check ; I have tried to dispel certain doubts, in giving a faithful delineation of the Man, about his real attitude towards them ; and now, after having satisfied myself about a question, which for some time troubled me, I shall light up another corner of the sectarian politics of Najd.

I was speaking one day with one of the Secretaries at the Palace. ' No one doubts,' I said, ' the sincerity of the Sultan's belief. He is the Imam of the Unitarians. But one thing still puzzles me about his militant purpose. Do you think he really believes that it is the duty of the Imam to fight the *mushrekin* everywhere—to wage war against them till they become Unitarians. I am going to ask him this question.' The Secretary : ' Do not do so. My own opinion is that the Sultan believes that it is the duty of the Imam to fight the *mushrekin*, and he also believes that it is not.' I was not satisfied with the Secretary's oracle-like reply. So, one evening I broached the subject by saying to the Sultan that I was puzzled by a certain question which he only can clarify, and that I was loath to leave Ar-Riyadh without submitting it to him. ' Ask me everything,' said His Highness ; ' and if thou departest from us carrying in thy breast a desire that can be fulfilled or an obscure question that can be illuminated, I shall never forgive thee.' I thanked him, and said : ' Do you deem it a religious duty to wage war against the *mushrekin* to the end of making them Unitarians ? '

' No, no,' he straightway replied, striking the carpet twice with his staff. And he continued : ' Take Al-Hasa, for instance. We have there thirty thousand of the Shi'ah, who live in peace and security. No one ever molests them. All we ask of them is not to be too demonstrative in public on their fête-days. Rest assured, *ya Ustaz*. We are not as some people imagine us.'

' Permit me to ask another question. My first question was : ' Do you deem it a religious duty. . . . But do you deem it a political duty to fight the *mushrekin* till they become " religious " ? '

' Politics and religion are not the same. But we the people of Najd desire naught that is not sanctioned by religion. Therefore, if religion sanctions our desire, the political measures we adopt for its realization must be lawful. If politics fail, then war. And everything in war is permissible.'

During my stay of six weeks in Ar-Riyadh, the Sultan visited me every evening at my apartment in the Palace ; and in all our discussions, which covered a wide field of subjects, he was always open and free. Nothing, indeed, could be more direct, coming from a ruler, than what has just preceded and what is now to follow. The Sultan Abd'ul-Aziz, like every great man, worries not if what he does to-day is inconsistent with what he did yesterday. He is not in politics and religion the same man ; for his rule in the provinces and cities which he has conquered, is based upon a certain recognition of tribal customs and sectarian beliefs. And he seldom appoints a governor in a city or a province who is not a native of it. It is a kind of decentralization, which only an extraordinary personality makes possible in such a widely flung country as the Sultanate of Najd...

Now, here is the other instance, alluded to above, of his extraordinary directness of manner. We had frequently discussed Pan-Arabism, or the establishment of an Arab Empire ; but one evening a few days previous to my departure the Sultan was more specific on the subject, making what may be considered an official statement. I wrote therefore a summary of his views immediately after he left, and submitted it to him on the following evening for approval.   He read carefully what I had written, and made one correction in it.   I give the reader the statement in both forms :

THE VIEWS OF THE SULTAN ABD'UL-AZIZ ON PAN-ARABISM. FROM THE EVENING CONVERSATION OF THE 21ST OF JANUARY, 1923.

I. He believes in Pan-Arabism, and will co-operate with those who work sincerely for it.   He would attend any convention to be held for this purpose, and would accept the leadership, the kingship of all Arabia, because he believes that he has the qualifications and the political power.

II. If the Arabs should choose another leader, he would accept ; and would continue to work for the success of the movement.

III. If Pan-Arabism should not be realized, and if, in its stead, an Arab Federation is organized, he would join it.

IV. If neither the one nor the other be possible, he will continue in his Najd policy and would welcome an alliance with a Foreign Power based upon a reciprocity of interest.

V. At all events, he is a man of peace in his own country and desires to encroach upon no one.   But he resents and would oppose any encroachment upon his rights.

To make sure the authenticity of the above I submitted it to the Sultan, who after reading it asked for my pencil and struck out the second statement, saying : ' Thou hast misunderstood us in this.   We will not utter a word, which the Ustaz Rihani may quote, if we cannot stand by it.   But this cannot be,' pointing to the second paragraph.   ' We know ourselves, and we cannot accept the leadership of others.'

CHAPTER XXII

IBN ABD'UL-WAHHAB AND WAHHABISM

In Wadi Hanifah, made classic by the poets and the learned men of Najd, appeared Musailamah, called the False, who fought against the Prophet Muhammad and was killed in battle by the Muslem general, Khalid Ibn 'ul-Walid ; and in the same Wadi, about a thousand years later, appeared Muhammad ibn Abd'ul-Wahhab, who preached against all idolatrous practices and super-stitions and brought the people of Najd back to the pristine purity of Al-Islam. They had been before that time stupefied by various religious and irreligious beliefs, which swept over the eastern part of the Peninsula from Al-Iraq as well as from across the Persian Gulf. Heliolatry and Sabianism were resuscitated among certain of the Bedu ; a form of Carmathian communism still existed in Al-Hasa ; and necrolatry, a practice of the Shi'ah of Persia and An-Najaf, had spread all over Central Arabia.

In fact, the Arabs, town-folk and Bedu, had drifted away from the Islam of the Prophet Muhammad, and were steeped again in the very superstitions which he himself had come to destroy.

They worshipped tombs, and rocks, and trees, making vows to them, supplicating them for favours ; they raised *walis* (saints) above Allah in their prayers ; they no longer could or would read the Koran ; they ceased to pay the *zakat*-money ; and they cared not about the pilgrimage to Mecca. They even did not know, says the historian, the direction of the Ka'ba when they prayed.

To be sure, there were learned sheikhs among them ; and although they followed Ahmad ibn Hanbal, who is the most rational of the five accepted Commentators,[1] their learning was fraught with the dogmatism of the mullas and was not wholly free from the mysticism of the soufis. The Ulema of Najd of those days resembled, in a sense, the schoolmen of the Middle Ages.

One of the most learned and distinguished among them was the grandfather of the founder of Wahhabism, a descendant of the tribe of the poets in Central Arabia, the once powerful tribe of Benu Tamim. He was not only a learned man, but also a man of justice and benevolence. He taught the Commentaries and the Hadith ; he occupied the post of Sheikh 'ul-Islam of Najd ; and his house was always open to those who came with questions, with grievances, or with appeals for assistance.

His son, Abd'ul-Wahhab, the father of the reformer, was also a learned as well as a generous and upright Arab. He sat as judge in the principal cities of Al-'Ared, was the author of several treaties on legal and religious subjects, and did not disdain to be the teacher of his own son. Indeed, one of his most noble qualities I think is that spirit of humility which distinguishes all true men of learning, and which led him to recognize the superior qualities of his son's mind and soul, and to adopt his opinions on important questions of religion and jurisprudence. ' I have often,' he says, ' in forming my decisions, been benefited by the opinions of my son Muhammad.'

Muhammad ibn Abd'ul-Wahhab ibn Muhammad ibn Abd'ul-Wahhab ibn Sulaiman ibn Ali of Benu Tamim was born in the year 1703 A.D. (1115 H.) in the city of 'Uyainah, which is, or was, in Wadi Hanifah of southern Najd. He was a precocious boy, physically as well as mentally ; for he finished the study of the Koran, when he was ten, ' and before he was twelve,' says his father,

---

[1] The others are Abu Hanifah, Ash-Shafe'i, Ibn Malik, and Abu-Ja'far.

' he had attained to maturity and I had him married.'
He then made the pilgrimage to Mecca and Al-Medinah ;
and returning to his native town he took up, under the
tutelage of his father, following the Imam Ahmad ibn
Hanbal, the study of law ; after which he travelled many
times to Al-Hijaz in pursuit of knowledge and to the city
of Basrah, where he studied the Hadith and the arts of
language, reading many books on the subject.

He did more than read in Basrah ; he also preached
there the Unitarian faith. ' Some of the *mushrekin*,' he
wrote, ' would come to me with questions, which I would
answer ; ' and they would sit ' dumbfounded,' as he
expounded the doctrine of the oneness of God. ' To Allah
alone is worship due : to *walis* and good men we owe
reverence. . . . We walk in the light of a *wali*, imitating
his example ; but we pray only to Allah.' He made a
few converts in that city, but he did not follow up his
success.

It was when he returned to 'Uyainah and then moved
with his father to Huraimala, however, that he started in
earnest to preach against the false worship and the idolatrous practices of his countrymen. And rapidly he made
enemies and friends ;—as rapidly as the idea spread in the
principal cities of Al-'Ared, from Huraimala to Dir'iyah
to Ar-Riyadh and down to Manfouhah. At this time
he wrote the first book, which is entitled, *The Book of
Unitarianism ;* after which he returned to his native town
'Uyainah, where the corner-stone of his mission was laid ;
or, to speak in a language adequate to the subject, where
the first gun in the great battle was fired.

Two events took place in 'Uyainah which were more
effective in spreading the movement and arousing people
against it, as well as making converts for it, than the
teacher's written or spoken word. I said that a form of
necrolatry was prevalent among the Arabs of Central
Arabia ;—more than that ; for they had started by
worshipping the *wali*, then the domed tomb of the *wali*,

and then the tree which they planted in the shadow of the dome. Indeed, there were certain trees in the caves of Jabal Twaiq and other parts of Najd which were supposed to be endowed with supernatural power ; and from far and near they were sought by devotees, who made vows to them and invoked their assistance.

Now, the first distinguished supporter of Ibn Abd'ul-Wahhab was the Ameer of 'Uyainah, Uthman ibn Mu'ammar ; and the first pledge of faith that the reformer asked of the governor was that he should help him to destroy the domed tombs and cut down the trees to which the people prayed. Ibn Mu'ammar complied ; and the two went out together to Jubailah, where some of the Prophet's Companions are buried, and had the domes above their tombs destroyed. They then ordered the trees cut down ; and Ibn Abd'ul-Wahhab took the axe in his own hand and felled a certain tree called Abu Dajjanah, to whom ' the maiden prayed for a groom ; and the barren wife, for a seed to bloom ; and the widow for some male to lighten her doom.' And when Abu Dajjanah was cut down by Ibn Abd'ul-Wahhab, the cry of woe and confusion went up in Wadi Hanifah and was echoed in the downs of Sudair.[1]

The second event is even more important, for it concerns the ' cutting down ' of a woman. According to a Koranic law, the adulteress should be stoned to death. Now, a woman was accused in 'Uyainah ; and after being duly tried—she herself confessing four times her own guilt, as the law requires, in addition to the four witnesses—she was sentenced to death. They stood her, therefore, in a ditch, deep enough to cover her up to the waist, and the Ameer 'Uthman ibn Mu'ammar cast the first stone. Thus did Ibn Abd'ul-Wahhab inaugurate his crusade for purity of worship and religion.

But the stoning of the adulteress was like a flame of chastisement which swept over the land ; it was felt and

[1] Pronounced Sdeir.

resented everywhere. The people of Al-Hasa, who were living most licentiously under a lingering shadow of Carmathian immunities, were infuriated ; and their Ameer Sulaiman, a very powerful and very wicked man, whose rule extended to Al-'Ared ('Uthman ibn Mu'ammar held office under him), sent to threaten the reformer with death if he did not stop ' agitating the hearts of the Muslemin and overturning their religion.' The reformer did not stop. The Ameer Sulaiman, therefore, sent to his Governor, the Ameer 'Uthman, an order to put to death Muhammad ibn Abd'ul-Wahhab. But the Ameer 'Uthman to save his friend and master—and to save himself in office—had him spirited away.

We next hear of him in Dir'iyah, which is about twenty miles south-east of 'Uyainah, the guest of one of his disciples Ibn Swailem,[1] who would bespeak for him the protection of the Ameer Muhammad ibn Sa'oud. But the Ameer of Dir'iyah was reluctant at first ; and his brothers,[2] who admired Ibn Abd'ul-Wahhab and later became his greatest supporters, tried in vain to prevail upon him and then appealed to his wife, who must have been a wise and discerning woman. But the historian, who goes deeper into the matter, tells us that when the brothers of her husband told her all about Ibn Abd'ul-Wahhab and his Mission, ' Allah cast into her heart the love of the Sheikh.'

. Therefore, when the Ameer her husband came to see her she spoke thus unto him : ' This man is sent to thee by Allah. He is a great boon : avail thyself of him.' Whereupon, the Ameer acquiesced. Says the historian again : ' And Allah cast into the heart of Muhammad ibn Sa'oud the love of the Sheikh.' So he decided to send for him ; but his brother Mushari was moved by a more generous impulse. ' Go thyself to him,' he said, ' to show

---

[1] The Swailems, who are one of the ancient and distinguished families of southern Najd, live to-day in Ar-Riyadh and remain staunch supporters of Wahhabism and Ibn Sa'oud.

[2] These are Mushari, Thunaiyan, and Farhan.

the people, who would persecute him, that he is much respected by thee.'

The Ameer Muhammad ibn Sa'oud went, therefore, to see Muhammad ibn Abd'ul-Wahhab in the house of his disciple Ibn Swailem ; and when they met, they greeted each other with mutual assurance. ' Be assured,' said the Ameer, ' of happiness in a town which is better than thine own.' ' And I assure thee,' replied the Sheikh, ' of increase of power if thou wilt ally with me.'

The alliance took place. And it was based, as it still is, upon the sword of Ibn Sa'oud and the faith of Ibn Abd'ul-Wahhab ;—it was based in its inception upon a living, fiery faith which could find adequate expression only in the sword. The sword, therefore, laid down the conditions. ' Thy faith is mine,' said Ibn Sa'oud, ' and that of my people, Allah be our witness ! And we shall carry it to the utmost ends of the land of the Arabs, *inshallah*. But thou must pledge thyself to remain here in Dir'iyah—to make it thy city and the pole of our religion ; and thou must pledge thyself, whatsoever may chance, to make no alliance with any other Ameer in the land of the Arabs.' The pledge was made ; and the alliance has now lasted well-nigh two hundred years.

Muhammad ibn Abd'ul-Wahhab was at that time forty-two years of age ; and in the same year the alliance was contracted (1744 A.D., 1157 H.), the war against the *mushrekin* and for Unitarianism was declared, and the first battle was fought in Ar-Riyadh between the forces of its Ameer Dahham ibn Dawwas and those of Ibn Sa'oud. This Ibn Dawwas was one of the two implacable enemies of the Sa'oud-Wahhab alliance ; and his rise to power was as extraordinary as his hold upon it, for more than thirty years, at a time when Al-'Ared was all aflame with religious disputes and wars. He was a menial in the Palace, the servant of a black slave, who ambitious for power killed the former ruler of Ar-Riyadh and fled away to save his own life. In the interval, Ibn Dawwas rose from his lowliness, his deep obscurity ; and in spite of the opposition of the inhabitants he declared himself the successor of his slave-master—the Ameer of Ar-Riyadh. He even sought the aid of Ibn Sa'oud to suppress the uprising in the city and strengthen his position ; and Ibn Sa'oud, when he became the protagonist of Unitarianism, invited him as a friend to its meadows of salvation. But Dawwas would no longer play second fiddle to any one in Najd or in Al-Jannat.

His one good quality it seems was pertinacity. For thirty years he fought against the Sa'ouds and the new creed, winning a town or a tribe to-day, losing it to-morrow ; but there was a time when victory seemed to be making her last choice ; for ten years after the first battle was fought, when Ibn Sa'oud had conquered all the cities of Al-'Ared except Ar-Riyadh, there was a general reversion, for which Ibn Dawwas was mostly responsible. And it was not the sword of Ibn Sa'oud that chastised apostasy and drove the apostates back to the fold, but the inspired words of Ibn Abd'ul-Wahhab, who assembled at Dir'iyah the leading Unitarians and re-lighted in them the fire of devotion and sacrifice.

Nevertheless, for twenty years after Ibn Dawwas continued, with varying fortune, to fight and coquet with Ibn Sa'oud ; he made four treaties of peace and piety with him ; he even once joined his forces against the *mushrekin;* and finally, after many oaths and betrayals, many battles and truces, he was defeated in 1773 by Abd'ul-Aziz son of the Ameer Muhammad, who entered Ar-Riyadh in triumph but did not capture Dawwas, who had fled to the desert. In this thirty-years war of Najd 4000 Arabs were killed, 1700 of the Unitarians and 2300 of the *mushrekin,* that is, only 133 every year died by the sword. But even this would seem exaggerated, if we consider that many of the battles were like the following :

Says the historian Ibn Bushr : ' And in this year, the Ameer Abd'ul-Aziz led his forces against Ar-Riyadh, where a great battle was fought, in which four of the children of error were killed and only one of the Muslemin.[1]

The other formidable enemy of the Sa'oud-Wahhab League was the Ameer of Al-Hasa, who succeeded Sulaiman and was more resourceful. 'Urai'er, as he was called, brought cannons with him, which were carried by camels across the Dahna, and which he used in his siege of Dir'iyah ; he had constructed also a huge box, which moved on wheels,—a crude form of armoured car, —and which could carry thirty soldiers to the bulwarks for direct attack. Besides, 'Urai'er was able to enlist the sympathy and the support of some of the people of Central Najd—those of the Washm and Sdeir—who were still holding out against Ibn Sa'oud. Nevertheless, he returned to Al-Hasa crestfallen, leaving his guns and his strategy boxes behind him. He then sent his son Sa'doun with more artillery to Yamamah, where he too was de- feated ; and he had to re-cross the Dahna sans cannons like his father. Nor were they, father and son, more successful in the Qasim, where they invested Buraidah, and after several months had to retire ignominiously from it. But in spite of all these failures, the campaigns of 'Urai'er in Najd had indirectly a fatal effect upon the cause of Unitarianism and Ibn Sa'oud ; for those who more out of fear than conviction accepted the creed— those who were ' made religious ' by the sword—were ready, whenever they saw an enemy banner in the land, to rally to it. Hence, the recurrent apostasies in the north and the south, which kept the indefatigable Abd'ul-Aziz trotting at the head of his Unitarian host from one end of the country to the other ; for as soon as he had won a victory in the Qasim, for instance, he had to hasten back to the south to chastise apostasy in the Kharj : and when Majma'ah became ' religious,' Manfouhah reverted to its ancient infidelity.

[1] The Unitarians are the Muslemin (Muslems) ; and all the others are infidels, *mushrekin*. See p. 145 for a description of another battle and an example of Ibn Bushr's style.

Many years before he succeeded his father Muhammad, who died in 1764, the Ameer Abd'ul-Aziz had started to fight for the Unitarian creed, was one of its great warriors ; and he continued after he became Imam to flourish the sword of religion, making as many as six *gazus* every year ; in districts so far apart as the Kharj, the Qasim, and Al-Hasa ; reaching in a south-westerly direction Wadi 'd-Dawasir. But his son Sa'oud, who like himself early in his youth, sallied forth on his own account, reached as far north-east as An-Najaf and Karbala, the Ka'bas of necrolatry, which he entered in triumph and wrought havoc among their domed tombs and shrines. Later, however, the Shi'ah avenged itself through one of its secret emissaries, who in the year of the Hijrah 1218 (1802 A.D.) came to Dir'iyah, and assassinated the Imam Abd'ul-Aziz while he was praying in the Mosque.

Fifteen years before his death, however, the Ameer Sa'oud was elected to succeed him ; was made Imam by the suffrage of the people at the instance of Muhammad Ibn Abd'ul-Wahhab. The old Sheikh had become the anointer of Kings ; but what was more gratifying to him was to see his mission spread and take root, through the exploits of the great Sa'oud ibn Abd'ul-Aziz, in every part of Arabia, from Al-Yaman and Asir up to the Mountain of Shammar, across to Al-Hasa, and down to Oman. But he did not live to see him enter into Mecca. He died ten years before that time, in 1791 (1206 H.).

For fifty years, from the time he first met Muhammad ibn Sa'oud until his death, he continued to live in Dir'iyah, which developed so rapidly in those days that it became the biggest city in Najd, perhaps in all Arabia. And Muhammad ibn Abd'ul-Wahhab was its central figure, its leading light—the luminary which sent its rays and its flames in every direction. In addition to the post of Sheikh 'ul-Islam, which he occupied, he taught religion in its purest form, preached on the oneness of God and true worship, continued to write and argue on

the subject, and sent his zealous disciples to the cities
and among the tribes to cultivate the seed which he had
sown.

The first chapter of a book of homilies, which is distributed free in Najd, and which is considered as an
auxiliary to the Koran, nay, as the Unitarian gospel, is
a catechism written by Ibn Abd'ul-Wahhab and prefaced
by these words :

> ' Know thou, Allah have mercy upon thee, that it is the
> duty of every Muslem man and woman to learn these three
> questions and live in accordance with them :
>
> ' First—That God has created us, and provided for us,
> and has not neglected us ; for he has sent us a Prophet.
> Whoso obey him, therefore, shall enter Al-Jannat, and
> whoso disobey him shall enter the fire (of hell). And the
> proof of this is the saying of Allah. . . . (Here he quotes
> from the Koran.)
>
> ' Second—That God dislikes to have anyone, neither a
> favoured angel nor a sent prophet, joined with him in
> worship. And the proof is his own word, praised be he. . . .
> (Follows the quotation from the Koran.)
>
> ' Third—That he who obeys the Prophet and unifies
> Allah must not befriend him who disobeys Allah and his
> Apostle, and though he be his nearest kin. And the proof
> is the word of Allah. . . . (Quotation from the Koran).'

Thus he returns, like Ibn Taimiyah, whom he greatly
admired, and like Ibn Hanbal their Imam, to what they
all consider the first and highest source of truth, the
Koran. Whatever is based upon it is positive and incon-
trovertible. Nor do the Hanbalis or the Wahhabis
disagree in this with the other acknowledged Imams.
They do disagree, however, in the interpretation of the
Book and about the right to do so ; the Ja'faris, or Shi'as,
on the extreme end, basing their secular and legal systems
upon it, often reading an esoteric meaning into the
sayings, often using interpretation as a door of escape from
the letter without, however, getting at the spirit ; and
on the other hand, the Hanbalis claim that the door of

interpretation after the four orthodox Khalifs, is closed, and that everything in the Koran is clear and must be accepted as it is—at its face value. Between the two extremes are the three other Schools—the Hanafi, the Shafe'i, and the Maliki—who use but do not abuse the right of interpretation.

Next to the Koran comes the Sunnat, or the Life of the Prophet as set down in the Hadith (Sayings) and the Commentaries. Now, every act or saying of the Prophet is traced back through its several reporters to the person that witnessed or heard it ; but not all of these acts and sayings are corroborated in the different Commentaries ; some are quoted in one or two only, others are variously quoted, and still others are questioned, even considered false, by one or more of the Commentators. Hence the differences in certain beliefs and practices which have arisen between the various sects.

But Ibn Hanbal, or the Imam Ahmad as he is called, who came after Abu-Hanifah and the others, undertook, for his better guidance, to sift the evidence ; and that he may arrive at a state of knowledge as positive as what is based on the Koran, he adopted the rule that only those acts and sayings that are corroborated in all the Commentaries should be accepted as authentic and binding. By this simplifying process much was rejected that was useless, and much that was harmful, indeed, because it sanctioned certain beliefs and practices which have the tendency of degrading religion. Thus, the Imam Ahmad, who does not acknowledge the right to interpret the Koran, has founded what may be designated as the rational school of interpretation in the Sunnat ; and Ibn Taimiyah, a fervent controversialist of the fourteenth century, took up the cudgels for him and is still considered as the leading teacher of the Hanbalist school. The book I have mentioned above contains several papers of his on such subjects as Forms of Worship, Intercession, Visiting Tombs, etc. Ibn Abd'ul-Wahhab was also a constant reader, as he himself tells us, and a great admirer of Ibn Taimiyah.[1] His father and grandfather, it will be remembered, were in their religious and legal decisions of the Hanbalist school ; and Wahhabism is in the main Hanbalism, or a revival of it. The more advanced Wahhabi of to-day, that is the liberal-minded one, prefers to call himself a Hanbali.

But a reformer need not necessarily be original ; he may find his material scattered around him, half buried in the past, dust or rust eaten, wilted, seared, or cobwebbed, and here and there still giving out a proof of life. This is his opportunity ; in this he finds his inspiration. Where there is life there is a seed ; and where there is a seed there is perpetuation and development. Ibn Abd'ul-Wahhab found Hanbalism in Najd still gasping out a breath of life, and he rescued it, infused into it his own genius, revivified it. Shall we then call him a revivalist ? But the word has acquired an unpleasant sense in these latter days. Shall we deny him the title of reformer ? He wrought

ONE OF THE ULEMA   of a certainty a great reform in Najd ; but he did not in a higher sense even point the way to a Reformation in Al-Islam. He harks back with a vengeance to the days of the Prophet ; destroys the superstitions, that is true, under which succumbed the vital truth of the oneness of God, but rakes up in the process all the old inhibitions which make Wahhabism insufferable. Shall we then call him a teacher ? He was more than that ; for, in addition to teaching the people of Najd a religion which they had forgotten, he infused

---

[1] ' I know of no one,' he wrote, ' who stands ahead of Ibn Taimiyah, after the Imam Ahmad ibn Hanbal, in the science of Interpretation and the Hadith.'

into them a spirit which, locked as they are in the heart
of Arabia, gave them the power to expand and to express
their superiority with the austerity, the confidence, and
the arrogance of the followers of the Prophet. And he
could do this only by sticking to the Koran, cleaving often
to the surface meaning of its word.

Take, for instance, the question of prayer and belief.
Abu-Hanifah was once asked if a man who believes in
God and the Prophet but does not pray, is an infidel, and
he replied in the negative. The same question was put
to Ibn Hanbal, who said, Yes, basing his judgment upon
the following words of the Prophet : ' I have been commanded to wage war upon people until they testify that
there is no God but Allah and that Muhammad is the
Apostle of Allah, and *until they pray and pay the zakat.*'
Hence, Ibn Abd'ul-Wahhab following Ibn Hanbal :
' He who does not pray from neglect or indolence should
be warned ; and he who does not repent and refuses to
pray should be killed.'

Take again the question of prayer and practice. If a
Muslem testifies that there is no God but Allah and that
Muhammad is the Apostle of Allah, but continues in his
prayers to ask the dead—meaning the saints—for favours
and invokes them instead of, or with, God, then he is a
polytheist and infidel and his blood is forfeit. Furthermore, says Ibn Abd'ul-Wahhab : ' The domes or other
monuments built above the graves, and the stones that
are kissed for their imagined blessing and to which vows
are made, nothing of such should remain on the face of
the earth.' For the Prophet himself hath said : ' The
best graves are those that are not visible.' And it is set
down in the Koran that ' to Allah alone all worship is
due ; to him the Kingdom of the heavens and the earth.'
Couple with this the command to fight the *mushrekin*
until they become Unitarians in faith and practice, and
you get the basis and justification of the militant spirit of
Wahhabism.

But how shall we know the real *mushrekin* from those who have but half-way strayed from orthodoxy? For non-orthodoxy in supplication, for instance, is according to Ibn Taimiyah of three degrees. First : To visit the tomb of a prophet or a *wali* and supplicate him direct for what can be given or performed only by God. This is polytheism, actual and complete ; and he who is guilty of it should be first asked to repent. If he refuses to do so he should be killed. Second : To ask a prophet, a *wali*, or a good man to pray for you, to invoke Allah in your behalf. This is permissible when he whom you ask is of the living not of the dead. (When one day, after the death of the Prophet Muhammad, the people prayed for rain they asked his uncle Ibn 'ul-Abbas to invoke Allah in their name ; but they did not go to the tomb of the Prophet to invoke him or invoke Allah through him.) Third : To supplicate others with God by inference, as to say, invoking the Omnipotent : for the love of thy Prophet, in the name of So and So who is near thee, grant me this wish. The Companions of the Prophet have never been heard to use this form of supplication ; and in their days, when people would appeal to Allah through a good man, they sought him not among the dead. Thus in the first degree only, according to Ibn Taimiyah and Ibn Abd'ul-Wahhab, are the blood and the property of a man forfeit ; while in the other two degrees, the guilt might be denoted as a misdemeanour or what is called, in Roman Catholic theology, a venial sin. Now, how are the Ikhwan, in battle with those whom they consider *mushrekin*, to distinguish the one from the other? This question did not seem to occur to either Ibn Taimiyah or Ibn Abd'ul-Wahhab.

CHAPTER XXIII

WADI HANIFAH

THREE times in my Arab travels has fear come upon me ; three times, I say, without philosophizing or apologizing, was I mortally afraid. In sooth, fear clutched at my heart, and stared at me an instant or two, shaking my will power and my faith. I knew then the biggest enemy of man, and I realized the meaning of security and peace.

The first time I was afraid of losing my life was when the soldiers of the Hawashib fired their guns to stop us for breakfast ; the second time I was afraid of losing at least my liberty, of being locked up in a gloomy castle, when in Mawia I was asked : Art thou a Hasani or a Husaini ? and the third time I despaired of the mercy of Allah when I was a captive of malaria at the Palace in Ar-Riyadh,— when for days the fever whispered in my heart that word in which is the end of all things.

Yes, I was afraid in Ar-Riyadh ; and I felt, moreover, for the first time in all my Arab travels that I was in a foreign land, far, very far from my own country and people ; far, very far from health, from doctors, from any means of treatment and recovery. But I found in that affliction, one great consolation, which Allah vouchsafed in the friendship of the first man of Najd, the lord of the land and of all generous deeds. He came to see me every day, bringing always with him, as I have said in another place, something to break the fever or to relieve it. But nothing did I find more refreshing and more reassuring than the smile and the words of the Sultan, and the shake of his hand.

Nevertheless, I was discouraged and in despair. I was afraid of losing my life,—I say, O thou brilliant one (with apologies to King Husein), afraid of losing my life. And it were not, by the life of thee, a precious thing, were it not for what its owner had been chosen to do, as the holy man would say. I was afraid of death, not because of its mortal terror—I say this in all humility—but because it was annoying to me. It threatened to interrupt my work at one of its most intense moments,—to strike me down treacherously in the midst of my travels. And when the thermometer read four above the hundred, the degree of a pardonable delirium, I would hear a tremulous voice repeating : The Washm, Wadi's-Sirr, 'Anaizah, Buraidah, Kuwait . . . to Kuwait . . . bring the map, O D'heim.

And D'heim,[1] in his dirty smock, moving about like a spectre—the very shadow of death : ' *Ibshir, ya Ustaz, ibshir* (coming).' But before he came with the map, I would have travelled, on the shoulders of the Jinn-fever, ten times to Kuwait and back. Besides, it was a very large map which seemed to exaggerate the distances and double the difficulties. As for my *rafiq*, Saiyed Hashem, he had become hardened through a protracted period of association or had reverted to his native humour. He was no longer sympathetic. I never shall forget him as he stood near the window with the mirror in his hand, fixing the *ighal* on his head and casually describing for my benefit the hardships of the road to Kuwait. And he would always, when he saw the map in my hand, take up the mirror to see if his *ighal* is on straight, and repeat while so doing, as one would hum a tune : *No water except in Al-Hafar.* Thus, would he give me the solace of departure, making life seem as an infinite series of arid deserts (who would not be glad, therefore, to escape it ?) and telling me so a hundred times a day. O give me woe, and tell me it is woe ![2]

[1] D'heim is the Najdi's abbreviation of Abd'ur-Rahman.

[2] Says the poet Abu'n-Nawwas : ' O give me wine, and tell me it is wine.' For he would have his ear also share in the joy.

To Kuwait ! There is nothing in the two words, if you are not in the heart of Arabia, to justify any fear or apprehension. Suppose you are in Bombay and Kuwait is your destination ; under the usual circumstances, peace will accompany you on a steamer tolerably equipped with the means of comfort and security. And if you were in Iraq and you said : Kuwait, steam will again respond to your call and carry you on wheels from Baghdad to Basrah, where a ship will take you down Shat 'ul-'Arab, —affording you through either of its banks a glimpse of Paradise—and bring you to a cove in the Gulf, which was carved out by the hand of time and to which have quietly strayed the sea and man.

But—To Kuwait, when you are in Ar-Riyadh, with the Dahna behind you and the Dahna and the Nufoud before you ; and you are not, O man, of the Dawasir or of Benu Murrah ; and you have nothing to carry you across but the camel ;—there is the calamity that comes exultant with her brother anguish and her cousin death. Yet the Saiyed Hashem, who had an overdose of me and my philosophy, would tie me neck and heels with the sister and her brother and her cousin for the sake of Sheikh Ahmad As-Sabah of Kuwait.

' Sheikh Ahmad is a good man, *ya Ustaz ;* educated, refined ; travelled in Europe. And in Kuwait you will forget Ar-Riyadh. Kuwait is the Paris of Arabia. You will find tobacco there, and whisky, and women. There, too, is a doctor and a hospital. . . . Where did you put the mirror, *ya Ustaz* ? ' And he would take it up to re-adjust his *ighal*, repeating the usual refrain : *There is no water except in Al-Hafar.*

' And I may die, O Saiyed Hashem, before I get to Kuwait.'

' Philosophers are long-lived, *ya Ustaz.* But suppose thou didst die on the way thou wilt not grieve : thou hast seen Ar-Riyadh and the Ikhwan, and for that thou wilt be admitted into Al-Jannat.'

'Al-Jannat is for thee, not for me. . . . Bring the map, O D'heim. . . . And bring the pitcher of water. I shall drink enough to hold me till I get to Kuwait.'

Saiyed Hashem, after he had adjusted his *ighal* and placed the mirror under the cushion : 'Dost thou not believe in Al-Jannat, *ya Ustaz ?* '

'No. Nor in thee.'

'But the Prophet and the Holy Book testify that Al-Jannat exists.'

'The Jannat of fools, as Al-Gazzali said. It is thine, a present from me.'

'Thou art jesting.'

'I am in earnest.'

'Wilt thou give me thy share in it ? '

'I have already done so.'

'Wilt thou write me a deed for it ? '

'O D'heim, bring paper and ink.'

Saiyed Hashem was quicker than D'heim in this. And sitting up in bed, while he held the ink-well, I wrote down the following : Granted that Al-Jannat exists, I hereby make a gift to Saiyed Hashem ibn Saiyed Ahmad of Kuwait, the Sunni, the Shafe'i, the Rufa'i, of my share in it.' I signed the paper and gave it to him. He read it and returned it to me, saying : ' *Billah ! ya Ustaz*, sign it also in English.' 'And dost thou think,' I said, after complying with his wish, ' that Radhwan has an English adviser or that the English hold the Mandate for Al-Jannat ? ' 'Allah is all-knowing,' he replied, as he folded the paper and placed it in his pocket.[1] He then took up the mirror . . . my silver hand-mirror—the only object of luxury which I carried with me—I am not exaggerating when I say that Saiyed Hashem hovered around it perpetually, asking it : How do I look ? more than twenty times a day. I saw that it had become one of the necessities of life to my friend ; and I would have been

[1] Later he showed it to a man in Bahrain, who took it in all seriousness and wrote to chide me for my infidelity.

unkind indeed had I deprived him of it.   Besides, a
mirror were a thing despised when Death is coquetting
with you.   So I said to him : ' I make thee the heir of
my mirror, too.'   He was overjoyed, and he called to
D'heim for coffee.

And I took up the map.   Here is Ar-Riyadh, and here
is the Washm—100 miles—and there is Wadi's-Sirr to
Shaqra, to 'Anaizah, to Buraidah—150 miles—and from
Buraidah to Al-Hafar, a hundred and fifty miles.

Saiyed Hashem : ' No water except in Al-Hafar.'

' We depend upon Allah.   And from Al-Hafar to
Kuwait is another hundred and fifty miles—all told 550
miles more or less ; a distance for an automobile of
twenty hours, and for an aeroplane of ten.   But we are
in a country which we do not desire to traverse motoring
or flying ; for we have loved it even in its desert wastes,
and loved its people and their camels.   And for the
increase of our knowledge and our love we would go
through it after the fashion of D'heim, like a snail.

When we were in Ojair one of the English officials said
to me : ' You have done well by going to Najd from here.
You will get accustomed gradually to the camel, and by
the time you get to the Qasim, you will be quite hardened
for the journey to Kuwait.'

It is, of a certainty, the most difficult road I have
known, the most difficult perhaps in all Najd.   For not
all the *zkirts*, when Hazlul was making up his list of
escorts and servants, were eager to go ; and in spite of
all the means of comfort and security, which the generosity
of the Sultan Abd'ul-Aziz had placed at my command,
I was often, in the hardships I have experienced, the
suffering and pain I have felt, an unenviable, a miserable
object of royal favour.

We walked out of Ar-Riyadh accompanied by two of
the Sultan's Secretaries and other friends, among them
Saiyed Hashem, who said good-bye to us in the northern
palm-grove ; and from its last green spot to the first of

Dir'iyah's we traversed about ten miles of hard, barren, level soil, broken here and there by a hillock or a ridge. It was at the end of January, and it had not rained in Najd ; otherwise at this season the clumps of seared grass would lend the barrenness a little green. We did come upon a solitary tree, a big tamarisk, about an hour from Ar-Riyadh, well known to travellers ; it is the last station—the dressing spot—of those coming to the Capital from the north. Here, too, is a *qasr* and a *masjid* together with a few palms to save them from destruction. The man who eats the dates keeps the roof over the few rooms and keeps the *masjid* open for the pious traveller.

Beyond that, except for a well of good water and the little town of 'Izrah to the left, there is nothing to arrest the attention until we reach the watch-tower on the hillock to our right, from which Ibrahim Pasha fired his cannons at Dir'iyah in the spring of 1818. Hazlul pointed to it and then to the ruins of the old capital about two miles away to the west, after he had told us, on the way, the story of the son of a ' slave-mother ' about whom Muhammad Ali, when he was in Constantinople, consulted the soothsayers before taking her to wife. She brought him ' the Shaitan Ibrahim who came from Egypt to destroy the capital of religion in Najd.' And he did so after a siege of five months, when the Ameer Abdullah ibn Sa'oud and those who were left had to surrender. Ibrahim Pasha then took Abdullah prisoner, banished the inhabitants, and completed the destruction of Dir'iyah ; after which, he marched through the country Atilla-like with fire and sword, his army reaching as far as Al-Kharj and eastward as far as Al-Hasa ; razing forts, cutting down palms, burning villages, treacherously massacring the inhabitants—leaving in its wake, in one brief year, an unspeakable horror of death and desolation.

' Shaitan Pasha ! ' said Hazlul, as we descended into the sunken gardens of the old capital. ' He was a double-barrelled gun of evil—a Turkish Pasha and son of a slave-mother.' I did not mind what he was saying at that time, for we were meandering through palm-groves spread with the vivid green of vetch between the new Dir'iyah, a village, and the old, whose ruins crown the western ridge. But the chief of the escort, mistaking my distraction for the lack of interest, was silent after that, even when he took me through the ruins.

We had entered into Wadi Hanifah, which runs from this point in a southerly direction, slightly east, to Yamamah ; and in a dry river-bed, which flows in the rainy season between the shadow of the ruins and the shadow of the palms, we crouched our camels. Hazlul gave his orders to pitch the tents and make supper, sent a messenger to the Ameer of the town for wood and fodder, and walked ahead of me to the height. In a few minutes we were strolling through the streets of the old capital of Wahhabism, which overlooked Mt. Twaiq to the north and Manfouhah to the south, between crumbling walls and fragments of roofs and bridges, across wide open squares, overgrown with seared grass and thistle, to what remains of the two or three story palaces of the Sa'ouds. The buildings, like those of Ar-Riyadh to-day, were of rough stone covered on both sides with plaster. But the extensive ground that some of the places occupied, the architectural designs, the bridges connecting one apartment or one palace with another, the big halls and courts, all testify to the greatness of the Sa'ouds and the importance of their capital a hundred years ago. It is not altogether deserted, however, if the poet has heard aright. For he speaks of it as

' A desolation and a loneliness,
In which the wailing of the Jinn is heard.'

When we returned we found that Misfer the cook had slaughtered a sheep and was cooking in two large copper vessels the supper, *i.e.* the rice and the meat ; and when we sat in a circle an hour later I found around me a dozen men, two of whom were *rafiqs* of the road. But they were all, when it came to service, ever ready and willing. The Sultan Abd'ul-Aziz was most generous and gracious to the last ; for we had with us two camel-loads of provision, including honey from the mountains of Asir and biscuits from London ; two camels carrying the baggage and the tents ; a herdsboy who drove before him six heads of sheep to supply us with meat to 'Anaizah ; and a military escort with letters to the Ameers of the different cities through which we were to pass.

We did not start early the following morning, because the people of Dir'iyah, in obedience to an edict of the Sultan setting that day for a public prayer for rain in Najd, had come out, men and women, and blocked our way through the river-bed, where the meeting took place. There was no kneeling or prostration, but only an invocation pronounced by the sheikh of the village and repeated after him by the people. It was very impressive ; and as we proceeded through Wadi Hanifah we realized that the rain was very much needed.

For an hour up the dry bed, we passed between the ruins on either side of Dir'iyah, which must have been a very big city in the days of the first Sa'ouds and Ibn Abd'ul-Wahhab. People came to it from every distant part of Arabia, not only to be taught by the Sheikh in the Unitarian creed, but also to trade, and to solicit the political favour of its Ameers. Beyond Dir'iyah we debouch into the Wadi, which is the work of the *sayl* (torrential rain) and which in a certain aspect is suggestive of the Iraq country along the Tigris ; for if that river dried up, it would resemble Wadi Hanifah in its deviousness and in the lack of vegetation along its banks. We meandered through the Wadi, going in every direction but one ; facing sometimes the south, sometimes the north ; but a zigzag line pointing north-west would fairly describe our course.

About ten miles from Dir'iyah, which was destroyed by the Egyptians, is Jubailah, which was destroyed by the Sa'ouds themselves in their fratricidal wars ; but it still can boast of a well of good water. And outside the town on an escarpment of the Wadi are buried a few of the Companions of the Prophet, whose domed tombs were destroyed, as I related in the preceding chapter, by Ibn Abd'ul-Wahhab and the Ameer of 'Uyainah Ibn Mu'ammar. I would not have noticed the place had it not been pointed out by Hazlul ; for no trace of the tombs is visible.

Half an hour from the ruins of Jubailah, is the native place of the Sheikh, as Ibn Abd'ul-Wahhab is called in these parts ;—the famous 'Uyainah, for whose destruction neither the Egyptians nor the Sa'ouds are responsible. Luqman the Wise had an eagle called Lubad, which threatened to live for ever, and was immortalized in Arabic poetry, at least, by a line of one of the poets of the Mu'allaqat, describing a city like 'Uyainah.

' Deserted, and the ruins on her frown ;
He worked her end who struck old Lubad down.' [1]

Amidst those ruins, in what seems to have been one of the city's principal streets, we made our way for an hour or more ; but nothing so much amazed me as the many *jalibs* (wells) we saw to the right and to the left of us ;—*jalibs*, deep and dark, well built with dressed stones, and revealing nothing at the end of the abraded steps, O thou who struck old Lubad down, O Time, but the greenish seal of desiccation. Some of them are stopped with rubble : all of them are dry.

'Uyainah, which is about four miles long, was built in the centre of the Wadi, where many streams of water must have flown in the past. The *jalibs* are a proof of this. But where are the subterranean streams to-day ? If there were any water at a tolerable depth in the vicinity,

---

[1] It is the first line of the poem of An-Nabigat 'uz-Zubiani. Literal translation :

It has become a wilderness, and its people have departed,
He struck her down who struck down Lubad.

there certainly would have been a new 'Uyainah, even as there is a new Dir'iyah. But the underground streams must have forsaken it, and man followed suit. Hence, the thorns in its courts and the grass in its streets. Can it be that a rib of the earth was broken under this town or an earthquake shook a few rocks into the streams, thereby changing their course and causing the wells to dry up and the deserted homes in consequence to fall in ruin ? I have seen in Najd other towns, which were deserted or were moved to a neighbouring spot, because of the deflection of the subterranean streams that fed their *jalibs* and supplied the inhabitants with water.

In the days of 'Uthman ibn Mu'ammar 'Uyainah was more flourishing than Dir'iyah ; the two were twin cities, when Ibn Abd'ul-Wahhab fled from the one to the other. In fact, Wadi Hanifah, in the days of the Companions of the Prophet, could boast an unbroken chain of towns from 'Uyainah to Dir'iyah ; but the Companions' tombs, and Musailamah's *dirah*, and the birthplace of the Sheikh Ibn Abd'ul-Wahhab are to-day like the *jalibs* underground, like the ruins above it :—the hand of desolation is upon them all. Even the birds and the flowers have deserted Wadi Hanifah ; and the only cheerful sight is the *athl* (1)[1] trees, whose graceful, willow-like foliage linger in the courts and inside the roofless houses of 'Uyainah to mourn the vanished past. But there too are the thorny *salams*(2) [1] darkening the dooryards and casting their shadows over the *jalibs*. Are they thy fangs in the heart of desolation, O thou who struck old Lubad down, or are they thy crown of thorns for the doomed cities ?

We continue up Wadi Hanifah, passing through a section of it called Haisiyah, where Ar-Riyadh gets its wood. The *salam* and the *talh* (3) [1] grow in what in those

---

[1] I have tried in vain to find the English names of these trees. As for the classic terms. I am not qualified even to search for them. But I find in Mr. Philby's book, *The Heart of Arabia*, the following : (1) Athl=tamarisk macrocarpa, (2) Salam=a species of acacia, (3) Talh=gum-bearing acacia.

parts is considered abundance. But the camels and the sheep give little chance to the tree to grow; what they have left in Haisiyah woods are doddered *salams*, denuded *talhs*, some thorny bushes, and the *harmal*, which every browser avoids. The woodman then comes to complete the work of destruction. No effort is made to plant new trees; and not many years hence, Ar-Riyadh will have to look elsewhere I think for its wood. Like the shepherd who comes from the south seeking *al-haya* (the life=green pasture), the woodman too may have to travel far to keep the coffee-fire, at least, burning at the Capital.

Many shepherds with flocks of sheep, goats, and camels have we seen going through Wadi Hanifah; and I was surprised to hear that they had come all the way from Wadi 'd-Dawasir seeking pasture, and were headed of the Dahna. Some of them even come from the souther-most end of the Wadi, from the confines of Najran, trudging behind their flocks to Al-Hasa, a distance of about seven hundred miles, where they hope to sell their live wealth and buy some food and clothes. At that season of the year many of the Bedu with their camels and their young were on the move. The children were carried in baskets, two of which are slung across the camel's hump; some of them are crude contrivances of wood and rope. But I have seen children riding the bare-back; and a boy of about four years of age swung the stick over the long neck like a man, without even holding to the hump-hair of his mount. They are rocked on the back of the camel, the babies of the Arabs.

A few of the Ikhwan, we also met on the way, who were walking to Ar-Riyadh, and behind them was a black carrying a bundle—their provision. ' They are going to read,' said Hazlul; that is, they are going to study at the Capital the Koran and the Hadith, and get into the bargain some new clothes. Those who are more diligent and intelligent than the rest will also get a largess in money. They salaamed us from a little distance, and our

Chief drove his *zelul* towards them to get their news.
They were as eager it seems to get ours. What we
heard, after the brief interchange of inquiries, was the
voice of one of the Ikhwan crying : ' Give us back our
salaam ! ' and the voice of Hazlul replying : ' we give
back your salaam. Get ye gone ! '

I had an inkling of what had happened ; for Hazlul
was ordered by the Sultan not to reveal my identity to
passing strangers. But the Brothers were not convinced.
No one comes from Syria to buy camels in Najd ; the
people of Najd, on the contrary, go to Syria with their
camels. This man, meaning me, must be of the Ingliz—
a Nisrani ; and the Brothers salaamed whom they thought
was a Muslem, a Wahhabi. They, therefore, want back
their salaam. ' I gave it back to them,' said Hazlul, as
he folded his cigarette, ' and wished them all in Juhannam.'
At that moment a little shepherd came running towards
us, and like all his fellows, after salaaming, he inquired
about the life, the green pasture. ' Where is *al-haya* ?
Where did you see *al-haya* ? ' ' In the Dahna,' one of
our men replied. ' In Al-Hasa,' said another. ' I wish
it were nearer for his sake,' said Hazlul. ' Not all the
Bedu are mad like the Ikhwan.'

We were now approaching the Washm plain, having
passed the affluent of Wadi Hanifah, whose course,
north by south, is the road between Huraimala and
Dhorumah. We had camped the night before near
'Uyainah, and we ate our supper on the third day in a
shelter of the surrounding hills, not far from the western
gate of the Wadi, which runs from that point in a south-
easterly direction to Dir'iyah and thence almost due
south to Yamamah.

As we near the Washm coming from the south or the
east, or turning from Wadi Hanifah to go up, by way of
Sudous and Huraimala, to the Twaiq hills, we come upon
a formation of soil which is quite remarkable. The
calcareous ridges break up along the west side into slopes,

as soft in places as sand dunes, over which at right angles rise several strata of soil, turret-like, in a uniform design. And between these ridges, which, with their promontories, are a picturesque feature of an otherwise monotonous landscape, are the *sh'ibs* (glens) so dear to the herdsman ; for they form, to the west and the south, the drainage of Mt. Twaiq, and are always, except in years of drought, vivid with ' the life '—*al-haya*—green pasture !

As we started out from our camping place the following morning, we left behind us a brilliant sunrise, which soon was veiled in clouds, very thin in spots, so that their reflection on the turreted hills beyond was cast in a deep blue merging into purple. This coloration, which does not last long, is common in southern Najd, and is observable, when the sun dips its brush in the clouds, at any hour of the day. I have often seen the purple mantle shifting from one hill to another—skidding, in truth, like the clouds themselves.

CHAPTER XXIV

THE WASHM

In eighteen hours, divided into three marches, we came from Ar-Riyadh through Wadi Hanifah, and to its western gate on the Washm plain, near which stands the town that belies not its name. Barrah it is called, which in Arabic means, in the open, outside. And Barrah, a walled village of less than a thousand souls, most of whom are of Mutair Arabs, holds the key to the Wadi and the Plain; has a promontory [1] bearing its name, which we pass as we approach it from the east; and can furnish the Sultan for the *jehad* with two hundred combatants. But we had to pay for firewood and fodder. The Ameer, who came out to see us—we squatted in the shadow of his palm-grove—told us that his town is poor, that the Imam knows it to be poor, and that for this reason, upon the Ameer's own entreaty, he exempted it from the ordinary duty of hospitality. ' *Billah!* ' continued the poor-mouthed Mutairi, ' we would hide in shame rather than face our guests.' But he would not accept the money for the green vetch and the firewood, the money on which he insisted, before he produced the writ of exemption over the seal of the Sultan, and showed it to me, saying : ' The testimony of poverty, *billah!* and of shame.'

Hazlul laughed when the Ameer went away with double

---

[1] These promontories west of Jabal Twaiq, near Barrah and Mudhnib, the Arabs call *khushms* (snouts).

the price of his provision, still swearing by Allah and mumbling words about shame and poverty. 'A Mutairi beggar,' he said ; 'many of his like come every day to Abd'ul-Aziz.' But notwithstanding we enjoyed our breakfast ; and breathing of the expansive air of the plain, which to me was a boon after the depressing atmosphere of Wadi Hanifah, we lingered in the shadow of the Barrah palms till noon, where I made myself better acquainted with my brothers of the road.

Hazlul, the Chief, is a grim-visaged Arab with a child's heart. He uses his mind and his hand in the management of the *qafilah* (caravan) before he uses words. I do not mean to say that he strikes the bungling or the lazy one. No : he tucks up his sleeve and helps him.

Baddah, the braggart, the salacious 'Ujmani, is already known to the reader, who has accompanied us from Al-Hasa to Ar-Riyadh.

Salem, the silent, a Shammari with a cosmopolitan manner, is the coffee-maker, and he enjoys nothing so much as digging a hole in the ground and building a fire.

HAZLUL, OUR CHIEF

Fares, the ex-*zkirt*, is a hindu half-breed, who sticks to Hazlul on the march because he is generous with the *sabil* (pipe).

Misfer, the cook is, like our Chief, a Dowsari,[1] and is the possessor of a physiognomy and a soul, which are rare, very rare anywhere in life, and which, outside of Shake-

[1] A Dowsari, of the Dawasir tribe.

speare and Hugo, are hard to match in fiction. Caliban-
Misfer will occupy with our Chief the diwan of honour
in the hall of the elect.

Hamad, Misfer's assistant, is a freed black slave, who
hails from Tarabah, where he had a wife and a sherif for
master ; he had to take both or leave both. He is the
most prodigal and the least dressed member of the
qafilah ; and he carries an old sword which he bought in
Ar-Riyadh, after returning from a *gazu,* to maintain his
reputation as a brave warrior.

Hamoud, the Mutairi, is a boy of seventeen who has
already been in half a dozen *gazus,* and who can pick
his way at night through the Dahna as truly
as a ' b'dewi ' of Benu Murrah.

HAMOUD :
THE BEDUIN BOY

Makhlouf, the Harbi, is our one-act
comedian, who carries a strip of white
sheeting in his saddle-bag, which he uses
to make up as one of the Ikhwan ; and
when he. winds it around his head and
carries his bamboo stick like a gun on his
shoulder, he gallops forth and back crying :
' Warrior of the Bamboo, Brother of him
who smokes ! ' The Arabic parody of the slogan of the
Ikhwan[1] has a rhyme and a ring, which impart to it a
comic opera flavour.

These (and others who in time will be introduced to the
reader) sallied out of the shadow of the Barrah palms
about noon of the last day of January, when the heat of
the sun was more like that of an Indian summer in New
York, to make the Nufoud of Tharmadah, about fifteen
miles thence, before the sunset prayer. We started, all
in fine fettle, at a *dirham* pace, and Baddah, unable to
resist the exhilarating air, and the freedom-enticing vastness of the plain, lifted his loud and broad voice in song.

---

[1] Their slogan is : Warrior of the Unity, Brother of him who obeys
Allah. The parody in Arabic is : *Khaiyal ul-Khaizaran, Akhu Sahib ud-
Dukhan.*

' O thou rider of a trotter fair,
   Who never brings her owner ill ;
In but a glance she whips the dust and air,
   And but a glance will hold her still ;
A ten days' march she makes in two, I swear,
   In two to do her rider's will.'

He was singing the praise of every *zelul* in the *qafilah*, except Salem's, which was a black, hirsute, and restive animal, very difficult to control : she would not go at a sober *dirham* pace, and she would not walk. So Salem would lag a few hundred metres behind, and then giving her the rein, he would gallop ahead, while the coffee utensils which hung from the pegs of his saddle-frame would clatter in applause. And lo, Haizaboun !—that is her name—she comes in a cloud of dust, blowing like a whale, and electrifies the whole caravan ; men and mounts prick up their ears ; Baddah calls to Hazlul ; Hazlul arouses Makhlouf ; and the bamboos are brandished—the signal for a charge. Salem the loon comes on his Haizaboun.

' In but a glance she stirs the dust and air,
   And but a glance will hold her still.'

In my first experience of the gallop, I felt something melting in my breast, creating what seemed a vacuum, making breathing for a thrice impossible ; and I imagined the saddle rising and falling under me like a rolling wave ; but gradually I was able to control myself and the rein, and to brandish the bamboo as if I were of the Dawasir or the 'Ujman.

A splendid exercise is camel-riding, and a sure cure for indigestion. For even in the walk, although you be lulled to sleep on that rocking eminence, you are still exercising the muscles of the stomach ; and the ride no matter how long, may be an unmixed joy, without fatigue, if the pace is changed regularly from the walk to the *dirham*, to the gallop, and back to a walk. Neither the rider in this case suffers nor the mount. An Arab who has any pity for his camel will not ride at a walking pace for more than an hour at a time. That is Hazlul's rule, which was not observed, however, till I became tolerably proficient in the *dirham*. ' Air the mounts,' he would say, after we had walked them for about an hour.

' Air the mounts ' is not a figure of speech ; and for the benefit of the reader, whose knowledge of the camel may only be elementary, I shall make plain its literal meaning. The most sensitive part of a camel's anatomy is the hump ; and the frame of the saddle is so made as to fit around it without pressing upon it. Thus, that collop of fat is exposed through the wooden frame to the air ; and thus, too, a pack-camel is happier than a *zelul*, because the burden, no matter how heavy, presses upon the sides and not upon the top of the hump. But the *zelul's* burden, and though it is lighter, is more onerous, because the hump is covered, smothered with the furniture of the saddle-seat ; and then comes the rider, who sits right upon it. Not only is it deprived of air, therefore, but is subject to constant pressure from above. Add to this the friction resulting from a swaying, horizontal movement, and you will have an idea of the plight of the poor beast. But when you change the walk to a *dirham* pace, the movement becomes perpendicular, and admits as you go up and down a little air to cool the hump and refresh its owner.

In alternating the walk with the *dirham*, we reached the edge of the Nufoud of Tharmadah before the sunset prayer, and we camped there for the night. Early the following morning we resumed our march, ploughing through the sands of this Nufoud, which runs north-west to Shaqra.

When we reached Tharmadah an hour before noon we had to stop to see who was coming upon us—upon me. It was Dame Malaria in a four-horse-power engine, —I mean, four degrees of fever. But she came slowly, stealthily at first, and then began to coast up hill—pardon a paradox—from my feet to my head. Here she stopped

—a breakdown—and we had to stop also to assist her and pack her off. Was this the result of the *dirham*, which shook old Malaria out of her sleep ? I am certain that locally, at least, the *dirham* had a fatal effect ; and I must here record my thankfulness to the carbolated vaseline and to the determination that saved it, together with a bottle of quinine pills, from Saiyed Hashem, when he requisitioned my medicines the day before I left Ar-Riyadh. Otherwise, I should have used the native remedy, which consists of the droppings of goats roasted in a pan and ground into a powder, and then made with clarified butter into a salve.

Tharmadah is the city of Benu Tamim ; and its Ameer, a worthy beard, is of the branch of Sa'd, which of old was the flower of the tribe. As soon as we had camped, his men came to us with firewood, fodder, and a sheep for slaughter. Later he came himself to make salaam ; and he was amused when I told him the story of Brother Nowwar, who refused to pray for my recovery.[1] ' Some men are born good,' he said, ' some develop to be good, and others cannot be made good even by the sword of Abd'ul-Aziz, Allah prolong his days.' He then told me that they had three hundred *jalibs* in Tharmadah and three thousand rifle-bearers. But when the Ameer of Shaqra read these figures in my notebook, he struck out a zero from each, and said : ' This is right :—30 *jalibs* and 300 rifle-bearers.'

There is no doubt, however, that the water in Tharmadah and its environs is plentiful and on the whole good ; even as the natural goodness of its people ; and I was sorry we left the city of the gentle Tamims on the following day, before we gave Dame Malaria a chance to depart. But would she have departed ? Her spectre was my unseen companion all the way ; my *radif*, riding behind me ;— riding in me, trotting through my veins fire-shod to my very heart ;—the enemy whom I have combated for two

[1] See Chapter XVIII, p. 211.

months with nothing but quinine. And every battle was followed by a truce, and every truce by a false peace. So much so that we despaired of peace, both of us, and wished that the war would continue till a decisive victory on one side or the other was achieved.

The battle was resumed in Shaqra, where I was furnished with reinforcements by its Ameer and the Collector of the Zakat in the Washm Muhammad Suba'i. Theirs is that generosity, that nobility of which the ancients sing. The Ameer, a Qahtani, offered me the citizenship of the town, a house, a *zelul*, and a wife, if I chose to remain with them and become ' religious,' *i.e.* a Wahhabi. And he assured me that their women were not like those of Tharmadah, who leave it because their men cannot be just to them. ' The women of Tharmadah,' he said, ' with the halter on the neck, you will see roaming about everywhere. Not so our women, who are demure and content ; they seek not beyond the city wall a proxy.'

We were the guests of Muhammad Suba'i, a frail little man with an infinite curiosity, an indefatigable tongue, and an ambition to go to America. He dresses in robes of brocaded cloth instead of the usual striped tunics, covers his head with a cashmere shawl, and is an artist after a sort. He has decorated his own *qahwah* (reception hall), covering its walls with fretwork and geometric designs. But the most dominating trait of Suba'i after his goodness is his curiosity. He is avid of knowledge. His conversation is a series of question marks.

After taking me into the best room in his house and helping me to undress, and bringing me with his own hand a bowl of the best *laban* I have tasted in those parts, he sat down for a chat ; but seeing how tired I was—the fever did not worry him : ' It will go as it came ; '—he vouchsafed me an hour of rest and then returned to discuss with me the problems of life and the universe.

He is keen on history and geography. Our world was a wilderness, he believes, before Allah sent the Prophets to

make it a fit place for human habitation.—' The Prophets
are the servants of Civilization. . . . Hast thou a medicine
for the digestion, O Ameen ? '

Dear frail little Suba'i was so eager to increase not
only his knowledge but also his appetite and his flesh.
He did not weigh more than ninety pounds.   The English
he thinks are very wise ; and having once travelled with
them to Bombay he is fond of imitating them, especially
before dinner.   How they would run up and down the
deck of the steamer—' like this, to sharpen their appetite.
Come, O Ameen, let us go to Bombay.'   Saying which
he would take me by the arm, and like the Ingliz we would
pace up and down—going to Bombay !—on the terrace
of his home.   And in spite of the exiguousness of his flesh
and vigour, my brave little friend sits up with his guests,
both to entertain them and to improve his own mind, till
two o'clock in the morning.

Muhammad Suba'i is also an inventor after a sort.   He
carries in his inner bosom pocket a wooden key of his own
making ;—a master-key which is always in the making.
To it all the formidable bolts of the doors of his many-
roomed house must yield.   The servant comes and whispers
a word in the ear of mine host.   Whereupon he takes out
the charmed key, which is in the form of a tooth-brush,
manipulates the little sticks (from six to twelve of them
in place of the bristles), and gives it to the servant.   He
also carries in another pocket several match-sticks (some
bolts require more teeth than others) which he uses in
changing the combination—in changing the teeth to fit
into the grooves of that particular bolt.

—' Thinkest thou, O Ameen, that I can sell my camels
if I bring them with me to America ? '   This while he was
changing the combination of his tooth-brush key to fit
the bolt of the door to the room containing the rare rugs,
which he wanted to show me.   ' We the people of Najd,
O Ameen, are happy in the treasure of our faith.   Said
the Prophet in the Hadith—I will read it to thee.'   And

forthwith he draws out the key, takes one of the little
sticks out of one hole and puts it in another, changing the
combination to fit the bolt of the closet door, behind which
is locked the Book of the Sayings of the Prophet. ' No,
we have no secretary. It is easy to find one, but it is
difficult to find one to whom we can trust our secrets.
We do all the work, therefore, and endure. We only
complain of a weakness in the body. . . . If ours were the
health and strength of the Bedu ! ' He did complain also
of the lazy, dirty good-for-nothing Bedu.—' Yet, when
they come to us we have to humour them and " love "
(kiss) them between their eyes, and carry the food to them
with our own hands, or they will curse us and say that
we are infidels. The beduin when there is aught good
will alight, and when there is not will take to flight.'
Another like saying I heard him repeat is, ' Who does
not come to us when the country is in danger we welcome
not when the country is at peace.'

But all the men of Shaqra have paid the tax to the
Unitarian Faith ; not one of them but has joined in at
least one or two *jehads*. Besides, there is always one thousand rifle-bearers ready for the call. This gives the city
a population of about five thousand souls, some of whom
are of Benu Tamim. But the majority are of Benu Khalid
and Benu Zeid : the latter are of Qahtan, the former of
'Aneza, which is a branch of 'Adnan. Hence they are, or
they were, ancient enemies ; but they all live in Shaqra
to-day as the brothers of one Faith in harmony and peace.
And although the Najd charges the Qahtani with miserli-
ness and jests about it, I have found him in Shaqra as in
Al-Yaman a kind and generous host. He invites you to
a princely spread and then apologizes, saying : ' We have
but two desserts in Najd, cold water in summer and a
good fire in winter.'

Indeed, Shaqra is distinguished in the Washm for its
excellent water, in praise of which the people still repeat
the word of a beduin who drinking of it for the first time

exclaimed : ' Get thee gone, O Rain ! ' But the rain, which the beduin often drinks even from a puddle on the road, is exceptionally generous to Shaqra, for it supplies as many as eighty *jalibs* within its wall of defence. It is also distinguished from other cities in the Washm in that its palms like its women stray not beyond the city wall. They are scattered among the houses, setting them off and relieving the white glare of sun and clay, which is intensified when, as in Tharmadah and Barrah, they surround the city.

The many *jalibs* in Tharmadah and Shaqra are a certain proof of the abundance of water in the Washm ; for the drainage of Mt. Twaiq runs in a south-westerly direction under this plain to the Kharj and the Aflaj, where it comes to the surface, even as it runs in a south-easterly direction under the Dahna and the Summan to appear in Al-Hasa. Not only in the towns but in the *qasrs* also, for which the Washm is famous, do we get a proof of the subterranean streams—a proof, too, that they are mostly going to waste. The *qasr* I have already mentioned ; but in the Washm, I must add, the *qasr* is a grange composed of a quadrangle, at each corner of which is a tower, with dwellings, pens, a *jalib*, a *qahwah*, and a mosque within. It is used as a fort in war time. And these *qasrs*, which are many miles apart, are surrounded by meagre zones of green, between which are stretches of land as barren as the Summan.

Now, if artesian wells were bored in the Washm and the land canalized, those little zones of cultivation would so expand as to meet each other, and the barren soil would disappear. This is true also of the Qasim.

But I am forestalling the reader. We are still in the vicinity of Shaqra ; for the first day out after a rest is but half a day, so much having to be done besides the farewell speeches and the osculations. An hour after we leave the city we get a view of Mushaiqer to our right, which is one of the two oldest towns in the Washm, the

other being Tharmadah. One of the most striking land-
scapes, too, does Mushaiqer present—a masterpiece in
massing. For there in the foreground is the green of
the palm groves, behind which are the soft red dunes,
over which rise the purple hills of Twaiq—a pastel by
Renoir. And it was exhibited on a wall of turquoise blue
with a wainscoting of pale gold, that is the sand between
it and us as we passed.

An adequate token at this juncture is a work of art ;
for we are on the highway that wore out of old the sandals
of the poets. Here, in sooth, is the *dirah* of the first of
Arab bards, the warrior and singer and king who said :

> ' O let us pause and moan the days of love and home and lea
> In Siqt'ul-Lewa, twixt the shades of Ad-Dukhoul and
> Howmali.'

I knew not whether Siqt'ul-Lewa is in these parts, and
whether Ad-Dukhoul and Howmali are between Tharmadah and the Nufoud ; but Hazlul, who is also a poet,
tells me that a few miles to our left is a town called
Athathiyah, which is the birthplace of the poet Jarir, and
that between Tharmadah and Athathiyah is Marat, the
town of Umru'ul-Qais the poet-king.

> ' And then to Tawdah and Maqrat of which the vestiges
> remain,
> Because the north and south winds heap and sweep the
> sands alternately.' [1]

But the Washm has been smitten in its poetry as in its
soil. No vestige of glory, no vestige of culture remains.
Even the Dawsari looks down upon its people, and the
hillman, the Sdeiri, counts them among the long-eared
kind. He often repeats, to prove his own superiority, the
following lines :

> ' Think me not a donkey of the Washm,—
> Of Tharmadah, Mushaiqer, or Marat.'

---

[1] These are the two first lines of the poem of Umru'ul-Qais, which is
considered the best of the Mu'allaqat.

Between Shaqra, which is the last town of the Washm to the north, and Wadi's-Sirr, is the Nufoud, or correctly speaking, the two Nufouds, the little and the big ; the first is called Al-Batra and is about five miles across, the other is called Al-Jazam and is about fifteen. We rode up and down the dunes, some of which are about three hundred feet in height ; and the view, as the camels slowly plough through the sands, is pleasant in its shifting forms—the variety in the composition although in two colours only, is striking. For the shades of grey of the burnt and denuded vegetation are splashed on the golden sands and wrought here and there into fascinating designs. Had it rained that season the opulent grey of the 'ubal and the 'arfaj would have been replaced by a rich green. Other plants, which are found in a state of decay, and which were recognized by the camels, who brushed their lips against their broken stems and passed, are the 'alanda, which is like the broom in stem, the qaisum, a thyme-like herb, and the thada which has a red bloom. The colocynth too abounds ; and its lemon-like fruit, which camels avoid, is given, I was told, to the sheep in summer, because it quenches their thirst and helps to make good milk.

The dunes are vividly expressive in colour only in the morning and about sundown ; but on a cloudy day at noon a purple something seems to undulate and brood. Before or after that, in the morning or afternoon hours, they are a study in grey. The clouds coquette with the sun ; the sands lose their lustre ; the velvety grey of the vegetation is subdued by a faded green ; and now and then under a feeble ray something glows here and there —a bright-eyed fairy winks and disappears.

Between Al-Batra or the Little Nufoud and Al-Jazam is about a mile of gritty soil ;—a circular patch, at the end of which is a heap of basalt rocks, black and greenish, of uniform size ; and not far from it is a sprinkle of ob- sidian, some of the pieces of which are like the knives and arrow-heads exhibited in museums of natural history.

Crossing the volcanic field we come to Al-Jazam and begin the ascent in a westerly direction, from one dune up to another ;—we go up a stairway, as it were, with landings hollowed by abrasion, revealing a smooth white floor as of cement. A floor sprinkled with sand—for the dance ! —of the fairies !

When we reach the last summit, the last landing in the staircase, which is about seven hundred feet from the bottom, we sight on the distant horizon the palms of the village called 'Ain or where the wells, 'Uyoun 'us-Sirr, catch the water that flows from the Nufoud or under it from Twaiq. And having descended to about the same level as the volcanic field we left behind us, we follow the stream that leads to the wells, and thence proceed through Wadi's-Sirr, due north to Mudhnib, which is to those coming from the south the first town of the Qasim.

CHAPTER XXV

THE QASIM

THE Nufoud, which we entered a few hours after we left
Barrah, lost sight of between Tharmadah and Shaqra,
and recrossed in two sections separated by a field of gravel
and obsidian to Wadi's-Sirr, continues to our right as
we go up the Wadi as far as 'Aushaziyah, where we diverge
from it, and connects I was told with another body of
sand which is between Buraidah and Zilfi. It would thus
be about a hundred and twenty-five miles long, and is
separated from the Twaiq hills by the plain, which in the
south is called the Washm. Its breadth, where we last
crossed it, is about twenty miles ; but it is lesser at other
points and only a little broader at its northern end
between Zilfi and Buraidah.

As we go up Wadi 's-Sirr, which is bordered on the west
with low-lying hills resembling, under a gradation of
purple shades mixed by the sun through the clouds, a sea
on the horizon, we keep within view to the east the
caravan of golden dunes which recedes every now and
then, however, and disappears behind an undulation or
what in Najd is called a rib in the soil. But it does not
disappear entirely ; for at intervals it lifts up its golden
pennant—a peak or a summit—to announce its reap-
pearance.

Northward we continue for a whole day till we reach
Mudhnib,[1] an unwalled town with a sense of security as

[1] The distance between 'Uyoun 'us-Sirr and Mudhnib on the map I carried
with me (scale : 1 inch, 48 miles, published under the direction of Col.

vast it seems as its spaces, and a well-being reflected by
the abundance of its palms. We rode through a boulevard
with gardens and houses on both sides, the first of its kind
I have seen in Arabia, and turning north as we issue out
of that pleasant thoroughfare we come in a few minutes
to the town itself, which has a big square and several
jalibs before its front door. Here we meet again with the
donkey, whom we left behind us beyond the Dahna and
the Summan ; but the Qasim animal looks not as pros-
perous, is not as portly, as that of Al-Hasa.

There is not much difference outwardly, however,
between the Arabs here and those we have seen in the
south. The Ameer, to whom we had sent a courier with
a note, had one of his men direct us to our camping-place,
a very pleasant spot surrounded with *athls* and palms,
where he had already dispatched wood for our fire, a sheep
for our supper, and fodder—dry grass—for our camels. A
worthy beard who came later in the evening to say
salaam and to inquire of Hazlul about the Shioukh, the
rain, the pasture, and other topics of the day. He also
smoked the cigarette which the Chief folded and presented
to him.

The Qasim is nine hundred feet above Al-'Ared, and
two hundred miles away from its centre of inordinate
zealotism ;—the character of the people, therefore, like
the air and the vegetation is a little different. The
kindness and generosity of those we have met in the cities
of the Washm may not be surpassed in any of the northern
towns ; but while my men could not smoke in Shaqra,
for example, except in secret, they smoked openly in
Mudhnib and with those in authority. They did not
relax, however, in their strict observance of the hours of
prayer, especially in the morning and at sunset ; and
when it was not possible to stop for the afternoon prayer

Sir S. G. Burrard, Surveyor General of India) is forty-eight miles, and that
between Mudhnib and 'Aushaziyah is twenty. This is a mistake ; for the
former is not more than thirty miles and the latter is twelve.

it was combined with the one that followed it, just as the
noon prayer was always combined with that of the
morning. This is permitted to a Muslem while travelling.

There is adjacent to Mudhnib a formation of soil
similar to that around Barrah as we come out of Wadi
Hanifah ; but the plateau here, though not as high as it
is in the south, breaks abruptly in several places forming
heads of land uniform in design, which look like ramparts
or foundations for fortresses. The same strata in them all
rise at a right angle above the rubble and earth, which
slope gently to the *athl* trees at their base. Another
feature of the soil between Mudhnib and 'Aushaziyah,
are the many loam floors of dried-up ponds or lakes,
which sink in places beneath the soft pad of a camel's
hoof. It is marsh land, and because of its salinity quite
barren. I was told in Tharmadah that mineral streams
run along side of the sweet water in their district. This
is quite possible considering the natural phenomenon of
which these saline marshes are the result.

This phenomenon which we behold before we approach
'Aushaziyah I first thought to be an illusion, even like
that of the purplish, bluish undulations on the western
horizon : a sea there, and a river here at the base of the
Nufoud. No, it is not a mirage ; nor is the broad white
ribbon, which runs for about three miles along the dunes
between the sable soil and the golden sand, a river of
water. I asked Hazlul and he said indifferently, ' That
is the *qa*'.' I asked Salem and he replied : ' The *qa*'.'
I turned to Baddah : ' What is the *qa*' ? ' Baddah :
' The *qa*', Allah keep thee, is the *qa*.''

The word in Arabic means plain, and it is correctly used
in Al-Yaman, where Qa' Yarim, for instance, means the
plain of Yarim. And there the colour of the *qa*' is green
or, if cultivated, dark brown. But here the colour is white,
white as snow ; and it did not change as we came nearer
to it. Nor was there observable on the surface any
indication of living water.

When we arrived at 'Aushaziyah, therefore, I went down, accompanied by Hazlul and Baddah, to explore the *qa'*—the river—the mystery. It was a relief to get out of the tent, which filled in a trice with flies. For what with the noonday heat, the saline soil, and the 'Ujmani choosing the worst spot for encampment, anything were preferable to being under canvas.

We crossed a grove of sparse and stunted palms and thence through thickets of *tarfa*, which is a dwarf species of *tamarisk*, we came to a stretch of dark muddy soil, in which we waded to the *qa'*—the river ! Yes, there is a river in Central Arabia, a frozen river of salt. Two inches thick at the edge, white as ice, and in places as smooth, the river is about a mile wide and ten miles long. My companions followed me gingerly across the dark, sticky muddy bank, and we stood on a white sheet with streaks indicating the fissures through which the salt water had oozed and subsequently dried up or evaporated. The surface is both dry and warm ; we sat down ; and the illusion of an ice-covered lake on which you could sit down without shivering, was fascinating. Indeed, I even wished that by some miracle a block of salt might turn into a block of ice.

' Hard as the rock,' said Hazlul, testing the surface with the butt of his gun before he stood upon it. ' Dry as the sand,' said Baddah before he sat down. It was the first time they ever visited the *qa'*. ' *Wallah*, ya Hazlul,' said the 'Ujmani, ' there are wonders in the land of Najd.' ' And the most wonderful,' said the Chief, ' is that we know nothing about them.' ' I know now what to reply when I am asked, What is the *qa'* ! The *qa* I would say is a river whose water is frozen and dry ! ' ' The *qa'*,' said Hazlul, ' is a sea of salt.' And as he applied his finger to the surface and then to his tongue : ' Aye, *billah*, this is the salt.' We cut a block of it, which was three inches thick, a vertical view of which revealed a quantity of dirt and straw. As one proceeds across,

however, it becomes purer and thicker. But judging
from the quality offered in the streets of 'Anaizah, where
it is sold in blocks and chunks like ice, I would say that
they do not venture very far into the *qa'* for their salt.

'Aushaziyah is a small and very poor village. Its
saltpan is the blight of its soil. There is hardly any
vegetation in its vicinity ; and its people have little or no
live stock. The Ameer who would send us but firewood
came to make his apology, and was most gracious about it.

But the people of 'Aushaziyah are the salt of the earth.
On our return from the *qa'* a gentleman met us in the
palm-grove and asked us to have coffee at his house. We
accepted. And he, the richest man in the town, took us
to his dwelling-place, which is a series of mud hovels, into
one of which we entered and had our fill of the thick
smoke of the coffee-fire before we had our coffee. But
our host with the wealth of his qualities made up in my
own poor estimation, not his, for what he and the town
lacked. He, however, was neither self-conscious nor
apologetic. While making the coffee he lighted a pipe
and offered it to Hazlul, who shared it with Baddah.

A servant then brought in a platter of what to me was
better than the coffee and the smoke. I had heard of the
'abit ; but it was the first time I had tasted of stoned dates
kneaded with butter and sugar into a paste. And when
I asked for more mine host joyfully exclaimed, ' *Wallah !*
thou art free like the people of Al-Qasim.' Later in the
day, when he came to see us, he brought with him some
'abit for me and a little tobacco for my *rafiqs.* ' *Wallah !*
we would have brought more,' said he, apologizing for
the tobacco, ' but it is very scarce.'—' . . . And why,' he
continued, ' did you not camp in our neighbourhood ?
It is a better shelter from the wind.'

Soon after supper we realized the truth of his words.
My tent was set north by south ; that of the men, which
was but a canvas lifted on four poles and closed at the
back, was open to the north. The fire was blazing before

it, and the men were sitting and chatting in the light of the blaze. Otherwise it was very dark. I was in my tent writing by the light of a candle when of a sudden it was snuffed out by the wind. I tightened the door-flap and sought my electric lamp, which I kept for emergencies, but the battery, the last I had, was exhausted. It was too early to sleep, so I walked out intending to join the coffee circle. But the wind, which had risen to a gale, was tugging at the canvas, wrenching it and scattering the fire sparks in every direction.

The wood blazed for a moment ; the smoke and ashes were blown into our faces ; but we turned our backs to the wind thinking that we could hold out till it subsided. Hazlul ordered the men to cling to the tent poles and fasten the pegs ; but the wind tugged more violently at the canvas and almost wrenched it away. ' Let it go,' said the Chief ; ' pull it down, quick.' He then ordered Baddah and two others to attend to my own tent and keep it standing. It was pitch dark ; the gale did not abate its force ; and while Baddah and his assistants were fumbling for tent pegs and driving them deeper into the earth, Hazlul at the head of his men took hold of the canvas, and in less than ten minutes made it turn about face to the south. Salem quickly dug a new fire hole ; Misfer and Hamoud with the few lighted sticks that remained ran from one side to the other as the wind blew what they carried into sparks and what they wore into balloons ; Hazlul moved the wood ; Makhlouf the coffee utensils ; and thus in ten minutes the manoeuvre against the attacking force was admirably and neatly accomplished.

To do the few things that are to them most essential in life, the people of Najd are well trained and equipped. They are quick, light, skilful, and thoroughgoing. Hazlul, who rated Baddah for choosing this camping spot and threatened that he would not send him again as advance-courier, seemed, nevertheless, to welcome this incident, which showed me what he and his men can do in a pinch.

His face beamed satisfaction as we resumed our sitting around Salem's new fire with our backs and the back of the tent to the wind.

Late in the evening when it subsided I heard what seemed like the fall of rain. It was a most pleasant sensation, one I had not experienced for six months, and I lay awake listening to the patter on my tent as to a piece of music.

Early the next morning we left 'Aushaziyah in a drizzle ; and I found that Hazlul notwithstanding his threat had despatched Baddah ahead of us with letters from the Sultan and from himself to the Ameer of 'Anaizah. Hazlul, veteran soldier, is satisfied with nothing but the best. So he writes letters, dictates them to Fares the scribe—*From Hazlul son of 'Ubaid to the Ameer so and so*—announcing our arrival and ordering food, fodder, firewood, and a palace. He assumes the Sultan's manner and often succeeds. ' Hear thou,' says he when he would have one take his word and heed it, ' I will inform thee, I will enlighten thee.' But he is always solemn and correct, though never unjust or overbearing, in the exercise of his authority.

He was indignant at the weather not only for the sake of Najd and its people, but also because he carried an umbrella. Why does it not rain when he Hazlul of the fierce Dawasir had come armed ? When it did rain, however, he was deprived of the use of his weapon ; for seeing that I myself had not an umbrella, he opened his and offered it to me. I refused it, saying that I enjoyed the rain. Besides, I had an esthetic feeling against anything so overshadowing above the head of one enthroned on the eminence of a camel's back. I pulled my *aba*, therefore, like the men over my head ; and the chief folding his cherished umbrella did likewise. He would not be so indecorous as to use it and be the only one among us so distinguished.

The country between 'Aushaziyah and 'Anaizah is the

hardest, rockiest, and most barren we have yet traversed. I do not think that outside the Harra is there such a fierce sterility. Were it not for the rain, which engaged and refreshed the spirit, it would have been for me most trying. To the native it is not any better or any worse than other soils. He looks not this way or that for relief from pain or from monotony ; he looks to Allah alone. The year of the Spanish fever, which visited even these desert wastes of Arabia, is called in Najd, ' The Year of Mercy ; ' for Allah had thought of those people—the many thousand victims of the Influenza—and drew them in fierce love to his breast.

CHAPTER XXVI

'ANAIZAH AND BURAIDAH

AFTER a ride of two hours across the plateau, the rocky waste called Safra, we come to the end of it, and lo ! an oasis surrounded by the red Nufoud and a city set amidst the palms. More like a stage scene it seemed at that hour —a dream-city—with the tall palms and the graceful *athls* in groups gracing its walls, and the sand of the dunes glistening in the first beams of the unveiling sun.

The queen-city of the Qasim and the Paris of Najd 'Anaizah is called. Of a certainty, a bird's-eye view of it surpasses that of Paris, which is neither crowned with emeralds nor zoned with gold. There may be something akin to it in the paintings of Manet or in the pages of the Arabian Nights. A small, humble and peace-inspiring city which has withal the advantage of contrast ;—a white temple half hidden in the palms and surrounded with *athls* which are half covered with sand ;—a pearl on a plate of jade on a cloth of gold. Indeed, Arabia is a land of strong contrasts—the green of the oases, the gold of the dunes, the purple of the hills, the sable of the land of death, the Safra—and there are no shades, no adumbrations.

We go down from the plateau in a sharp incline to a hollow in the land about three miles long by two wide, surrounded on three sides, north and west and south, by the hilly Nufoud. In that hollow is the city and its palm-groves ; and around the city wall are zones of *athl* trees, which are planted there to keep back the sands. Thus, 'Anaizah and the Nufoud are enemies and ever at war.

For this reason, too, it cannot expand. Its thirty thousand souls are crowded within its double wall, and bridges are built across its streets, and extensions above the bridges to overcome in a measure the crowded condition. But 'Anaizah has an extensive bazaar of one main and many minor streets, well lighted by the sun, where you may find things that remind you of America and England or transport you to India and Japan, and where you hear spoken, besides several Arabic dialects, English and French and Hindustani.

Yes, there is a cosmopolitan accomplishment but not without a tinge of pretension in 'Anaizah. Of a certainty, the faces of the people are more open, more friendly and appealing than those of the south. Wahhabism here has lost its sting. I have even seen some *athl* trees recently planted in the cemetery. As for tobacco, it is not used or sold freely, but it is to be found. One man in the *Souq* said to me in English, ' It is sold in private.' Nor do they take advantage of the prohibition to make a fortune. In Najd, cupidity goes not with *allahu akbar*.

A traveller may be noticed but not as a stranger in 'Anaizah ; for many of its citizens have also travelled in foreign lands, and some of its best families [1] have commercial and banking connections with houses in Basrah and Bombay as well as in Damascus and Cairo. It is moreover the custom of the better class to entertain the stranger, whether a native from other parts of the Peninsula or a Nisrani from beyond the seven seas, by asking him to coffee—*We would ' coffee ' thee*—at their homes.

This invitation to coffee is like the invitation of the English to tea ; there is in both, besides the social brew, a delectable something, a florescence not only of esteem or curiosity or both but also of genuine friendliness.

[1] The Sleims, for instance, the Bassams, the Zkeirs, and the Qadis.

And the Arab host, like the English hostess, serves his guests with his own hand ; but unlike many a hostess, he does so in a simple and unaffected manner.

' You are invited to coffee at the house of Abdullah ibn Yahya,' said our attendant as we were coming out of the house of the Ameer an hour after we had arrived. And Ibn Yahya, a genial old sheikh of the Sleim family, met us at the door of his qahwah and led us to the cushions of honour around the fire-place, where he took his seat behind a formidable array of coffee and tea pots. The qahwah, as the reception room in all Najd is called, is as a rule the most interesting and the most pleasant part of the house. It has a high ceiling, which is supported on columns of stone covered with plaster, and a double row of small windows high above each other which are opened and closed with cords. The design cut in the white plaster is more elaborate and finished than what I have seen in Ar-Riyadh. A zone of circles enclosing stars and flanked by V's, scalloped, is a common design ; another is a simulation of crenelles ; and between the two are panels in which are inscribed lines of poetry or verses from the Koran. The ground is the rough plaster, and the effect is that of point lace on an Arab smock. Here, too, the contrast between the elaborate mural decorations and the crude ceiling, which is of *athl* rafters and palm ribs, is characteristic. On the whole, especially when the walls and rafters are stained with the smoke of the qahwah-fire, the effect approaches the classic. It is expressive of ancestral dignity and gloom.

An alcove for the firewood and a closet for the utensils are built behind the fire-place or along side of it, in both instances within the reach of the host and his assistant, who sits near him ; and before them in a row are the brass coffee pots, always burnished bright, of various sizes, from the one that serves a few guests to the one that serves a hundred. The assistant pulverizes the coffee in a stone mortar with a long pestle also of stone, making it ring in rhythmic measure of the joy of the moment, the joy of the host in welcoming his guests.

Speaking of Abdullah'l-Bassam, Charles Montagu Doughty [1] says : ' His mortar rang out like a bell of hospitality when he prepared coffee.' He once mentions tea, the use of which was not then so extensive in Najd. But no host these days serves coffee without following it with a brew, the major ingredients of which are sugar and milk. It is nevertheless called tea ; but I have heard people speak of it as sweet coffee. It is served in glasses, and is an indispensable part of the ceremony. After the tea the host rises with the incense burner in his hand, which he offers to his guests, three or four times in succession, and they perfume their beards, sniffing the fumes of aromatic wood, or place the burner under their *gutrahs* and their *abas* to perfume the head and breast. A leisurely manner marks the whole entertainment—I should say, ceremony—which is generally prolonged for the sake of conversation. After the incense, however, the guests may rise and go, saying to the host, Allah favour thee, Allah honour thee.

But their manner at meals is curt and may seem to the stranger crusty. The people of Najd eat but twice a day ; their first meal about ten in the morning is called dinner, and their second, between the afternoon and the sunset prayers, is supper. That they do not converse while eating is generally known ; but even after meals no reception is held, for there is a tradition which enjoins dispersion directly after they wash their hands.

The Prophet Muhammad once said : ' After ye are fed, disperse.' This is because he was too often annoyed by those who came to his spread. They ate, and lingered, and talked, and bored him, when he would desire privacy or prefer to spend the evening with his harim. But he could not say to his guests in crude human speech, Now that ye have eaten, begone. One of the

[1] *Arabia Deserta.*

fruits of faith, one of the proofs, according to the Ulema is a sense of shame. So the Prophet Muhammad was helped out of his difficulty by the Angel Gabriel. Hence the divine dictum, ' *After ye are fed, disperse*,' which the people of Najd strictly observe. That is why coffee is not served after meals ; only soap and water—and then a brief salaam.

That is why too I have always preferred to be ' coffeed ' in 'Anaizah than fed, particularly when my host was a Sleim or a Bassam. Abd'ul-Aziz ibn Abdullah Aal Sleim who had entertained us several times between the two prayers and after—in the afternoon and the evening—at his home and in his palm garden, was eager to know everything about 'Amrikah ; ' but he included in his curiosity both geography and dentistry. He deplored the fact that there are no dentists in 'Anaizah, and said : ' One day we might go to ' Amrikah ' to verify the fame of its doctors of the teeth and to see its tall buildings.'

His nephew Abdullah, the Ameer of 'Anaizah, who put us up in a palace recently built on the site of the oldest house in the city, for the Sultan Abd'ul-Aziz when he visits the Qasim, was so cosmopolitan as to converse with us at the many meals we ate at his house ; and he surprised me the morning of our departure with a pastry cake called *hunaihah*, which combines the excellencies of both the *khabis* [1] and *'abit*,[2] and which is served in a platter over an earthen brazier containing live coals— the 'Anaizah Arab's chafing-dish.

The Ameer Abdullah, like his uncle, is a landowner who does not disdain to work on his plantation ; but notwithstanding the deep interest he takes in agriculture, he is still like all Arabs a captive of its ancient traditions. He asked me about oil-engines and artesian wells, and

---

[1] See Chapter XI, p. 119. [2] See Chapter XXV, p. 281.

First the *khabis* is made, then the *'abit*, which is added to it, and the two are cooked together in clarified butter and made into what resembles a plum pudding.

R.I.S. T

then said : ' We have heard that the Sultan Abd'ul-Aziz is going to use them in Al-Hasa. When he does we shall follow him, *inshallah.*' ' In religion,' runs the Arabic saying, ' people are after their king.' And in agriculture also it seems.

Even Abdullah ibn Muhammad 'ul-Bassam confirms what I say ; for in spite of his knowledge and his experience, and his modernity in many of the affairs of life, he will not go ahead of the Long-of-Days at Ar-Riyadh. But let me begin with Abdullah at the beginning. I was surprised the evening he first invited me to coffee when he told me in the light of an arc lamp that he was the friend and protector of Khalil (Charles Montagu Doughty). His face, which looked ridiculously young in the limelight, certainly belied history ; for Khalil adventured through Central Arabia fifty years ago. Nevertheless, Abdullah was his understanding friend and his protector against the fanaticism and inhumanity of the people. What a heroic spirit that wandered in those days among a people who closed their hearts and homes to the Nisrani ! And what a noble spirit that opened to him, in those days, the door of hospitality—of security and peace !

When I saw Abdullah the following day in his palm-grove, he was true to his years in spite of his dyed beard. He has a pleasant smile and a genuine cosmopolitan spirit. He is also a progressive farmer after a sort and a reader of books. He told me that Khalil had no tact, and that Al-Kenneyny, his host and persecutor in those days, was the last of his generation. No one in 'Anaizah to-day will beat a stranger, a Nisrani, if he does not go to the Mosque to pray. Indeed, the people of 'Anaizah have advanced ; for since the days of the Criminal Dowla and the fanatic Wahhabi sheikhs, several European travellers —Shakespear, Knox, Leachman, Philby—have passed their way and claimed their hospitality.

Said Abdullah 'l-Bassam : ' I was a young man when Khalil came to 'Anaizah, and Al-Kenneyny was his first friend and protector. He too was cursed by the people and called an infidel like the Englishman. Forty-five years have now passed and I have witnessed the change. Yes, there is a big change. Only three in those days dared to openly befriend the stranger and protect him. Three only. But to-day, if Khalil came back to us, he would not meet with anyone that might offend him in word or deed.'

If Kenneyny was the last of his generation, Abdullah 'l-Bassam is the first of his. And he has the great satisfaction of seeing it flourish in his own days, even like his beautiful garden in the desert. We walked out of the city northward into the Nufoud, where Abdullah had dug a deep *jalib*—made the very rocks under the red sand gush forth with the first principle of life—and planted within the big wall a grove of palms. His men were still at work. The long blocks, quarried in the vicinity of the Safra, are carved like gargoyles and laid into canals through which the sweet water flows amidst the brilliant green of the vetch to water the pomegranates and the palms as well as the vegetation beneath their shade.

Abdullah's *jalib*, whose water passes through an iron vein and is, therefore, ' a tonic—better than any medicine made in Europe,' he said—is the biggest in 'Anaizah. It is 25 by 15 by 75 feet deep, 35 of which are carved in the living rock without blasting ; and it was finished in less than three months at a cost of 3000 Marie Theresas, or $1500. I asked him what he paid for labour. ' Some receive a real for every three days,' he replied, ' others a real for four days, but to the few skilled labourers I pay a real every two days.' In other words the scale runs from ten to twenty-five cents a day.

When we arrived the camels were drawing water from the *jalib*; the men who were seated in a circle had just finished eating their dinner and were sipping coffee poured out of shining pots of beaten brass ; the silvery water was flowing among the palms ; and all around beyond the garden wall the desert smiled upon the enchanted scene. One thing I missed—flowers. Nowhere in Najd have I seen a flower pot or a nursery bed.

But Abdullah had a compensating surprise. Amidst the palms was set a house made of palm branches, its floors spread with clean red sand, and all around were leaning pillows of clay. This is his summer residence. ' And here,' said he, as he took me through it, ' is the harim quarter.' The Arab loves his privacy and is fastidious about it. The custom of secluding women imposes upon him what has become an art. The harim quarter whether of the poor or the rich may not be always exceptionally clean, but is seldom so bad as the tenements in a big city.

This, of Abdullah'l-Bassam's summer residence, is composed of more than ten palm booths curiously involved, in which a male stranger might fatally lose himself. But the two most interesting features of the place are the *qahwah*, at the door of which the water flows in rocky ducts, and a walled circular path leading to a rock-cistern—the bath—which is open to the sun and sky and fed by a running stream. Here be a luxury in primitive fashion, voluptuously conceived ;—the cool sweet water flows at your door, the hot sun falls impotent upon your roof, and the palms shelter you and your harim from the gaze of the curious ;—a desert atmosphere moulded to the whim of a man of the world.

There is plenty of water it seems as well as plenty of sand around 'Anaizah ; for while they are always planting *athls* around its wall to keep back the advancing Nufoud, their efforts in digging into the heart of their enemy for water is no less remarkable. Other large *jalibs*, when I visited the garden of Abdullah'l-Bassam, were being constructed outside the city. And it is remarkable what skill they can command when it is a question of prime necessity. After digging six or seven feet in the sand a square of 15 by 15 feet, a scaffolding of *athl* logs is built

over it, into which is mounted a wheel with its tackle for
their use as they go deeper down ; at the same time a
frame is set up around the sides of the portions dug to keep
the sand from falling upon them ; and if they do not find
water when they reach the solid rock, they bore into it
sometimes as deep as thirty feet. After which they begin to
build the sides of the *jalib* with dressed blocks of stone in
such a way as to make one wish that their houses were
similarly constructed. But they reserve their good material and their best skill for securing the prime necessity—
water—*al-haya*—the life. Given water they can put up
in booths of hair and be happy. In fact most of the
people of 'Anaizah move into the Nufoud for the spring
season, taking their cattle and sheep with them to pasture ;
and thus they live in tents for three or four months of
the year.

Another instance of their inventive skill is the *jalib*
wheel, which without any scientific knowledge they
construct scientifically. It is generally made of *athl* wood,
the hardest in the land ; and the hub, the spokes, the rim,
the teeth, they are all fitted together skilfully, solidly and
without a single nail. For they must have found out by
experience what water will do to a nail, and what a rusty
nail will do to the wheel.

But the most remarkable in the gear of the *jalib* is the
rope, which is neither of hemp nor of cotton, nor of flax.
The rope at which the camel pulls to draw water for the
thirsty land ; the rope that sings a duet with the wheel,
and holds out even longer than the wheel in patient toil ;
the rope that once sweated and groaned in the service
of man and now sweats in the service of the soil ;—that
very rope at which the camel tugs is drawn out of the neck
of the camel.

Strange, indeed, are the uses of this solemn and ever
groaning beast—stranger in death than in life.

I have even seen a butter in the *Souq* made of the marrow
which is extracted from the bones of the camel. And here,

O thou child of prosperity and well-being, is the climax in the tragedy of man and beast in Central Arabia. It has been written in books sacred and profane that in lean years the Arab eats the locust, the jerboa, the *dhob ;* that is true ; but it has not yet been recorded in the World's History of Necessity and Invention that he also eats the hoofs of the camel. He does it in this way. The hoofs are roasted, ground into powder, and kneaded into a cake.

The same spirit of economy and invention is observable in the architecture of 'Anaizah, which the Nufoud, as I have said, will not permit to expand. Bridges with houses upon them are therefore built across the streets ;—an economy which New York might imitate in its slums if it would make them more dark and dank. I have seen the same feature of construction in Shaqra. The street is a passage through the ground floors as it were of the tenements.

But the *Souq* is open to the sky, though not always to the buyer. Only a few hours of the day are vouchsafed for trade. When I asked the attendant about nine in the morning to go out with me, he said : ' The *Souq* is not yet open.' On another day I wanted to go out about noon. —' The *Souq* is closed ; the people are at prayer.' And about four in the afternoon, the time of the third daily devotion, it closes for the day.

Thus it is that while Japan is competing with America in grey sheeting, and Abbadan with Texas in oil, the citizen of 'Anaizah, who uses both and prefers the best at a higher price,[1] opens his shop from four to five hours a day and has ample time after prayers even for a game of checkers outside the city wall on the desert sand. Young men and old have I seen seated in the shade of the *athl* or the palm, with several rows of holes dug in the sand

[1] American sheeting is sold for ten reals a piece, the Japanese for eight ; and although the latter has a few more yards to the piece, the former because of its quality is more popular. And notwithstanding that Standard oil is one real more a case than the Anglo-Persian, it is more in demand in Central Arabia.

between them, playing a game which is a cross between checkers and backgammon. And they may be grave and staid merchants of the bazaar or hawkers who run up and down the street crying their wares as they do in Ar-Riyadh. But they run faster in 'Anaizah, perhaps because they have trysts for a game or a chat on the Nufoud sand.

To a traveller coming from Ar-Riyadh the *Souq* of 'Anaizah is as attractive as an arcade in a big European city. Here you are likely to find anything that you think *not* of—even a woman with a pumpkin on her head and an invitation in her peeping eyes. Dry rosebuds and sandal wood powder for mylady's toilet ; aromatic wood and frankincense for mylord's *qahwah ;* the dried skins of the pomegranate for the sheikh to dye his turban ; a looking glass which the blood with long braids may carry in his pocket ; heavy silver anklets with which the bud in an *izar* may make her gait more graceful ; kohl for his and her eyes ; unguents for his and her hair ; sulphur rock for the camel's itch ; and what to me was a more welcome sight than anything, a thermos bottle (having broken mine) which some traveller must have given to a *zkirt*, who in his turn must have sold it to a merchant in the *Souq.*

There is also a fodder market, where veiled women sit on the ground with bundles of grass, dry or green, of this year or the last before them. And here I have seen the strangest thing, two of the strangest things, offered for sale. Before one of the women was a bowl containing date stones, which are good for the camel's digestion, I was told, and which help the cow to make good milk. The other strange thing was a calf with the blood still fresh on its naval. The woman needed the milk of the mother, and so she brought the poor *dayling* to market for sale.

The women's bazaar is in a separate *Souq*, where men may pass but not tarry ; for the shops are kept by women, who prefer to do their business unveiled. And there the ladies of 'Anaizah may find everything necessary for gracing or covering their beauty ;—for making odalisques of themselves within the four walls of rapture and tears, or bundled forms for the unwalled world. Judging from their feet they have white skins ; and judging from some of the girls who had not reached the veil-age, they do not lack beauty. Otherwise, they are moving shapes, bundled and humbled, which stand close to the wall and turn their backs when they see a man pass.

We surprised a group of them one day at the public spring, and they hastened to cover their faces without screaming. Hazlul even addressed one of them asking the direction to the western gate, for we were going to explore the city wall. And the reply was an opulent voice, which suggested grace and candour. ' Imshi ! (walk ahead),' said the stern Chief to the lingering traveller. Aye, aye, we must explore the city wall.

The standing army of 'Anaizah are the *athl* trees ; and only by walking around the wall does one realize how the battle is waged. The sand dunes are beating in places at the rampart, have heaped their forces to its height, even higher, and the *athls* are doing their utmost to maintain their stand and keep them back. One *jalib*, which was being operated by three camels, is at the foot of the dune whose slope is covered with these trees ; nevertheless the sands are heaped around it and it seems to be doomed.

In the north-east the situation is more hopeful ; for there besides the open space is the old part of the town, called Al-Janah, and in it are the oldest and largest *athls*, some of which have been there for three centuries past.

'Anaizah itself was built 670 years ago ; and while its name is derived from the famous 'Aneza tribe, it must not be confused with it. 'Anaizah is the diminutive of 'Aneza ; and although it harbours to-day a mixed population and has lost its tribal power as a free city, the Benu Khalid and the Benu Tamim still maintain in it a certain prestige. The oldest house, the site of it rather, is where we were staying ; where now stands a three-storied palace elaborately planned, with the roof as a fourth story, since it is divided into rooms that require but roofs. It was to me tantalizing. Most all the roofs of the city are thus hedged about, and command but one view, the sky. Otherwise, the inhabitants would have no privacy in the summer nights.

From our roof I could also see two minarets ; and when about sundown I would go up for a moment of repose, the two muazzens with their palms clapped to their ears would be calling the faithful to prayer. Their voices always clashed, and the currents of my own mind were always deflected to the Nufoud and the ever advancing sand dunes. Without the *athls* both minarets might have been submerged long before our day, or they might still be partly visible as shrines above 'Anaizah's tomb.

Before we leave the queen-city of the Qasim I would introduce to the reader its blind bard, who afforded us one evening a rare entertainment.

A word first about poetry, which in Najd is still elemental, but no longer pure. Most of the poets of the present day write and improvise in their native dialects, and often their verse has to be translated into pure Arabic to be understood by the scholar. When this is done, however, all the fine qualities of the ancient bard—his fervour, his eloquence, his imagery, his turn of thought and phrase, even his brag—are vividly revealed.

The poets of Najd do not even transcribe their verse. What they produce they chant in the *qahwah* and on the road, and is carried by the traveller to town and encampment distant and near. One of their famous poets is Shuwai'er, whose monument, a cairn, stands at the eastern edge of the Dahna—we passed it coming from Al-Hasa —and whose *qasidahs* are transmitted by one generation to another. Shuwai'er has a sense of humour as well as dramatic appreciation. His irony and his imagery are native, but not uncouth. He chanted about two hundred years ago, when Ibn Sa'oud and Ibn Abd'ul-Wahhab first appeared together, and was the first to aim his shafts upon them.

> ' They both profess that God is one ; but I know well
> That many dark designs in their profession dwell.'

To Shuwai'er also belongs the honour of having run, with his rhymes about the ages of man, in the same channel with Shakespeare. Now I come to the noted present-day blind bard of 'Anaizah, Ibn Husais, whom our Chief Hazlul ferreted out one day and brought him in the evening to our house. A tall figure in a beduin smock of grey sheeting, with a *gutrah* loosely covering his head, and a face that recalled to mind Anatole France, he slipped his sandals at the door and walked up, with the stoop of an English nobleman, to the centre of the hall, where he sat in a kneeling posture and then salaamed.

Shuwai'er is the favourite poet of Ibn Husais ; and after he had made a few preliminary remarks about him, he started to chant from his verse in a tone and gesture that were to me unique. With his hands clapped to his ears, his eyes closed for ever by fate, his face, long and sharp and distinguished bowed over his breast, his elbows on his knees, Ibn Husais bewitched our circle with his intonations and the shades of his vocal art. There was nothing studied, nothing artificial ; he commanded his voice and made it suit every tone of the poet's speech and manner.

Poetry in Najd is not read but chanted. And invariably the chant is a dramatic recital, natural, direct, with pauses and effects, and a gesture more in the expression of face and voice. Ibn Husais's hands framed his classic features ; but every now and then his right would dart out and his fingers snap to underline a dash of colour in his speech. This is not the height of his art, however ; for gradually he reaches the point when the *gutrah* is cast off ; and the circle, wrapped in attention, enchanted responds to the spontaneous emotion which is the prelude to the ecstasy.

Every one by this time lay flat on his bosom with his hands supporting his chin and his eyes fixed upon the bard, who seemed to sense every pulse of his audience.

He had chanted enough of Shuwai'er's verse. And now that the spell is on, a moment after he had cast off his *gutrah*, he stood up and began to chant some of his own amatory rhymes, while lightly with his hand he beat his left breast as if it were a tambourine. To the silent rhythm he swayed his tall and graceful form ; and then, with a step forward and a gesture of the torso, he launched into a dance. It was most effective and in parts fascinating. But he did not sustain his effort, or he leaped beyond it. Inevitably every such performance is diluted more or less with the sensual ; and Ibn Husais, in his ecstasy, became libidinous.

Indeed, the classic performance degenerated into a stomach dance, which was very funny—and very pathetic. The noble character, esthetic in mood and gesture, distorted itself into a caricature ; the which, however, made the figures stretched bosomward on the floor rock with laughter, even like a New York audience in full dress. They rolled also, for that was quite convenient and proper. But even then he had not reached the orgasm which marks the fall of the curtain. There was a lull in the performance, an undertone rather, which was preliminary to the final spurt ; and this came when he doubled himself, his head almost touching the floor, and continued to beat his breast tom-tom-like, puffing simultaneously and blowing like an ox. That, in our Western speech, brought down the house ; and in Arabic vernacular, it made everybody, in this instance, literally sit up.

' Give him the *sabil*,' cried one ; and Fares, the Hindu half-breed, who was smoking all the while handed him reverentially the little pipe. What followed is characteristically Arabian. Every one became a generous prince. Baddah took off his *ighal* and placed it on the head of the bard ; Hazlul slipped off his outer garment and covered him with it ; Salem gave an *aba ;* Misfer a *gutrah ;* and I contributed some money. The latter he seemed to appreciate the most.

'To-morrow,' said he, as he placed the coins in his bosom pocket, ' *al-hurmah* (the old woman) will have some rice for dinner—she is toothless and blind, Allah save thee. And to-morrow, praise be to Allah, then to thee, I shall get me a young wife.' The following day, about noon, I saw him squatting near a door in the street and rather flippantly I asked, ' Is this where she lives ? ' ' Look thou upon this beard,' he replied ; ' not even the dye will correct it. And remember, Allah keep thee, the line of the poet :

"The words of night are by the dawn effaced." '

·   ·   ·   ·   ·   ·   ·

The distance between 'Anaizah and Buraidah can be covered by a *najjab* in two hours ; but we could not make it in less than four, chiefly because there was war that day between me and my mount. I broke upon her head my cherished bamboo and lost in the bargain my cherished illusion. No, one cannot afford to lose any sympathy upon a camel. I had treated mine for the past ten days with the utmost consideration, using the stick only to direct her ; I had always been patient when, finding her favourite grass or shrub, she stretched her neck for a bite ; and withal in 'Anaizah she had five days of green grass and rest. Now, one would expect of her, after all this extra-vagance in sympathy and food and attention, a decent foot, a glad foot, a trotting disposition. Nothing of the kind. I had spoiled the beast. She walked out of 'Anaizah that morning as if she were being led to slaughter; and at the sight of the first shrub familiar to her appetite her mouth would water and she would draw her neck to the ground. After all the feed she's had, the camel !

Well, my patience was exhausted and the bamboo was put to its right use. I first taught her to walk alone ; for her wont was to follow, rubbing her lip against her sister's hind. But she avenged herself upon me whenever we had a dune to descend. Halter or no halter, even though I made a ring of her neck, holding it back, she would go at a *dirham* down hill and make me most miserable. But when we came to the opposite slope the *qafilah* would have to wait for us at the top of the dune. Much is to be attributed, of course, to the temper of the rider. When the *zelul* behaves, is brisk in the walk, fleet in the *dirham*, you dance on her back, your power of endurance increases with your joy, and you become more humane than a member of the S.P.C.A. But often in moments of friction both the rider and the mount are to blame. It takes two to make a quarrel.

An hour and a half after leaving 'Anaizah we came to its Wadi, a rift in the Nufoud planted with *athls* and palms, which is a part of Wadi 'r-Rummah, and thence we plunge into the heart of the dunes. The horizon line, shadowy and frail, undulated at times into nothingness, disappearing in the glare of the sun ; but now and then it would stand out again clear and firm in a contrast of chromatic grandeur, when even a touch of purple on a globe of gold would melt into pearly tints and flashes of flame.

Two hours from the Wadi, through the Nufoud, and we sight the *khuboub* of Buraidah (*khuboub*, pl. of *khabb*), which are little oases in the laps of the dunes. A *khabb*, in other words, is a hollow in the sand-hills, a bottom floor of loam with water in it, which the citizen of Buraidah discovers and makes it serve, through a *jalib*, one or two of the purposes of life. Hence the palm-groves, the mud huts, and the *athl* garrison to keep back the sand. The *khabbs* are trenches occupied by the soldiers of peace, and Buraidah is girdled with them. The first impression one gets, however, as we advance towards it is that of vastness and impeccability. Here be a city set in the clean palm of the desert and adorned with a girdle of emeralds in a chain of gold. The dunes recede from it ; the verdure

302 IBN SA'OUD OF ARABIA

stoops low before it ; and everywhere around it between it and the *khabbs* is a vastness which gives wings to the most depressed spirit.

The sanded streets of Buraidah are cleaner than those of 'Anaizah and Ar-Riyadh ; and in its *Souq*, which boasts a few of the crafts, you hear the tinsmith's hammer and the carpenter's saw as well as the inevitable auctioneer. The brass pots and kettles they make are excellent ; but they have to buy their brass outside of Najd. The carpenter, on the other hand, has the palm and the *athl*, which are sufficient for his purpose ; while two of the colours—red and yellow—which he uses to paint and decorate the doors he makes, are extracted from the berry of the *athl* and the crocus. But the blues and greens are imported from India. Buraidah is also noted for its sandals and other works in leather, which are titivated in the Mexican or the American Indian manner. More important than any native industry, however, and more conspicuous in the trading of each day, is the camel.

Nowhere in the Qasim, in all Najd, is there another market like that of Buraidah ; camels of every quality and colour, from Oman as well as from Iraq, the best and the worst, are brought to it for sale or for barter. To camel square, which is in front of the Palace, the most vicious beasts are also driven and soon schooled in obedience by a multitude of would-be purchasers. One such I saw run amuck, and lo ! upon its back and neck and hind a hundred bamboos. Every one took a hand in the discipline, for anyone might be the last bidder. Another camel I saw dragging its owner behind it—he held to its tail—while he continued to cry : ' Twenty, twenty ! ' Those who were bidding cut off its line of retreat, and the sound of the switches on its hide was like the patter of rain. ' It is not worth a bamboo ! ' a boy exclaimed. ' Twenty, twenty reals ! ' persisted the owner. ' Twenty ! Allah bless thee with it ' (which is the Arab auctioneer's equivalent for Sold).

Camel Square during business hours suggested in its babble and tumult the Stock Exchange. Instead of hands in the air, however, there are bamboo sticks ; and instead of clerks running in every direction there are men riding up and down the Square, at a walk, at a gallop, to exhibit the qualities of the animal they would sell or buy.

To the camel market of Buraidah come also the *'Uqailis* (camel dealers) who buy in large quantities and go north to Syria or to Palestine with their stock. During the month of March, when the land begins to glisten with the green pasture, they move northward in companies of from 200 to 500 people, with a stock seldom less than 2000 camels and several times more of sheep. The journey from Buraidah to Damascus is made in two months ; for leisurely they travel, pasturing the flocks as they go. Not only to Syria and all parts of Arabia, but also to Egypt does the business of the Buraidah market extend. About 15,000 camels, a conservative estimate, are sold every year.

It was here that Swailem ibn Swailem the Acting Ameer, upon hearing of the misbehaviour of my *zelul*, bought another for me and had it branded on its neck with the brand ($_o{}^o_1o$) of Ibn Sa'oud. In Buraidah, too, did we replenish our stock of provision, and, lingering for a week, also our strength.

It was a week of rest at the Palace, for the people of this city, unlike those of 'Anaizah, seldom entertain : their favourite occupation is to buy and sell. They are the Philistines of Al-Qasim. Their contact with the Bedu is more frequent and genuine ; and their connections with the big cities, as Kuwait, Basrah, Damascus, Al-Medinah, is solely for trade. They scarcely have time, one would think, for anything else. And yet, they are not unlike the citizens of 'Anaizah in their business hours. But their manner is more beduish than urban ; for Buraidah is the magnet of the Bedu of Central Arabia. Mutair, 'Utaibah,

IBN SA'OUD OF ARABIA

Hutaim, Harb, they all contribute to its population. If 'Anaizah is the Paris of Najd, Buraidah is its New York.

But I have found in Ibn Swailem, who is a worthy descendant of the Swailem that harboured the founder of Wahhabism when he fled to Dir'iyah, and a travelled official of the Sultanate of Najd, I have found in him a generous Arab with the manner of a Parisian. No ruler of an unruly people can be more soft-spoken, more gracious, more patient, or more just. For hours I would sit at his *majlis*, when the bawling Bedu would come in complaining, asseverating, cursing ; and never once did I hear him raise his voice or use harsh words upon them. —' Soften, Allah give thee strength. Be brief, Allah keep thee.' And if these words did not have the desired effect, his staff, with which he strikes the ground in the manner of the Sultan himself, would forthwith command silence and right behaviour.

The view from the roof of the Palace at sundown first suggested to me the soul of Ibn Swailem—a tranquillity swept by a subdued fire, with delicate shades languidly clinging to the sand. But there too are the vast spaces inviting the children to play ; the green of the graceful *athls* vibrating in a greyish mood ; the little girls in red driving home their little flocks of goats ; and out of the desert, returning from pasture or from a long journey, a train of camels slowly plodding towards the city. Never shall I forget the idyllic charm of that vast scene, especially when the colours settled down into solids, the flocks into groups like the *athls* and the palms, thus transforming the picture into a masterpiece of cubism.

The Palace of Buraidah is an organic, ramified structure, which has developed through a series of revolutions and conquests. A part of it was built in the days of the Muhannas, the former rulers of the city ; a part by Ibn 'ur-Rashid when he annexed it to his dominions ; and the wing in which were our quarters is of recent construction. But there is a homogeneity in the plan, a consistent growth ; for the turreted wall, the wings, the two vast courts, as well as the halls of audience, all bespeak a single mind.   The whole structure with its three lines of defences, its three fortresses, one within the other, is set in front of the city facing the open desert.   It has more than a dozen square turrets with a running path between them along the walls and funnels, in addition to loopholes and lookouts for shooting down at the enemy.   It also has a *masjid* for its garrison of a hundred soldiers and a zealous commander, whose voice early in the dawn and a little before sunset supplemented that of the mauzzen. ' Get ye up and pray !   Come ye and pray ! ' I would hear him cry.   And once I saw him with staff in hand driving to the *masjid* the delinquent and the supine.

Four hundred years ago Buraidah was a watering-place belonging to a sheikh of the 'Anezas, who sold it to a man from Shaqra, an 'Ulaiyan of Benu Tamim.   Soon after more 'Ulaiyans moved thither, built houses around the wells, and encouraged others to do so.   Rapidly the settlement grew into a city, and the 'Aneza Arabs became an important factor in its development.   But the rivalry between 'Aneza and Tamim led to a conflict in which the Muhannas of the former tribe defeated the 'Ulaiyans and supplanted them in authority.   Since that time Buraidah has been the prey of revolutions and conspiracies fomented by the two rival houses ; and often, when one party would invoke the assistance of Ibn 'ur-Rashid, for instance, the other would invite Ibn Sa'oud to rule the city.   It was natural, therefore, that they both lose their authority and power, first to Ibn 'ur-Rashid and eventually to the conqueror of Ibn 'ur-Rashid, the Sultan Abd'ul-Aziz ibn Sa'oud.   The last of the Muhannas is now with the Rashids in Ar-Riyadh enjoying a lifelong vacation.

Having given a brief account of the beduin city of Al-Qasim, from which we are now to set out on the longest and most difficult of desert journeys—a journey of fifteen days through arid wastes and seas of sand in which even the children of the desert, without a guide, are lost—it is befitting at this juncture to call up the escort for a brief review.

Our Dawsari Chief Hazlul, after a week of preparation, was worrying about his sword which he had left in 'Anaizah to be polished. ' We must start to-morrow,' I said, ' Yes, *billah !* ' he replied. But on the following day he came with a circumlocution about an extra mount, which will come to-morrow morning, ' and *inshallah !* we shall set forth.' *Inshallah*, after *billah*, abetted my doubt; but he avowed that the armourer in 'Anaizah was responsible for the delay, and that he will dispatch one of the men to bring the sword. ' And why the sword, O Hazlul ? ' I asked. ' We are not going on a *gazu*.' ' And would I enter Kuwait,' he replied, ' I Hazlul, a man of the men of Abd'ul-Aziz, without a sword ? That is not meet, nay, *wallah !* ' He showed me the letter which he had dictated to the Sultan. He did not start it I noticed with the usual formula, *From Hazlul son of 'Ubaid to So and So*, as he does in writing to his equals. Form, forsooth. With the Arabs, whether urban or Bedu, it comes next to Allah and the Prophet. Aye, Hazlul was lost without his sword.

Even his scribe Fares, the Hindu-Arab, who carried a bamboo, nursed an ambition to carry one day a sword and walk behind the Long-of-Days. And why not ? Is he not a *zkirt* and a scribe, the only one in the *qafilah*, forsooth, who can write ? And what matters it if he cannot read his own writing ? I had seen the letter he indited to the Sultan. It was a masterpiece of solecism and ambiguity. Fares does not believe in monosyllables ; and whenever two or three come together he not only yokes them with the following, but also with the preceding, word. ' Thus is written the language of the people of Najd,' he had the boldness to tell me. I do not think that a half-breed is ever without an enormity of some sort.[1] Fares

---

[1] Without warning, he left the caravan at the last hour of departure.

did not know his father, and he was quite frank about it.
'But I know that I am a *zkirt*, and I can read and write
the language of the people of Najd.
Why then should I not carry a sword
and walk behind the Long-of-days
the Sultan Abd'ul-Aziz?'

But Baddah, who had crossed
many times between Buraidah and
Kuwait and who assured me that we
needed no guide while he is with us,
was nevertheless crestfallen. For he,
Baddah the 'Ujmani, who coming
from Al-Hasa lorded it over the
b'dewi Majed and the Basrah cook,
was not only outfaced by a half-
breed Arab, but had to also take
orders from a Dawsari with a sword.
How the mighty have fallen.

FARES, THE SCRIBE
OF HAZLUL

Salem too was in the suds, but not because of anything
or anybody connected with the journey. He received a
letter from Ar-Riyadh telling him that his wife gave birth
to a baby girl. So he wrote back saying, Allah be praised,
who alone is praised for things evil.

But Hamad the comely black, who drags his dirty
tunic and frilled *aba* listlessly like a girl,
was not afraid of going to Kuwait.
'No, *billah*. Is not Tarabah farther than
Kuwait, and have I not travelled to
Al-Hijaz many times back and forth?'
—'And why art thou thus sad?'—'In
Tarabah is my wife.'—'And dost thou
love her?'—'Aye, *billah!*'—'And what
is love, O Hamad?'—'Love, ya Bey'
(coming from the Hijaz, this Turkish
mode of address was still on his tongue),
'love is death.'—'And the brand upon
thy forehead, O Hamad?'—'When a boy, Allah keep

HAMAD, THE PRODIGAL
BLACK

thee, I was much troubled with headaches : the fire cured me.'

Hamoud also had the blues ; but he was neither a disappointed father nor a lackadaisical husband. Hamoud the Mutairi boy with the girlish voice was longing for the *gazu*, the only life to him worth living. I asked him why he did not wash his garment, and he lifted it up to his waist to show me that it was the only one he had.—' But did not Hazlul buy you a new one ? ' (I had given the Chief some money to purchase new garments for them all)—' Aye, *billah*. And I shall wear it when we come to enter Kuwait.'

And here is Caliban-Misfer bringing his smock with him. ' Be thou favoured of Allah,' he said, thanking me, as he unfolded it. I was too angry to speak or laugh. Why did Hazlul purchase for Misfer such a garment—a garment made of the odds and ends of Japanese unbleached sheeting. But I wronged the Chief in my mind. It was Misfer's own choice ; he fancied what was printed upon it in blue—Made in Japan, 30 yards, Kane Mills, etc., which he called ' the decorations.' He does not know, be he ever favoured of Allah, that Caliban is not a clown. But there is often a delicate irony in the speech of Misfer, who is himself a satire upon humanity. I examined one day Hamad's seat on the pack camel and was surprised to find nothing there but the wooden frame ; but Misfer, who was helping him to load, threw a piece of burlap upon it saying : ' Give him a little luxury.' And when I asked him to tell me why were ' our Brothers,' Hamad and Hamoud and Salem and Baddah, all so overcome with sadness, he replied : ' They have been too long in the lap of idleness ; their humour will be corrected when we start again on the march.'

But before we made our last remove I must tell thee, O reader, that I have found a real luxury in Buraidah ; yea, I have made two discoveries in the *Souq* for the distant journey. Truffles I chanced upon ; and they are as cheap as potatoes, even cheaper—about two cents a pound—in years of plenty. Misfer's broth will now taste better ; and Salem tells me that he knows of other ways of ' decorating ' —preparing—the truffle. We shall see.

The other discovery is *iqt*, which, I think, is evaporated milk. I will at least tell you how it is prepared. The milk is first made into *laban* (lactoferm) ; the *laban* is then churned and placed in a kettle over a slow fire to inspissate; after which it is kneaded, broken up, and placed in the sun to dry. The traveller buys it in that state, grounds it to powder and sugars it (one-third of sugar to two-thirds of *iqt*) ; and when he is thirsty he puts a little of this powder into a bowl and adds water. This makes an excellent drink. But the *iqt* has other virtues. If the water is dirty or brackish it corrects it ; and if it is rare the *iqt* will help you to economize. A drink of it will drive away the thirst for a whole day.

Three hundred miles ahead of us, with only two wells on the way about a hundred miles apart ! But I have two *qirbahs* to myself, a gun to defend them, and a bag of the blessed *iqt*. Add a few truffles a day, and a fig for your Dahna, O my pious Brother, and your Nufoud ! Blessed are the hands that made thee, O *iqt*, and thrice blessed the hand that dug thee, O truffle !

CHAPTER XXVII

IN THE DAHNA

THE Sultan Abd'ul-Aziz had ordered the Ameer of Buraidah to send with us four extra men—a guide, a cameleer and two soldiers. Our caravan was increased therefore to six transport camels and six *zeluls*, besides my own—in all thirteen ! But when we stopped to fill a few skins of water at the well of 'Ain Thumaid outside the city, I found that we were only eleven, and I noticed that Hazlul's sword did not hang from the tree of his saddle. It was still at the armourer's shop in 'Anaizah, and Hamoud the Mutairi boy was sent to fetch it.

An hour later I missed Baddah, and the Chief told me that the 'Ujmani had forgotten my skewers in Buraidah and was sent back to get them. Now, my skewers, the Chief had the good sense to realize, were as important as his sword, if not more so. For was I not a victim of fever as well as of strange messes, concocted at the two queen-cities of the Qasim ? And did not my stomach turn even against boiled lamb and rice steeped in butter ? Roast lamb, therefore, lamb on the skewer—thanks to the Buraidah smith—would I have for a change, nay, for a remedy. So, after a march of but two and a half hours that day, we waited in Sh'ib'un-Naqib for what was very essential to the health and the moral well-being of our party—for a sword and skewer.

Much had been added in Buraidah, as I have said, to our gear and provision ; for Hazlul and his men, to whom seldom comes such a commission, considered themselves on a grand vacation. Indeed, to travel leisurely through the land of the Arabs ; to have rice and lamb every day ; to be invited to feasts in the big cities ; and to have the freedom of the desert for a *sabil* and a song—this were a boon for which, be it said to their credit, they thanked their Sultan many times a day.

But Hazlul, in looking after himself and his men, did so through a subtle consideration for the Sultan's honoured guest. ' It is the pleasure of Abd'ul-Aziz,' he would say, ' that everything be done for the comfort of this man. He is now to us Abd'ul-Aziz.' What could I say in thanking the Dawsari Chief but that he was a true poet, equally eloquent and generous. I even forgave him the indifference he sometimes showed to the interest of his sovereign. —Economy, not on such an expedition shalt thou accompany us. In many a *gazu* and many a battle have we lived on dates—but a few a day ; and *iqt* was a luxury denied even to the Imam. But now a sheep a day, O thou Misfer, or thine own head will roll on the sand, aye *billah !* And the best of preserved dates did Ibn Swailem provide ; and the best of rice ; and the best of coffee and tea ; and twelve live chickens in a cage made of two petroleum boxes for ' the friend of Abd'ul-Aziz.' Hazlul is an astute diplomat. Every third or fourth thought is for ' the worthy one,' who has come from America to give him and his chosen ' Brothers ' a vacation.

Hay'ala, hay'ala ! A cry of joy and thankfulness in the camp ; for our Brothers have arrived at a gallop, and with them were my skewers and the sword of our Chief— the sword that flashed in a hundred *gazus.*

But one man did not cheer, and that was Khalaf our guide. A tall Mutairi Arab, with a beak and a scowl and a strut, is Khalaf ; for he has travelled far and wide in the land of the Arabs ; has been the companion of the great ; has fought in the World War with the Turks, then with the Sherif, and afterwards with Ibn Sa'oud against the Sherif's son Abdullah. Khalaf has also a voice, which comes up from the very bottom of his being and is, therefore, both rich and sour—a voice to make even the Bedu tremble. And when he wraps himself in his *aba* and stands aside to give his orders, he is monumental—in selfishness and conceit. On the third day, when we arrived at Al-Asyah, an assistant cook, one Ibrahim, for the sake of Khalaf, was attached to the *qafilah,* because poor Misfer's last platter of rice and lamb was unduly salted.

KHALAF, OUR GUIDE

All of which augured a rivalry between the guide and the Chief. But Mubarak and Ju'aithen, whom Khalaf considers as his aides, will make up in their energy, geniality, and devotion for what is sorely lacking in him.

On our way to Al-Asyah we passed by Turfiyah, which is the battle-ground where Ibn'ur-Rashid and Ibn Sa'oud have often contested the sovereignty of the Qasim. Battles and the wells! These determine in this land the fate of the people and their cities. For when the underground water sinks or changes its course the walls dry up and the people have to move ; or when a battle takes place the town is sacked, the palms are cut down, and those who survive must choose another place of habitation. Turfiyah did not have to move far ; the ruins of the old town are within a stone's throw from the wall of the new.

Praised be Allah ! Here is the first flower I've seen in Najd—a wild violet. There were patches of it around Al-Asyah, where water abounds ;—patches which Baddah, were he accustomed to notice flowers, would have called gardens. For as we were nearing the town he pointed to a strip of green at the feet of the rose-coloured Nufoud and said : ' There runs the river of Al-Asyah.' When we arrived I asked him to show me the river. ' Where the camels are drinking,' said he, ' come.' I saw the camels,

but not until we were within their shadow did I behold
the river !—a thin stream of water which runs through
the palms. ' When the rain descends,' said the 'Ujmani,
' the river overflows. There are the marks of the inunda-
tion of last year.' What he pointed to were irrigation
channels.

Al-Asyah is in the shadow of the Nufoud, or what is
called the 'Uroudh, between it and Qibah,[1] which is a
settlement of the Ikhwan. Behind the 'Uroudh is the
Dahna, and behind tha Dahna many hard and arid
deserts. Allah irrigate thy heart, O Saiyed Hashem.
How often in the 'Uroudh did we envy thee in Al-'Ared.
No water except in Al-Hafar ! And between us and Al-Hafar
are mountains of sand, one summit beyond another, and
seven days of travel.

We filled our *qirbahs* and water-skins [2] at 'Ain Fuhaid,
which is one of the best wells outside of Al-Asyah, and did
not start out till the sun was well in the sky. But no
sooner were we amidst the dunes than the cry, *mudhahha*
(the crouching place for the first meal of the day) was
heard on every hand. It was about noon, more than an
hour late, and the food corrected the humour caused by
our delay in moving out of Al-Asyah.

But about three hours later it was I, overcome by
fatigue not by hunger, who wished that the *mu'ashsha*
(the place for the last meal of the day) was near. For

---

[1] Qibah—pronounced I'bah. Here is an example of how Arabic
proper nouns often lose their identity in transliteration. I have said
elsewhere that in Najd the ق=q in certain words is pronounced j, and
the vowel in the first syllable of certain words is silenced. Qibah by the
first rule, therefore, is Jibah, and by the second J'bah. Now, the
European traveller who hears this, writes it down in his notebook—and
then in a scholarly work of two volumes—thus : Ijba. Another example
is : Dahna. He hears the beduin say D'hana, and after supplying the
eleptic vowel retains the vernacular ' a ' and writes the word on the map
thus : Dahana.

[2] The *qirbah* is made of sheep or goatskin and is carried by the traveller
on his *zelul*. The water-skin, which is called *ruwi*, is made of camel hide,
has a capacity of about five *qirbahs* full, and is used for cooking and washing.
A camel carries two *ruwis*.

having had to avoid Qibah, we took a southern course
cutting through the virgin dunes. Dunes? Do I say
dunes again?

The 'Uroudh are a series of ridges—the natives call
them the ribs of Al-Asyah—running lengthwise northwest
by southeast; the height of each ridge is from 400 to 500
feet; from summit to summit, for the descending and
ascending *qafilah*, is about four miles; and there being
eleven 'Ribs' in all, the distance east by west, *i.e.* the
width is therefore from 40 to 45 miles. But every mile's
ride across this most difficult of Nufouds we have yet
crossed is equal to five; and Khalaf our guide did not
know evidently that he had an invalid to guide. He
would ride sheer down a slope and we would have to
follow; the *zeluls* cutting virgin paths in the ridges, their
soft hoofs sinking five inches in the sand; and albeit at
a tossing, tumbling pace.

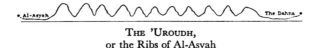

THE 'UROUDH,
or the Ribs of Al-Asyah

There are eleven 'Ribs' of from 400 to 500 feet in height, with a
distance of about four miles from summit to summit

I said that fatigue, not hunger, made me wish that the
hour for supper was near. But after going down another
ridge I realized that it was neither fatigue nor hunger;
it was Dame Malaria who compelled me about 3 p.m. to
ask for a halt. And when I descended I threw myself on
the sand and asked my *rafiqs* to cover me with all the *abas*
they had. I was shivering and my teeth were chattering
with the chills. Soon the tent was set up and I shuffled
to my cot with five degrees of fever coursing through
my veins. But towards evening the thermometer regis-
tered 100 F., and by the help of quinine and Eno's I was
able to get up the following morning and resume the
march.

Indeed, Dame Malaria was beginning to have taste and manner ; for she no longer prolonged her visits. She was become sensitive to the outspokenness of Eno and the irony of the Sugar Pill ? Or was it because of the madcap ride down the sand-hills, which shakes the very ligaments of one's bones, that she was stirred to anger and she came rushing at me with the stick of warning ?

But what could be done ? My *zelul* this time was a headstrong beast with a long step and a jealous disposition. She would not let even Khalaf's get ahead of her ; and to keep her back or make her go down a steep sand-hill in a zigzag course, required more strength than a fever-ridden traveller could command. During the afternoon of the second day in the 'Uroudh, therefore, the chills would have unseated me had I not surrendered, and waited, stretched on the sand under a covering of six *abas*, until the spell was spent. Then came the fever. But we could not stop to humour Dame Malaria on the road to Kuwait and in the Nufoud every time she came. For consider that our water supply was limited, and between us and Al-Hafar—*no water but in Al-Hafar !*— were five days more of travel. Get thee in thy saddle, O man, and depend upon Allah. I was a true Wahhabi in that unique plight, for I depended upon no one else. I even felt, forgive me Allah, that while Dame Malaria was my back-rider, my own halter, as well as that of my *zelul*, was in Thy hands.

'O my *zelul* (thy name, to rhyme, must be in English, Star),[1]
O my *zelul*, the water-skin is leaking and the way is far.'

It seemed farther than ever in those few days of the 'Uroudh—in that sea of sand whose billows are tossed mountain-high—when even Khalaf the guide complained of a ' straitness of the breast ' and Hazlul himself, wondering when the ridges would end, invoked the mercy of

[1] Najmah, her name, is the feminine of Najm = star.

Allah. At last the eleventh ridge loomed on the horizon, and Khalaf exclaimed : ' The back of the 'Uroudh : from there we behold the Dahna.'

The back of the 'Uroudh, the last Rib of the Ribs of Al-Asyah, the last step in the ladder of torture ! We praised Allah again and again. And when we ascended to that height of blissful exhaustion, about sundown, every one fetched a breath of relief and Baddah went galloping to the camping place and crying : ' *Allahu akbar, allahu akbar !* '

I could not resist walking up to the top of the dune near our encampment to see the sunset ; but there were only two colours in the heaven and in the vastness of the 'Uroudh as the sun went down behind the ridge we crossed in the morning—two colours only, a solid red against a solid blue. The dune itself is more interesting, more fascinating. Not a footprint, not even the trace of a bird's promenade was upon it. And its back is as sharp as a sword. It is a hill in the shape of an obtuse angle made by the simoom, blowing from the south, and the *mahabb* (cold blasts) blowing from the north. We walked across its edge, leaving rude footprints behind us ; and when we went back to our tent the sword looked in sooth like a saw. ' Aye,' said Baddah, ' and the wind will sharpen it again and anon.'

Strange are the ways of the wind with the sand ; strange are the whims of the wind in the Nufoud. Here is a down as smooth as the cheek of a babe ; there is a scaled ridge, whose uniform scales are, as it were, stereotyped ; beyond is the apex of a pyramid rising behind an edge like alsirat ; and in the bottom, between the ridges, are the wondrous horseshoes whose loam or rock-floors are swept clean of sand. Even more fascinating is the colouration at certain hours of the day. I transcribe a page from my Diary :

The Nufoud—Thursday Evening, *February* 22.

The colour of the dunes this afternoon was of various shades. The summits in the distance were suggestive of pressed rose leaves ; the tint of the summits beneath them was of old gold ; vermilion whispered in the one ; saffron lisped in the other. And not far from us, as we rode through the vale—the trough between two ridges—rose a form as soft in outline as in slope, whose virgin sand, free of a herb or a root, reflected in the slanting sun a rich copper with glows of vermilion ; and above it, the azure blue of the sky was toned with shreds of silver clouds ; the whole forming a landscape so beloved of the artists of fairyland.

When I was writing the above Baddah came in to say that the coffee circle is composed and Khalaf is telling stories. Now, I had heard Khalaf for the past four days telling stories, even when his *zelul* would be ploughing down the billowy 'Uroudh ; and although I could not understand him, I was willing to try again, since he promised the last time to speak slowly for the sake of ' the Sahib.' He has wandered in his travels, you see, beyond the land of the Arabs.

But ' the Sahib ' was again disappointed ; for Khalaf's pace was not changed, could not be changed. He tells his stories so fast that even a son of the desert has to gallop after him, or he gets nothing. In sooth, Khalaf has a galloping tongue. When he recites verse—what he knows will fill a volume—he stops after every third or fourth line to explain ; and the difference between the explanatory and the reciting tone is hardly perceptible. I could not tell, in sooth, whether his explanation was verse or his verse was an explanation. No, there are no Nufouds in his voice—no dunes in his tone.

Khalaf too had evidently come out on a holiday ; for he was determined not to ride more than six hours a day and to ' coffee ' himself every hour. My recurrent fever had partly served his wish ; and when he came to see me in my tent he lifted his finger towards heaven and, even like Brother Nawwar, praised Allah. He meant, of course, that Allah could have made things worse.

On another occasion I asked him—was he not our guide ?—about a certain place mentioned in the map.

He did not know. I asked about another and he shook his head. But after a brief silence, in which he seemed crestfallen, he spoke. ' Is there . . . on the map—between Thamami and Al-Hafar ? ' I looked and made reply. He asked again about another place, and again I had to say, No. Whereupon Khalaf said, as he raised his head triumphantly : ' The men of science in your land write down what is nothing to us, and do not write down what is important.'

We resumed early the following morning our march across the plain which separates the 'Uroudh from the Dahna ; but about noon, ' for the sake of the Sahib,' seeing that he was still weak, Khalaf wanted to camp for the day. I knew better ; and although I was more than weak I told Hazlul to continue. But our guide had a powerful ally ; for at one p.m., when the hot sun was beating upon me and another sun was burning within me, I longed for a shade—for the tent—and I surrendered.

Besides, when one has the fever the *iqt* does not quench the thirst ; and I found that the water on the fifth day had changed in colour and taste—even in my own *qirbah*. But Hazlul and Khalaf did not mind so long as they had a sheep a day ; and it was their most essential business to keep a circulating eye on the horizon. ' There is a sheep,' says Hazlul. ' I see the flock beyond that ridge,' says Khalaf. And straightway our two good scouts, Ju'aithen and Mubarak, are sent forth to make a purchase. Nothing was requisitioned ; and once or twice the Chief paid out of his own purse.

But I was weaned for four months from vegetables ; and finding a little herb on the way (Mubarak found it and gave it me to eat), my eyes, like my *zelul's*, were turned to the soil for sustenance. And they were not turned in vain. For we were now approaching the little cistern of Zubaidah, or the remains of one of the many cisterns on the old Zubaidah road, which the famous and benevolent wife of Haroun'r-Rashid had built from Baghdad to Mecca for the benefit of the pilgrims.

Allah be gracious unto thee, O Sitti Zubaidah, and give thee an honoured place among his chosen ones, if he has not done so yet. And would that thou hadst to-day a little sister in the world of Al-Islam to repair, at least, the road which thy name still honours, not only for the sake of the pilgrims, but for the safety and well-being of man and beast in this land of the Arabs.

But a fringe of thine own blessing remains green around this dilapidated fountain of mercy, where beast and man, even to-day, will linger and browse and give thanks. Indeed, near the cistern, which still holds a little water when it rains, I too found my heart's desire. Nay, it was again Mubarak, the herbalist of the *qafilah*, who found it for me.

' Here is the *hanbasis*,' he said, offering me a few leaves, which had a pleasant sour taste ; ' we use it to flavour the *iqt* also.' He then led me to the pasture ground, where I found other edible herbs, among them one familiar and dear to me, even as the *irta* is to the camel. Aye, here is one of our Mt. Lebanon garden salads—here is the garden cress ! And how I browsed, my fellow countrymen (ye sons of Mt. Lebanon and of Manhattan) ! Even like Nabuchodonosor on all fours did I grass, praising Allah and then Sitti Zubaidah. I suspect that the *hanbasis* and the cress which had a magical effect, chased old Malaria away. Or was it that my reversion to type, if but for a quarter of an hour, corrected for a few days, at least, all my bipedal corruptions ? Of a truth, I was not only reconciled to the universe, but I felt that I was an honest and healthy part of it, after browsing around the cistern of Sitti Zubaidah.

And here is the Dahna spreading its white carpets of welcome. But let me tell you before we proceed wherein it differs from the Nufoud. First—the Dahna is a long and narrow body of sand which rises northwest of the

Qasim and meanders, like a river, in a south-easterly direction till it reaches the Vacant Quarter ; secondly— the colour of its sand is white except along the edges where it is slightly reddish ; thirdly—there are no dunes or ridges in it, but only mounds of sand not more than a hundred feet high ; and fourthly—it has a variety of herbs and shrubs which make it the pasture ground of the Bedu. Considering its length, which must be about six hundred miles, its breadth is insignificant—forty miles at the most ; and the Arabs in crossing it always choose the narrowest point. Thus is the Dahna much less difficult to traverse than any of the Nufouds ; it is even easy and pleasant ; and only when the beduin loses his bearings and wanders lengthwise in it, is he in danger of perishing of thirst.

We now cross it from the west to Kuwait, after having crossed it from the east to Ar-Riyadh ; and Baddah, who was then our guide and is still our *rafiq*, again raised his voice in imitation of the Bedu who come to it seeking *al-haya*. ' By the father of thee,' he cried, ' we're at the head of th' D'hana ! ' while Mubarak was repeating in a beduin sing-song manner his favourite lines :

> ' O ye to whom all good may come,
> Ye children of the strong and free,
> The brother of my soul is with ye,—
> Allah bring him back to me.'

And Ju'aithen, who always rides beside him, drones his refrain— w-i-n-n-n-n-eh—which is another version of the bumblebee's, at the end of each line.

This part of the Dahna must be the narrowest ; for we crossed it, along the old Zubaidah road, which is still the highway of caravans, in three hours. It cannot therefore be, as the crow flies, more than six miles—the breaking

JU'AITHEN, OUR GOOD SCOUT

point. I was told that in the north it actually breaks ; which must be in these parts a few miles south, where Wadi 'r-Rummah makes its way through it, and where also must be the end of the 'Uroudh.

We crossed the Dahna at a slow walking gait for the sake of the camels who found a luxury in its pasture ;—a luxury in the green foliage of the *irta* bush,[1] for which they scrambled. For the sake of Khalaf, too, who in a condescending mood went out with his scouts on a hunt and came back carrying in his hand a rabbit, we ' coffeed ' ourselves thrice in three hours, and were sorry that he, our guide, did not choose a wider section for the crossing.

But I was anticipating an extraordinary entertainment that evening—a monster bill, as the theatrical manager would call it—because every one had promised to do something when we come to the Dahna. Aye, the Dahna, which is the hereditary foe of the Arab, and which the Arab has conquered, that very Dahna has become the Valhalla of his freedom. Even the austerest Wahhabi here gives way, becomes human.

But Misfer is no austere Wahhabi. Every time I asked him to dance, however, he said : ' Wait till we get to the Dahna.' Now, before he comes forward to make good his promise, let me tell you a few more things about him. Misfer is the chief cook, the chief steward, and the captain of the transport corps :—a quartermaster-general, who is also a butcher and a blower in the fire. He has the hand that shrinks not from work, especially from slaughter ; the eye that sleeps not ; the waist that always bristles with daggers and knives ; and behind him on his pack-camel he carries the chickens and an axe.

---

[1] The *irta*, which is also called *'abal*, has a berry-like fruit, a needle-shaped leaf like the pine's, and a bark which yields a yellow dye. I can only give the Arabic names of other herbs and shrubberies in the Dahna, as the *'ulqah*, which is a bush with greyish bark and winter foliage ; the *qaisum*, a thyme-like plant ; the *'arfaj*, a thorny shrub ; and the *'alanda*, which in its twig resembles the broom. Any one of these is a good browse for the camel.

But the face of Misfer is what they call in Najd mildewed : in other words the skin, or that part of it which  the beard is unable to conceal, is covered with a filmy something, which is copperish in the scale, greenish in the furrow ; and which no soap can improve, no cosmetics can overcome, no chemicals can remove. Were this possible, however, the chemicals would still be unable to correct a nose that sprawls upon his cheeks, a mouth that reaches for his ears, a forehead that retires modestly between the shag of his head and the shag of his brows, and an eye that merrily babbles about our fellow simians.

MISFER-CALIBAN, OUR COOK

Moreover, Misfer is so original in his dress that you cannot tell whether he be a Najdi, a Yamani, an Iraqi, or a Hijazi. The head-kerchief and the black cord, which he presses lightly over it in a cocked manner, are in fact his only outward marks as an Arab. For he wears shoes instead of sandals—heavy army shoes in which his feet, were they of brass, would rattle when he walks ; and between the Arab and the European ends of him is a pair of pantaloons, which were white once upon a time ; over which is a tunic of the same colour and cotton material cut like a Cossack coat, and bound with a girdle that bristles with daggers and knives. But nothing of this individuality is evident when he is seated, sinking amidst the bundles on his pack-camel ; one of the bundles is he, and nothing more.

This is Misfer in his outward shape and significance. But inwardly he is a proof that the divine is not withheld from the most grotesque of God's creations. Aye, in that rusty face is a smile whose magnetism can hardly be surpassed by any feminine charm ;—a smile that fascinates and amuses ;—a smile that makes you laugh and forget his mouth, his nose, his forehead, and all the simians, and all the Ribs of Al-Asyah as well.

Yes, *billah* ! And there was not among our men, there is rarely to be found among men, one who is more genial, more gracious, more kind, more tender in feeling, and more willing withal to be of service to others than this grotesque and noble being.

But let me go back to his tunic to give you an example of his unexampled usefulness. His tunic, with its pockets and their contents, is a veritable store.—Dost thou want a button and a needle and thread ? Dost thou desire some salt or pepper or a little lemon powder ? Is it pen and ink and paper that thou wouldst have ? Or is it an *araak* stick for thy teeth, or a little kohl for thine eyes ? To hear is to obey. I was not surprised when I first saw Misfer use the kohl, with which most of the Arabs, men and women, enlarge and strengthen their eyes. But I was struck with wonder when one day we were having coffee he took a smooth stone, placed upon it a few live coals, and then, thrusting his hand into one of his pockets, he drew a little wooden box, which he opened with the studied slowness of an esthete who would prolong the pleasure of an esthetic moment, and placed upon the live coals a little of its contents—aromatic wood !—to scent his brothers of the road. No one but Misfer carried this precious object, this luxury of the esthetic life, with which he treated us after each meal.

But I could not resist laughing when he pointed with his index finger to his head as if to say, Misfer forgets nothing, and then took out of his bosom pocket a little round mirror, which he offered me to see my own face and fix my *ighal* before starting on the march. That mirror he cherished more than any other object he carried with him ; and often I would see him, as he swayed amidst the bags and bundles on that unenviable eminence of the pack-camel's chine, looking into that mirror, gazing intently upon the face I have described.

But what is the motive of his interest ? Is he bewitched or beguiled ? Does he see what other people see in his face, or what God, the equalizer of all things, beholds ? Or is it the simian in him who wonders at such an object as a piece of glass which can reflect his own face, and is bewitched ? What say my Masters, the professors of psychology and metaphysics ? Do they not wonder a little that the victim of such ugliness, which moves people to laughter and to tears, does not plunge into his heart one of the daggers he carries with him when he sees his face in a glass ? But is it not self-love, as I think, which protects us against ourselves when the naked eye beholds the outward distortions ? Indeed, were it not for self-love, that blessed seed which God has sown in every sociable and unsociable animal, there would be more suicides in life, chiefly for this reason, aye, chiefly because the hand of the potter shakes.

Forgive me this outburst, dear reader. But others have written novels whose heroes are modelled after Misfer ; and were Caliban and Guinplaine to meet him in the flesh, they certainly would offer him the first place of honour. After all, Guinplaine and Caliban are shadows, and Misfer is a reality ;—one of the shining realities of these travels ;—the same Misfer who slew a sheep a day for us, perfumed us with incense, often spoke about his wife and children in Sudous, and is now to dance for us the dance of the Ikhwan.

We sat in a circle around the fire under a limpid sky in which the stars shone the more bright because of the absence of the moon, and the camels were contentedly crunching in another circle around us. The blaze of our fire, thanks to Misfer's assistant, Ibrahim, who sat leaning against the wood pile, did not abate ; and the flames, rising in spirals and set off by the surrounding darkness, were a fitting prelude to the performance. Hamad the black, with a skillet in his hand, Hazlul with a tray, and Baddah with a tin pan, were ready to furnish the music, when Misfer came out of the tent with the sword in his right hand and the dagger in the left. ' Wood on the fire ! ' he cried, as he stood in the centre of the circle, swaying his torso lightly from side to side ; and Ibrahim heaped the dry *'arfaj*, which expressed the jubilant spirit of the evening. ' A hand ! ' cried Misfer, who was still stepping lightly around the circle ; and Hazlul gave the order for his brass orchestra to begin.

Ta ra ta taa ra ta tum tum, Ta ra ta taa ra ta tum tum.

' We are the people of Allah,
   Brothers of those who obey him ;
 We are the sons of Al-'Awja (another name for Ar-Riyadh)
   Slayers of those who betray him.'

Misfer began singing the first two lines, which were repeated by the circle, while dancing a graceful and slightly sinuous step, by no means a prelude to a war dance. But gradually, as he shook the sword with one hand and twirled the dagger with the other, the spirit of fire and steel leaped into the arena and over the blaze.

' We are the people of Allah,
   Brothers of those who obey him.'

And he leaped over the flame with a flourish of the sword and the dagger, crying : Ulu lu lu lu lu li !

The Chorus : Hay ala, hay ala !

The Orchestra : Ta ra ta taa ra ta tum tum, etc.

This is a prelude to the song of the Ikhwan in battle, *The winds of Al-Jannat are blowing.* The tempo changed, and Misfer, stepping briskly around the circle, threw the sword and dagger in the air and caught the first with the left and the second with the right hand—Wood, O Ibrahim ! The brass, O Hazlul !

' The winds of Al-Jannat are blowing,
   Where are ye who Al-Jannat desire ? '

Those winds, blowing into the hearts of the men, fanned them to flames, and every one was eager to leap into the arena. The sword of terror was unsheathed ; the tempo was quickened ; and it was the Ikhwan, not my brothers of the road, who were now repeating in chorus after Misfer :

'The winds of Al-Jannat are blowing.'

And Misfer, having attained the pinnacle of ecstasy, took his *gutrah* and *ighal* off his head and threw them into the fire. Whereupon, every one exclaimed :

'Where are ye who Al-Jannat desire ? '

And taking up the slogan, Warriors of the Unity are we !—*ahl it-tawheid*—they continued to repeat it in a most realistic abandon till the fire went out. For Ibrahim, soaring to Al-Jannat, let the performance end in smoke and darkness.

.   .   .   .

The fire, O Ibrahim. Second Act : Story-telling. The first was Hazlul, who related of a battle he had with the Jinn one night in Wadi 'd-Dawasir. They pursued him to the mosque where he killed two of them, *billah !* and wounded many. Followed Baddah, the prime lecher of the *qafilah* by his own testimony, who told a love story of which he himself was the hero.—'And she hid me in the trunk when she heard a knock at the door. It was her husband, *billah !* who came in cursing her and her parents. She showed surprise. He did not believe, but continued to curse her. She then cursed him and cursed his parents. "Divorced !" he cried, "thrice divorced." For this she praised Allah, and called the servant to carry her trunk away. The servant did so, wondering what was in it. I did not move. She walked behind us, *wallah, billah !* and when we were outside the house I could hear her laughing.'—'And after that, O Baddah ? '—' Ask not, O Hazlul.'

Hamoud then spoke : ' I was carrying a letter from the Shioukh to the Ameer of 'Anaizah, and I crouched my camel in a *sh'ib* (glen) of Wadi Hanifah. I was alone ; the night was dark ; and after binding my *zelul* I gathered some wood for a fire. But as soon as I lighted the fire I heard the voice of a woman crying out : " Tear not our veil, Allah keep thee." I looked around, and under the tree I saw a face, life of Allah ! like the sun. In a twinkle of the eye it appeared and disappeared. Again I lighted the fire, and again she cried : " Light not the fire, Allah save thee from the fire (of hell). Veil us, protect us." She is the bride of the Jinn, a very kind Jinniyah.' And Hamoud swore by Allah that she kissed him, while begging him to go his way and leave her and her companions veiled with the veil of night. He did so ; but for many days after he suffered from a burn in his face. ' *Wallah !* *ya Ustaz*, she kissed me here, and her mouth was like a live ember. Life of Allah, I speak the truth.'

Hazlul nodded, and Misfer said that he once had a similar experience. But he told us of a *gazu* in which he was very successful, and closed his story saying : ' I killed fourteen, *billah !* among them Ibn Tawalah, who is still living.' He meant that Ibn Tawalah, who witnessed his heroic deeds, is still living to testify to them. But he was not given the chance to say so. Every one laughed, and the laughter of Baddah, which was as usual louder and more disagreeable, offended Misfer, who drew out one of his knives and cried : ' Be silent or I will slay thee, *billah !* ' And Baddah, still laughing : ' As thou didst slay Ibn Tawalah.' Which infuriated Misfer, who leaped over the fire seeking the blood of the 'Ujmani. But Hazlul held him back and with appeasing words made him sit down. He then ordered Baddah to pour the coffee for Misfer with his own hand.

It was now the turn of our coffee-maker Salem the grave, Salem the silent.—' *Wallah !* *ya Ustaz*, I have no stories. I have a draft on King Husein for a hundred and fifty pounds, which I will sell thee for ten rupees.'—' And thou sayst thou hast no stories ? Tell the story of the draft.— Aye, aye, the story of the draft. So, reluctantly complying, he told us that he was a water carrier in the transport corps of the Ameer Abdullah's army when, after the Armistice, they marched from Al-Medinah against Tarabah. And when they entered that town in triumph he applied to the Ameer for leave and pay. The first was granted to him and the second was given in the form of a draft drawn by the Ameer Abdullah upon the King his father. With which draft Salem went to Mecca by way of At-Taief, where he stopped to visit a friend. Baddah : ' He speaks in the masculine when he should speak in the feminine. A pretty little she-friend—I know her.' Salem paid no attention. He remained a few days in At-Taief and then went down to Mecca. Meanwhile, the Ikhwan had entered Tarabah the night of the very day of the Ameer's triumph, and put his army to slaughter. A report of the calamity was sent by a *najjab* to King Husein ; and when Salem arrived and presented his draft His Majesty said : ' The recompense of Allah to us and to thee, O my son. We have lost everything.'

' And what did they lose ? They still have plenty of gold.' It was Ibrahim who spoke. But before he is given the floor, he deserves a word of introduction. A purblind ex-*zkirt*, down at the mouth as well as at the heel, is Ibrahim. The one thing in him that offended me, however, was his castaway frock-coat, oily, torn, patched, buttonless, and large enough for two Ibrahims. Only a *zkirt* who had been out of Najd could be guilty of such a sartorial enormity. He reminded me of my friends of the road in Al-Yaman. But Ibrahim had been to Syria, where he graced the halls of pashas and picked up a few crumbs of knowledge from their tables. He could tell a story, therefore, in a familiar dialect ; and he was always up and ready for the march at any hour of the night.

I retain a picture in my memory of Ibrahim sitting

around the fire, his *gutrah* pulled over his eyes, which were always leaking, his moustachios flowing over his mouth, his hand ever in pursuit of something creeping under his arm or down his back, and—'Hearken, O Ameen, Misfer knoweth not. I will inform thee.' He interrupted everybody, although he was of the lowest 'caste' in our 'society,' and often justified his shocking conduct. If a story was being told he told it better ; and when a piece of false information was given, he corrected it. 'That is not exact, O Ameen,' and the hand, which had been in pursuit of the creeping atom, is shaken over the fire. He even knew the road better than Khalaf, our pompous guide. 'I cannot see, *billah !* but this is the road, O Ameen.' He seemed to smell the road, and he was never wrong in his direction.

'When I was in Syria, O Ameen, I used to be employed in digging wells. Once we were digging for a Bey and we found a buried treasure—a kettle full of gold. The men would conceal it and have it divided among us, but I did not think it was right. I told the Bey, and he made them give up the kettle.

But two of the labourers reported to the Governor, who sent soldiers to the Bey with orders to deliver to them the kettle. 'The land and everything in it belongs to the Sultan,' said the Governor. But the two labourers waylaid the two soldiers and slew them, and wore their uniforms, and came to the Bey at night and forced him to give them the gold. I saw them, O Ameen, and knew them ; but I did not dare to speak. I was afraid, and Allah has punished me. I have not seen a gold piece since that time. If one were even placed in my hand I would not recognize it.'

.   .   .   .

Third Act : A Catechism.—It was one after midnight when Ibrahim finished his story. The camels were still contentedly chewing the cud ; Salem was still making coffee and tea, one brew after another ; and we did not feel the need of sleep. Nevertheless, we all retired ; and about two hours after that I heard Hazlul calling as usual, 'Up ye, up ye, and pray ! Baddah, Salem, Hamoud, Hamad, Mubarak, Ju'aithen, up ye all, up ye, and pray.' . . . Misfer was the muazzen. *Allahu akbar, Allahu akbar.* . . . *Haste ye to prayer.* . . . *Prayer were better than sleep.* . . . *La ilaha ill' Allah.*

And Hazlul, who watches with paternal care over the souls as well as the bodies of his men, delivered from his high seat, as we sallied forth under the stars, leaving behind us a smouldering fire, a sermon worthy of a *motawwa'* of Ar-Riyadh. He told us that Allah is merciful, in sooth, but also relentless. ' If thou committest adultery and repentest, and repeatest not the offence, Allah will forgive thee ; if thou slayest a man and repentest, and repeatest not the offence, Allah will forgive thee ; but if thou dost repeat it, thou wilt of a certainty lose the mercy of Allah. . . . Deal with us in thy mercy, O Allah, and not in thy justice.'

He continued to sermonize, expanding upon the idea of Allah's justice and mercy ; and he made it clear that after all Allah is most gracious. ' For did he not say : " When a man moves toward me a span, I move two ; when he moves a mile, I move five ; and when he walks to me, I run to meet him." These are the words of Allah. Let us be thankful always and pray. We are not bad, we the people of Najd ; but some of us are wanting in prayer. Look ye, how Allah in his justice sends us the north wind to chill our bodies this morning, and how, in his mercy, he creates the *irta* and the *'arfaj* for our fire. Go ye ahead of us, O Mubarak and Ju'aithen, and kindle a fire to warm our feet.' Mine were ice in my boots and I welcomed the idea.

Mubarak and Ju'aithen galloped forth and soon a fire was blazing ahead of us. We descended, thanking our two good scouts, and after warming ourselves we resumed the march. There was another fire about half a mile away :

it was Misfer and his men, who had, like us, received their inspiration from the north wind.

Our pious Chief was still in his religious mood. He taught us that morning, by precept and catechising, the first principles of Wahhabism,[1] the five pillars of Al-Islam, the ceremonies of ablution and prayer, and the branches of the faith. ' If they ask thee,' said he, ' " What are the three fundamental doctrines ? " say thou : " That the slave (man) should know his God, his religion, and his Prophet Muhammad." And if they ask thee : " Who is thy God ? " say thou : " My God is he who created me and created all mankind. He is my worshipped one, and I worship none but him." And if they say, " How didst thou know thy God ? " make reply : " Through the wonders of his creation. And of these wonders are the night and day, and the sun and moon." '

He then turned to Baddah and asked : ' What are the five pillars of Al-Islam ? ' ' I know them all,' replied the ignorant 'Ujmani. ' But thou art now our Ameer and our teacher. I will repeat them after thee.' And Hazlul, the man of simple faith, was more than willing. ' The testimony that there is no God but Allah and that Muhammad is the Apostle of Allah,' he said ; and Baddah counted—' One.'—' The prescribed prayers.'—' Two.'— ' The rendering of the *zakat*.'—' Three.'—' The fast of Ramadhan.'—' Four.'—' And the Pilgrimage.'—' Exactly. Thou knowest them all, *billah !* '

Baddah then asked Hazlul : ' Dost thou know the saying about the eyes ? ' ' Tell it,' replied the Chief. And the 'Ujmani gave utterance to his favourite homily, which I had so often heard him repeat, ' All eyes shall weep on the day of Judgment, except three : the eye that defendeth the sacred things of Allah ; the eye that shedeth tears in the fear of Allah ; and the eye that watcheth at night for the sake of Allah.'

—' Thou hast taught me something, O thou 'Ujmani.

[1] See Chapter XXII, p. 238.

Allah reward thee. And what are the conditions of prayer ? '

—' I know them. First, Al-Islam.'

—' Al-Islam. And second ? '

—' Continue, O Imam.'

Hazlul enumerated, while Baddah repeated, all the conditions that make prayer acceptable. These are sanity, discretion, ablution, the covering of one's shame, the prescribed time, the turning towards the Qiblah (or Mecca) and the intention.

Baddah thanked the Chief, who continued his catechism.

—' And what are the rules of ablution ? '

—' To wash the face is one.'

—' And the mouth by gurgling,' said the Chief.

—' To wash the head is two.'

—' And behind the ears,' the Chief corrected.

—' Thou seest that I know them, O Hazlul. But repeat them for the benefit of those who know them not.'

—' To wash the hands and up to the elbow is three ; and lastly, to wash the feet up to the ankles. Now tell me what are the nullifiers of ablution.'

Baddah swore that he knew, but the Chief's own speech was so delectable that he would like to hear him repeat them. And Hazlul, knowing Baddah well, and knowing too that there are others among us who are as ignorant, but not as bold, told us that eight things nullify a Muslim's ablutions. Whatever pollutes the body, of course (several forms of pollutions are unprintable in English), and insanity, and the eating of camel flesh, and the washing of the dead, and sexual intercourse.

—' When she is near, Allah keep thee, my ablution is null—null completely. But tell us, O Imam, what are the pillars of faith.'

—' The pillars of faith, O Baddah, are six : the belief in Allah, and in his angels, and in his books, and in his Prophets, and in the Last Day, and in predestination. It is written also that faith is a tree with seventy odd branches, the highest of which is, *There is no God but Allah*, and the lowest is to remove a thing of injury from the road. Know thou further, O Baddah, that a sense of shame is one of the branches (of the tree) of faith.'

—' A branch which Baddah knoweth not. Shame is an enemy to him.'

It was Misfer who gave utterance to these words. Whereupon, Baddah : 'Thou art right, O Musaifer (Little Misfer) of Sudous. But I have the first and the last, the beginning and the end of faith. And were it not for the Ustaz I would prove it by removing thee, thou noisome one, thou worse of injuries, from the road.'

—' *Brrrrrrr! Wallah, billah!* ' And with his dagger drawn, he urged his camel and drove at Baddah. But the Chief was quicker in dashing across and standing his *zelul* between the two.

—' Is this aught of faith ? Allah sift thee, O Misfer. Allah subject thee, O Baddah ! ' [1]

—' But when did a son of the 'Ujman insult a son of the Dawasir ? '

—' I shall punish the 'Ujmani. Attend thou to the *hamlah*.[2] Go ! '

Misfer turned away, murmuring slaughterous words. And Baddah, coming towards me, said : ' Misfer likes not the joke. But we like to chafe him for thine entertainment.'

[1] The people of Najd, unlike the Syrians and the Egyptians, are neither blasphemous in their expletives nor profane. If they are angry at one they say : Allah sift him, *i.e.* sift the evil out of him. And if the offender merits more violent treatment, they say : Allah subject him (*to the devil*).

[2] The transport section of a caravan.

CHAPTER XXVIII

AL-HAFAR

ON the second day, after leaving the wells of Al-Asyah, the water in our *qirbahs* achieved a colour ; on the third it had a taste ; on the fourth it smelt ; and on the fifth there were shreds in the bowl which Baddah brought me to drink. These shreds, which looked like gelatinous matter, as well as the colour, the taste, and the smell, are not inherent, but acquired, qualities of the H_2O of Al-Asyah ;—acquired from the new skins which were bought in Buraidah. For a new skin, no matter how well seasoned, will continue to flavour and colour the water and shed in it of its inner substance, until it has had a practical seasoning of at least a year's use. Even when I boiled the water, as I have always done, it retained all of its acquired qualities ; and filtering through a silk handkerchief robbed it only of its colour. Science, how-ever, gave me the assurance that in boiling alone, despite taste and smell, is perfect safety. To which I added the belief of the Muslem, repeating as I filled in the morning my thermos-bottles for the day, ' To the pure all things are pure.' But neither my belief nor my science had any effect upon Dame Malaria, who continued to honour me with her visits. I was surprised, however, that on the last two days before we reached Al-Hafar, when the water was like a cold broth with vermicelli in it, she did not come. The joys of the Dahna and the expectations, which were soon to be realized at the famous wells, must have crowded her out.

334

Be the water then what it may. Here we are in Al-Batin, which is a continuation of the famous Wadi 'r-Rummah, or the part of it that runs down to Iraq. This Al-Batin is historic, for in it, the Najdis tell us, was the *dirah* of the famous Arab tribe the Benu Helal. Here were their towns and their battle-ground ; but nothing on the surface remains. Underground, however, are those masterpieces of construction the *jalibs*, which proclaim the energy and daring of those warring Arabs. We passed several of them of remarkable depth ; threw a stone into one and counted four seconds before it struck bottom. But they are all dry. The subterranean streams, which long ago must have turned from the Wadi, were the allies of war against Benu Helal ; those who survived the fratricidal slaughters succumbed to famine and the drought or deserted the *dirah* that was made sterile with blood. Even vegetation has forsaken the land ; and the only plant to be seen is the colocynth, whose tendrils like snakes creep on the ground, and whose fruit is a most befitting symbol—the apple of bitterness in the *dirah* of desolation.

As we go through the Wadi we come upon some ruins near which is a cemetery with blank tombstones ; but Hazlul, after a brief survey of the scene, explained it thus : ' There are no *jalibs*, and no remains of a *masjid* here ; this is not a city, therefore, but a battle-ground. The circles of stones are the remains of defence towers, and these are the tombs of those who were killed in battle.' A plausible explanation.

But what divided the attention was the colocynth harvest which the camels were trampling upon ; the fruits of last year, the yellow, shrunken, dried-up apples of bitterness, still clinging to their mother-vines, cracked under the soft hoof ; and the sound of the slowly moving caravan was reminiscent of a ferryboat crunching through the ice. Here and there was a *ramth* bush ; and the *ramth*, according to the Arabic lexicographer, is a plant with a sour taste, which the camels browse. But the camels did not come near it, much as they longed for a browse in Al-Batin. The reason given by Baddah is not without interest to the lexicographer. Said the 'Ujmani : ' The *ramth*, Allah keep thee, is to the camel what sugar is to man. It creates thirst. And only where there is water, in familiar *dirahs*, is it a desired pasture. But the *ramth* is good for the fire.' ' I know of one camel,' I said, ' who did not like it even for firewood.' And I quoted the line of the poet Al-Mutanabbi, in which he says of his *naqah* :

 ' She turned away from the smoke of the *ramth* of her
  native land,
 Seeking the fire of those who burn the ambergris.'

As we issue out of the narrows of Al-Batin, parts of which are not more than forty feet wide, with high banks of calcareous and sand strata (the river of Wadi 'r-Rummah here flowed in the past, and still flows, I was told, once every forty years), we come to a spot called Umm'ul-Hashim, where the bed widens and gradually losing its banks, opens upon the vast plain. There, as we rode ahead, Khalaf our guide was proud to point out and to give me the names of five places not mentioned on the map. But Umm'ul-Hashim, Matruhah, Mawiyah, Zunaib 'uz-Zib and Hulaibah, which is three hours from Al-Hafar, are empty spaces with a tree or a cairn to distinguish each place. *Khabrahs*, Khalaf called them ; and a *khabrah* is a hollow spot that gathers rain water and draws to it, therefore, the tent-pegs of the Bedu.

The vastness and the vacancy of the plain are appalling ; the eye turns from its shadowless spaces even as the heart from its infinite sterility. Nevertheless, beyond it or in it, somewhere in its almost imperceptible folds, is the anticipated paradise—the paradise of travellers and caravans between Kuwait and the Qasim. Three hours before dawn, therefore, our camp at Hulaibah was struck down, and we were ready for the home stretch, at the end of which I imagined an oasis, running water, cool shades, green vegetation, and flowers ! Even when I curbed my imagination I pictured a place no better and no worse than any other watering-ground I have known in Najd. It was not madness, therefore, to be up a few hours after midnight and be on the last march to Al-Hafar, where we are to have at least clean water, a day's rest, a wash, a change of clothes, and—thy pleasure, O Khalaf—a head of something for slaughter. For passing through the wilderness we had not encountered, the past two days, any flocks of sheep or goats.

But we were still in the wilderness when we had reached Al-Hafar—Al-Hafar, the grave of my illusion !—Al-Hafar, the bludgeon on the head of sober thought !—Al-Hafar, the watering-ground and the battle-ground of the Arabs, who drink their water mixed with the blood of their brothers. Here in sooth is the barrenest of all wastes— not even the colocynth creeps upon the ground—and the levellest of all desolate spaces. The road is effaced, the horizon is like that of the sea, and the traveller at night must find his way by the stars. Moreover, despite the fact that in a radius of several miles from the wells the soil is richly fertilized by the flocks—camels, sheep, goats —that come to the water every day, I did not see a blade of grass or a root, a green or a withered leaf anywhere.

Why is this ? Because Al-Hafar has always been the battle-ground of the tribes, and was always changing hands ; one day belonging to the Dhafir Arabs, another day to the Shammars ; at one time ruled by Ibn'us-Sabah, at another by Ibn'ur-Rashid. Indeed, many a battle around these wells has drenched the good soil with the blood of Rabi'ah and Mudhar, drenched it with the blood of thine own sons, O 'Adnan ; [1]—and not even the colo- cynth does it nourish to-day, and not even the beetle can it shade.

There are eight wells at Al-Hafar, and all are in need

[1] Most of the tribes of Central Arabia and Al-Hijaz are descendants of 'Adnan through the two principal lines Mudhar and Rabi'ah.

of repair. The depth of some of them is about a hundred feet ; the water of two or three is good ; the principal one has a scaffolding for a pulley : but not one of them is supplied with tackles. A traveller must have his own rope and bucket, or, if no one happens to be at the wells to lend him his own, he goes away with an empty *qirbah*. The wars in the past have bred this inhuman feeling. The wells are mine to-day, but they may be my enemy's to-morrow. Why then should I repair them ?

Thus, no one has ever felt secure in his tenure, secure enough to build even a scaffolding for a wheel and pulley. This was the feeling of the tribes, the Dhafirs and the Shammars of Iraq, who held Al-Hafar in the past ; this was the feeling even of Ibn 'ur-Rashid when it was under his dominion. But the authority of Ibn Sa'oud extends to-day to Al-Hafar and beyond ; peace and security reign supreme in his land ; Irtawiyah, the first and biggest of the new settlements, is only fifty miles to the south, and its powerful Mutair Arabs are always able to defend the wells. There is no reason, therefore, that the conditions of the past, the inhumanity of the past, should continue to prevail.

On the other hand, it must be said that there is not in Arabia any real national feeling ;—no : a feeling of nationality based on race, co-operation, and common interest, does not yet exist. It may be in the making. But in the political realities of the present, the Peninsula is still dominated by two supreme sentiments, religious and tribal ;—the religious sentiment renders the Arab in-different, even inimical, to progress ; and the tribal sentiment condemns any progress which may benefit the other tribes. Notwithstanding, Baddah thinks that the Arabs are not bad. ' There are four devils in the world,' he once said to me ; ' one in the land of the Arabs, and three in the land of the Ingliz.'

Is that why Mr. Philby was jubilant when he arrived at Al-Hafar ? Baddah, who was with him, saw him dance

with joy ? And why shouldn't he ? Why should not anyone, especially if he is a European, who crosses safely
the 'Uroudh, the Dahna, and the other deserts, be happy
when he gets to this point where, at least, the water-skins
may be replenished ? I had a doublefold right and reason
to dance like Mr. Philby ; for I had passed the dangers
of the road and the dangers of fever ; but nevertheless,
when we crouched our camels at Al-Hafar my heart was
like the fruit of the colocynth.

We occupied the place for a day, but not alone ; the
other occupants were the four winds. They have a
permanent joint-lease on Al-Hafar, and two of them always
and all of them at times, as on the day we arrived, are in
possession, nay, are fighting for possession. One wind
comes thundering from the north, the other galloping
from the south, the third charging from the east, the
fourth trotting from the west ; and the battle was on, as
I said, when we arrived. I entered into my tent, laced
the door-flap and threw myself on my cot, feeling that
the house of my day would topple any moment upon me.

In the afternoon Caliban-Misfer came to ask me
if I would like to swim. Swim ? Thinking it at first to
be a joke of his I answered laughing, Yes. But I soon
recalled that ' to swim,' in the language of the people of
Najd means ' to bathe.' An hour later, therefore, he
carried into the tent one of the large cooking vessels full
of hot water. ' We shall swim in the flesh-pot, O Misfer,
Allah bless thee.' ' But I have washed it,' he replied,
disregarding my banter—' I have washed it with sand
and hot water.'

A little later he came in with a tin plate in which the
aromatic wood was burning, and offered it, saying, ' Be
thou perfumed.' His hand was then thrust into his bosom
pocket, and lo ! his greatest treasure—the little round
mirror.—' Adjust thine *ighal*—hold thou the mirror—I
will adjust it for thee.' He also helped me to put on my
boots ; and walking ahead of me to the big tent, he

seemed proud.—'Congratulate the *Ustaz* on his swim.'
'A perpetual bliss,' said Hazlul, which every one repeated.
But the winds said : ''Thou shalt eat thy supper cooked
with dirt.'

The winds were right. For how could Misfer or anyone else of the noted cooks of the world keep the dust and
the soil out of the vessel, although half-buried in the fire
hole, while the four winds were madly blowing around it ?
And how could Baddah and Mubarak and Ju'aithen or
any of the other brave and daring Arabs fill the water-
skins without being buffeted around the wells and repelled
from them, and without getting into their buckets much
of the very dust under their feet, blown by the very four
winds which would spoil Misfer's supper ?

But no food in the desert is ever sufficiently spoiled to
be rejected. After supper, as if sent by the four winds,
came to our camp one of the Ikhwan ;—a Mutairi youth
with fine features and the usual stage voice—stentorious
and sonorous—of the Bedu. *Eigh, billah !* He has camels,
and land, and a house of stone, and he sows and reaps.
But when he was asked if he would go with us to Kuwait,
he said that he would only go down there to make those
people 'religious' or put them all to the sword. *Eigh,
billah !* And he clapped the palm of his right hand on the
fist of the left. He then asked who I was.—'Does he
pray ?' And he shook his head in answer to his own
question. After which he asked Hazlul for some coffee
beans. He had guests—*eigh, billah !*—and his stock of
coffee was exhausted. When he went away, quite
satisfied, Hazlul said that he was not a real Brother ; for
if he were, he would not have salaamed me.

The north wind continued to blow at night, my tent
flapped incessantly, violently, and I could not sleep.
Besides, I was impatient to move out of this Hafar, this
benighted heritage of the winds and the Bedu. So I got
up about two hours before dawn, and assuming the part
of Hazlul I walked out to wake up my companions, four

of whom, wrapt up like mummies from head to foot, slept around my tent, thanks to the Chief's thoughtfulness and protecting grace.—' Up ye ! ' I cried, adopting also his voice and his mood, ' up ye and pray ! Baddah, Misfer, Salem, up ye and pray ! Hamad, as soon as I mentioned his name, replied, *Labbeik* (at thy order) ! and the purblind Ibrahim, who must have been like myself awake all night, recognized my voice.—' Allah reward thee, O Ameen, for waking up the sluggards.' But Misfer, who denounces no one, except occasionally Baddah, considered it a great favour that I should wake him up to pray. More than once during the day he thanked me and offered me the little mirror.

It was not the hour for the morning prayer ; but we were travelling, and the Prophet himself on such occasions broke the rule. My brothers and companions prayed while the winds were still howling. The battle of the winds was in fact renewed at that hour, and we loaded and pulled out of Al-Hafar under clouds of dust and in the din of the storm. The camels themselves stepped heavily, tremulously, turning the neck this way and that, as if struggling up the sand dunes of the Nufoud.

Nevertheless, and in the teeth of the wind, Hazlul delivered the morning sermon. He praised Allah for the bounty he has chosen to bestow upon them the people of Najd and upon all the Muslemin ; for the peace and security that reign in the land of the Arabs ; for the personification of justice and wisdom, the Sultan Abd'ul-Aziz, who makes the Bedu tremble and the foolish reflect ; and—last but not least—for the jewel of faith, Unitarianism. They are genuinely thankful, my pious companions ; and not one of them seemed conscious of the woeful desolation and the abominable atmosphere of Al-Hafar.

The winds were still pursuing us when we crouched our camels in a sandy hollow for breakfast ; and each of us took some bread and food in his hand and squatted on the ground, pulling the *aba* over his head and tightening its ends under his feet. Nevertheless, the sand got ahead of the food into my mouth. And Salem's coffee was sanded while he was pouring it out. It was a most strenuous day ; for riding in the wind storm is even worse than crossing the ridges of the 'Uroudh.

The ground, as Al-Hafar recedes from view, becomes a little animated ; but among the stubble were only two green shrubs, the *ramth* of the season's growth and what is called *bu'aitharan*, a plant resembling the anise, with a yellow corymb and a pungent smell, and which, like the *ramth*, does not tempt the camel.

In the air too was a pleasant sign of life, palpitating in the north wind, playing with it, daring it, and riding sometimes ahead of us upon it. It was amusing to see the greenish-winged little birds carried away—gliding, their wings outspread and still, they went ;—and then, when the wind turned, they were blown swiftly backward as if shot out of the mouth of a cannon. The rude and ruthless north wind.

It was the last day of February, the time of storms in Syria. And is not the day that follows the beginning of the Ides of March ? But the birds and the corymbed anise-like plant did not mind ; for in Central Arabia, in spite of the long arm of the March north wind, the sun is pleasantly warm in the day, although at night the cold bites through to the bone.

Even ' the cheek,' as they call the face of the earth in Najd, was attaining some colour ; for the farther we got away from Al-Hafar the more inviting was the pasture in the fields and in the glens. The Bedu came to meet us from every direction, some running from a distance and waving their sleeves for us to stop. Hazlul disappointed none of them.

—' *Salaam alaikum* ya Ikhwan ! Allah greet the Muslemin. How are ye ? and how is Abu Turki ? [1] and what

---

[1] The name of the Sultan Abd'ul-Aziz's eldest son, who died during the War, was Turki, and the Bedu still call the Sultan Abu Turki, following the time-honoured custom of giving the father the name of his first-born son.

are your tidings ? ' They then ask about the pasture.
' How is " the cheek "—what's the colour of " the cheek,"
where you've passed ?—What's the colour of " the
cheek " of the glen ? ' And Hazlul would answer every
question, directing them to the best pasture we had passed.
Some of them, whose *naqahs* with their foals were browsing
near by, insisted on milking for us ; and the bowl, with
a froth four inches thick rising from the brim, looked
beautiful, tasted delicious, and had a most wholesome
effect.

On the second day, after leaving Al-Hafar, when we
were coming to a place in Al-Batin called Ar-Riq'i,
where travellers diverge to go to Kuwait, our guide
Khalaf lost his bearings and took us through a hilly ground
south of Al-Batin before he had reached the bifurcation
of the road. But we applauded afterwards his mistake,
for it was a short cut to Dibdibah, which we were to enter
after turning at Ar-Riq'i to our right.

Dibdibah is a plain of about twenty thousand square
miles lying south-east of Al-Batin, between Al-Hafar and
the Shiq, and is divided in half by the 23rd degree of
latitude. It has always belonged to whoever held sway
at Al-Hafar ; but a small section of it is included to-day
in the territory of Iraq. A vast plain, severely level, but
not severely monotonous ; for it fairly glows in long
stretches with green pasture. Most of the vegetation is
the same as that of the Dahna, and the way is more
bewildering. The road is often effaced or lost in the
shrubbery, and travellers at night are guided by the stars.
If one is going from Al-Hasa to Iraq the direction is
simple ;—' put the pointers between your eyes and you
will not go astray.' There is also good game in the
Dibdibah, especially the hare, the gazelle, the sand-
grouse, and the bustard. But water is very scarce. On
either of the two roads from Al-Hafar to Kuwait, the
direct road to Khabrat'ud-Dawish and the one through
Al-Batin to Jahrah, there is not a single well. Nevertheless,

the Dibdibah has an assuring atmosphere ; and its air, like that of the Washm, is exhilarating.

Once we were on the plain the vastness revived the mood, the sharp breeze abetted it, and we were all on the fast *dirham*, galloping abreast, imitating the Ikhwan on a *gazu*, repeating their war-cry, and shaking the bamboos at an imaginary foe. I was even given an exhibition of a *qafilah* attacked by the Bedu. It was Baddah's idea, who is, after all, of an enviable humour—a fellow of quips and jests. The party divided itself into travellers with a *hamlah*—our transport corps—and the bandit-Bedu, who were Baddah, Mubarak, and Ju'aithen. Misfer, leading the *hamlah*, came behind ; and we the travellers were going ahead when the three strangers, half-masked, approached us. Their spokesman was Baddah, who questioned us about our going and coming, about the Ikhwan, about Kuwait, etc., and then revealed his purpose. He and his brothers are Arabs of the north, without water and without food, ' The way to Kuwait is not safe : you need an escort.' Hazlul spoke for us. We were the men of Ibn Sa'oud : we required not their protection, etc. But the parley was cut short by Mubarak, who struck Khalaf with his stick and thus started the fight. Followed a tilt with bamboos, which developed into a hand-to-hand encounter, and every one struck out, bending from his saddle, and snatched whatever he could from the other. Meanwhile, Baddah was shooting his rifle in the air, and Misfer, who had just arrived with the *hamlah*, jumped to the ground from his high seat, gun in hand, and began to shoot at Baddah and his gang. It was an amusing performance, which ended in the defeat of the bandits, who galloped bareheaded away. The victory in the tilt was to him who could snatch the other fellow's headgear, or the rein of his *zelul*, or even pull him from his seat to the ground. No one was able to do this, although at one time I saw Salem and Mubarak earnestly tugging at each other while bravely managing their

zeluls, keeping them going around as if they were performing in a circus ring.

It was natural, after thus whetting their appetite, that
the *gazu* should be their only subject of conversation in the
evening at the coffee circle ;—a serious discussion it was,
in which even Salem participated. I give you the gist
of it. Four out of five of the Bedu prefer the *gazu* to the
pastoral or the agricultural life, because there is loot in it.
True, there is also peril ; but its daily presence, in one
form or the other, had made it familiar. Their flocks, if
they have any, are subject to the perils of the desert and
the weather. No rain, no life : hence the preference of
the *gazu.* If peril always exists, therefore, why not with
it the chance of gain ?

I asked my companions—eleven Arabs of different
tribes and occupations—what was their own preference.
And the result of the plebiscite, which was taken in the
Dibdibah on the evening of the 3rd of March, the year
of Grace 1923, on the 15th of the 6th month of the year
of the Hijrah 1341, is as follows :—Six of them preferred
the gazu ; three the agricultural life ; and two were
dissatisfied, dreamed of adventures in other lands, desired,
in sooth, to come with me to America.

' There is no blessing in the spoils of the *gazu,* nor in
the money of the *gazu,*' said Salem. ' *'Adl* (just),' assented
Misfer, who nevertheless is of the majority. He then told
us the story of how his last *gazu*-money went.

' I had been six months away on the *gazu,* Allah keep
thee, and I killed twelve men, *billah,* and came back to
Buraidah with thirty reals in my bag. In Buraidah I
bought a camel for twenty reals to take me to Sudous,
the whereabout of my wife and the children ; and I
carried the remainder—ten reals—as evidence of my
success, and went across the Nufoud *dirhaming bilhail*
(trotting strong) to 'Anaizah. But further the camel
would not go. She was vicious and stubborn. So I sold
her in 'Anaizah for fifteen reals and bought another for

twenty. What remained of the money? Five reals,
Allah keep thee. I galloped to Shaqra; but right outside
the city wall the camel fell flat on her four knees and
would not move. I walked into the city and found,
Allah be praised, a buyer. Ten reals—the beast was sick
—I was glad withal to get ten reals. Two days in Shaqra
and I found another *naqah*, a good-looking black, which
I bought for fifteen reals—all gone, the *gazu*-money!—
And down to the Washm I went, *dirhaming bilhail*, and to
Tharmadah, and across to the foot of Jabal Twaij, where
the accursed one tripped, fell down, and would not get
up again. I invoked Allah and the Prophet—it was dark
—no one could see or hear me. I could not make the
vicious one get up even with a stick of fire under her tail.
There is no resource and no power except in Allah. I
left her at the foot of the Jabal and I walked to Sudous
clean of hand and clean of purse. That is the *gazu*-gain.
No blessing in it, as says Salem. But I would tire of sitting
at home with the wife and the children. My eyes would
get sore, and my breath, she tells me, gets bad. The *gazu*
—life in the *khala* (the open) and on the *zelul*—polishes
the body and makes it smell good.'

On the other hand, the Arab has an instinct for trade,
nay, a mania for buying and selling or exchanging things.
If your companion of the road cannot sell you his cloak
or his sandals or something he might be carrying, he will
ask you to exchange bamboos, for instance, or head-
kerchiefs with him. Mubarak, who is travelling on duty,
is like the wide awake American, even more so, combining
with duty both business and pleasure. He is carrying
with him six dozens of Buraidah sandals to sell in Kuwait.
But Hamad the black, who cannot keep anything, has
not the shrewd business instinct of the Semite. When he
returned from a *gazu* once he had, like Misfer, thirty reals
in his bag; and instead of a camel he bought with two-
thirds of his capital a sword, which he sported as he
swaggered idly in the *Souq*, to make people believe that

he had won it in the *gazu*. Soon, however, the remainder of his capital was spent and he was on the point of selling the sword when Allah sent him Hazlul, who employed him as assistant to Misfer. Thus was the weapon destined to grace our *qafilah* from Ar-Riyadh to Kuwait, stuck one day under Misfer's packs and dandling at another from the saddle-tree of Baddah. But Khalaf, who had set his eye upon it ever since he left Buraidah—a rival of the Chief must also have a sword—succeeded eventually in getting Hamad to sell it to him for thirteen reals, thereby losing seven. And when I gave Hazlul some money to buy new garments for his men, he bought one for Hamad, but did not give it to him until the morning of our entry to Kuwait, when he made him wear it. ' Otherwise,' said the Chief, ' he would have sold it. I know the boy.'

The *gazu* and this haphazard way of acquiring things and disposing of them are closely associated with the Arab's improvident and disorderly spirit. But the exceptions, a few of which I have already noted, may not be so conspicuous to the traveller—especially the European traveller —as the rule. What the Arab has learned to do, what he must do, I say again, he does well—as well as his means permit. But he has neither the inventive nor the dynamic mind. He can be taught to be orderly and methodical ; and he can acquire with little practice the thoroughgoing manner. The best example of this among my *rafiqs* was Salem, and I shall now tell you how he made coffee and tea.

Every time we descended for the day the first bit of business that struck my attention was that of Salem with axe in hand digging a hole in the ground. He then sniffed the wind, which decided the direction of the tent. After the hole was dug, he and two others were soon gathering wood or plucking up roots ; and if there were none at all in the place we had chosen for the encampment they would gather *jilla* (camel dung). Salem then kindled his fire

and took out the *ma'amil*, or coffee utensils and cups ;
these were placed in a long brass tube, each one wrapt in
a piece of cloth, and those in a bag made of burlap with
pockets in it each the size of the object it held.   Thus was
he able to carry the *ma'amil* behind him and trot with
us without any damage to them or to himself.   No, I do
not think that Salem broke a single cup or lost a stirring
stick during the whole journey.   His efficiency in this
business is admirable.   But he never could lace his shoes ;
—his patent leather shoes which he wore in the cities,
slipping them on and off as he would a pair of sandals.
It was not laziness in Salem ; but he did not know, he
confessed to me, how to tie a cross knot.

But I am now speaking of Salem the coffee-maker.
After the fire is kindled into a blaze he sits before it
cross-legged and sets his utensils in a row beside him.   A
special pot for water is filled and left to boil, while he
roasts the beans (the roaster, the stirrer and the tongs
are all long-handled implements) and grinds them in a
brass mortar.   By this time the water would be boiling
and one of the brass pots would be used to make a first
brew, which is left to boil while stirring with a stick for
about five minutes.   He then makes another brew in a
smaller pot, using with the coffee the grounds of the previous one ; and thus the residue of a previous brew is
always used in the brew that follows.   The contents of
the two pots are then poured into a third, with palm fibres
as a filter in its spout, from which the coffee is served.
The people of Najd use the cardamom in big quantities
with the coffee ; I have seen Salem ground the seeds as
he would the coffee beans and use as much as a cupful
in a brew.   He was equally skilful in making tea, which
he never boiled over a fire ; but, even like a Persian or
a Japanese epicure, he would pour the boiling water over
it and discard the first infusion.

In the evening Salem also made a special brew of
coffee sufficient to fill a *zamzamiyah*—a jar of earthenware

—for the following day during the march. For when we stopped to be ' coffeed ' between the two meals no time was lost in roasting and grinding and brewing. The contents of the *zamzamiyah* are poured into a pot, heated in a few minutes over a fire of dry shrubs, and served. Indeed our coffee ' department ' was the most modern and attractive of our ' establishment.' No one, not even the most fastidious and sophisticated, could wish for more order in it or efficiency or taste or cleanliness. The latter especially was amazing. But the Arab everywhere, in the city or in the desert, is oldmaidish about his brass coffee pots. They must always be shining just as his fire must always be burning, or he is not an Arab gentleman. Judging him by this standard, Salem was the first Arab gentleman of our caravan.

Would I could say this about Misfer. But he, Caliban-Misfer, shall not be judged as cook or butcher or chief steward. He carries the incense and the mirror :—he is our high priest and master of ceremonies. I forgot to tell you, however, that he is also a baker. Which I would never have discovered had I depended exclusively upon my observations during the day. But one night in the Nufoud, as I was going out of my tent, I saw in the blaze of Misfer's fire (we always had two fires, one for the coffee, another for the cooking) a man raising something rather heavy with his two hands, raising it above his head and throwing it with force upon the ground. He picked it up again, brushed it with his hand, and repeated the operation three or four times. The shadow and the motion near a fire at night were indeed weird. I walked across, curious and apprehensive ; but it was none else than Misfer, who was beating on the sand a loaf of bread ! How he makes it ? and why this operation ? After the flour is kneaded—little or no salt is used—it is made into a round loaf, ranging from the size of a bun to the size of a cushion, according to the immediate need, placed in a pit made for it alongside the fire and covered with hot

ashes. There it is left to bake. Every now and then
the ashes are removed and the loaf is turned over ; and
when it is sufficiently baked he takes it out and puts it
through the process I have described to remove from it
that layer of ashes and sand and smudge. It is then broken
up in a pan or a platter, immersed in butter, kneaded
again and served for breakfast. With the rice and mutton
—cold, left over from the previous day for dinner, but
freshly cooked for supper—they ate little or no bread.
What was brought for me from Buraidah, about thirty
of the round thin loaves—leaves—lasted till we had
crossed the Dibdibah.

And with them, at the end of this plain, ended the good
fortune which had accompanied us the past four days.
For what with the change of air, the pleasant landscape,
and the easy riding ground ; and what with the green
pasture for our camels and the fresh truffles for ourselves ;
and what with the feeling that this long and arduous
journey was nearing its end, we were all, of a certainty,
in clover. Four good days, four delightful days, and then,
and then—Dame Malaria !

Nothing so much helped to bolster up my spirit in
those dark hours, when D.M. was a visiting guest, as my
imagination which, strange to say, never soared on the
dark side of the world. For were we not always moving ?
And is not in movement change ? And in mortal movement both change and an end ? There it was, indeed,
and only thirty miles away.

Behold us, then, a bonny crew, bringing peace and goodwill to Kuwait ;—Hazlul our Chief and Khalaf the
pretender with swords drawn heading the procession ;
Baddah, Salem, Mubarak and Ju'aithen shooting their
rifles and exclaiming, *Allahu akbar !*—and I, wrapt in my
aba, hands across the breast and bamboo stick across the
shoulder, Bedu-fashion, following them ; while Misfer
is marching behind at the head of the *hamlah*, carrying
a yellow flag. After all, and in spite of the health of the

mounts and the riders, we are escorting an invalid, a
neuritic and malaria-ridden traveller, who depends not
wholly upon Allah. For does he not carry bottles with
him, and does he not eat *kinkina* ? . . .

'Up ye, up ye and load ! Up ye !' It was again
Hazlul waking us from sleep. The hour was two a.m.
and the desert was suffused with moonlight when we set
out on what was to be the last march. But three hours
later the cold air of dawn asserted itself, especially in
Khalaf's ends, as he said ; and he was the first as usual
to inquire about the time and to ask for a few minutes
of rest. We alighted ; and after kindling a fire and making
coffee and saying the morning prayer we resumed our
march.

The moon was still on the horizon at dawn, when we
were making for Jahrah by the sea, or rather on the Gulf.
How welcome is the sea after four long months in the heart
of Arabia ! The sea, or just that blue ribbon on the
horizon, how beautiful it seems, how generous, and how
significant. The desert takes you away from the world ;
the sea brings you back to it :—the desert brings you near
to God ; the sea invites you to familiar strands and revives
the loving thought of home and friends :—the desert is
contemplation ; the sea is love. But I conceal not from
the reader that the long divine companionship is at
intervals too monotonous, almost insufferable, to one who
has not conquered nor ever did attempt to conquer the
flesh ; and although I admire St. Antony of the Thibaid
and St. Simon of the Pillar (who, I think, is my ancestor),
I must confess that, after two months on a rocking pillar
of camel-flesh in the shadow of Allah, Who, I once felt,
shared the same pillar with me to reinforce me against
the fever—after all this divine luxury, I say, I longed for
the mortal things, the simple things, aye, even the frivolous
things of life. Once in Ar-Riyadh I had the fear that my
eyes were never again to behold the sea. But here I am,
Allah be praised, only a few parasangs away from a

seaport and a bit of civilization to boot, run by steam
on the water ! [1]

Jahrah is a village in the shadow of Mt. Zour at the
head of an arm in the Gulf, which runs westward from
the bay of Kuwait ; and the distance between it and the
Capital is not more than fifteen miles. Jahrah of the
Wells ! There are about fifty of them outside the town,
which needs not more than one or two, and the water of
all of them is good. The Sheikh of Kuwait has a palace
here, which he visits when he is shooting sand-grouse.
But Jahrah would not have been known in the Peninsula,
were it not for the Ikhwan—the Fierce Brotherhood—
who wrote its name with blood upon the map.

There was, in sooth, a war, and the cause was the camel.
Cherché la femme, we say in the West ; *cherché le chameau*,
in Arabia. Some of the Bedu of Kuwait had stolen the
camels of some of the Bedu of Najd ; and so Ibn'ud-
Dawish at the head of five thousand of the Ikhwan,
marches out of Irtawiyah on a punitive expedition. He
would either make the people of Kuwait ' religious ' or
exterminate them. What he did was to frighten them
away ; for when they heard he was coming they took
refuge under sails in the Gulf. Those who had the courage
to remain got some of the Bedu together and came with
them to Jahrah to reinforce its armed population. But
the Ikhwan marched on Jahrah, slaughtered five hundred
of the *mushrekin*, the infidel Kuwaitis, besieged Salem
Aal Sabah in his palace, and only on the promise that he
would become ' religious,' an *akhu* of the Ikhwan, did
they spare his life. But Sheikh Salem played false ; and
were it not for the British Government, he would also have
lost his Sheikhdom. For when he escaped from his palace

---

[1] In Book XII, p. 134, of my *Notes of Travel in Arabia*, I find the following :
Saturday, March 10.
Curious coincidence : I left Basrah November 10 on the S.S. Barjora,
and I returned to Basrah from Kuwait March 10 on the S.S. Barjora ! . . .
It is so good to eat with a knife and fork again, and to look into a book-
case, and to read a page or two of George Meredith.

and his promise, the Ikhwan pursued him to Kuwait and would have entered the city had it not been for an English man-of-war and a message dropped among them from an English aeroplane. Now the mothers of Kuwait frighten their children with the Ikhwan. Hush ! the Ikhwan are coming.

I did not think we were going to stop at Jahrah ; but Hazlul would not enter the city of Kuwait unannounced. We camped, therefore, outside the wall on a sand-hillock and Baddah was dispatched with letters to Sheikh Ahmad Aal Sabah informing him of our arrival at Jahrah and our purpose of entering into his Capital on the morning of the following day.

The Ameer of the Qasr—here too the keeper of the palace is called Ameer—and other distinguished Jahrites came to see us and invite us to coffee. Their hospitality, like that of the people of Al-Qasim, is flavoured with a pleasant social feeling ; and while sipping coffee I tried to get from them what might have filtered through the Capital of the news of the world. But they are more interested, it seems, in the news of Najd and the Ikhwan. They told me that Jahrah, like Al-Hafar, is also exposed to the winds, particularly to the *mahabb*, or north wind. But I do not think they dread it as much as they do the simoom—the winds of Al-Jannat—which blow from the south.

I dread both the simoom and the *mahabb*, and I praised Allah that on the Jahrah stage the day we arrived there was nothing but vacancy and silence. But when we were returning from the village in the afternoon, Hazlul noticed a heavy cloud over Mt. Zour and said : ' It is the *mahabb*, Allah ward it off.' Nevertheless, the heavy black clouds— pregnant they seemed with rain—continued to move slowly across the mountain from the north-west.

We hastened to the camp, where the men were seated around Salem's fire drinking tea and chatting uncon- cerned. Hazlul rated them.—' Open your eyes and look

R.I.S.   z

above you.' He then ordered them to quickly knock down their tent and tighten the pegs of mine. No sooner was this done than the vanguards of the storm were upon us.

The order was given to pack and load, and Misfer and his men tucked their sleeves. But the camels growled and brayed ; the *mahabb* which first blew from the north-west was now blowing also from the south, or another wind from that direction had joined in the attack ; and the tunics of the men were flying and flapping while they were bravely doing their duty. They moved to a shelter on the other side of the tent, but the wind, which increased in volume and power, tugged at it and almost hurled it upon them.

' Hamad and Hamoud and Ju'aithen, get hold of the ropes. Mubarak and Baddah fasten the pegs.' Saying which, the Chief took another rope, threw it over the tent to Khalaf, who fastened it at his own end. The winds from three directions increased ; the sand was piled against the tent and up to the crouching camel's breasts ; and all around there was a dark screen between us and the world. One could not see more than ten feet ahead ; and when I stood outside, the wind blew the sand into my eyes through the very felt of my goggles' frame.

It was about sunset and Misfer had cooked a good supper which could not, of course, be eaten outside. They therefore gathered in the little tent where the mat was spread ; and Misfer and Ibrahim came in with the two big kettles, which they poured into the brass platters after skimming from them the layers of sand. But the wind continued to blow through the slits adding the extra spice to Misfer's mess.

I sat down and ate with them. It was our *last supper ;* —a supper of rice and sand ; but under a shelter and in a circle of genuine brotherhood, we did not mind. *They* did not mind, and I tried to be as heroic and brave.

After the supper, the sunset prayer ; but they had to

face the storm if they prayed outside. Which was impossible even if they shut their eyes, for the sand pierced
the skin like needles. The mat was therefore removed
and at my suggestion they also prayed in the little tent,
and I prayed with them.

It was a fitting close, a beautiful ceremony, the sacra-
ment and the seal of brotherhood in a sand storm. And
we sat huddled in the little tent after that, while Hazlul
recited some of his own verse and Khalaf told stories till
about midnight, when the storm subsided. The moon
had then risen, and the wind whispered its assurance ;
after which a calm, a warmth, and the level spaces, all
inviting to the march. Hazlul gave the order, and
within thirty minutes Misfer and his assistants were on
their laden camels facing the east. We followed after
drinking the tea which Salem was quick to make. Three
hours of blissful swaying in the moonlight, and we
alighted once more that another important ceremony
might be performed.

We were but a few miles from Kuwait, and my *rafiqs*
and friends had to change their clothes and make themselves presentable for the city by the sea. Hamad wore
his new tunic over the old ; so did Misfer and a few others.
But Hazlul and Baddah and Khalaf and Salem, who are
more travelled and more particular, indulged in a complete change, wore also their bandoliers and took the
rifles out of their cases. Every one *kohled* his eyes, and
Misfer's little mirror, by the help of the moon, was very
serviceable. Faces smiled to it, as it passed from hand
to hand.

I sat near the fire watching them, and, strange to say,
I was the captive of a melancholy which I tried to conquer
or conceal. It was in sooth the first time it really dawned
upon me that we were on the last march, the last hour of
the long journey. And how often I have wished and
longed and prayed for the end. But at that hour, when I
realized that the moon would no more shine upon us,

upon my *rafiqs* and myself—at that hour, the hour of parting, I wished that Time would vouchsafe us another day in the Dahna and another night around Salem's fire, when Misfer would dance again the dance of the Ikhwan and Ibrahim would feed the blaze until it is shot with the gold threads of the sun.

No, it is not without a deep pang that I leave my Arab Brothers. How kind and thoughtful and obliging, each in his own way, they were to me, it is a duty to record and will always be a pleasure to recall. I have never had so many servants and attendants ; I have never been so guarded and honoured in travel ; and I have never had a cook like Misfer, who can only cook rice and lamb, but whose face and genial spirit are a joy for ever ;—nor have I ever come in so close a contact with the Bedu, nay, with the gentlemen of Najd.

They are real brothers, these people, and not Ikhwan. It was Baddah's wont to cry out whenever the hand of weariness was heavy upon us, ' Smoke, ya Ikhwan ! Tobacco drives away the Shaitan.' They were, indeed, the target of my brother's jest.—Pass the *sabil*, O Mubarak. . . . Light up, O Brother Salem ! It is Baddah's idea that the Ikhwan of the new towns ought to plant tobacco and get rich quick.

Thus, in sooth, did the jest lighten the heavy whiles and shorten the long languishing hours of fatigue and pain. Aye, even to the end of the journey. ' Is my *ighal* on straight ? ' asked Misfer of Hazlul, as the city of Kuwait, looming in the diaphanous silvery veil of dawn, was slowly unveiling itself before us. Hazlul : ' If thy head were straight, O Misfer, thine *ighal* would also be straight, *billah !* ' . . . Come, come. Be we again the children of thy favour, O Hazlul. And the Dawsari Chief repeated the verses he had recited in the little tent but a few hours ago (which shall always be to me, *but a few hours ago*) :

' Oh, what a sigh, my brothers, I have sighed,
    When you rode away on the fair reds of Oman !

I wish that I were with you, even though
    I have to walk behind the caravan ;—
I wish that I were with you but to hear
    The talk that giveth joy to lovers wan.
O thou who hath Al-Jannat made, and Fire,
    O thou the Lord of every tribe and clan,
Send them a pregnant cloud ; forget them not :
    For with them is the man I love—the man
Whose braided locks and lustred eyes and smile
    The fire of infatuation fan.
I never shall forget him though my grave
    Be many fathoms deep—I never can.'

A TIME SCHEDULE OF THE JOURNEY FROM AR-RIYADH TO THE QASIM

The Day's March.	Hours.
First Day—From Ar-Riyadh to Dir'iyah - -	3.15
Second Day—Slept in Wadi Hanifah - - -	6.35
Third Day—Slept in Kushm'ul-Barrah - - -	6.30
Fourth Day—Camped in the Nufoud of Tharmadah	6.15
Fifth Day—Camped outside of Tharmadah - -	3.30
Sixth Day—Remained in Shaqra two days - -	5.00
Ninth Day—Slept in the Nufoud - - - -	5.00
Tenth Day—Slept in the Nufoud - - - -	7.30
Eleventh Day—Wadi's-Sirr - - - - -	6.00
Twelfth Day—Camped outside of Mudhnib - -	8.30
Thirteenth Day—Camped at 'Awshaziah - -	3.45
Fourteenth Day—'Anaizah - - - - -	2.30
	64.20

A *najjab* can cover the distance between Ar-Riyadh and 'Anaizah in four days.

A TIME SCHEDULE OF THE JOURNEY FROM BURAIDAH TO KUWAIT

The Day's March.	Hours.
First Day—Camped at Sh'ib'un-Naqib - - -	2.30
Second Day at Al-Asyah—From Buraidah to Turfiyah, 4h. 30m. ; and from Turfiyah to Al-Asyah, 5 h. - - - - - - -	7.00
Third Day—Camped in the 'Uroudh - - -	5.30
Fourth Day—Camped in the 'Uroudh - - -	7.00
Fifth Day—Camped in the 'Uroudh - - -	5.30
Sixth Day—Camped near the Dahna - - -	8.00
Seventh Day—At Umm 'ul-Hashim - - -	8.00
Eighth Day—At Hulaibah - - - - -	9.00
Ninth Day—At Al-Hafar - - - - -	4.30
Tenth Day—In Al-Batin - - - - -	6.30
Eleventh Day—Dibdibah - - - - -	8.00
Twelfth Day—Dibdibah - - - - -	9.00
Thirteenth Day—Dibdibah, near the Shiq - -	5.30
Fourteenth Day—Camped outside of Jahrah - -	5.45
Fifteenth Day—Kuwait - - - - - -	4.30
	96.15

310 Miles : 96 hours $= 3\frac{1}{4}$ Miles an hour.

A *najjab* covers this distance ordinarily in six days. But Abdullah 'l-Bassam told me that he once rode from Kuwait to 'Anaizah in three and a half days. He slept but four out of twenty-four hours.

At Al-Asyah, Al-Hafar, and Jahrah there is both water and pasture ; at all the other places, pasture only.

INDEX

Aal (family, house), xi.
Aba, The, 132, 133.
Abbaside Khalifs, 6.
Abha, xiv, 57, 177, 178.
Abd'ul-Aziz ibn Abdullah Aal Sleim, 289.
Abd'ul-Aziz ibn Mit'eb ibn 'ur-Rashid, 165, 166, 173, 174.
Abd'ul-Aziz ibn Muhammad ibn Sa'oud, xvi, 146, 190, 243-245.
Abd'ul-Aziz ibn Sa'oud, King of Najd and Al-Hijaz, xvi, xvii, 1-4, 9-15, 17-22, 27, 30, 37-49, 61, 62, 69, 71, 81, 91, 96-98, 99 *n.*, 101, 105 *n.*, 134, 137, 138, 140-146, 149, 151-166, 168, 170, 171, 173, 175-180, 182-185, 201, 202, 204-206, 209, 210, 212-214, 225, 227, 228, 251, 255, 289, 290, 305, 311, 312, 338, 341 ; his character, 18-22, 40, 51-55, 58, 78, 197, 198 ; his generosity, 151, 229-231, 258 ; his physical characteristics, 38, 46, 50 ; flag of, 26 ; on American and European political policy, 43-46, 64, 223, 224 ; and Arab unity, 64-67, 236 ; on Arab fundamental needs, 39 ; and the English, 49, 61-68 ; and Najd-Iraq Treaty, 59-62 ; and Ojair Conference, 74-89 ; his attitude towards *Mushrekin*, 234, 235 ; his career of conquest, 56-58 ; handling of the Bedu, 20, 190-196 ; justice of his rule, 215-220 ; yearly stipend received by him from British Government and revenues, 76, 78, 222, 223 ; progress and innovations introduced by him, 233.
Abd'ul-Latif Pasha al-Mandil, 38, 76, 84.
Abd'ul-Muhsin ibn Jlewy ibn Sa'oud, xvi.

Abd'ul-Wahhab, 238.
Abdullah, Dr., 77, 86, 158.
Abdullah branch of Rashid dynasty, 166, 167, 173, 174.
Abdullah ibn Abd'ur-Rahman ibn Sa'oud, xvi.
Abdullah ibn Ali ibn 'ur-Rashid, 172, 174.
Abdullah ibn Faisal ibn Sa'oud, xvi.
Abdullah ibn Husein, Ameer of Trans-Jordania, 62, 311, 328.
Abdullah ibn Jlewy, xvi, 24, 98, 99, 111, 219, 220.
Abdullah ibn Misfer, 78.
Abdullah ibn Mit'eb ibn 'ur-Rashid, 45, 165, 169, 170, 173, 174, 176.
Abdullah ibn Muhammad 'ul-Bassam, 288-292, 359.
Abdullah ibn Sa'oud, Ameer, xvi, 256.
Abdullah ibn Talal ibn 'ur-Rashid, 169, 170, 173, 174.
Abdullah ibn Yahya, 287.
Abdullah 'l-Qosaibi, 3.
Abd'ur-Rahman ibn Faisal ibn Sa'oud, xvi, xvii, 56, 72, 73, 152, 178, 182 *n.*
Abd'ur-Rahman ibn Hasan ibn Sa'oud, xvi.
Abha, 78.
'Abit, 281, 289.
Abu Bakr, Khalif, 193.
Abu Dajjanah, 240.
Abu Hanifah, 92, 238 *n.*, 247, 249.
Abu Ja'far, 238.
Abu Jefan, *see* Jefan.
Abu Taher, 188.
Abu Turki, 342 *n.*
Abu'n-Nawwas, 252 *n.*
Ad-Dahna, *see* Dahna.
Ad-Dawasir, *see* Dawasir.
Ad-Dukhoul, *see* Dukhoul.
Ad-Dulaimiyah, *see* Dulaimiyah.
Aden, 1, 2, 6, 18.

Adh-Dhubai'ah, *see* Dhubai'ah.
'Adnan tribe, 272, 337.
Adultery, 240.
Aesculapius, 100.
Aflaj, 273.
Ahmad As-Sabah, Sheikh, 253, 353.
Ahmad ibn Hanbal, Imam, 238, 239, 246, 247, 248 *n.*, 249.
Ahmad ibn Jaber, 155.
Ahmad of Kuwait, Saiyed, 15.
Ahmad Pasha as-Sane' (Mutasarrif of Basrah), 14, 20.
Ahqaf, *see* Vacant Quarter.
'Ain, 276.
'Ain Dar, *see* Dar.
'Ain Fuhaid, *see* Fuhaid.
'Ain Thumaid, *see* Thumaid.
Aja, Jabal, xiv.
'Ajam, 190.
Akhdhar, Al-, 199.
Al (family, house), xi.
Al in words and place-names, xiii.
Al. Place-names such as Al-Hasa, Al-Medinah, etc., are alphabetised Hasa, Al-, Medinah, Al-, etc.
'*Alanda*, 321 *n.*
'Alat, 34, 35, 45, 91-94, 122, 218.
Ali, Benu, *see* Benu Ali.
Allah, 196.
'Amarat, 77, 78.
'Amarat tribe, 59-62, 74, 76-79.
American political policy, 43-46, 64, 223-225.
Amir, Ameer, xii.
'Anaizah, xv, 96 *n.*, 128, 255, 258, 281, 283, 285-304, 358, 359.
'Aneiz, Jabal, xiv, 61.
'Aneza tribe, 48, 60, 61, 74, 75, 230, 272, 296, 305.
Anglo-Persian Oil Co., 83, 84.
An-Najaf, *see* Najaf.
Aqaba, xiv.
Ar. Names beginning with Ar as Ar-Riq'i, Ar-Riyadh are alphabetised Riq'i, Ar-, Riyadh, Ar-.
Araak, 184 *n.*
Arab mind, 347, 348.
Arab unity, *see* Pan-Arabism.
Arabic transliteration, xi.
Area of Najd, xiv.
'Ared, Al-, xiv, 1 *n.*, 71, 120, 125, 126, 157, 181, 188, 193, 196, 204, 238, 239, 241-243, 278, 313.
'*Arfaj*, 321 *n.*
'Arja, 198.
Armies, Arab, 180, 194, 198, 207-210, 229.

Arratoon, J. A., 5.
As-Sadeqah, *see* Sadeqah.
As-Sanam, *see* Sanam.
As-Sawh, *see* Sawh.
As-Sihaf, *see* Sihaf.
As-Sirrar, *see* Sirrar.
As-Suhoul, *see* Suhoul.
Ash-Shafe'i, 238 *n.*
Ash-Shi'b, 198.
Ash-Shubaikiyah, 199.
Asir, xiii, xiv, 7, 10, 78, 81, 147, 177, 178, 189, 245.
Asyah, Al-, 312-314, 316, 358, 359.
Athathiyah, 274.
'Atiq, Al-, 199.
At-Taief, *see* Taief.
Auctions, 129, 130, 134, 302.
'Aushaziyah, 277-281, 283.
'Awazim, Al-, tribe, xv, 199.
'Awja, Al, *see* Riyadh, Ar-.
'Awshaziah, 358.
Az-Zabba' Zenubia, 97.

Babylon, 12.
Baddah, 102-106, 110, 113, 114, 116, 119-121, 265-267, 279-283, 307, 308, 310, 312, 316, 317, 320, 325-327, 330-334, 336, 338, 340, 341, 344, 347, 350, 353-356.
Badr ibn Talal ibn 'ur-Rashid, 166, 172, 174.
Baghdad, 2, 3, 5-13, 68, 78, 87, 99, 253, 319 ; Residency, 18, 66, 76.
Baghdad, Khalifs of, 98, 99, 188.
Bahrain, 1-6, 13-23, 25, 27, 48, 67, 81, 82, 84.
Bahri tribe, 224.
Baidhah, 105.
Bakr ibn Wa'el ibn Jadilah, xvi.
Bandar ibn Talal ibn 'ur-Rashid, 166, 172, 174.
Barjora, S.S., 80.
Barqah tribe, 198.
Barrah, 264-266, 277, 279.
Basrah, 13-15, 18, 21, 68, 135, 188, 239, 253, 303, 352 *n.*
Bassam family, 286 *n.*, 289.
Batin, Al-, 96 *n.*, 335, 336, 343, 358.
Batra, Al-, 275.
Beards of Wahhabis, 19, 20, 70.
Bedu, 20, 21, 58, 188-199, 202, 212, 218, 219, 222, 225, 229, 237, 261, 272, 303, 304, 320, 345, 352, 356.
Beggars, 124, 125.
Beirût University, 152.
Bell, Gertrude, 7-12, 20.
Benak, 199.

Benu Ali tribe, 230.
Benu Hajir tribe, 199, 217, 218.
Benu Helal tribe, 335.
Benu Khalid tribe, 272, 296.
Benu Murrah tribe, xv, 196, 199, 217, 218, 220, 253.
Benu Tamim tribe, 238, 269, 272, 296, 305.
Benu Zeid tribe, 272.
Bida', Al-, 199.
Binwan, 199.
Bisha, 146.
Bolsheviks, 67.
Bombay Political Department, 2-6, 9.
Book of Unitarianism, 239.
Booty, sharing of, 210.
Boundaries, xiv, xv, 60, 64, 66, 77-79.
Bread-making, 349.
Bridges with houses built on, 294.
British India Company, 27.
British-Iraq Treaty, 8.
British-Najd Treaty, 77, 86.
British political agents, 2, 6, 8, 9, 84.
Bu'aitharan, 342.
Buckhner, ——, 90.
Buraidah, xv, 152, 193, 244, 255, 277, 300-310, 358.
Buroud, Al-, 199.
Burrard, Col. Sir S. G., 278 n.
Bushire, 84.
Busht, 133.
Butter extracted from camel's bones, 293.

Camels, 28, 29, 32-34, 95, 103, 104, 111, 112, 196, 210, 230, 231, 267, 268, 293, 294, 300, 302, 303.
Canopus, 30 n.
Carmathians, 100, 188, 237, 241.
Cherd, 125.
Churchill, Winston, xiii, 79.
Cities of Najd, xv.
Climate, 132, 133, 225, 226, 229.
Clothing, 143, 144 ; state distribution of, 134.
Coffee, 64, 128, 286-289, 348.
Coinage, 129, 130, 222.
Colocynth, 335.
Commentaries, *see* Koran.
Contentment amongst Arabs, 213.
Cordova, Mosque at, 131.
Cox, Sir Percy, 8, 10-13, 31, 32, 48, 52, 55-57, 59, 61, 71, 73-80, 84, 86, 87.
Cox, Lady, 86.

Criers of Arab ameers, 37.
Crime, punishment of, 24, 215, 219, 220.
Ctesiphon, 12.
Cursing, 73 n.
Custom amongst Arabs, 138.

Dahham ibn Dawwas, Ameer, 188, 242, 243.
Dahna, Ad, 198.
Dahna, The, xiv, 14, 27, 101, 102, 105-112, 116, 122, 180-182, 193, 212 n., 217, 244, 253, 261, 273, 297, 313 n., 316, 318-334, 339, 343, 356, 358.
Damascus, 86, 152, 222, 303.
Damascus, Khalifs of, 99.
Dame, Dr., 84.
Damlouji, Dr. Abdullah, 38.
Dancing, 299, 324.
Dar, 'Ain, 199.
Darin, 106 n.
Darwin, Charles, 90, 91, 110, 135.
Date stones, 295.
Dawasir, Ad-, 199.
Dawasir, Wadi 'd-, xiv, 57, 146, 189, 231 n., 245, 261, 326.
Dawasir tribe, xv, 196, 217, 253, 274.
De Sacy, ——, 16.
Dhafir tribe, 59, 60, 62, 76-79, 230, 337, 338.
D'heim, 143, 252, 254, 255.
Dhorumah, 262.
Dhouma (Dh'ruma), 1 n., 3, 6.
Dhubai'ah, Adh-, 199.
Dhuraiyah, 198.
Dibdibah, 343-345, 350, 358.
Dickson, Major, 20, 31.
Dirham, 51.
Dir'iyah, 188, 239, 241-245, 256-258, 260, 262, 304, 358.
Distances reckoned by prayers, 111 n.
Divorce, 206.
Diwan, 15 n.
Donkey, 278.
Doughty, Charles Montagu, xii, 288, 290.
Dowla, 290.
Dubai, 230.
Dukhnah, 193, 199.
Dukhoul, Ad-, 274.
Dulaimiyah, Ad-, 199.

Education, 20, 21, 193.
Egypt, 18, 303.

Europe, Ibn Sa'oud on, 44-46, 223-225.
Executions, 220.

Fadl 'ud-Din, Dr., 81.
Fahd ul-Hazzal, Sheikh, 48, 49, 51, 60, 61, 74, 75, 87.
Faisal, house of, xvii.
Faisal, King of Iraq, xiii, xvii, 6-8, 10, 59, 62, 65, 77-79.
Faisal ibn Abd'ul-Aziz ibn Sa'oud, Ameer, xvi, 4, 177-180, 186.
Faisal ibn Hamoud ibn 'ur-Rashid, 45, 64, 165-168, 170, 174, 177, 182-184.
Faisal ibn Sa'oud (the Great), xvi.
Faisal ibn Turki ibn Sa'oud, xvi.
Falcons, 16.
Faras, Al-, muazzen of, 26.
Fares, Sheikh, 137.
Fares, servant, 265, 283, 299, 306, 307.
Farhan ibn Sa'oud, 241 n.
Farouq, Wadi, 102.
Fatimah Sibhan, 168, 170.
Fireplaces, 128.
Flannels, washing of, 149-151.
Flies in the desert, 47.
Flogging, 203, 216, 219.
Flowers, 292, 312.
Fossils, 118 n.
Fraisan, 198.
Freike, 86.
Fudoul, Al-, 96.
Fuhaid, 'Ain, 313.
Funerals, 162.

Gatgat, 193, 198.
Gazalahs, 32 n.
Gazu, xii, 345, 346.
Gazzali, Al-, 254.
George, Lloyd, 12.
Gharb, 125, 126.
Ghrazzu, xii.
Graves dug before doors, 225.
Graveyards of Wahhabis, 127.
Gutrah, The, 133.

Hadda, xiv n.
Hadith, The, 97, 99, 192, 238, 239, 247, 248 n., 261, 271.
Hafar, Al-, xi, 252, 253, 255, 313, 315, 318, 336-343, 353, 358, 359.
Haiel, xv, 57, 134, 152, 165-167, 173, 184, 189, 212 ; Ameer of, 63, 64, 74, 165-170, 172.
Haisiyah, 260, 261.

Hajir, Benu, see Benu Hajir.
Hajji Ali Ridha Zainal, 3.
Hajrah, xii.
Hamad, servant, 266, 307, 308, 324, 330, 341, 346, 347, 354, 355.
Hammer-Purgstall, ——, 16.
Hamoud, servant, 266, 282, 308, 310, 327, 330, 354.
Hamoud ibn 'Ubaid ibn 'ur-Rashid, 166, 174.
Hanafi, 247.
Hanbalis, 246, 248.
Hanifah, Wadi, 181, 237, 238, 240, 257-265, 279, 327, 358.
Hannat, Al-, 199.
Harb tribe, xv, 192, 193, 199, 304.
Harim, The, xii, 152, 160-162, 292.
Haroun'r-Rashid, 319.
Harra, The, 114, 115, 284.
Harra of Khaibar, 96 n.
Hasa, Al-, xiv, xv, 11, 14, 15, 18, 23-25, 27, 31-34, 55, 57, 59, 60, 71, 90-101, 107, 146, 152, 188-190, 217-219, 221, 222, 235, 237, 241, 244, 245, 256, 261, 273, 278, 297, 343 ; oil concession, 79-87.
Hasan ibn Mushari ibn Sa'oud, xvi.
Hasani, 251.
Hashem, Saiyed, 15, 17, 18, 21, 26, 27, 29, 31, 32, 35-37, 41, 42, 70, 79-86, 88, 90, 91, 95, 101, 102, 104, 110-117, 121, 129, 135, 143, 148-153, 159, 160, 163, 175, 205, 206, 252-255, 269, 313.
Hasi, Al-, 199.
Hauran, Wadi, 48, 87.
Hawashib, 251.
Hayathem, Al-, 199.
Hazlul, 255-257, 259, 261, 262, 264, 265, 267, 268, 274, 278-283, 296, 298, 300, 306, 308, 310, 311, 315, 318, 325-327, 330-333, 335, 340, 342-344, 347, 350, 351, 353, 355, 356.
Hazza' ibn Sultan ibn Zaied, 230, 231.
Hazzal, tribes of, 52.
Helal, Benu, see Benu Helal.
Heliolatry, 237.
Hijaz, Al-, xiii, xiv, 18, 19, 39, 63, 77, 182 n., 192, 228, 239, 307 ; sherifs of, 40.
Hijaz, Al-, King of, see Abd'ul-Aziz,
Hijaz railway, xiv, 78.
Hijrahs, xii, 191-193, 198.
Hisat, Al-, 199.

Holmes, Major Frank, 81-87, 158 n.
Hoover, Herbert, 80, 81.
Horse-racing, 175-177.
Houses of Najdi, 127, 128, 157.
Howmali, 274.
Hudaidah, 6, 81.
Hufouf, xv, 35, 96-100, 111, 116, 122, 129, 135, 180, 217-220, 222.
Hulaibah, 336, 358.
Hulaifah, 199.
Humaidah Wells, 101.
Humaidan, the Little Poet, 105.
Hunaiz, 199.
Hunaizal, 199.
Huraimala, xv, 1 n., 3, 6, 145, 239, 262.
Husaini, 251.
Husein, King, 28, 29, 37, 39, 62, 63, 65, 92, 95, 96, 157, 165, 177, 178, 194, 198, 224, 252, 327.
Hutaim tribe, 199, 304.
Huwaidi, 90, 91, 102-104, 109, 113, 114, 116, 119, 120, 142, 143, 147-150.

Ibn 'ul-Abbas, 250.
Ibn Abd'ul-Wahhab, see Muhammad ibn Abd'ul-Wahhab.
Ibn Bushr, 96 n., 243, 244 n.
Ibn Dakhil, 230.
Ibn 'ud-Dawish, 352.
Ibn Dawwas, see Dahham ibn Dawwas.
Ibn Hanbal, see Ahmad ibn Hanbal.
Ibn Hathlain, Sheikh of the 'Ujman, xi.
Ibn Husais, blind bard of 'Anaizah, 298-300.
Ibn Malik, 238.
Ibn Mijlid, 230.
Ibn Mu'ammar, of Najd, 188.
Ibn Muwaishir, 230.
Ibn Naif, 230.
Ibn-ur-Rashid, 19, 37, 57, 58, 60, 63, 72, 78, 146, 158, 174, 190, 231 n., 304, 305, 312, 337, 338.
Ibn 'us-Sabah, 190, 337.
Ibn Sa'oud, see Abd'ul-Aziz, King.
Ibn Sibhan, 166-168.
Ibn Swailem, 241, 242, 304.
Ibn Swait, 230.
Ibn Taimiyah, 246-248, 250.
Ibn Tawalah, 327.
Ibn Zaied, Sultan, 230.
Ibrahim, the cook, 312, 324-326, 328, 329, 341, 354, 356.
Ibrahim ibn Jumai'ah, 231 n.

Ibrahim ibn Thunaiyan ibn Sa'oud, xvi.
Ibrahim Pasha, xvi, 99, 256.
Ibsher, 32 n.
Idrisi, The, 65, 198.
Idrisi, Saiyed, 81.
Ikhwan, 14, 18, 141, 158, 163, 168, 170, 178, 179, 181, 192, 195, 198, 207-214, 228, 234, 261, 313, 324, 340, 352, 353, 356.
Imam, 47 n. ; see also Abd'ul-Aziz, King.
'Imar, Al-, 198.
Imbayedh, 198.
Intoxicants, absence of in Najd, 135.
Iqt, 309.
Iraq, xiii, xiv, 1-3, 6-12, 18, 19, 48, 60-62, 67, 81, 88, 125, 214, 230, 237, 258, 302, 335, 343 ; boundaries, 60 ; Kemalist attitude towards, 65 ; Nationalist Party, 10 ; Iraq-Najd Treaty, xiv n., 10, 59-62, 68, 77-79.
Irrigation, 95, 96.
Irta, 321.
Irtawi, Al-, 198.
Irtawiyah, 193, 198, 338, 352.
Islam, Al-, 58, 131, 140, 152, 158, 188, 190, 192, 200, 209, 212, 237, 245, 248, 331, 332.
Islam, Sheikh 'ul-, of Najd, 238.
Ithlah, Al-, 198.
'Izrah, 256.

Jabal. Place names beginning with Jabal are found under the name following, i.e. 'Aneiz, Jabal.
Ja'faris, see Shi'as.
Jafourah, xiv, 33 n.
Jafr, Al-, 94, 199.
Jahrah, 343, 351-353, 358, 359.
Jaizan, 81.
Jalbouts, 23 n., 27.
Jalib (Qalib), 125, 126, 293, 335.
Janah, Al-, 296.
Jannat, Al-, 131, 196, 209, 213, 243, 246, 253, 254, 325, 326.
Jarir, the poet, 274.
Jasrah, 34, 105.
Jawf, Al-, 79, 173, 214, 230 ; Ameer of, 168.
Jazam, Al-, 275, 276.
Jeddah, 135.
Jefan, Abu, 101, 103, 108-110, 112-116, 118, 119, 122, 182.
Jibrin, 78.
Jibrin, Wadi, 219.

Jishshah, 33 n., 35, 94, 96, 122.
Ju'aithen, the scout, 312, 318, 320, 330, 340, 344, 350, 354.
Jubail, 27.
Jubailah, 240, 258, 259.
Jufair, Al-, 199.
Juhannan, 196.
Justice, 215-221.

Ka'ba, 237, 245.
Kafir (infidel) tribe, 145.
Kamin, 145.
Karbala, 12, 88, 129, 245.
Kemalists, 65.
Kenneyny, Al-, 290, 291.
Khabis, 119, 120, 289.
Khabrahs, 336.
Khabrat 'ud-Dawish, 343.
Khalaf, the guide, 311, 312, 314-318, 321, 329, 336, 337, 343, 344, 347, 350, 351, 354, 355.
Khalid, Benu, *see* Benu Khalid.
Khalid ibn Abd'ul-Aziz ibn Sa'oud, xvi.
Khalid ibn Sa'oud (the Great), xvi.
Khalid ibn 'ul-Walid, 237.
Khalifah, Aal, Shiuokh of, 17.
Khalifs, 247.
Kharj, Al-, 27, 196, 199, 244, 245, 256, 273.
Khurmah, 63.
Kindersley, A. F., 4.
Kissing, 69.
Knox, ——, 290.
Konfudha, 177.
Koran, The, 49, 200, 201, 207, 210, 211, 215, 237, 238, 240, 246, 247, 249, 261 ; the Commentaries on, 61, 238, 247.
Kushm'ul-Barrah, 358.
Kuwait, xiii, xiv, 16, 20, 56, 57, 60, 66, 67, 76, 79, 95, 106 n., 135, 166, 205, 213, 217, 222, 223, 252-255, 303, 306-308, 320, 336, 343, 352-359 ; Sheikh of, 352 ; Consul of, 48, 49.

Labour, Cost of, 291.
Lahaj, 1.
Lausanne Conference, 46, 67, 78, 88, 224.
Leachman, Lt.-Col. G. E., 122 n., 290.
Life of the Prophet, 99, 195.
Luqman the Wise, 259.
Lux arc-light, 73.

Magneto-electric machine, 185.
Majed, servant, 28, 29, 35, 36, 92-94, 102-104, 109, 113-115, 117, 120, 121, 218, 225, 307.
Majed ibn Hamoud ibn 'ur-Rashid, 174.
Majlis, 15 n.
Majma'ah, xv, 244.
Makhlouf, 266, 267, 282.
Malaria, 141, 268, 269, 314, 315, 334, 350.
Maliki, 247.
Malsouniyah, 105.
Manama, 17, 23, 24.
Manfouhah, 157, 239, 244, 257.
Mann, Dr., 158.
Mansour ibn Abd'ul-Aziz ibn Sa'oud, xvi.
Map of Arabia, 146-148.
Marat, 274.
Markets, *see* Souq.
Marriage, 162, 205, 206.
Mascat, 67.
Masjids, 130, 131.
Matruhah, 336.
Mawia, 251.
Mawiyah, 336.
Meals, 288 ; state distribution of, 124, 154.
Meat, raw, eating of, 116.
Mecca, 19, 62, 124, 182 n., 188, 223, 237, 239, 245, 319, 328, 332.
Medinah, Al-, xiii, 167, 182, 230, 239, 303, 328.
Misfer, the cook, 257, 265, 282, 300, 308, 309, 311, 312, 321-327, 329, 331, 333, 339, 341, 344-347, 349, 350, 354-356.
Mish'el ibn Abd'ul-Aziz ibn 'ur-Rashid, 166, 167, 174.
Miskah, 198.
Mit'eb ibn Abd'ul-Aziz ibn 'ur-Rashid, 166, 167, 174, 184.
Mit'eb ibn 'ur-Rashid, 166, 172, 174.
Money, *see* Coinage.
Mosques, 130, 131.
Mosul, 67, 68.
Motawwa', 26, 202, 203, 208.
Motor-cars in the desert, 180-182.
Mountains, xiv.
' *Mowta*,' 34.
Mu'allaqat, 227, 259, 274 n.
Mubarak, servant, 312, 318-320, 330, 340, 344, 346, 350, 354, 356.
Mubarak of Kuwait, Sheikh, 57.
Mubarraz, 99.

Mudhar tribe, 337.
Mudhnib, 264 n., 276-279, 358.
Muhammad, M'hammed, M'hammad, Mehemmed, xi.
Muhammad, the Prophet, xiii, 191, 200, 210, 237, 250, 288, 289, 331.
Muhammad Ali, 256.
Muhammad Effendi, 100, 119.
Muhammad Suba'i, 270, 271.
Muhammad ibn Abd'ul-Aziz ibn 'ur-Rashid, 166, 167, 174.
Muhammad ibn Abd'ul-Aziz ibn Sa'oud, xvi.
Muhammad ibn Abd'ul-Wahhab, 58, 127, 162, 188, 189, 203 n., 209, 237-250, 258-260, 298.
Muhammad ibn Abd'ur-Rahman ibn Sa'oud, xvi, 45, 57.
Muhammad ibn Faisal ibn Sa'oud, xvi.
Muhammad ibn Mushari ibn Sa'oud, xvi.
Muhammad (the Great) ibn 'ur-Rashid, 56, 166, 172-174.
Muhammad ibn Sa'oud, Ameer of Dir'iyah, xvi, 189, 241-243, 245, 298.
Muhammad ibn Talal ibn 'ur-Rashid 165, 170-172, 174, 184, 186
Muhammarah Conference, 59, 60, 76, 77.
Muhannas, 304, 305.
Muharraq, 17.
Mulaih, 198.
Munaisef, Al-, 199.
Munasir tribe, 217, 218.
Muntafiqs, sheikh of the, 224.
Muqren ibn Markhan, xvi, 188.
Muqren ibn Muhammad ibn Sa'oud, xvi.
Murad, Sultan, 99.
Murrah, Benu, see Benu Murrah.
Musa'ed ibn Abd'ul-Muhsin ibn Sa'oud, xvi.
Musailamah, 181, 188, 237, 260.
Mushaiqer, 273, 274.
Mushaireqah, 199.
Mushari ibn Abd'ur-Rahman ibn Sa'oud, xvi.
Mushari ibn Sa'oud (the Great), xvi.
Mushari ibn Sa'oud, xvi, 241.
Mushrakin, Mushrekin, xii, 19, 242, 243, 244 n.
Music, 130, 131.
Muslemin (Muslems), 92, 244 n. ; no difference of rank amongst, 46 ; see also Wahhabism.

Mustapha Kemal, 46.
Mutair tribe, xi, xv, 193, 198, 264, 303, 338.
Mutanabbi, Al-, 336.
Mutawakkil, Al- Al-Laithy, 232 n.

Nabuchodonosor, 319.
Naief ibn Talal ibn 'ur-Rashid, 174.
Najaf, An-, 12, 88, 188, 209, 237, 245.
Najd-British Treaty, 77, 86, 147, 223.
Najd-Iraq Treaty, xiv n., 10, 59-62, 68, 77-79.
Najran, xiv, 57, 261.
Na'lah, 102, 122.
National feeling, lack of amongst Arabs, 338.
Nawwar, 210-212, 317.
Necrolatry, 237, 239, 245.
Nifei, 198.
Nisrani, 231 n., 262, 290.
Nouri, 61.
Nouri Sha'lan, Ameer, 230.
Nowwar, 269.
Nufoud, The, xi, xii, 14, 27, 33, 34, 43, 48, 59, 94, 110, 122, 180, 182, 218, 253, 266, 268, 274-277, 279, 285, 286, 291-295, 297, 301, 312-316, 319, 320, 358.
Nukair, 198.
Oases, xiv.
Oil, 79-88.
Ojair ('Uqair), xiv n., 13, 16, 21, 23, 26-33, 35, 52-55, 57, 59, 61, 69-71, 78, 122, 125, 182, 216-218, 255 ; Conference at, 74-89.

Omaiyads' Mosque of Andalusia, 131.
Oman, 29, 32 n., 67, 222, 223, 230, 245, 302.
Oqair, see Ojair.

Palestine, 222, 303.
Palm tree, 95.
Palmyra, Queen of, 97.
Pan-Arabism, 39, 40, 64-67, 78, 235, 236.
Pearl fisheries, 217.
Persia, 60, 237.
Persian Gulf, xiv, 6, 65, 67, 95, 96 n., 237.
Philby, H. St. J. B., 122 n., 222, 231 n., 290, 338, 339.
Plaster wall and door decorations, 127, 128, 287.

Pleiades, 30.
Poetry, 227, 228, 232, 233, 259, 274, 297, 298, 336, 356.
Political agents, *see* British political agents.
Polytheism, 188, 250.
Poona, 9.
Population of Najd, xiv.
Prayers, 24, 41, 47, 91, 92, 111 *n.*, 135, 240, 249, 258, 278, 330-332.
Pride amongst Arabs, 138.

Qa', 279, 280.
Qadis family, 286 *n.*
Qahtan tribe, xv, 190, 199, 272.
Qahwah, 62 *n.*
Qalib, see Jalib.
Qariah, Upper and Lower, 198.
Qasim, Al-, xi, 57, 58, 60, 134, 135, 152, 193, 196, 213, 244, 245, 255, 273, 276-285, 289, 297, 302, 303, 305, 312, 320, 336, 353, 358.
Qasr, 30, 273 ; Ameer of the, 26, 27, 29, 30, 35, 69, 82, 353.
Qatar, xiv, 95, 217, 223.
Qatif, Al-, xiv, xv, 16, 20, 27, 33 *n.*, 60, 78, 84, 217, 219.
Qibah, 199, 313.
Qiblah, 332.
Qiblah, newspaper, 62, 63.
Qirbahs, 313.
Qonfuzah, xiv.
Qorain, Al-, 199.
Qoraiyat 'ul-Milh, 79.
Qosaibi, Al-, 17, 21, 23, 52, 53, 55.

Rabi'ah, house of, 61, 337.
Radhwan, 254.
Rain, 223, 225, 226.
Rajhan, 35, 36, 90-94, 102, 109, 117.
Rajil, Wadi, xiv.
Ramadhan, fast of, 200.
Ramth, 335.
Rashed, servant, 23-26.
Rashid dynasty, 165-174.
Ras'ul-Mish'ab, xiv.
Ras'ul-Qilliyah, xiv.
Rawdah, Ar-, 198.
Rayn, Ar-, Upper and Lower, 199.
Red Sea, xiv.
Religion of love better than religion imposed by the sword, 141.
Religious sects of Najd, xv.
Revenues, 223, 229.
Review ('*ardhah*), 179.
Riq'i, Ar-, 343.

Riyadh, Ar-, xv, xvii, 14, 18, 19, 56, 57, 71 *n.*, 78, 86, 87, 101, 111-113, 116-120, 122-164, 175, 178, 180-182, 188, 194, 203-207, 214, 220, 225, 230, 235, 239, 242, 243, 251, 253, 255, 257, 260, 261, 287, 295, 302, 305, 320, 325, 358.
Rope from camel's neck, 293.
Rowdat-M'hanna, 173.
Rowdh'ul-'Uyoun, 199.
Rubaidah, 102, 122.
Rufa'i, 254.
Rujmat'ush-Shwai'er (Cairn of the Little Poet), 101, 105, 106.
Rummah, Wadi'r-, xiv, 96 *n.*, 301, 321, 335, 336.
Ruqah tribe, 198.
Ruwaidhah, Ar-, 199.
Ruwala tribe, 60, 61.
Ryiad, Ar-, 182 *n.*

Sabianism, 237.
Sa'd ibn Abd'ul-Aziz ibn Sa'oud, xvi.
Sa'd ibn Abd'ur-Rahman ibn Sa'oud, xvi.
Saddle-frames, 32 *n.*
Sadeqah, As-, 199.
Sa'doun, 244.
Safety of person and property in Ibn Sa'oud's territory, 217.
Safra, 285, 291.
Saiyed Hashem, *see* Hashem.
Saiyed Idrisi, *see* Idrisi.
Sajer, 198.
Salem, servant, 265, 267, 279, 282, 283, 300, 307-309, 327, 329, 330, 341, 342, 344-350, 353, 355, 356.
Salem Aal Sabah, 352.
Salt river, 280.
Samarra, ruins of, 12.
Samm, 33 *n.*
Samover, 133.
San'a, xiii, 1, 14, 91, 129, 135.
Sanam, As-, 198.
Sanjan, Jabal, 94.
Sa'oud, Aal, Genealogical table, xvi ; Kingdom of, 60, 145.
Sa'oud (the Great), xvi, 145, 159, 189, 190, 245.
Sa'oud ibn Abd'ul-Aziz ibn 'ur-Rashid, 166, 168, 169, 173, 174.
Sa'oud ibn Abd'ul-Aziz ibn Sa'oud, Ameer, xvi, 195, 196.
Sa'oud ibn Faisal ibn Sa'oud, xvi.
Sa'oud ibn Hamoud ibn 'ur-Rashid, 162, 166-168, 173, 174, 183.

Sa'oud ibn Muhammad ibn Muq- ren ibn Markhan, xvi, 172.
Sa'oud ibn Thunaiyan ibn Sa'oud, xvi.
Saqia, 125.
Sarif, battle of, 57.
Sarrar, xi.
Sawh, As-, 198.
Schools, *see* Education.
Sdeir, 27, 244.
Sdeiri, 274.
Shafe'i, 247, 254.
Shafe'i, Ash, *see* Ash-Shafe'i.
Shakespear, Capt. W. H., 290.
Sha'lan, Benu, Sheikh, 60, 61.
Shalhoub, 129, 133, 152-158, 163, 164.
Shamiyah, 60, 62.
Shammar Mountains, 57, 212, 245.
Shammar tribe, 165-173, 199, 337, 338.
Shamsiyah palms, 126.
Shaqra, xv, 255, 268-275, 277, 278, 294, 305, 358 ; Ameer of, 269, 270.
Shar', 215, 219.
Shat 'ul-'Arab, 30, 253.
Sheikh, 105 n., 202.
Shi'a, 88.
Shi'ah, 188, 235, 237, 245.
Shi'as (Ja'faris), 246.
Shi'b, Ash, *see* Ash-Shi'b.
Sh'ib 'un-Naqib, 310, 358.
Shi'is, xv.
Ships, Arab, 23 n., 25 ; Arab mode of life aboard, 15.
Shiq, 343, 358.
Shubaikiyah, Ash, *see* Ash-Shu- baikiyah.
Shuwai'er, the poet, 297-299.
Sihaf, As-, 199.
Singing, Arab, 25, 26, 131, 325 ; forbidden in Najd, 211, 212.
Siqt'ul-Lewa, 274.
Sirhan, Wadi, xiv.
Sirr, Wadi's-, 255, 275-277, 358.
Sirrar, As-, 199.
Sitti Fatimah, *see* Fatimah Sibhan.
Sitti Zubaidah, 319.
Slaiy, Wadi, 120.
Slave-girls, 152, 153.
Sleim family, 286 n., 287, 289.
Souq, xi, 129, 130, 294-296, 302.
Sports, 175-187.
Stick or staff, 208.
Stoicism of the Arab, 144, 213.
Story-telling, 326-329.

Stuart, W., 5.
Subai' tribe, xv, 199.
Sudair, 198, 240.
Sudous, 262, 324.
Suhoul, As-, tribe, xv, 199.
Sulaiman, Ameer, 241, 244.
Sulma, Jabal, xiv.
Sultan of Najd, *see* Abd'ul-Aziz, King.
Sultan ibn Hamoud ibn 'ur-Rashid, 166-168, 173, 174.
Summan Desert, 102, 103, 105, 107, 111, 112, 114, 116, 118, 126, 180, 273.
Sun, Satanic horns of the, 92 n.
Sunnat, The, 200, 201, 247.
Sunnis, xv, 212, 254.
Sûq, *see* Souq.
Suras of the Koran, 189.
Swailem ibn Swailem, 303, 304, 311.
Syria, 12, 18, 61, 62, 116, 152, 212, 230, 262, 303, 328, 329.

Tabari's *History of Arabia*, 97-99.
Tabouk, 78.
Taibism, 199.
Taief, At-, 328.
Taima, xiv.
Talal ibn Naief ibn 'ur-Rashid, 174.
Talal ibn 'ur-Rashid, 166, 172, 174.
Tamim, Benu, *see* Benu Tamim.
Tarabah, 19, 63, 307, 328.
Target-practising, 175.
Tea, 53, 288.
Terabi, plain of, 182.
Terabi, Wadi, 116, 122.
Thaj, 199.
Thamami, 318.
Tharmadah, xv, 266, 268-270, 273, 274, 277, 279, 358.
Theft, punishment of, 24, 215, 220.
Thumaid, 'Ain, 310.
Thunaiyan ibn Sa'oud, xvi, 241 n.
Tigris, 6, 9, 258.
Tihamah, 177, 178.
Tobacco smoking forbidden, 135, 203, 211, 212, 278, 286.
Tooth-brush, Arab, 184.
Trade, Arab instinct for, 346.
Trans-Jordania, xiv n., 62, 67, 77, 79, 214.
Treaties, xiv n., 8, 10, 59-62, 64, 67, 68, 77-79, 86, 147, 223.
Trees endowed with supernatural powers, 240.
Tribes, chief, of Najd, xv.
Tribute, collection of, 218.
Turfiyah, 312, 358.

Turki ibn Abd'ul-Aziz ibn Sa'oud, xvi, 342 *n.*

Turki ibn Abdullah ibn Sa'oud, xvi, 47 *n.*

Turks, 57, 60, 67, 68, 99, 217, 218, 221.

Twaiq, Jabal, xiv, 126, 129, 240, 257, 262, 263, 264 *n.*, 273, 274, 276, 277.

Typewriting, 148.

'Ubaid branch of Rashid dynasty, 166, 173, 174.

'Ubaid ibn Ali ibn 'ur-Rashid, 174.

'Ubaid ibn Majed ibn 'ur-Rashid, 174.

Ubaireq, 199.

'Ujair, Al-, 199.

'Ujamn tribe, 190.

'Ujman, Al-, tribe, xv, 102, 110, 111, 190, 199, 217, 218.

'Ulaiyan tribe, 305.

Ulema, xii, 134-137, 192, 194, 200-206, 233, 238.

'Ulqah, 321 *n.*

Umm'ul-Hashim, 336, 358.

Umm uz-Zarr, 33, 34, 45, 46, 91, 218.

Umru 'ul-Qais, 274.

Unitarianism, *see* Wahhabism.

'Uqair, Al-, *see* Ojair.

'Uqlah, Al-, 119, 122.

'Urai'er, Ameer of Al-Hasa, 244.

'Urairah, 199.

'Uroudh, 313-318, 321, 339, 358.

'Urwah, 198.

'Usailah, 198.

Ustaz, 36 *n.*

'Utaibah tribe, xv, 192, 193, 198, 303.

Uthman ibn Mu'ammar, Ameer of 'Uyainah, 240, 241, 259, 260.

'Uyainah, 188, 238-241, 259, 260, 262.

Uyoun 'us-Sirr, 276, 277 *n.*

Vacant Quarter, xiv, 87, 217, 219, 320.

Wadis, xiv.

Wadi. Names beginning with Wadi are under the name following, *i.e.* Dawasir, Wadi.

Wa'el, 61.

Wahhabism (Unitarianism), xv, 30, 127, 141, 170, 189, 190, 192, 193, 200-206, 209-212, 234, 258, 272, 331-333 ; its foundation and development, 145, 237-250 ; asceticism and unsociability of the Ulema, 134-136 ; the *masjids* and Grand Mosque, 131, 132.

Washm, The, 27, 244, 255, 262, 264-278, 344.

Water, digging for, 291-293.

Wilson, President, 43, 44.

Wilson, Sir Arnold, 84.

Winter in Central Arabia, 132, 133.

Wusaitah, Al-, 199.

Yahia, Imam, 65, 197.

Yamama, 113.

Yamamah, 181, 244, 257, 262.

Yaman, Al-, xiii, 7, 10, 14, 90, 95, 98, 99 *n.*, 110, 125, 147, 193, 209, 245, 272, 279 ; Saiyeds of, 209.

Yarim, Qa', 279.

Zakat, Zikat, xii, 223.

Zeid, Benu, *see* Benu Zeid.

Zelul, 29.

Zilfi, 277.

Zioud of Al-Yaman, 98.

Zkeir family, 286 *n.*

Zkirt, 136, 211.

Zour, Mt., 352, 353.

Zubaidah, 318, 320.

Zuboun, 121.

Zuhair ibn Abi Sulma, 230.

Zunaib 'uz-Zib, 336.

LaVergne, TN USA
23 September 2009

158728LV00003B/12/A